Prayer

A Lifelong Conversation with God

Prayer

A Lifelong Conversation with God

<u>Two Bestselling Works Complete in One Volume</u>

What Happens When We Pray for Our Families

~

What Happens When God Answers Prayer

EVELYN CHRISTENSON

INSPIRATIONAL PRESS

First Inspirational Press edition published in 2003.

Inspirational Press
A division of BBS Publishing Corporation
450 Raritan Center Parkway
Edison, New Jersey 08837

Inspirational Press is a registered trademark of BBS Publishing Corporation.

Published by arrangement with Chariot Victor Publishing,
a division of Cook Communications.

Library of Congress Catalog Number: 2001012345

ISBN: 0-88486-303-4

Printed in the United States of America.

CONTENTS

WHAT
HAPPENS
WHEN
WE
PRAY
FOR
OUR
FAMILIES

CONTENTS

DEDICATION

To my wonderful extended family who traveled this sometimes arduous but always victorious road of prayer with me.

To Sally Hanson, the other half of my ministry, for her nineteen years of untiring and humble seeking of God's wisdom for the uncharted path and awesome doors He was opening to us.

To my faithful board members for never ceasing to pray for my family and me as we have needed them so desperately.

But, most of all, to my Heavenly Father, who has performed all these incredible things for my family in answer to those prayers.

MY HUSBAND, CHRIS, AND I celebrated our fiftieth wedding anniversary on Valentine's Day 1992. When we were married, prayer already was an important part of our lives; but as we faced the complexities of the new marriage relationship and rearing a family, prayer soon became our automatic, spontaneous lifestyle. And for all these years God has answered in many different and sometimes unexpected ways. But He has answered. So through prayer we have had fifty years of indescribable help, specific divine guidance, wonderful comfort, and awesome love—from our Heavenly Father—for our family here on earth.

Many have asked how I know what I should pray for my family members. First, I pray asking God to show me what He wants me to pray. Then I just wait on God to tell me—either as I read His Word, the Bible, or during prayer by His calling to my remembrance the Scripture He wants to be the basis of my prayers for them. Then I write down and date what God said, either in the margin of my Bible or in notes I keep on file. Then I pray. So the whole process is *God*—from Him and then back to Him in prayer. (These two methods are described fully in my book *Lord, Change Me!*)

I have used our favorite family names throughout this book, but for clarity, here are the names of our family members in the order they appear in the picture on the back cover:

Evelyn and Harold (Chris) Christenson.
Daniel and Nancy Thompson with daughters Cynthia Joy (Cindy) and Kathleen Mae (Kathy) Thompson.
Kurt and Margie Christenson with son James Kurt.
Spencer (Skip) and Jan with son Brett Jezreel and daughters Crista Alisse and Jennifer Diane (Jenna) Johnson.

You may recognize some of the experiences I recount, having told about them in former books and in speaking. It was impossible to draw a complete picture of our family praying without using some of them in this book. Since this book is not fiction, I could not make up illustrations.

The thing that has been hardest in writing this book is that there are thousands of exciting and important prayer answers that could not be included in a book of this size. Deciding what to leave out was my hardest task.

My prayer for you as you read this book is that you will discover not only the awesome power of prayer in your family as we have in ours, but the incredible God who answers by reaching down from heaven into your family too. If you have not already done so, I trust that you also will make prayer the spontaneous lifestyle of your family.

More Than Ever, Our Families Need Prayer

OUR CHRISTENSON FAMILY all rejoiced with our daughter Nancy and her husband Dan Thompson when he took a position in 1981 as a financial analyst with a U.S. government agency and went to work in St. Paul for the agency's regional bank. Then in 1985 Dan was transferred to the national office in Washington, D.C. By 1987 it was obvious that he had become an extremely valuable worker, for he was honored as the employee of the year in the agency. And there were prayers of thanksgiving within our family.

Then in May 1988 we got shocking news. When Dan refused to accommodate his boss by falsifying a report to Congress about irregularities in the books of the agency he discovered, his job was suddenly terminated. The word *Incompetency* was stamped on his file. This kept him from finding another financial position elsewhere. And even when the Merit Systems Protection Board ruled six months later in Dan's favor, he still could not get another job because his former employer appealed the case—with no time limit forcing a conclusion of the matter.

Our family will never forget the three and a half years that we bombarded heaven with prayers, upholding Dan and Nancy through each emotional and financial crisis.

Later in this book I will tell you about God's amazing answers to these prayers. This I will say now, God is faithful to hear and answer prayer when we earnestly seek Him for our loved ones—whether in relation to a job matter, illness, the birth of a child, the death of a family member, or the salvation of someone we deeply love. And certainly in such problems as rebellion, alcohol and drug addiction, infidelity, and divorce.

Prayer should be the spontaneous lifestyle of every Christian family, especially today because the family as the world has known it for centuries is disintegrating before our eyes. Consider these phone calls and letters that have come to me:

- Texas: "This is Laura calling. My supposedly Christian husband is bringing home pornographic videos and viewing them with our two teenage sons. They contain not only kinky but violent sex, and I have become the brunt of their anti-women abuse."

- Illinois: "My father was brilliant but became a full-fledged alcoholic. His drinking made him so violent our very lives often were endangered. Finally, he was unable to cope with his top management job, settling for janitorial work. Now my married sister blames our mother and for years has not allowed Mother to even see her grandchildren."

- Michigan: "Our daughter rebelled and ran, taking her two children with her. We haven't heard a word from her for two years."

- Minnesota: "My husband and I established a Christian home the day we were married. And we brought up our son 'in the way he should go,' but he did depart from it! He moved out of our house, is on drugs and alcohol, has been in jail several times. Where did we go wrong?"

WHAT IS HAPPENING TO THE FAMILY

Children in many families today have rebelled and blatantly turned their backs on everything they have been taught in their homes. Some have broken all ties with their families and established a new godless life-style, frequently involving drugs, illicit sex, and even violence.

It seems popular these days for family members to betray and accuse other members for past inadequacies, leaving confused parents and siblings bleeding in a shattered family unit that seems beyond repair.

For several years now sexual, physical, and emotional child abuse have been escalating at a terrifying rate, and wife abuse is alarmingly common with even increasing numbers of cases of husband abuse reaching the courts.

Marriages broken by infidelity, separation, or divorce are multiplying at an alarming rate, leaving bitter children and an exhausted spouse to hold together what is left. Many one-parent families are struggling just to exist with incomes below the poverty level, bitterly remembering happier days of adequate necessities, good relationships, and a respected family image.

It is not uncommon to find a family member shuddering alone when a devasting tragedy has struck because nobody cared—or even knew. With the current humanism ideology resulting in individuals looking out for themselves, much of our society and even many of our families have ceased caring for each other.

Financial disaster after financial disaster has left many families' faith in God stretched beyond the breaking point and survival all but impossible.

In our ever-aging society, many senior citizens feel utterly forsaken by those who should be loving them while increasing numbers of adult children, themselves aging, are staggering under the heavy burden of round the clock care of a parent.

Still others stand stymied by complex family decisions that need to be made in the ever-increasing confusion of our modern society.

What we are experiencing in our families today sounds frighteningly like the description of the last days in 2 Timothy:

> For men will be lovers of self, lovers of money, boastful, arrogant, revilers, disobedient to parents, ungrateful, unholy, unloving, irreconcilable, mali-

cious gossips, without self-control, brutal, haters of good, treacherous, reckless, conceited, lovers of pleasure rather than lovers of God; holding a form of godliness, although they have denied its power . . . always learning but never able to come to the knowledge of the truth (3:2-5, 7).

IS THERE NO HOPE?

Is there hope for today's family? Your family? Yes, there is. Although these symptoms are becoming more and more prevalent in even the best of families, there is an answer. And the answer is prayer. Not just an SOS prayer now and then, but an automatic calling out to God in prayer in every family need. A lifestyle of prayer.

Our daughter-in-love Margie said to me recently, "I need to learn to pray and not worry. I have a tendency to work things out myself. Think them through and come up with my own answers. But God's Word says it is *prayer* that works."

The answer to today's disintegrating family is a spontaneous lifestyle of prayer. "The effectual fervent *prayer* of a righteous man [person] avails much" (James 5:16, italics added).

HUMAN HELP IS NOT ENOUGH

Won't counseling and friendly advice help just as much? Might not the results be even better if we seek top human professional help? No, because prayer invites not just *any person* but *a certain Person* into the family situation—a supernatural, divine Being to intervene, assist, direct, instruct, rebuke, solve the problems—and heal.

There are many helpful resources available in books, seminars, and counseling today (some also are very bad), and the good ones certainly can help in the important step of identifying the family problems. And, if following biblical principles, they can lead through many of the steps of recovery and reconciliation. However, secular intellectual human help is not sufficient by itself. *Only God has the power to reach down and complete the final healing step that mends the broken family members.*

The "Age of Enlightenment" as a cure-all is fizzling because as knowledge has increased, evil has escalated. Social reform through godless communism is dead. Materialism in our families has failed to bring sought-after peace. These things didn't work. Why? Because there is another dimension in us that needs curing—the spirit. "The fool has said in his heart, 'There is no God'" (Ps. 14:1).

Also, prayer relies on the God who can run a family without ever making a mistake. It invites the God who knows the outcome from the beginning of every situation to be in control of the family.

Why should prayer be the automatic, spontaneous lifestyle in our families? *Because from the everyday hassles to those devastating family catastrophes, prayer enlists the help of the omnipotent, omnipresent God of the universe who is willing and even eager to release His divine power into the lives of our family members.* Only God, not humans, can do that!

> Be anxious for nothing, but in everything by prayer and supplication with thanksgiving let your requests be made *to God* (Phil. 4:6, italics added).

Mary George, a tiny Philadelphia woman known to longtime friends as "the girl of prayer," tells of a time when she and her six sisters and a brother were facing eviction, since the owner wanted to convert their home into an apartment house. Their parents had died, and the house they lived in was in dire need of repair—a leaking roof, a broken water heater, and ceilings about to fall.

The condition of the old house prompted a friend, Susie Bahner, to write a song based on the tune "This World Is Not My Home," the first verse and chorus going like this:

> This house is not our home,
> We're just existing here;
> The ceiling's falling down,
> And Esther's full of fear.
> The kitchen's full of things
> That run around at night,
> And the dining room ceiling is really a sight.

O Lord, You know that we must all be out;
On January 24th we'll wander all about.
We only need a dime to open our front door,
And we don't feel at home in this house anymore!

Yet the landlord had given the family notice that they had to move, and finding a house large enough for the family of eight, and one they could afford, wasn't easy. They prayed and prayed about a place to go, both individually and as a family.

Inquiring about a house a block away, they were informed a potential buyer was settling the next day. But the owner phoned later to tell that family of children that the buyer had backed out on the deal, and she would rent the house to them.

Mary recalls, "The next day we signed the lease, and word got around the neighborhood how God took care of the Georges. Immediately, we had neighbors and friends volunteering to help us clean and do repairs, and make the house livable. The next few days, up and down the streets, people were heard saying, '*Have you heard how God took care of the Georges?*'" *Family prayer!*

PRAYER INVOLVES GOD

How can a simple thing like prayer do such a monumental job in our families? When our children have rebelled and broken the family ties, prayer calls on God who always can and will reach down to them no matter where they are scattered around the earth. He will intervene in their lives no matter what they are doing. This is the God who can muster ten thousand angels to protect them in the the most dangerous situations and rescue them in all crises—*if we pray.*

When there has been a betrayal or hurtful accusation by another family member, how wonderful it is to be able to turn to our God. The God who is absolute truth in the midst of deceit, denial, and duplicity of family members to one another. The God who never has memory lapses like us humans or who remembers incorrectly. The God who is absolutely impartial, who is always 100 percent fair, and never sees through prejudiced eyes. Our God who never is spiteful or petty like we family members sometimes are but always does all things for all the family members' good. Yes, He even helps us forgive when we can't and helps us love when we are unable or unwilling. Prayer breaks down barriers we have built for days or even years. The God of our prayers melts stony, stubborn hearts.

In the midst of abuse and mistreatment that some family members are powerless to avoid, the suffering ones can cry out to their God who reaches down and holds us close to His loving breast. And in the years of recovering from past abuses, it is *only* our God who can bring that complete and permanent healing so desperately needed for full emotional, physical, mental, and spiritual restoration.

In broken marriages, prayer invites the Heavenly Father into the headship role of the remaining family. A family head who loves unconditionally and never breaks a promise.

In our loneliness, prayer will bring the God who never forsakes or betrays any family member. For the aging parent, prayer calls on a Person who never slumbers or sleeps, who never ignores, or who never is too busy to give His undivided attention—all of the time.

In financial disasters, we can trust the God who will provide, sometimes in miraculous ways, for our needs. Prayer may or may not remove the difficult circumstances, but it will give grace and courage to face them. Prayer doesn't necessarily remove every storm, but it definitely will calm the family in the storm.

Prayer guarantees a Companion in our homes when tragedy strikes. A Friend who will gently hold our hand or hold us close to Himself in His everlasting arms. Or even pick us up and carry us when we cannot go on. The Great Physician. The One who comforts in all our deepest family sorrows.

In our family's confusion when we have lost our way, prayer introduces an omniscient, all-knowing God who gives wisdom and peace. Who always knows which decision we should make. Who knows the "what if's" of our intended course of action. Knows what disasters would happen if our human plans—not His—were followed.

Prayer gives the family the privilege of depending on an all-knowing, all-powerful and all-caring Person—who can be with every family member every minute—everywhere. God!

FIRST PRAYER IN THE BIBLE IS
ABOUT FAMILIES

The first time the word *prayer* was used in the Bible, it was in a family situation (see Gen. 20:7 and 17). After Abraham deceived Abimelech into thinking Sarah was his sister to keep from being killed, God revealed the truth to Abimelech in a dream telling him to restore Sarah and then Abraham would *pray* for him. The Lord had closed fast all the wombs of the household of Abimelech because of his taking Sarah; and then "Abraham *prayed* to God; and God healed Abimelech and his wife and his maids so that they bore children" (Gen. 20:17, italics added). And prayer has been a critical part of biblical family life ever since.

SO WHY DO SO FEW PRAY?

While being interviewed by a Christian counselor in California, I was asked a very profound question. "Evelyn, since all Christians know that there is power and guidance in prayer, why is it so few of them really pray diligently and fervently?"

"There are many reasons," I answered, "but one of the main ones is pride. It is hard to admit we need help or that our way of doing it may not be right. In fact," I continued, "deep down in their hearts many Christians are saying '*I can do it myself, God!*'"

Also many people glibly say, "All's well that ends well." But this is just wishful thinking and not true if they haven't included God in their human handling of circumstances and events.

How foolish it is to depend on our inadequate, limited, and biased opinions and wisdom—when we don't pray.

How foolish to deprive our families of all that fantastic good—when we don't pray.

How surprising that Christian families grope and stumble and sometimes break up—because they have not bothered to call for God's help.

The Bible clearly says one of the main reasons we don't have solutions to our family problems is that we have not asked God for them. We have not prayed. "You have not because you ask not" (James 4:2).

But when we do pray, God releases His divine power into the life of our family members for whom we are praying.

Our prayer groups in our "What Happens When Women Pray" church joined a devastated mother and father praying persistently for their son. He had left his family's Christian lifestyle for one of organized crime. It took years of their praying—and ours. But prayer did work. Today he is the father of a fine family and on the board of a good church.

As I was typing this page, a member of that church called to say hello. "I want to tell you that prayer really does work, Evelyn," said the caller, a father. "One of our sons was in the lowest one-fourth of his high school class and almost flunked out of his first year of college. And now he is a dedicated math teacher in our very fine local Christian high school. And prayer did it!"

Another family from that church had a daughter who was breaking their hearts. She rebelled at the Christian leadership lifestyle of her parents and many times refused to go to high school. She ended up running from the family, on drugs, and in a very godless lifestyle. But our prayer groups joined her praying parents also—praying almost daily. And now she and her husband have a successful ministry in Hollywood reaching those in the movie industry for Jesus.

OUR FAMILY'S LIFESTYLE

God literally has run my family through prayer. Our multiple family problems have kept us on our faces before God. Many, many times our dependence on Him has been our means of survival. But God has been in control of our family decisions, relationships, joys, and trials. In these fifty years of marriage, our family literally has had a spontaneous lifestyle of prayer.

Since becoming a mother and a grandmother, I know what the Bible means by the admonition "Pray without ceasing" (1 Thes. 5:17).

It is not just the bedtime praying of my husband and me which always includes each of the family members. Not just my daily morning devotions when I always intercede fervently for my family members. It is not just the formal times we pray together for each other, or the spontaneous quick prayers when a need suddenly arises. No, family prayer is the lifestyle of our family—independently and with each other.

Also, each of my family members does not get the same amount or intensity of prayer each day. Family prayers are not a formal listing of each member in a prayer diary to be dutifully or even perfunctorily prayed through. *No, the time spent on each is directly in proportion to that individual's need that day.*

Prayer is sweeping my grandchildren into my arms when they are afraid—thanking God with them for His protection. It is pacing with an infant granddaughter with colic, breathing a continuous prayer for relief. It is including God's comfort along with the bandage on a skinned knee. It is asking for God's healing as a hand is laid comfortingly on a sick tummy or fevered forehead—or for a husband during surgery. It is clinging in faith to God while pacing the floor with the unwashed grandbaby while the surgeons race to save a daughter's life. It is agonizing through sleepless nights for a wayward child.

Prayer in our family isn't something we do occasionally; it is a way of life. *A life lived moment by moment with the most important member of our family—the God of the universe.*

And God is longing to be the most important member of your family too.

PRAYER IS NOT A COP-OUT

People frequently tell me they believe we often use prayer instead of handling a problem ourselves. They believe prayer is used by people who aren't smart enough or brave enough to run their own lives. That is not true. Prayer is just one step in the process of identifying the problem and then getting the instructions as to how to handle it from God. But it is by far the most important step.

Prayer is including God in our course of action instead of bungling through with our incomplete, biased, and sometimes inaccurate human thinking. Only by seeking God—in prayer—do we have His divine wisdom and input into the family situation.

Of course, after praying, we "put feet to our prayers" and obey what God has directed us to say or do or be. Prayer is not *in place of* action, it is just getting the wisdom and power *for* that action.

PRAYER ACKNOWLEDGES GOD AS DIRECTOR OF OUR FAMILIES

I have had special days that I waited in prayer on God for special Scripture verses of guidance. For example, back in our pastorate time in Rockford, God would give me the same New Year's Scripture year after year—Proverbs 3:5-6:

> Trust in the Lord with all your heart, and lean not on your own understanding. In all thy ways acknowledge Him, and He will direct your paths (KJV).

At first I was thrilled at knowing He wanted to direct me and my family the next year, and enthusiastically practiced letting Him do it. But as the years passed, and He kept giving me the same Scripture, I became impatient. Was God in a rut? Or had He run out of new ideas for me?

But now I realize that this was a very deliberate repetition, reinforcing the greatest lesson of my life: *If I DON'T lean on my own understanding, and if I DO trust in Him, and if in all my ways I DO acknowledge Him— then, and only then, will God direct my own and our family's paths.*

And how do I acknowledge Him? By running my life by prayer. Depending on Him instead of myself.

I have found this guidance as precise, tangible, definite, and accurate as the star of Bethlehem leading the magi to the Christ Child (Matt. 2:9). When they left Herod, the star appeared again very clearly to them and directed them to the Child. So also with me. The same words apply to my life. *He will direct our paths*—through prayer.

WHEN WE DON'T KNOW HOW TO PRAY

However, there are those times when we don't know how to pray for our families. But God has provided me the solution to that problem too. The Father gave us the Holy Spirit to live in us—who prays to Him whatever is the Father's will—when we don't know how to pray.

> And in the same way the Spirit also helps our weakness; for we do not know how to pray as we should, but the Spirit Himself intercedes for us with groanings too deep for words; and He who searches the hearts knows what the mind of the Spirit is, because He intercedes for the saints according to the will of God (Rom. 8:26-27).

Our daughter Nancy called recently saying that her five-year-old Kathy was going through a stage—arrogant, bossy, and aggressive. Remembering her older sister's similar attitude and the spiritual warfare prayer against Satan that changed her completely, I started to pray the same for Kathy. But somehow it wasn't right.

Finally, kneeling at my prayer pouf in the living room, I prayed, "O Holy Spirit, I don't know how or what to pray for Kathy. Please take my 'not knowing how to pray as I ought' to the Father according to His will."

What a relief! The pressure to figure out just *what* to pray left me. I knew God knew exactly what Kathy needed—and the Holy Spirit would take my inadequate prayer to the Father exactly according to the Father's will."

Talking to Nancy the next day, I asked about Kathy. A little surprised, she said, "Oh, she seems so much better." I thought, *I wonder how God answered my prayer of not knowing what to pray? Well, I don't need to know as long as God knows—and answers!*

One of the greatest helps to me in my family praying throughout the years has been the burden the Holy Spirit has lifted from me when I don't know how to pray in family situations.

NO PRAYER IN THE GARDEN OF EDEN

God's original plan for Planet Earth did not include prayer. When God put the first family in the Garden of Eden, there was no family prayer. Why? Because Adam and Eve didn't need it. In the first home established on earth, there was perfect one-on-one communication with God. "They heard the sound of the Lord God walking in the garden in the cool of the day" (Gen. 3:8).

And God carried on direct conversations with them, asking them questions and getting answers from Adam and Eve. They were open, personal friends.

So, why do we need prayer now? Because of *sin*. When Satan brought sin to earth through our first parents, God drove Adam and Eve out of their perfect environment and relationship with Him. Sin destroyed humans' perfect two-way communicating with God.

But God's communicating with people did not cease; it just changed form. *He then instituted prayer.* In Genesis 4:26 we read this about Adam and Eve's son Seth: "Then men began to call upon the name of the Lord."

And we can see prayer developing throughout the Bible until today when we have communication with the Father restored by Jesus on the cross. Adam and Eve's perfect communion with the Father is available to us, His children. Sweet, unbroken communion has been restored by the shed blood of Jesus Christ—for our families.

> Having therefore, brethren, boldness to enter into the holiest by the blood of Jesus (Heb. 10:19, KJV).

Once we have availed ourselves of that cleansing and redeeming blood of Jesus in salvation, we are eligible for this ideal relationship of unbroken communication with God.

PRAYER RECOVERS FOR US WHAT WE LOST THROUGH SIN

God provided prayer as the means of recovering those things which humans lost when sin took over Planet Earth.

First, in the Old Testament prayer restored people's communication with God, and prayer in the name of Jesus restored human beings' perfect communion with God. Jesus said:

> Until now you have asked for nothing in My name; ask and you will receive, that your joy may be made full (John 16:24).

A second thing restored by God is *boldness* in people's coming to Him in prayer. Are you afraid tó approach the holy God of heaven with your family needs? Afraid He won't want to be bothered by your problems? Afraid He won't answer? Adam and Eve had no inhibitions about talking to God—until they hid themselves from Him because of their sinning. But God provided forgiveness for our sins through Jesus—and confidence to come to His throne.

> "Let us therefore [because of our High Priest Jesus] draw near with confidence [boldness] to the throne of grace" (Heb. 4:16).

Amazingly, a third thing lost to humans through Adam and Eve's sin—and was restored through prayer—is *dominion.*

When God created the first parents and placed them in the Garden, He said to them, "Be fruitful and multiply, and fill the earth and subdue it; and rule over . . . every living thing that moves on the earth" (Gen. 1:28). But at their sinning, the whole world fell into Satan's domain. The human race had forfeited its right to rule the earth. And 1 John 5:19 is still true today, "The whole world lies in the power of the evil one."

After the Fall God chose a new way to let His children help Him rule the earth. It is through *intercessory prayer.* This, of course, is not the direct dominion it would have been had humans not sinned; but, nevertheless, prayer does assist God today in ruling the earth.

Andrew Murray, my favorite devotional author, wrote, "Most churches don't know that God rules the world by the prayers of His saints." And that includes our families—here in the world.

We must never forget that God is sovereign; but all through the Bible we find promises that when we pray, He will act. In prayer, we move the hand that moves everything in the world—including our families.

> Ask, and it shall be given to you; seek, and you shall find; knock, and it shall be opened to you. For everyone who asks receives, and he who seeks finds, and to him who knocks it shall be opened (Matt. 7:7-8).

When through rebellion or separation we feel we have lost all influence or control over the wayward family members, we can pray up to God, who in turn reaches down to them. And He brings His holy influence to bear upon them. There may be nothing we can do directly because of their having broken our relationship, but God can—and will.

PRAYER WORKS!

Since Chris and I celebrated our fiftieth wedding anniversary, I no longer have to say about family prayer, "I think" or "I hope" it will work. No, after our family has prayed for a half century, I now *know* that prayer really does work.

When I was young, I had to take so much on faith. But not anymore! Frequently, it takes years for us to see the final answer to prayers prayed with and for the family. And some we don't recognize as answers. Some we even forget we prayed for. And some we won't know the answers until we get to heaven. But, nevertheless, God *is* answering!

One of my most exciting answers to prayer in our family came when our son Kurt applied for the doctoral program in physics at the University of Illinois. After going to classes all day, he had to take three-hour entrance exams on two consecutive nights. And I had promised to pray while he took them. I spent those two three-hour evenings staying only in prayer, alternately moving from pleading on my knees to seeking direction from God in my Bible. From struggling long over releasing my son to God's will, not mine—to the piano to worship God for being in control of our family—to praising Him in advance for however He was going to answer.

I had gone to bed exhausted—and prayer *is* hard work—after I knew

Kurt finally was finished. But my heart leaped with joy as I sleepily answered the phone and heard the telephone operator struggling to say, "Will you accept a collect call from physics doctoral candidate Kurt Karl Christenson?" His way of announcing that God had answered my prayers! He had passed.

A few years later my daughter-in-love Margie wrote me a letter soon after her marriage to Kurt. "I appreciate the personal example you have set for your family as a praying mother, and I guess this is really what inspired me the most and keeps on inspiring me. I've thought a lot about you praying for three hours just for Kurt. A person's life tells the best story."

Then there also are those squeezes of my hand with a grateful quick smile and, "Thanks, Mom, for praying."

Or the "Call-the-prayer-chain-quick,-Mother" phone call when calamity strikes them or a friend.

Or the endless sighing, "Please pray *again,* Mom," when a hurting problem still hasn't been solved.

Our daughter Jan just told me that she heard their six-year-old Crista vomiting in the bathroom and she dashed in to help her. Our Jan said as she pulled Crista's hair back out of her face and held on to her, Crista gasped, "Pray for me, Mom. Pray!"

In fifty years of marriage, Chris and I have left many imprints on our family, some good and some not so good. But the greatest legacy we ever could leave our children and their children is their seeing and knowing the importance and power of family prayer.

Prayer should be, and can be, the spontaneous lifestyle of every Christian family.

Crisscross Praying

WHEN A BRIDE AND GROOM establish a new Christian home, they start to weave the fabric of which their home will be made. Of all the things they begin to weave into their newly formed family, prayer is by far the most important. Love, fidelity, mutual respect, support, and serving each other are all vitally necessary—but prayers are the threads that weave the fabric which God uses to hold a family together.

Fifty years ago when Chris and I were married, we founded our family on prayer. Through the years we have experienced disasters, deaths, rebellions, and going to war. But the fabric of undergirding prayer we wove has stood the test of time; God Himself has been crisscrossed through the fabric of our home.

When a new couple starts building their home on God through prayer, they begin crisscrossing their individual and mutual strands of prayer. These form the warp (the threads extending lengthwise in a loom) and the woof (the threads that cross the warp) of a potential impenetrable woven foundation for their home and marriage.

CHILDREN CAN ALSO BE PRAY-ERS

Through the years the family praying expands. As the children mature, they also can become pray-ers, not just the objects of prayer. The threads of prayer then come from several directions for each other. From the time our first child, Jan, started kindergarten to when our last child, Kurt, graduated from high school, Chris or I prayed with them at the door, sending each off with the Lord protecting and guiding. It was so reassuring to our children and us that they weren't going out to meet the world alone but going out under God's care. It gave confidence, quelling the fear of what they might encounter. Yet it was always Chris and I—the parents—praying for our children.

However, one day a new kind of prayer emerged in that "front door praying." I had just finished praying for our grade-schooler Nancy, when I said, "Honey, Mother has a problem today. Would you please pray for me too?" And joy filled that front hall as my child took her little, immature but oh-so-sincere thread of prayer and wove it haltingly into the fabric we called family prayer.

I have brought our children up absolutely knowing that I need them to pray for me—because I tell them. Frequently, what they pray is the Scripture verses God gives them for me. While writing one of my books, I struggled to have enough courage to say the things God clearly was telling me to say. Our daughter Jan wrote me a note with her prayer for me from Ephesians 6:19-20:

> Pray for me also, that whenever I open my mouth, words may be given me so that I will fearlessly make known the mystery of the Gospel. Pray that I may declare it fearlessly, as I should.
> Love, Janny

I taped her note to my computer, rereading it whenever my boldness started to falter—and never once writing less than what God told me to. God answering my daughter's prayers for me! And that note is taped up by my computer to this day.

Children's prayers are heard by the Heavenly Father. The chairman of our Metropolitan Prayer Chain told me that all her children received Jesus before she and her husband did. "It was my children's prayers for our salvation," she told me, "that brought their father and me to Jesus."

Crisscrossing prayers has spilled over into our extended family. For example, our medical doctor son-in-law Skip Johnson (I call him my "son-in-love") was teaching a Sunday School class, and Jan and their two little daughters, Jenna and Crista, had gone alone to pray for him while he taught. However, the next week, the older daughter, Jenna, was in the class listening to him. She asked her dad if she could be excused to go to the bathroom, but later told him her reason was to go there to pray alone for him while he was teaching.

As our three children's praying for us parents grew, an exciting and powerful dimension of family prayer developed. Crisscrossing with our children emerged. And the fabric of our family praying solidified day after day, year after year, as we all wove our threads of prayer every which way—sometimes with bursts of enthusiasm, sometimes with urgency, and even sometimes with apathy. But little by little the weaving progressed.

PRAYER—HOPE FOR ONE-PARENT FAMILIES

Today almost half of the children across the land are from one-parent families. Is there no hope for them? Does it take the traditional family of a father, mother, and children to have an effective prayer life? Not so. I have seen an unusually strong prayer base develop in many one-parent families as they struggled to survive financially and emotionally. When their forced dependence on each other turns also to a dependence on God in prayer, an incredibly strong fabric of support from the omnipotent God of the universe weaves through their family relationship.

I have received many phone calls and letters about a straying husband and father—and occasionally about a straying mother. In each instance a traditional family has been shattered. And I am astounded at how many mothers say, "My children and I are praying for our daddy every day. We're praying that he will turn back to God, and then that he will come home to us." Frequently, they expect my praying to bring him home immediately, so I gently remind them that God gave everybody, including their daddy, a free will. A straying father still can, and frequently does, choose to live in his sin; and it is only prayer that can reach him. So I join in praying that God will reach down, convict him of his sin, and call him back first to Himself and then to his family. This is a situation in which the children of a fragmented family can join Mother (or Father) with their strands of prayer—for a reunited family.

WHEN THERE'S ONLY ONE PRAY-ER

Even in many traditional Christian families, all too often there is only one member—a wife, husband, mother or father, or sometimes a mature child—who intercedes for other family members, perhaps for a family member who has strayed from godly teaching and is living in sin. The lone pray-er may pray fervently month in and month out or even year after year, weeping and agonizing before God.

In my many years of ministry, the vast majority of phone calls and letters I receive have come from faithful Christian wives and mothers asking prayer for their husbands and children. Not long ago a mother home-schooling her six children came to one of my prayer training sessions to get a new lease on her praying. Her husband was in prison, and the burden she carried all alone was almost more than she could bear.

Yes, if only one parent or another pray-er believes in the power of prayer, there is hope for that family despite a pulling in opposite directions of priorities, lifestyles, and goals. There may be open opposition and even ridicule about depending on God through prayer. But it can work even if there is only one pray-er. It worked in my own home as I was growing up. My mother was the one who prayed, never giving up, teaching us the Scriptures and living her Jesus before us.

In the case of a lone believing parent, the New Testament bears out that it is definitely possible to bring up a child the scriptural way he should go. Timothy was the "son of a Jewish woman who was a believer, but his father was a Greek" unbeliever (Acts 16:1). The Apostle Paul attests in 2 Timothy 1:5 to the fact that his young co-worker, Timothy, became a Christian through his mother and believing grandmother and mentions it further in chapter 3 (vv. 14-15):

> You, however, continue in the things you have learned and become convinced of, knowing from whom you have learned them; and that from

childhood you have known the sacred writings which are able to give you the wisdom that leads to salvation through faith which is in Christ Jesus.

Again, it may seem so lonely and sometimes almost futile, but God does hear and answer those prayers woven all alone by just one pray-er through days and even years.

The effectual fervent prayer of a righteous person avails much (James 5:15, KJV).

PRAYING GRANDPARENTS

As indicated earlier, Grandmother Lois evidently played an important role in the spiritual nurturing of Timothy. The praying of the grandmothers (now great-grandmothers) in our own immediate family have produced changed lives and an ongoing stability and security in our extended family as well.

Our Grandma Chris started praying for every one of her family members more than seventy years ago upon receiving Jesus as her Savior and Lord when she was twenty-one. As the years passed, she prayed while working at the kitchen sink, a Bible promise stuck up in the window, or as she knelt in her bedroom. Now at ninety-one, too feeble to kneel, Grandma Chris still continues to pray in her rocking chair, each day reminding God of the needs of each child, grandchild, and great-grandchild. Though helpless to do anything personally when family needs arise, she knows who can help—her Heavenly Father.

Because of the myriad of answers to prayer through all those seventy plus years, she has immovable faith in God's prayer promise. So unshakable was her faith in God's answering prayers that when her husband, Rudolph, died, leaving her with two children, ages nine and twelve, to bring up alone, day in and day out her anchor in prayer was: "As thy days, so shall thy strength be" (Deut. 33:25, KJV). When there wasn't food for the table or coal for the old furnace, there was always her never-failing God answering her prayers.

My own mother had an especially hard life when I was a child. My parents operated a greenhouse and retail florist business. Mother had serious asthma, but would always take her turn to go down two flights of stairs in the middle of the winter nights to stoke the big furnace with coal. Even when pregnant, she never stopped carrying big loads of plants, soil, and pots. But prayer sustained her.

When things got really difficult, we knew where to find our mother—in the middle of the calla lily bed, with the almost ethereal purity of those huge waxy white flowers surrounding her, as she stood serenely praying. And pray she did, until God called her home five years ago. She prayed according to 1 Thessalonians 5:17—"without ceasing." She prayed while she worked, while she made as many as a hundred quilts a year for missionaries, while she rolled thousands of bandages for medical missionaries until the wee hours of the morning. The hours of intercessory prayer she managed to carve out of her very busy schedule were basically for her offspring. She prayed us through difficult births, deaths, times of rebellion, financial disasters, educations, career changes—anything else that came up. And we all knew it. So we would call our mother immediately when our world started to fall apart—because we knew that her hotline to heaven never shut down.

BLESSED ARE THOSE WITH "PRAYER ROOTS"

Many newly married couples bring into their marriage a strong prayer network from one or both of their birth families. However, as they leave their father and mother and become one flesh (see Gen. 2:24), they do start weaving a new fabric of prayer for their own emerging family. Before a new family unit is organized, godly parents may have spent many, many years praying for that future family unit. All of this prayer is used by God to help weave the new family's prayer fabric.

After our marriage Chris and I as a new family unit had that kind of support. We had three praying parents, all of whom prayed for years that each of us would marry the person God intended for us. Chris' father was a "godly spiritual giant." With my new husband fighting in World War II as a bomber pilot, I spent many nights in the home of Chris' parents.

But I never could get up earlier than Grandpa Chris. Every morning I would find him kneeling in prayer—even huddling over the heat register on a cold Michigan winter morning absorbing the little heat that his newly laid coal fire was sending his way. His powerful prayer life, along with Grandma Chris', gave our marriage a spiritual send-off with God.

With such a heritage, we also prayed for years and years for the mates God knew were right for each of our children. And God over the years answered!

THE MULTIPLYING FAMILY

When the children eventually take a spouse of their own, they not only form their own new family, but their continued prayers for the other members of their families strengthen the original family unit. And, of course, when other family members pray for them, their new undergirding fabric of prayer is continuously strengthened by the other prayer threads weaving in and out. This is not just being prayed for by the original parents, but results in crisscrossing prayers flowing in all directions. The seemingly haphazard pattern actually is producing an amazingly strong network of woven support of prayer for the multiplying family.

So, through the years, an actual *network* of prayer develops with as many starting points as there are family members, weaving in as many directions as those members choose to pray faithfully for their siblings, parents, grandparents, close and distant relatives.

However, that crisscrossing is not just an inert, lifeless network. No, it is everchanging in intensity and frequency as family members' needs come and go. And changing personal relationships within the family determine the quality and quantity of the praying. This, of course, changes the strength of the prayer network—for better or for worse.

The first time my daughter-in-love Margie heard me speak, she and our son, Kurt, were newlyweds. I found myself carefully guarding my illustrations of answered prayer so as not to intimidate her or overwhelm her with what she might consider a "preachy" mother-in-law. But a note passed up to me during the seminar quelled my fears and thrilled my heart:

I love you so much. We are enjoying being here, praying together—and with God. Keep preaching it! We're praying for you in the back pew! Love, Margie and Kurt

Crisscrossing prayers produce strong family ties—not just based on tradition, fun, and family celebrations—but on a deepening *caring* as the prayers continue to weave a stronger and stronger family network.

When a dog almost bit off the nose of one of our granddaughters, God performed an absolute miracle; there were virtually no scars in answer to desperate family praying. After my husband, Chris, underwent cancer surgery, he said, because of so many prayers, he felt as if his body were on air, not even touching the hospital bed. Our family prayer network has undergirded one family member during a period of deep financial distress. Entrance tests to colleges and advanced programs have been prayed through by the family. There was a prayer vigil during labor and delivery of all the new babies in the family. The list is endless. But in each need, the dimension producing the results was *family prayers*.

When our original family unit lived in Rockford, Illinois in the 1960s, a tornado passed through while I was alone with our three children. Lightning hit the outside electric wires and traveled through two rooms to an outlet in the living room. En route to another state, our daddy kept track of the storm's path by radio; and, as soon as it had passed our home, he called long distance. Stunned, I picked up the phone and answered that, yes, we all were safe, but the house had just been hit by lightning.

The city firemen left though they still felt heat in the walls where the lightning had traveled—and still smelled smoke. I listened in awe as they informed me not to go to sleep but to keep watching for a possible outbreak of fire. The excitement of the big hook-and-ladder fire truck, the curious gawking neighbors, and the fear of fire still someplace in our walls had the children and me fearful and on edge. But then the children and I all knelt by Nancy's bed to pray before they tried to settle down. And it was Kurt, still in grade school, who calmed us all with his immediate prayer, "Dear God, thank You that we don't need to be afraid." We continued to keep alert, but the danger passed.

Family crises, large and small, have sent our whole family to our knees through all these years. A book could be written on all the times God has intervened, rescued, and performed miracles—*when we prayed for each other.*

THE EXTENDED FAMILY

Our family praying extends an incredibly long way out, because what we consider family includes aunts, uncles, cousins, nieces, nephews, and even "second" and "third" relatives. Although these are usually prayed for only when deeper needs arise, it is a joy to stretch our threads of family prayer beyond our immediate family unit to those even remotely connected to us.

When my only brother Edward's only son, Bud, was murdered some years ago, much of our praying was for his only son, Budde—left fatherless and very bitter toward the police for doing such a seemingly incomplete investigation of the crime. Our extended family fervently and persistently prayed for God to take over in the boy's life. And we especially asked God to bring a good Christian man to help fill the void left by Budde's father's death. Just two years later we were thrilled at how he had lost most of his bitterness toward the police and was amazingly well adjusted. God had brought the right man, a man who took him through the Eagle Scout badge in Boy Scouts and guided him as he attended a good church. *Extended family praying!*

Our grandniece Kirsten was finishing some necessary teaching degree college credits and living temporarily with us when our daughter Nancy called from Virginia. Distraught, she asked us to pray immediately for a Christian school for Cindy, since the one in which she was registered was closed for a minor infraction of a rule—and she had just until 2 o'clock that day to enroll Cindy somewhere else.

A few quick phone calls revealed that my prayer chain members had all scattered for the holiday weekend, and neither was I able to contact any other family members. So Chris, niece Kirsten, and I bowed our heads at the kitchen table calling upon God to intervene. Then Kirsten prayed with profound insight, "Dear God, put Cindy where it will be best for her. You know how devastating the first day of a new school can be. Protect her emotionally in her fear and in the horror of not being included in a school her first day away from preschool at her own church."

Shortly after 2 P.M. our Nancy called, spilling out the details of finding an academically sound, prestigious school. But, without Nancy knowing it, that school had a bus pickup at Cindy's old preschool, where her sister, Kathy, would be going every day—and where many of Cindy's friends would be boarding the school bus with her. Cindy could continue with her usual after-school care the days both parents had to be working—and with both her friends and little sister, Kathy! How we needed that prayer from an extended family member—Kirsten—a grandniece!

RIPS AND HOLES

In all families there are times when a few individuals or even all family members squabble and have misunderstandings, ripping holes in the undergirding fabric which has been woven by prayer. Some holes are easily patched and hardly affect the strength of the network at all; in some cases squabbles rip huge gaps in the prayer fabric, causing a serious disruption in the flow of family prayers or even a ceasing of praying altogether.

But again, it is the threads of prayer that can mend the snags and gaping holes in family relationships. During the Depression of the 1930s, I used to watch my mother darn socks. She would take one strand of darning thread and painstakingly weave it back and forth until what was a hole was stronger than the original sock. That is how prayer mends a family's rips and holes.

Through the years, my prayer many, many times has been in the words of the Apostle Paul's desire for the family of believers in Corinth when there were quarrels among them:

> Now I exhort you, brethren, by the name of our Lord Jesus Christ that you all agree, and there be no divisions among you, but you be made complete in the same mind and in the same judgment (1 Cor. 1:10).

So it is with just one, or perhaps a few, family members taking their threads of prayer and patiently, often painstakingly, weaving to mend the family fabric. Sometimes the weaving accomplishes its purpose quickly, but sometimes it takes faithful weaving for years before the rift is mended. Much mending prayer is done in weeping and even agonizing of spirit. But, stitch by stitch, God takes His holy hand and pulls those threads of prayer in place, supernaturally mending those hurtful holes.

WHEN OTHERS PRAY FOR MY FAMILY

I haven't tried to pray for my family by myself since 1964, but instead have enlisted help in praying for our immediate family. For twenty-eight years there have been organized prayer groups, telephone prayer chains, and individual non-family members praying for our family. We feel unusually blessed of the Lord to have had this rare privilege.

From 1964 through 1967, Signe Swan, Lorna Johnson, and I met every week to pray for our church—and also for our families' needs. Then in 1968 during our "What Happens When Women Pray" experimentation, we organized the first telephone prayer chains. And until we left that Rockford pastorate three years later, according to our carefully kept records, our family needs were voiced to God an average of four times a week on those telephone prayer chains. That prayer experimentation had a great influence on our whole church. When the most difficult disaster came to our parsonage family, the whole church undergirded us in prayer. On one unbelievably hard day, the deacon board divided up the day and kept up unbroken prayer for us for twenty-four hours!

Immediately following our move to St. Paul, I organized a group of praying women into a monthly ministry supporting prayer group and a telephone prayer chain, which kept daily prayer for me and my family going up to our Heavenly Father for fifteen years. Then in 1973 we incorporated our United Prayer Ministries, and until this day my telephone prayer chairman calls me by 6:20 A.M. three times every week. This is my ministry prayer chain involving some thirty women, but always included are the prayer needs for my family. I share our needs—and they all pray! Then at my monthly board meetings we pray at least half of the time, and all deep needs of my family are included with other families' needs.

Then I have a host of people around the world who have picked up family needs from my illustrations in seminars, prayer warriors who not only pray for us but enlist their prayer groups and chains to do so also. I am continually surprised as notes and phone calls tell me God has laid on their hearts to pray for my family. Frequently, it has been even beyond what I understood the problem or need to be—but God knew and told them to pray. This is an overwhelming privilege which I don't deserve but for which I am so grateful!

So this too has become a way of life for our family. It is just second nature for our children to "call the prayer chain." The last time I was in India, Grandma Chris went into a coma, not expected to live. Our daughter Jan immediately called the prayer chain—and they joined family members in praying God's will and God's timing. Then, getting word to me in Calcutta, my national chairman there alerted all the city chairmen where I was to speak of the possibility of my having to go home. And immediately they all mustered their pray-ers all over India. To the astonishment of the doctors, Grandma Chris rallied— and I could continue my prayer tour of India laying the groundwork for the first national women's movement ever in that country—a prayer organization.

MY SPECIAL PLACE OF PRAYER

My old green prayer chair has been replaced. When we moved into our present house, there was not room for that big old green chair which had been my place of prayer—my "prayer closet"—for so many years. Now I have what I call my "prayer pouf."

Since my ministry was prayed into existence around my vice president's prayer pouf over twenty years ago, I had wanted one in my house. A few years ago we ordered an oversized tufted footstool to serve as my prayer pouf. My heart leaped with ecstatic joy, and tears sprang up in my eyes as I checked it in the warehouse before it was delivered.

After my excited granddaughters Jenna and Crista watched the big truck deliver it, I suggested that the three of us practice so we could teach their mummy and daddy how to pray there. But six-year-old Jenna replied, "I don't have to; I already did!" All practiced up!

The first time we knelt around it to pray, it was an invitation to three-year-old Crista to crawl up on Grandma's back and play piggyback. Sometime afterward, several family members were casually discussing the name I had given that new piece of furniture—the "prayer pouf." Suddenly Crista decided we should pray right then. "I know how to kneel," she announced, and she promptly knelt to show us. When her invitation of "let's pray" came so uninhibited out of her mouth, we all eagerly knelt and called the rest of the family to join us. When Crista's daddy, Skip, suggested, "Why don't you pray first, Crista?" there was a short pause, and we could almost hear her wondering, *What do I do now?* But then she bravely launched into her prayer about the thing uppermost in her mind right then, "Thank You, Lord, for the wonderful food we just had."

Her little, sincere prayer was so precious, prompting the rest of us to take turns praying deeper and deeper as we knelt about that new place of prayer. My heart almost burst with joy inside me. "O God," I prayed, "thank You for the joy and privilege of family. Please fill this prayer pouf—our place of prayer—with Yourself. When we kneel here, may we feel You. Fill this whole house with You. Fill us with You."

And then Chris also prayed asking God to come in a special way to our new place of prayer. Skip prayed next, and after he finished praying, he told us it seemed that a shaft of light came down and surrounded us all.

After Jan closed in prayer, I wondered, *Have I merely replaced the old green chair?* Possibly. But much more than that. This is a place for not only my private praying—*but corporate family prayer!*

It was just five days later that several family members again gathered at the prayer pouf—this time the night before my husband's cancer surgery. The prayers of thanks flowed: "Thanks for the privilege of a family praying together." "Thank You for having taken us through so many hard things—so that we can trust you for Chris' surgery tomorrow." "Thanks, Father, that You have never let us down." Then came the plea,

"Put Your arms around him and hold him close, dear Lord." Skip's prayer from his medical doctor's perspective was next. "Protect his mind while he is under anesthesia, please, dear Lord."

As I reached over and laid a hand on my husband's shoulder and head, I prayed, "O God, fill him with Yourself. Holy Spirit of God, fill him right now with Your peace, courage, and even Your joy."

Last, Chris prayed and gave himself completely to God for His will in handling the cancer in his body. And he closed telling God he was so grateful for our family caring and for their prayer support.

That prayer pouf has been the scene of many deep family prayers. I remember my knuckles turning white as Kurt squeezed my hand so hard as we begged God to reveal His will to Kurt for his future career after college. Then later his wife, Margie, newly married to Kurt, was there as all three of us knelt after Kurt and Margie had responded to several mission board invitations at the Urbana Missions Conference. We agonized in prayer for God to show them if He wanted them on the foreign field or to stay in America.

When my only sister Maxine, and her husband, were en route to the Philippines for short-term missions in their retirement, the depth of love and closeness we experienced as we knelt with them at the prayer pouf—sending them off with God enfolding them—was indescribable joy. Another most meaningful time was when Maxine and I—the only remaining members of our immediate family—knelt there and prayed, "O Lord, pass the mantle of prayer on to our children."

Home—a place to gather to fellowship. A place to enjoy family meals together. A haven in the storms of life. But, most of all, *a place to pray!*

WHAT FAMILIES ARE ALL ABOUT

Our medical doctor daughter Jan called one Monday night, sobbing about a problem faced by her doctor/husband. "Skip has a very ominous looking growth on his ring finger." We spent hours of prayer bombarding God's throne for our Skip. The very next day God, knowing our concern over a fatal type of cancer, gave both Jan and me the same Scripture verse to comfort us: "The Lord knows the days of the blameless, and their inheritance will be forever" (Ps. 37:18).

Then as our family sat together in our family room, not knowing until the next day that the lab test would show the growth to be benign, Skip began apologizing. He told us he was sorry for putting the whole family through such agony because of a growth on his finger. But our Nancy responded with the essence of our crisscrossing family prayers: "Skip, that's what prayer is all about. And that's what families are all about."

Praying Family Members to Christ

HAVE YOU WONDERED after you have prayed and prayed and prayed about your children's rebellion, sinful lifestyle, or lack of interest in Christian things why God hasn't answered? Why your children don't live the way you taught them? Why they don't practice a godly lifestyle? It may be they are just searching for independence—or their own personal identity. Or it may be just plain rebellion against God or family standards. However, a likely explanation is that they never *really* received Jesus as their Savior and Lord. They still have their old nature.

By far the most important prayer to pray for every family member is to receive Jesus as personal Savior and Lord. Without a genuine salvation experience, your children and other family members are still in the spiritual condition of everybody before they are made alive spiritually by accepting Jesus. Their condition is described in Ephesians 2:1-3:

> And you were dead in your trespasses and sins, in which you formerly walked according to the course of this world, according to the prince of the power of the air, of the spirit that is now working in the sons of disobedience. Among them we too all formerly lived in the lusts of our flesh, indulging the desires of the flesh and of the mind, and were *by nature the children of wrath,* even as the rest.

Dr. Bruce Wilkinson, president of Walk Thru the Bible Ministries, in his "The Seven Laws of the Learner" series gives these startling statistics about teenagers in America today:

- 65 percent of all Christian high school students are sexually active.
- 75 percent of all high school students cheat regularly and think it is OK.
- 30 percent of all high school seniors have shoplifted during the past 30 days.
- 40–50 percent of teenage pregnancies are aborted, the young mothers killing their child.
- 3.3 million teenagers are alcoholics (1 in 9).
- 1,000 teenagers try to commit suicide every day.
- Up to 10 percent of high school students either have experimented with homosexual behavior or are living a homosexual lifestyle.

Dr. Wilkinson went on to list a major national magazine's seven big school problems of 1940 contrasted with today. In 1940 the problems in schools were: talking, chewing gum, making noise, running in the halls, getting out of line, wearing improper clothing, and not putting paper in the wastepaper basket. Today, however, the seven big school problems are: drug abuse, alcohol abuse, pregnancy, suicide, rape, robbery, and assault.

You are hardly alone if you have a child or children who are not living for God. It is obvious that something is drastically missing today. While it is true that Christians sometimes are guilty of gross sins, could the main reason possibly be that even those who call themselves Christians really are not believers—that they have not received a new nature and still are living according to their old sinful nature? Ephesians 2:4-5 goes on with the answer to this problem:

> But God, being rich in mercy, because of His great love with which He loved us, even when we were dead in our transgressions, made us alive together with Christ (by grace you have been saved).

To have a child or any family member living a godly lifestyle, the prayer we must pray first is for him to have Jesus living in him as Savior and Lord. In themselves, family members never will be able to live godly lives, or even have the desire to do so. A real salvation experience actually makes us new creations in Jesus. Second Corinthians 5:17 explains this new being that we become:

> Therefore if any man is in Christ, he is a new creature; old things are passed away; behold, all things are become new (KJV).

IS IT A REAL SALVATION EXPERIENCE?

The church our family has attended during vacations for over forty years had a tremendous shock not long ago. The son of one of their finest families had as a lad seemingly received Jesus, been baptized, and had participated as part of the church family for years. Then he went into military service and steadily moved farther and farther away from God, ending up on drugs and in trouble with the law. A definite wedge developed between him and his whole family as time went on.

Coming home from the service with a wife and new family and facing his mother who suffered with life-threatening cancer, he got into more trouble and ended up in jail. It was then that he realized that his life was empty and hopeless and his claim to knowing Jesus was not real.

Soon after that he stood before the congregation of his boyhood church and told them that, though he had gone through all the proper steps, he really had not become a genuine Christian as a lad. But now, he said, he really had received Jesus as his Savior and Lord of his life. "I want you all to know that I love the Lord," he testified as he requested to be re-baptized—this time as a real believer. The stunned church congregation watched as he stepped into the baptismal waters for his first *believer's* baptism along with his young wife, a new Christian. It was a baptismal service the congregation would long remember.

Jesus said to Nicodemus, "Truly, truly, I say to you, unless one is *born again,* he cannot see the kingdom of God. . . . Do not marvel that I said to you, 'You must be born again'" (John 3:3, 7, italics added). It is frightening to even consider that any of our own children—or other family members—may not be truly saved, born again.

A close friend has been a pastor of liturgical churches all his adult life. Having just retired, he told me he is going to write another book, this one about the many, many young people he watched go through their confirmation classes, memorize all the right Scriptures, and correctly answer all the questions. "But as soon as confirmation was completed," he said, "that's the last the church saw of many of them." Then he sadly added, "These, I firmly believe, never had a real experience of salvation."

My only brother, Edward, evidently was one of those, though no one but God knows for sure if his childhood profession of faith was genuine or not, or knows whether it was just peer pressure, family prodding, or just the honest good intentions of a young boy—but nothing more. Edward seemed to be such an eager little Christian, passing out Gospel tracts and being so faithful at church. But then peer pressure in junior high school and the temptations of tobacco and alcohol won out. Within a few more years it was the wild lifestyle of a traveling highway contractor, three wives, a prison term for accidentally shooting a girlfriend to death, and finally deciding there wasn't a God at all.

Had he really received Jesus—or was it just the church environment in which Mother kept us? Or was it just, as a boy, doing what everybody in his young church social group was doing? We'll never know. But for thirty years He lived completely away from God, denouncing even His existence.

It took thirty years of agonizing, persistent, daily prayer by our mother—and much prayer by the rest of us. And then it took a near-fatal accident to bring him to Jesus—for the last two years of his life here on earth.

No matter how long it takes, their personal salvation should be the number 1 prayer that we pray for each of our children and family members.

REPENT AND BELIEVE

As I talk with parents, I realize children turning their backs on all they have been taught is a very common occurrence. One overseas missionary, agonizing over her own teenage daughter's rebellion and plans to marry a communist, told me she believed that many young people brought up in the church really haven't had a *valid* born-again experience. They went through the proper classes, passed with their buddies, joined the church with the group. "But was there ever real repentance and acceptance of Jesus not only as Savior but as their Lord?" she asked me. She answered her own question with a sad, "I think not."

Why is this so? It takes more than the head knowledge of believing that Jesus is the Son of God. Even the demons do that, but they certainly aren't saved. Somehow we have reduced becoming a Christian to only accepting intellectually what the demons believe—that Jesus the Son of God came to earth, died on the cross, and rose again the third day. It takes more than that. Many have forgotten that Jesus started His preaching with "repent and believe" (Mark 1:15) and have lost the fact that the early church immediately was built on both repenting and believing in Jesus (see Acts 2:38). Then after Peter explained to the believers in Jerusalem that God had called him to bring Jesus to the Gentiles too, they replied: "Well, then, God has granted to the Gentiles also the *repentance* that leads to life" (Acts 11:18, italics added).

The hours before I received Jesus as my Savior, I was miserable. The evangelist had preached about everybody needing his or her sins forgiven, and I, as a nine-year-old child, had cried all afternoon over my sins. My mother and new-Christian older sister, Maxine, hovered over me like midwives—expectant, eager for the new birth. They spent hours instructing, answering my questions, and explaining my terrible burden of guilt. But when that preacher finally ended his evening sermon and gave an invitation to come forward and receive Jesus, I was the first to shoot out of my seat. As I knelt repenting, with our Sunday School superintendent at my side, the guilt was swept away. And as I prayed for Jesus to come into my heart, I knew I was a Christian—ecstatic, thrilled, born again, *forgiven!*

For He {God} delivered us from the domain of darkness, and transferred us to the kingdom of His beloved Son, in whom we have redemption, *the forgiveness of sins* (Col. 1:13-14, italics added).

So, what should we pray for our unsaved family members? Pray that they will see their sinful condition, repent, and truly receive Jesus as their Savior.

THE MATTER OF RIGHT BIRTH CIRCUMSTANCES

There are many rites of passage methods into church membership and Christianity that may or may not produce real Christians. A church staff member, the mother of a daughter approaching adolescence, said to me recently: "I am scheduled to go away for further theological education next year, but I don't think I should go. That is the year my daughter will be the 'right age' to go through the church's membership class, and I need to be home to supervise her entrance into Christianity." Shocked, I wondered "where in her previous theological training had she missed that becoming a real Christian is more than being the 'right age' to enter Christianity through a church class?"

Then there are those who believe that *where* one is born makes him a Buddhist, Muslim, Christian, or whatever. I actually have had people say to me in all sincerity that they knew they were Christians because they were born in Christian America. That is no more true than the old cliche that being born in a zoo makes one an elephant.

Also, the widespread belief that being born into the "right family" automatically produces Christians is not New Testament teaching. When Jesus said, "You must be born again" to Nicodemus, he was talking to one who was a Pharisee and a ruler of the Jews, a follower of Jesus' own religion. Jesus even looked at the religious leaders of His own church who did not believe on Him and said, "What makes you think *you* will escape the sentence of hell?" (Matt. 23:33, italics added)

An honest look into Christian families reveals that many members are not true believers, born again and destined for heaven.

My own father rested all his life on what his parents' church had done to him as a baby. All of our prodding and twenty-five years of praying for him to receive Jesus and change his extremely worldly lifestyle brought no results—until his doctors told him he was dying. After calling his clergyman (whom he never even had met) to administer last rites, he said to my mother, "There's more to it than this, isn't there?"

"Do you think so?" she gently countered.

"Yes. Call your pastor." And my dad received Jesus. Surprisingly, he lived two more years as an invalid, but frequently with his Bible open on his lap, communicating with His newfound Lord Jesus. It took twenty-five years of persistent prayer for his salvation—and we are so glad that we never gave up!

INDIVIDUAL BELIEF A SCRIPTURAL MUST

In His conversation with Nicodemus, Jesus insisted on a personal, individual acceptance of Him as Savior and Lord. He said, "For God so loved the world, that He gave His only begotten Son, that *whoever* believes in Him should not perish but have everlasting life" (John 3:16, italics added).

I recall how the emphasis of a personal salvation in my presentation affected so many in a large seminar I conducted some years ago in South Africa. Most of those in attendance were church members who assumed they were Christians because they had been born into the "right family," one affiliated with a certain denomination. However, after I invited listeners who were not sure they knew Jesus personally to pray aloud in their groups, attending denominational leaders were shocked when about seven-eighths of that audience prayed to make Jesus their personal Savior and Lord.

Their belief stemmed from the teaching of "household salvation"—that is, that the decision of the head of the household brings salvation to the members of the household. However, God's Word does not teach "household salvation." When the Philippian jailer cried out, "What must I do to be saved?" Paul and Silas replied, "Believe in the Lord Jesus, and you will be saved—you and your household" (Acts 16:30-31, NIV). But a careful reading of the passage indicates that all members of his household were old enough to believe: "The jailer . . . was filled with joy because he had come to believe in God—he and his whole family" (16:34, NIV).

The same explanation applies to the account of Cornelius who was promised by an angel that "you will be saved, you and all your household" (Acts 11:14). However, earlier, the Bible says that Cornelius was a "devout man. . .*who feared God with all his household*" (Acts 10:2, italics added). So, *all* the members of his household already were old enough to fear (reverence) God. This could not have included babies and young children, who themselves must personally receive Christ in order to be born again when they are mature enough to believe and fear or reverence God. Faithful praying on the part of believing members of a household can be a means of working in the hearts of young family members calling them to personal salvation. (See pages 53–54 regarding how God cares for young children before they reach an age of accountability.)

"HOW CAN I BE SURE, MOTHER?"

It was our daughter Jan's first child. She searched my face for an answer as she asked, "Mother, how can I be absolutely sure Jenna will be saved and go to heaven with me?"

"You can't be absolutely sure, Honey," I replied. "God gave your precious little baby a *free will* just like He gave everybody else on earth."

With tears in her eyes she cried, "What can I do then? Can't I do *anything* about it?"

"Oh, yes, Jan, there are many things you can, and must, do. First you yourself must *live* your Jesus in front of her every minute. In all you do and say, she must see Jesus living in you. You must teach her the things of God and surround her with music and stories about Jesus. You must keep her encased in a good church family."

This is what Chris and I promised God we would do at the important time of dedicating our infants—but really ourselves—to God.

"But, Jan, by far the most important thing you will do for her is *pray.* Pray continually that she will find Jesus as soon as she is old enough to understand. Although God gave Jenna a free will, He will move in her heart in proportion to your praying. Pray, pray, pray!

"No one can make that decision for your child, not even you, her parent. Even Jesus didn't assume that authority over anybody. Although Jesus wept over Jerusalem, longing to gather them to Himself, they would not. Although those He was weeping over were born into Jewish families, they chose not to follow Jesus. Nothing you can do, Jan, will guarantee that Jenna will go to heaven. *That is strictly a personal decision every person must make—no matter who their parents are or what ritual or rite of passage they have gone through."*

And the prayers for Jenna's salvation were answered. While Jenna still was a preschooler, as her parents were praying together with her at bedtime, she prayed so sweetly and sincerely, "Jesus forgive my sins and come into my heart."

TRAIN UP A CHILD

What about "train up a child in the way he should go, and when he is old he will not depart from it" (Prov. 22:6). I have had many parents almost defensively say to me, "But I *have* trained up my child in the way he/she should go. So why isn't he/she living a Christian life?"

First, that verse doesn't say that the child will *never* go through the "prodigal son" stage, rebelling against God and family. It says "when he is *old* he will not depart from it." That explains temporary "departings."

Also, I have been astounded at the lifestyle of some parents who honestly believed they had brought up their children "the way they should go." Their gods had been money, careers, social status, or pleasures instead of the godly lifestyle the Bible dictates. Examples in the home of self-centeredness instead of the biblical caring for others, amassing treasure on earth instead of heaven, putting the body above the soul in priorities—all directed the child away from, instead of toward, God.

But there are Christian households in which children are trained to go God's way, and the children go wrong. There is no apparent condemnation of the New Testament father whose son became the famous prodigal. Therefore, believing parents who have faithfully trained their children in the way they should go should not feel they are failures. Once I was discussing these matters with our daughter Nancy. She commented, "Mother, the danger of a good Christian home is that the children learn to say all the right things and learn all the right Scriptures —but they may never internalize them into their own lives. And they may never make their salvation personal."

When parents have done the very best they could, but the children turn their backs on everything the parents hold dear, rebel at all that has been taught them, and pick friends that horrify the parents—it is time to reevaluate their child's actual relationship with Jesus. Of course, this may be just their cutting the apron strings or trying their wings to find out who they are. But it is important to make sure your child actually has the *new nature* the Bible promises:

> For by these He has granted to us His precious and magnificent promises, in order that by them you might become *partakers of the divine nature,* having escaped the corruption that is in the world by lust (2 Peter 1:4, italics added).

THE PRAYER FOR SALVATION

Yes, the prayer for salvation is the most important prayer I, as her mother, prayed for Jan and her sister, Nancy, and brother, Kurt. I persisted, frequently agonized in prayer, until I had listened to each of my three children invite Jesus into their lives. It also was the most important prayer my mother prayed for me.

I remember the family prayers that brought me to Jesus. I was born into a family that knew nothing about this personal relationship with Jesus. In fact, my family knew little of Jesus Himself. But when my mother trusted Jesus as her Savior when we children were young, her first thought was for our salvation too.

Nobody taught my mother to pray. There were no prayer seminars and "how-to" books available to her. She just listened to the older saints in Wednesday night prayer meetings—and started to pray. And her first prayers were for her children's and her husband's salvation. As mentioned earlier, I was only nine years old, but it was my mother's zeal for Jesus and fervency of her prayer that brought results that very year.

Never question if it is right to pray for a family member's salvation. The Bible clearly says that "God . . . desires all men to be saved and to come to the knowledge of the truth" (1 Tim. 2:3-4). And again, "The Lord . . . is patient toward you, not wishing for any to perish but for all to come to repentance" (2 Peter 3:9).

Although Paul apparently never married, it was for his whole extended Jewish family that he said that his "heart's desire and my prayer to God" was for their salvation (Rom. 10:1). And I have joined Paul in making this the number one prayer for my whole extended family too.

Have you made it your prayer for your family?

HOW OLD MUST A CHILD BE TO COME TO CHRIST?

The age a child can understand he or she needs sins forgiven and Jesus as Savior varies tremendously depending on his or her training and exposure to Jesus. There are steps in a child's development starting at grasping "Jesus loves me" to the ultimate awareness of being a sinner and needing the Savior.

My son-in-love Skip reinforced that needing a Savior from their sins develops at different times in children. "There are tears in my eyes," he said to me, "when I think back to our Crista saying when she was just twenty-two months old, 'I yove Jesus.' Then when she was just three-and-a-half-years old, after listening to a Bible story on a James Dobson radio program, her spontaneous and unprompted prayer was, 'I'm sorry, God, for breaking Your rules.'" It was just two days later in church that she had her dad write a note and put it in the offering plate saying, "I love Jesus . . . (signed) Crista." And after falling asleep that Easter night, she opened her eyes and said, "He is risen," and went back to sleep. *Her Savior*!

Crista's own daddy was a little boy when he sat on the knee of the child evangelist and received Jesus—again the product of praying parents who cared enough for lost souls to have started in their living room a now-thriving church.

The concept of doing wrong may develop earlier in a child than we expect, and we must keep alert to make sure we help children translate that into receiving Jesus when it is time.

A NUTURING ENVIRONMENT

It happened very early in Jan, Crista's mother, our oldest child, too. It was two months before Jan's fourth birthday when I found her facing the wall on her bed, crying. She had just listened to her daddy preach through an Easter series of sermons. When I asked her what was wrong, she sobbed out that "the awful, awful naughty things" she had done had hung Jesus on that cross.

Sensing immediately that God clearly was dealing with her, although I hadn't dreamed she had started to understand, I gently led Jan through the prayer of asking God to forgive all those bad things she had done— and then asking Jesus to come into her heart and be her Savior. It was one of the most definite, and thrilling, salvation prayers I ever have heard— and it's still holding to this day! God answered my prayers much more quickly than I had expected.

One of the greatest days of my life as a mother was when I had the un-believable joy of praying with my last child, Kurt, as he asked Jesus into his heart as a seven-year-old grade schooler. *All of my children saved!*

Kurt's father (my husband, Chris) had received Jesus at the same age as he and his parents were returning home after his mother had preached an evangelistic sermon in a mission. Young Chris asked his dad to stop the car because he wanted to ask Jesus into his life. For years young Chris had heard his father pray fervently for him and for the lost people his parents were trying to reach for Jesus. And repeatedly, young Chris had heard his mother explain in their meetings how to become a Christian.

In relation to Kurt's coming to Christ, his dad had preached the Gos-pel in his hearing. And I had prayed every day while Kurt was in my womb, and after he was born I had rocked him to sleep with songs about Jesus. As with our other children also, I had prayed at his crib every night until he was ready for me to pray *with* him. So our son also was ready— ready to bow his head with his parents and receive Jesus as his Savior, as his own dad had done at age seven.

MAKING SURE

Our second child, Nancy, also prayed with me asking Jesus into her heart while a preschooler, but she remembers a step she took later. She definitely felt she already was a Christian, and clearly remembers talking to God in prayer. In fact, she told me, she remembers praying a lot with her Grandma Moss, frequently saying, "Father, if there is anything in my life that is wrong, forgive me." But at age eight she attended a kid's evangelistic meeting and felt she needed assurance of salvation. She then rededicated her life to Jesus. "The 're' was important, Mother," she told me. "I didn't question my salvation, but that day I cemented it."

This step often is necessary when children have made their first commitment to Jesus early. Some really might not have been mature enough, and this actually is their initial accepting of Jesus. And, even though it was a sincere first prayer, more maturity is frequently needed for the child to understand completely the meaning of making Jesus not only Savior but the Lord of his or her life.

Also, there are children who do not reach that "age of accountability" or spiritual maturity until later in grade school or perhaps even junior high school. But it is never too early to start the praying for children to find Jesus as their Savior. Yes, the prayers for our children's salvation started before their births—and continued until God answered.

PRAYING FOR GRANDCHILDREN

I have grandchildren, but God does not. He only has children. We only can become the children—sons and daughters—of God, not His grandchildren.

> But as many as received Him [Jesus], to them He gave the right to become the children of God, even to those who believe in His name (John 1:12).

My prayers for the ultimate salvation of my grandbabies started before they were born, and mingled together with their own parents' prayers. So the prayers for these precious little ones entrusted by God into my children's families multiplied and multiplied until one by one they have received Jesus.

Our son-in-love Dan told me that their Cindy (our first grandchild) definitely reached the "age of accountability" at four. She had a deep understanding that there was a God who sent His Son Jesus into the world to die for her own sins. And she knew she needed to ask forgiveness for her own sins, and very emphatically prayed that prayer with her daddy.

"She was our ponderer, our thinker," Dan said. She understood the good and the bad guys in the universe, and wanted to make the choice for God. One day she said, "Daddy, I have Jesus in my heart now. Satan can't hurt me anymore."

Cindy and her sister Kathy had a lot of early training about Jesus both from their parents and the Christian preschool they attended. From the time they could talk, the school taught those little ones a simple Bible verse for every letter of the alphabet—beginning with "A is for 'All have sinned'" and "B is for 'Believe on the Lord Jesus Christ and thou shalt be saved.'" Through the alphabet they memorized the steps of salvation, the essence of Christianity, and a child's responsibility. I remember how surprised I was when three-year-old Kathy rattled off all those verses for me plus Psalm 23 and dozens of songs about Jesus.

They also learned to pray honestly to God as their Friend at preschool. So it was natural for Kathy to receive Jesus as her Savior, repeating her prayer a couple of times to make sure. Then while still three she popped up in Sunday School and clearly explained that Jesus was living in her heart—the concept that seemed to jell best in her little mind.

No matter how young or old your child is, it is important to start praying now that when your child is ready, he or she will receive Christ.

EVEN BEFORE THEY UNDERSTAND?

A close friend was following the casket holding the body of one of her triplets. "That's my baby; that's my baby in there," she sobbed.

"Mother, will you talk with her?" our Jan pled. "People are telling her that her baby will be in hell eternally."

It was a deep privilege to talk with her about my own four babies I thoroughly expect to be waiting for me in heaven. To explain to her that I am sure my two unborns lost in miscarriages, my full-term stillborn, and my seven-month-old Judy (too young to understand when she died) are in heaven with Jesus! Why am I sure? Because David so definitely said about his dead child, the son born to Bathsheba, "I shall go to him, but he will not return to me" (2 Sam. 12:23). And:

> They were bringing . . . babies to Him [Jesus] so that He might touch them, but when the disciples saw it, they began rebuking them. But Jesus called for them saying, "Permit the children to come to Me, and do not hinder them, for the kingdom of God belongs to such as these" (Luke 18:16).

These Scripture passages make me know that I, with David, will be able to go to my infant offspring too. And, if my two small grandsons' lives here on earth would end before they could understand accepting Jesus, I know our James and Brett will join us in heaven too.

A DYING MOTHER'S LETTERS

It isn't only for a better and holier lifestyle here on earth that we pray for our family members to receive Jesus. Their salvation also determines their eternal destiny—either in heaven or hell.

My mother had a clear biblical picture of every one of her family members without Jesus being forever in hell (Rev. 20:15). Her consuming passion was their salvation. I wept as I read two letters my mother wrote while I was a high-schooler. One was to my father and one to us three children written on the eve of her very serious surgery. It was the same surgery that had taken her mother's life, and somehow she was convinced that it would take hers too. Here are what she thought were her final words, written in the hospital, to my unsaved dad:

Dearest Daddy:

As I am facing an operation I do not know but perhaps it might be God's will to take me home that way, so I want to tell you that I am very happy in the Lord and am resting on His precious promises.

I have prayed much for you, Daddy, that you might be saved. I love you so. I feel that God has spoken to you many times through sickness in our family, and now once more He is speaking. It may take the life of one precious to you before your eyes will be fully opened; but, Daddy dear, I gladly give my life if it will be the means of your salvation. Just ask Pastor Larson or any good Christian to show you the way, and I will be waiting for you on the other side. To know Him is life eternal. You will find several salvation texts in the front page of my Bible. Read them and believe them.

If I must leave you, Daddy, I hope you can find a good Christian woman to come in and keep house. The children will need someone to mother them and to continually remind them to keep looking up, to keep praying, and no matter what happens to just put their whole trust in Him who died for them.

Do not let my going hurt you so that you give up, Daddy Dear, but rather give thanks to God that you have found your Lord and that you know we shall meet again and be together for all eternity.

Mother

Yes, the most important prayer to pray for our family members is for their eternal salvation!

How to Pray When Loved Ones Hurt

MOST PRAYERS FOR FAMILY members are uttered because someone in the family is hurting. It is watching our loved ones suffer that drives us to our knees, begging God to intervene. Sometimes God's answer comes immediately, the hurt is handled, and a quick "thank-You" finishes it. But there are other times when the problem causing the hurt persists—hours, days, even years. How do we pray then?

In the Bible I received for my eighteenth birthday from my then boyfriend, Chris, I underlined in red God's answer to that question in Hebrews 11:6—*faith!*

> And without faith it is impossible to please Him, for he who comes to God must believe that He is, and that He is a rewarder of those who seek Him.

And through all these years it has been God's rule for my praying—*in faith.*

FAITH THAT IS TRIED

But sometimes the depth of the suffering or the duration of the need severely tries our faith. I'll never forget how my daily prayers deepened in intensity month after month as our entire family prayed for our son-in-law Dan Thompson when he suffered his job loss for refusing to lie to Congress in connection with the irregularities he discovered in the books of the Farm Credit Administration for whom he worked as a financial analyst. As previously mentioned, he could not find another financial position despite the fact the national Merit Systems Protection Board had ruled six months later in Dan's favor—all because his former employer had appealed the case. Dan and Nancy were plunged into a nightmarish situation.

As I prayed during the early weeks of this ordeal, I began to feel a gnawing fear for Dan's reputation and future forming in the pit of my stomach. One night I was awake, pleading with God for several hours. The next morning I knelt at my prayer pouf several more hours, imploring God to bring truth and justice to the situation. Early the following morning I was desperate. As I picked up my Bible, I prayed, "Father, I *must* have an answer. Please—*today!*" With tears in my eyes, I began reading devotionally in Luke 8 at the story of Jairus.

Jairus, a ruler of the synagogue, was entreating Jesus to come to his house because his twelve-year-old daughter was dying. But when a messenger came with the news that his daughter already was dead, what Jesus said to Jairus almost jumped off the page at me:

Don't be afraid any longer; only believe, and she will be made well (Luke 8:50).

I cried out, "O God, I believe Dan will be healed. Increase my faith."

The fear suddenly evaporated, vanished, lifted from me like a heavy cloud. Yes, the problem was still there, but my heart soared as I wrote "*promise!*" in the margin of my Bible.

I couldn't wait to phone Dan and tell him what God had promised me, and was disappointed when Dan was not at home. But God didn't want me to tell him—He wanted to tell him Himself! That same day, God gave Dan the very same verse, and in shock we compared notes that evening. The message—that was to carry us for three and a half years—came from God almost simultaneously to both of us 1,000 miles apart: "Only believe!" *Have faith!*

FAITH REMOVES FEAR

I was reading in the *New American Standard Bible,* and two explanatory words have been added after Jesus said, "Do not be afraid." They are "any longer."

Jesus is not surprised at human fear when we are encountering the unknown, facing a calamity, anticipating excruciating pain, or experiencing a devastating disaster. Jesus understood the fear in that father's heart—and in mine. I remained kneeling in silence several minutes, engulfed by the wonder of my Lord, overwhelmed at how He understood my human frailty. The tears turned to praise and thankfulness—and worship of my wonderful Lord.

That was the end of my fear. Although the problem was not solved for three and a half more years, that fear didn't rear its ugly head again. "Don't be afraid any longer!" said Jesus. "I'm here!"

It was a whole year later, still in the midst of the devastating problem, that Jesus summed it up when He gave John 16:33 to me for Dan and Nancy:

> These things I have spoken to you, that in Me you may have peace. In the world you have tribulation, but take courage; I have overcome the world.

BASE FAITH ON SCRIPTURE

It is important to base our faith, not on our own whims and wants, but on what God says in the Bible. Faith is not blind faith in what we ourselves decide we want. It is faith in what God says to us in His Word, the Bible. It is God giving us His doctrine, reproof, correction, and instruction in righteousness (2 Tim. 3:16) out of the Bible that forms the basis of what we pray in faith.

The Jairus promise was just one Scripture, although a very important one, that God gave for Dan and Nancy. There was a three-and-a-half-year running account of promises, warnings, and instructions. Here are a couple examples of a specific Scripture for a specific need at a specific time:

In May 1988 while Dan was struggling in prayer and rationalizing whether or not he should expose the financial discrepancies, God gave me Ephesians 5:11 for him:

> Do not participate in the unfruitful deeds of darkness, but instead even *expose* them (italics added).

And just before that, God had given Jesus' position on truth out of John 3:20-21:

> For everyone who does evil hates the light, and does not come to the light, lest his deeds should be exposed. But he who practices the truth comes to the light, that his deeds may be manifested as having been wrought in God.

It is human nature to pray for things to come out all in our favor—whether we deserve it or not. But prayer doesn't allow that, for it is petition to God. And His treatment of His creatures conforms to the purity of His innermost nature. Justice is a fundamental quality of God—the revelation of His holiness.

Through those years I never had the freedom to pray anything for the outcome of Dan's problem except justice. God would not let me pray, "Restore everything to Dan—income, his reputation, his job." Rather the Holy Spirit led me to pray, "Father, You alone know all the facts. Know which things Dan actually does deserve to have restored—and if there are some he doesn't. Lord, we want only Your all-knowing justice."

> Does God pervert justice or does the Almighty pervert that which is right? (Job 8:3)

Jesus clearly stated the answer in John 5:30:

> I can do nothing on My own initiative, as I hear, I judge; and My judgment is just; because I do not seek My own will, but the will of Him who sent Me.

God used innumerable Scriptures about His justice to instruct and encourage us, including passages stating that those who do the wrong will receive the consequences without partiality (Col. 3:25), and God will give relief to the afflicted when Jesus returns (2 Thes. 1:7). "Who will bring a charge against God's elect? It is God who justifies" (Rom. 8:33). *God's justice!*

I have all the Bibles I have used devotionally since I was eighteen, with dates and notes of what the Lord had for me to pray right then. Through my fifty years of marriage, God always has given me exactly what and how He wanted me to pray—for myself and my family members. And when He said it, I have stepped out, confidently or shakily, praying in faith.

ENCOURAGEMENT FROM OTHERS TOO

Members of my United Prayer Ministries board prayed for Dan all those years too, and God gave them Scripture verses for him also. Amazingly, those who were going through the deepest trials with their own families often were the ones God gave the most insightful Scriptures for Dan and Nancy. One member, whose heart was still breaking over her own daughter who disappeared just before graduating from medical school taking her two daughters with her, sent this incredible promise to Dan:

> God will not reject a man of integrity, nor will He support the evildoers. He will yet fill your mouth with laughter, and your lips with shouting (Job 8:20-21).

Another board member's daughter had a baby out of wedlock, for years kept running away, dealing drugs, and then vanishing for weeks with the infant, or leaving the baby with its alcoholic father, who abused the baby with cigarette burns. The board member's verses from God to Dan were:

> "And they will fight against you, but they will not overcome you, for I am with you to deliver you," declares the Lord (Jer. 1:19).

"For I know the plans that I have for you," declares the Lord, "plans for welfare and not for calamity to give you a future and a hope" (Jer. 29:11).

"But," said that board member, "all that trouble increased our faith. And we really learned to hang on to God in faith and pray without ceasing." Then smiling, she said, "But God has answered all those prayers of faith. Our daughter now is an honor student in her third year of college."

Most of my board members have had deep hurts in their family members. So it was from personal experience that they decided on November 7, 1988 before Dan had any ruling from the Merit Board that this was God's Scripture for him:

And indeed, all who desire to live godly in Christ Jesus will be persecuted. But evil men and impostors will proceed from bad to worse, deceiving and being deceived. You, however, continue in the things you have learned and become convinced of, knowing from whom you have learned them; and that from childhood you have known the sacred writings (2 Tim. 3:12-15)

But my board members didn't just pull out a Scripture verse they thought fit. Oh, no. They had learned to wait on God for His words in their own hurts, so they waited on God for Dan's too. And then month after month at board meetings, and daily as I sent through specific needs on our telephone prayer chain, their current Scriptures formed the basis of their praying.

Also people from all over the United States phoned or wrote to assure us they were praying. One seminar chairman not only prayed for months, but contacted her U.S. senator about the injustice.

Some dear friends, whose own bank president son-in-law is spending time in prison after a questionable ruling by a judge, called to say they were claiming Psalm 25:1-3 for Dan:

To Thee, O Lord, I lift up my soul. O my God, in Thee I trust. Do not let me be ashamed; do not let my enemies exult over me. Indeed, none of those who wait for Thee will be ashamed; those who deal treacherously without cause will be ashamed.

PRAYING IN FAITH FOR OTHER
FAMILY MEMBERS

When I was praying and God gave me the Jairus promise for Dan, I also was in intense prayer for our son, Kurt, and his wife, Margie, who were making a decision that would affect his whole career. Just finishing his doctoral educational program in physics, Kurt was struggling over his next step. Kurt, Margie, and I all had knelt several times together by the living room prayer pouf asking God to direct them clearly, and it had been a deep subject of prayer for them and all of us for a long time. That morning my prayers for Dan and Kurt were mixed, and God knew I needed the "faith" promise for both. After praying, "O God, I believe Dan will be healed. Increase my faith," I immediately added, "I *believe* you will send Kurt and Margie where You want them!" *Faith!*

Our family members have hurt in many ways. God gave the word *faith* when our Jan and Skip had been married ten years, and still desperately wanted their first baby. After years of their praying (and mine) for our daughter to be able to conceive, I was reading in Hebrews 11, the Bible's great faith chapter. It surprised me that after the passage emphasized the faith of Sarah's husband, Abraham, the list of males of faith abruptly changed to a female's faith—Sarah's. And, as that verse quickened my heart, my own faith soared.

> By faith even Sarah herself received ability to conceive [the power for the laying down of seed], even beyond the proper time of life, since *she* considered Him [God] faithful who had promised (v. 11, italics added).

This was added to the wonderful promise God had given to Jan's husband, Skip, just as he had to Abraham, Sarah's husband. And our Skip too had clung to God's promise with unshakable faith.

WHEN FAITH DOES NOT SEEM REWARDED

It is important to read all of that Hebrews faith chapter in the Bible because there were many other Old Testament heroes of the faith who, although they had gained approval through their faith, did not receive what was promised. Some were tortured, stoned, mocked, scourged, chained and imprisoned, put to death, afflicted, ill-treated, and even sawn in two (vv. 35-39). They did not see the promise.

Not all of our prayers of faith have been answered the way we wanted them here on earth either. The biblical reasons are many. Dan had felt strongly that God, in His waiting to give answers to our prayers, was teaching us. We have discovered that to be true in our family trials through the years. Chapter 6 of this book will give the things God was teaching our family while He was silent during our praying in times of trouble.

Most importantly, the time for the proof of our faith is coming.

> In this you greatly rejoice, even though now for a little while, if necessary, you have been distressed by various trials, that the *proof of your faith,* being more precious than gold which is perishable, even though tested by fire, may be found to result in praise and glory and honor at the revelation of Jesus Christ (1 Peter 1:6-7, italics added).

FAITH IN WHAT—OR WHOM?

In what—or whom—do we put our faith when praying? Faith in our ability to have faith? Faith in the words printed on a page of the Bible? No. The faith must be in the God who gave the Bible's promises.

Jesus interrupted His interaction with Jairus to give a tremendous visual lesson about the object of our faith—Himself. A woman with an issue of blood for twelve years had come up behind Him and touched the hem of His cloak. And immediately her bleeding stopped. Although the crowd was pressing around Him, Jesus demanded to know who had touched Him in the special way that He felt power go out of Himself. When the woman fell trembling at His feet declaring why she had touched Him, Jesus explained what had healed her—her faith in Him—even just touching the hem of His garment.

> Daughter, your faith has made you well; go in peace (Luke 8:48).

This prepared Jairus to receive his simple "only believe" from Jesus. The Lord had just proven before the eyes of the mourners that He had power over physical problems. And, although the mourners scoffed without faith, Jairus and his wife had the thrill of watching Jesus take their dead daughter's hand, telling her to arise. And her spirit returned to her—resuscitated. The result of faith!

Through the years of seeing God answer family prayers in our hurts makes it easier for us to have faith in God too. Four years ago, as mentioned earlier, a doctor found a small growth in my husband, Chris. But even before we received the results of the biopsy telling us it was cancerous, Chris and I both prayed together that night, "Thank You, God, that You never have let us down in all our deep things. This could be one of the worst we have to face, but it is so good to be able to trust You completely for our future. Thank You, Lord, for this assurance we both have tonight."

Knowing who God is is an important part of our praying in faith. After we received the biopsy result of "cancer," our daughter-in-love Margie sent the following Scripture to us uttered by Jeremiah calling to the Lord from the depths of the pit. She reminded us that this hope can bring us through every trial if we will only call it to mind:

> Yet this I call to mind and therefore I hope: Because of the Lord's great love we are not consumed, for His compassions never fail. They are new every morning; great is Your faithfulness. I say to myself, "The Lord is my portion; therefore I will wait for Him." The Lord is good to those whose hope is in Him (Lam. 3:21-25, NIV).

Then it was Margie who gave these same verses to our Nancy when she was behind in her studying for her R.N. degree because her little Kathy had broken her leg—and Nancy herself had been in a car accident the day before, causing her back and neck to ache, this in addition to deep nausea that morning. *Faith in God—producing hope.*

Yes, our faith begins and develops in our Lord—not ourselves.

> Fixing our eyes on Jesus, the author and perfecter of faith. . . . Consider Him . . . so that you may not grow weary and lose heart (Heb. 12:2, 4).

PERSEVERE IN PRAYER

No, praying in faith doesn't necessarily bring instantaneous results. Many of our family problems have persisted for long periods of time—while we persisted in prayer. Sometimes it is hours, such as the three hours each of two consecutive nights while our Kurt took his entrance tests for a physics doctoral program. And when I became sleepy after just the first hour of praying, God shaking me with Jesus' words in the Garden of Gethsemene, "What, could you not watch with Me *one* hour?"

Sometimes it is persevering consecutive days such as when our Jan, ten days overdue with her first child, took her medical board exams for eight hours two days in a row. Before starting, I had wondered how I would be able to stay in prayer that long, but the Lord kept reminding me, "Pray now for her aching shoulders as she bends over those papers so long." Or, "She's cold." "Pray for clarity of mind." "The day is getting too long." Then, "Pray for Me [God] to take My holy hands and lift that heavy burden pressing in her womb." The next day Jan and I compared notes as to what times she had needed those specific things. And, to our amazement, every one was exactly when God had told me to pray!

But most of the time our persisting prayer is for those ongoing, day-by-day nagging troubles that hassle a family. Jesus taught us a valuable lesson about keeping on praying in His parable of a family situation where the unjust judge gave in to the widow's request because she kept bothering him so much.

> Now He was telling them a parable to show that at all times they ought to pray and *not to lose heart* (Luke 18:1, italics added).

Every family member does not get equal prayertime each day—reciting by rote each name during a formal prayertime. Our praying for each other is in proportion to the need of each. There are times one family member requires concentrated prayer from us right then—sickness, surgery, giving birth, danger, unfair treatment, emotional or spiritual needs.

Much of the time it is those immediate, imperative situations that demand our prayer right then. The first day of Dan's Merit Board hearing in August 1988, most of our family was on vacation on the shores of Lake Michigan. We promised Dan that would be our day of prayer, and there was much individual prayer and at meals. But in the afternoon we gathered in the shallow water to pray. Jan was on the big yellow supertube as Skip knelt on one side and I on the other with the waves lapping over our feet. Chris came and stood in the water as we all prayed for Dan.

That morning Skip had spent time studying biblical truth and justice in his devotions, and he formed the words first. "Truth and justice is what I am praying, Lord." The same words were mine. "Jesus, give the judge eyes to see the truth. May justice, only justice, prevail. Not unfair settlements. Just justice." One after the other prayed that prayer. Then we prayed for clarity of mind as Dan testified. For peace. For God's arms to be around Dan.

The next month when ABC national television interviewed Dan in the office of U.S. Senator Grassley, chairman of the Senate Investigating Committee, my grandniece Kirsten and I knelt at the living room prayer pouf and poured out our hearts to God. We prayed for God to make Dan Christlike, that people would see only Jesus in him. We prayed for great wisdom from God. "Take away all thoughts *he* thinks he should say. Put in his mind, Holy Spirit, exactly the words *You* want him to say. Protect his mind. Keep it clear, sharp. Keep his attitude Christlike at all times. Please!"

Then Kirsten prayed for Nancy—for her peace, her physical needs, her nervousness, her tension. Then I prayed for God to come into her whole being and fill her with Himself.

Later the prayer was for God to protect every word Dan had said. To keep *truth* there, not the way the news media sometimes twists things.

WHEN WE DON'T WANT TO PRAY

When a family hurt drags on for weeks, months, and even years, it is hard to keep on praying as instructed in Ephesians 6:18:

> With all prayer and petition pray at all times in the Spirit, and with this in view, be on the alert with all *perseverance* and petition for all the saints (italics added).

Dan's wife, our Nancy, ran out of patience several times. "Mom, I just prayed, 'Do something, God!'"

When the pressure got too great, Dan even admitted getting angry with God a couple of times, praying much as the psalmist often prayed. "God, You *can* do something. Why *don't* You? Why are You so silent—so long?"

I remember one day sagging under the ongoing load of so much praying, and complaining, "Lord, I'm sick and tired of praying these prayers!" And I was. That kind of prayer is hard work. And I was tired.

But those attitudes were sin—and we knew it. Being able to confess them melted those fleeting negative feelings, and we settled into the regular prayer routine again.

WHEN WE DON'T KNOW WHAT TO PRAY

The day after our deep family praying for Dan on the beach, I had a surprise. At 5:45 A.M. I tried to pray for him, but my utterances were just perfunctory words. I would pray for other family members, and then come back to Dan again. But still nothing. At 8 o'clock I finally said, "Lord, I don't know how to pray for Dan today. There is nothing there. After hours of wrestling in prayer for him yesterday, I just don't understand it."

Finally, after praying about my own cleansing and any other hindrance I could think of, I blurted out, "Father, I don't know how to pray for Dan today. Holy Spirit, please pray *for* me. Romans 8:26-27 is where I am today." Then I recited the passage:

> And in the same way the Spirit also helps our weakness; for we do not
> know how to pray as we should, but the Spirit Himself intercedes for us
> with groanings too deep for words; and He who searches the hearts knows
> what the mind of the Spirit is, because He intercedes for the saints accord-
> ing to the will of God.

Then the Holy Spirit took over, and for fifteen minutes *He* prayed. I
formed no words except "Dan" and "Holy Spirit" for the entire time.
What a precious relief!

ELEVENTH-HOUR ANSWERS

Sometime later Dan was at our summer cottage. Looking up from
his dinner plate, Dan asked, "Why does God so frequently wait until the
eleventh hour to answer, when He knows all along how He is going to
answer when we pray about a problem?" He shook his head and wondered aloud, "Why am I still making mortgage payments on two houses
with no income?"

"I've struggled a lot with that one, Dan," I replied. "In fact, I'm questioning having the right to write a book on family prayers with such a big
one still outstanding in our own family."

Why did God wait until the very last minute to rescue Peter when
Herod was about to kill him just as he had killed the Apostle James—in
spite of so much prayer being made for Peter?

> And on the *very night* when Herod was about to bring him forward, Peter
> was sleeping between two soldiers, bound with two chains. . . . And be-
> hold, an angel of the Lord suddenly appeared, and a light shone in the
> cell; and he struck Peter's side, saying, "Get up quickly." And his chains
> fell off his hands (Acts 12:6-7, italics added).

We have had intermediate eleventh-hour answers too numerous to
mention, but the big one came the night before I was scheduled to start
writing this chapter. I had resigned myself to having to report that we are
still in the waiting stage—*in faith*. Perhaps, I thought, it was God's will

for us to be waiting because so many Christians reading this book would be in that same situation in their family prayer life. But God wanted the victory to be written in this chapter—our faith praying rewarded!

As I was about to begin writing this chapter the next day on praying in faith for loved ones when they hurt, I was still in North Carolina following a speaking engagement. When I called home that night, Chris just exploded the good news over the phone. "Dan won his case! The Merit Board has not only upheld its first decision but has cleared Dan's name completely—and actually praised him for his stand and integrity."

The Associated Press put it succinctly in a news release:

> A Farm Credit Administration (FCA) employee who refused to lie to Congress was back at work Monday, three years after a judge ruled he had been fired illegally.
>
> Daniel J. Thompson was fired in May 1988 after he accused the agency of destroying internal studies [Dan's] that showed the Farm Credit System was in deeper financial straits than its then-chairman . . . wanted to reveal to Congress.

Then the AP quoted Senator Grassley, who headed the government's investigation:

> It's obvious Thompson was wrongly fired, and it's also clear that Congress got incomplete information four years ago [when Congress approved a $4 billion bailout of the system]. As the court order states, he was fired in retaliation because the information would have been embarrassing to the chairman of the FCA.

The press release concluded with,

> Grassley said Thompson has been awarded back pay, but "this alone cannot make up for all that he has lost because he elected to be forthright and honest."

When your family members hurt—*pray in faith. It works!*

How to Pray When Loved Ones Hurt Us

A YOUNG WOMAN sought me out at a convention. "I am a psychiatric nurse with a master's degree and just have been offered a full scholarship for a doctorate at a fine university," she began. "God has told me to have you pray for me as to whether or not it is something I should accept." As she told me about her success with some of the most difficult patients, I realized she knew the dimension that is frequently missing in this field—*God*. She adds prayer, making her very needed and uniquely qualified to help victims.

Here is one of her experiences that convinced me. "I was assigned a violent psychiatric patient who had not shaved for fourteen years, with a tangled beard down to his waist. He had physically hurt so many caregivers that nobody wanted to go in his hospital room, and he hadn't let anybody touch him all that time. Fourteen years ago his family, not being able to get him to change something wrong in his life, agreed with a counselor that what he needed was an 'intervention procedure.' So his family had gathered and pounced on him, brutally accusing him and exposing his wrongdoing. It so shocked him that he mentally snapped— and he has been in this condition in that psychiatric hospital ever since.

"But," the nurse continued, "*I am a Christian. And I prayed and prayed about that man.* Finally, ignoring his fierce threats of 'You know I can really hurt you,' I walked into his room and began a slow process of tenderly working through his hardened shell—while I prayed. And,' she bubbled, "it *is* working. He gradually has let me touch his hand—and even pray for him!"

Assuming someone in his family was a believer and could have prayed for him, what part could prayer have played if it had been applied earlier in the handling of this man's wrongdoing? What might have been avoided if God had been included fourteen years earlier? How would God, in response to their praying, have given divine wisdom to those seeking to help that erring family member? If they really had followed God, He could have added His reproof, healing, reconciliation, and restoration of this family's oneness again.

When a family relationship is ruptured that badly, is a lifetime like that inevitable for the victim? Or could prayer—then and even now—help?

PRAYER—WHEN WE HAVE BEEN HURT?

The hardest time to pray in regard to family matters is when we have been hurt by loved ones. All of us are wounded from time to time by those we love (and certainly we all also wound loved ones). I do not believe there is any person who has escaped being hurt at sometime within his or her own family. Even Jesus' own kinsmen must have hurt Him immensely when they came to take custody of Him "because He had lost His senses" (Mark 3:21).

This hurting by loved ones usually is unintentional, and frequently the family members are unaware they have wounded each other. Most of these hurts result from thoughtless acts, words, omissions, or neglect. In the close proximity of families, we accidentally step on each other's toes so easily.

Then there are those times when the words or actions have been with the best of intentions, but have backfired, causing deep wounds in our family members.

And, of course, there are those times when the motive for hurting another family member is revenge—or feeling justified in using some cruel means to accomplish an end the family member has decided must be accomplished. And even when the criticism is deserved, the pain could have been avoided had it been handled in a less hurtful way.

Occasionally, there are those shattering hurts from other family members that absolutely devastate people. They render their victims unable to cope with everyday living (like the man with the fourteen-year beard). Leave them bitter, not caring or, in extreme cases, not even wanting to live. At those times their motive or reason for hurting doesn't seem to count. Whether it was deliberate or unintentional, for our good or theirs, doesn't enter into our thinking. And it certainly doesn't ease the immediate pain.

I'm by nature a hugger. I constantly reach out to hurting people in my ministry's autograph lines and committees. But I vividly remember saying after I'd been deeply hurt by several family members, "It hurts too much to hug them—with this knife sticking in my back."

HOW DO WE PRAY WHEN WE
HAVE BEEN HURT?

Pray? How are we able to pray at those times when we feel betrayed, excluded from their intimate communication, even unwanted? How do we pray while we are just barely treading water ourselves? Or, how do we pray when the little everyday hurts just chip away at us?

It is not the being hurt, but what we *do* with the hurt that will determine our future relationship with that family member.

The prayers at these times can be what keeps a family together. Neglecting to pray, and to pray the right kinds of prayers, almost insures a family split of some kind—physical or at least emotional. *The prayers we pray will determine our future relationship with the family members who hurt us.*

WHAT DO WE PRAY?

There are many prayer *Steps of prayer* in the family healing process. A particularly devastating confrontation in our extended family clearly reminded me of these steps. Immediately after it took place, I had to leave for an important speaking assignment in a college in a neighboring state. Completely shattered, I crawled into the bed in back of our van and desperately cried out to God as my husband drove me to the meeting two and a half hours away. I wept as I prayed. "Lord, what should I do? How should I handle this?" How should I, could I, pray? I begged, "Lord, please give me the attitude *You* want me to have. Other advice can be so confusing, so conflicting, and sometimes so wrong. But never *Your* advice!" I sobbed. "How do I pray when I am bleeding this hard?"

As a result of my prayertime in the van, I began to focus again on the forgiving formula from 2 Corinthians 2:5-11 that I had taught and used personally hundreds of times. I sorted through those points one by one: forgive, comfort, and reaffirm your love—in order that Satan cannot take advantage of the situation. Out of this experience I outlined eight prayers that we should pray when we are hurt by loved ones.

• *Prayer No. 1—"Lord, change me."* God answered me by immediately bringing to my mind that I first should ask the Lord to search my heart and enable me to change my attitude toward the loved ones who had hurt me. I was not surprised. God had taught me that secret for living with others twenty-three years before, and I had written about it in my second book, *Lord, Change Me!* It is the prayer I have prayed more often than any other, frequently several times in a day. And here it was again. Me!

For the first two hours in that van I wept and agonized in prayer, crying, "O Lord, change *me;* change *me!*" "Forgive *me,* Father, for everything that is *my* fault. Lord, make *me* absolutely clean before You!"

It was two hours of Psalm 139:23-24:

> Search me, O God, and know my heart;
> Try me and know my anxious thoughts;
> And see if there be any hurtful way in me,
> And lead me in the everlasting way.

"Lord, forgive me for retaliating verbally," I pleaded. "Lord, cleanse me from my ugly reactions and un-Christlike attitudes." (Through the ensuing months, I recorded innumerable tear-filled prayers of "Lord, change me" as steps of the incident unfolded.)

But only when I felt in that van that I had my own attitudes and my relationship with God in order was I ready to turn to my relationship with those who had hurt me. This sequence is crucial. It is impossible for us humans to forgive others until we have settled our own relationship with our Heavenly Father.

• *Prayer No. 2—"Lord, help me forgive."* The most important prayer in the whole family healing process is prayer that leads to our being able to forgive loved ones—not just in words but truly in our hearts.

So, that last half hour of the trip I spent asking God to help me forgive those family members who had so wounded me. And I did—immediately, within hours after I had been hurt!

I was right back to Jesus' words that I have taught so often in seminars for over twenty years to everybody else. In Matthew 6:14-15 and Mark 11:24 Jesus said that if we forgive others, God will forgive us; but if we don't, He won't! Jesus said it didn't do any good for me to pray those two and a half hours asking God to forgive me if I wasn't willing to forgive also!

I wondered if God had brought Jesus' words to Stephen's mind when he forgave the people who were hurting—and killing—him, the first martyr for Jesus (see Acts 6:8–7:60). It was a scene of terror as the angry mob gnashed their teeth at Stephen, snarling like a pack of attacking dogs. And when he gazed intently into heaven and told them he saw the glory of God and Jesus standing at His right hand, they exploded. Covering their ears, the whole snarling mob erupted into terrifying yells. Shouting, they pushed and shoved Stephen out of the city, and suddenly he felt the stabbing pains of stones crashing against his whole body. Knowing he was dying, Stephen cried out, "Lord Jesus, receive my spirit!" But the remarkable part of Stephen's response to their anger is his dying request. Falling to his knees, he shouted above the angry mob,

"Lord, do not hold this sin against them!" How similar to his Savior's dying words on the cross, "Father, forgive them for they know not what they do!" The secret—*forgiving.*

Many families have gone through times when the bitter words, shouted accusations, and snarling attacks felt like the sharp stones that mutilated Stephen. In most of my seminars, I listen to devastated family members spill out similar horror stories.

So what do we do when family members hurt us? We first settle our own relationship with God, letting Him prepare us and give us the ability to forgive (which may take considerable time). And then, as I in my heart did in that van, we fall before God and forgive.

Jesus put a high priority on being reconciled. If you remember that a fellow believer has something against you when you are giving your offering, first go and be reconciled before you present your offering. God doesn't even want our money if we aren't willing to forgive and be reconciled: "First be reconciled to your brother, and then come and present your offering" (Matt. 5:24). And Jesus warns that God will punish those who, having been forgiven themselves, refuse to forgive someone else: "So shall My Heavenly Father . . . [punish] you, if each of you does not forgive his brother from his heart" (Matt. 18:35).

I was surprised to find out from a "Dear Abby" newspaper column that there is an annual International Forgiveness Week at the end of each January. Abby gave this beautiful thought from George Roemisch:

> Forgiveness is the fragrance of the violet that clings fast to the heel that crushed it.

Forgiving does not mean that we condone what people have done. And it does not absolve the sinner of accountability to God—or responsibility to the one hurt. *Forgiving is the step God, in His omniscient wisdom, provided the victim, to heal his hurt, mend the relationship, and restore the God-intended unity in family relationships.*

• *Prayer No. 3—"Lord, help me comfort those who hurt me."* In addition to praying "Lord, change me" and to enable you to forgive, the next step is to pray to be able to comfort those who have hurt you. The Apostle Paul wrote concerning treatment of "any [who] has caused sorrow . . . forgive and comfort him" (2 Cor. 2:5, 7).

Early one morning at my prayer pouf, I randomly had turned to the story of the end of Joseph's life in Genesis 50. After Joseph's brothers had sold him into slavery, they were starving in a famine, and God used Joseph to rescue them. The brothers who had hurt him worried, "What if Joseph should bear a grudge against us and pay us back in full for all the wrong which we did to him?" What if Joseph hadn't forgiven them? And I wrote in the margin of my Bible, "What if I should hold a grudge?" What would happen?

But Joseph calmed their fears by saying, "Do not be afraid." Joseph had no intention of retaliating. He had forgiven his brothers for being so unfaithful and mean to him. Then he comforted them by speaking kindly to them.

Suddenly hot tears blinded my eyes. This is to be *my* attitude! Months before I had decided no accusing confrontation until some touchy circumstances cleared themselves. But now God confirmed that comforting and speaking kindly was to be my attitude *always*. I mentally considered each of the family members involved, resolving that there would be no attitude of retaliation toward any of them—ever. And the peace of God settled in all around me.

● *Prayer No. 4—"Lord, enable me to pray for those who hurt me."* When loved ones hurt us, we must pray *for* them, not just *about* them. Praying for them not only involves God in their healing process, it changes us also while and because we pray. Jesus said, "But I say unto you, love your enemies, and *pray for those who persecute you*" (Matt. 5:44, italics added).

Immediately after our Dan had illegally lost his government job because of refusing to lie to Congress, his family was praying together about it. There were all kinds of prayers flying up to God concerning their rights, their emotional and financial survival, and God dealing with the agency head who had fired Dan. But suddenly Cindy, their then six-year-old, prayed, "Dear God, what that naughty man needs is Jesus. Please save him!" She alone had grasped the need to pray *for* the troublemakers. The rest of us had to catch up with her insight in obeying Jesus' words in Matthew 5:44, "Pray for those who persecute you."

It is easy to pray telling God "to get even for us," "to heap coals of fire on their heads," "to give them what they deserve." Praying *for* them when they have hurt us is more difficult.

It frequently takes time to come to this place. A local pastor had sexually abused more than a hundred young boys in his churches, and the hurts were incredibly deep. But now, two years later, many of the parents of the victims have finally been healed enough by God to be able to forgive—and now are praying *for* that pastor while he is incarcerated. God has taken them through the stages of grief so necessary to be able to forgive, so that praying for him is possible.

Infidelity is one of the deepest hurts in a family. It isn't easy, for example, for a wife to pray *for* a husband who is having an affair with another woman. But a beautiful, meticulously groomed woman at a seminar handed me a note about how she was praying even for the other woman in her husband's life. "I'm praying that God will so fill the needs of my husband's girlfriend with Himself that she won't need to be fulfilled by my husband anymore."

• *Prayer No. 5—"Lord, help me love."* Again, in His Sermon on the Mount, Jesus included *loving* in His instructions to pray for those who persecute you: "*Love your enemies,* and pray for those who persecute you" (Matt. 5:44, italics added).

A woman at a recent prayer convention told me she was deeply hurt by her son's choice of a wife, and kept praying for the Lord to change her daughter-in-law. Suddenly the woman realized that *she herself* needed to change her own attitudes, so she prayed, "Lord, give me the *love* You want me to have for my daughter-in-law." And, she said, that prayer changed things completely!

The prayer "Fill me with Your love, Lord" has had amazing effects upon me in my family relationships through the years. It has turned my negative attitudes into love for those who have hurt me instead of "just obeying" Jesus' command to pray for those who have wounded me. It is hard to fathom that such a little prayer could have such profound effects.

The Bible's warnings to Christians in 1 John about *not* loving are truly frightening:

> By this the children of God and the children of the devil are obvious: anyone who does not practice righteousness is not of God, nor the one who does not love his brother (3:10).

> If someone says, "I love God," and hates his brother, he is a liar; for the one who does not love his brother whom he has seen cannot love God whom he has not seen (4:20).

One of the most precious memories I have is of the late evening one of my daughters and I sat alone in her darkened living room, working out a deep hurt. The rift had come so unexpectedly. Though she had had the best of intentions of fixing a need in our extended family, the situation had suddenly erupted into accusations flying and loved ones vocally defending their own points of view. That night as our time of praying and talking came to an end, we sat with our arms entwined around each other. The tears streamed down our faces and mingled into one as we murmured over and over, "I love you, Mama"/"I love you, Darling."

Loving each other is the powerful glue that holds our families together.

> And beyond all these things, put on love, which is the *perfect bond of unity* (Col. 3:1, italics added).

• *Prayer No. 6—"Lord, enable us to pray together."* If at all possible, set up a time to pray *with* the family member who has hurt you. Or quickly take advantage of any opportunity to turn your discussing, arguing, or humanly trying to resolve the differences into prayer.

However, his or her continuing anger, embarrassment, or indifference may make this impossible or even inadvisable. Or he or she may not be ready yet for that depth. But one of the most healing steps in broken family relationships is together inviting the impartial, loving God into the relationship through prayer. His holy presence does wonders in the healing process.

• *Prayer No. 7—"Lord, call others to pray for me—and us."* There are times when we are so shattered by a family hurt that praying for ourselves, and a family member who has inflicted the hurt, is impossible. Words simply won't come. This is when the crisscrossing prayers of other family members take over for us.

And this is also when I call my prayer chains. For over twenty years I have had my ministry's board members organized on telephone prayer chains ready to pray for me and my family—and I for them, as previously mentioned. When I send through a prayer request, they don't expect all the gory details—just that I need special, intense prayer right then. It is so wonderful to feel God lift the burden *while* they pray! And it is exciting to watch Him answer—*because* they prayed!

My phone rings several times a week—sometimes a day—with a broken spouse, parent, or child asking us to pray for them because they just can't handle being hurt by a family member. And we always do. But then I encourage them to get into some local prayer group of people who care and will pray for them. Or, if not available, to organize two or three Christians who will faithfully hold them up in prayer through their trial. Or I encourage them to use their church's telephone prayer chain, telling them that having a few pray-ers right around them in ongoing problems produces profound results in the problem—and in them. I know!

WHEN THEY WON'T HUG, WHAT DO WE PRAY?

The ones who hurt us may still feel anger even though we have forgiven them and are praying for them. There are still things about which they may be angry—justifiably or not. Perhaps they have not forgiven us or accepted our forgivness. Or they may not see their own responsibility for their actions, not feeling there is any initiative they need to take. Or they aren't ready in their healing process to hug yet.

So, what do we do when *they won't hug?* Over that we have have no control. We are only required to follow the Bible's admonition in Romans 12:18-19:

> If possible, *so far as it depends on you,* be at peace with all men. Never take your own vengence, beloved, but leave room for the wrath of God, for it is written, *"Vengence is Mine, I will repay," says the Lord* (italics added).

"Never take your own vengence, beloved" is hard, especially when we feel we have done everything we were instructed to do in the Bible, and still the hurting goes on. When unfair words cut into us, when uninvited thoughts of defensiveness pop into our minds, when a martyr complex starts to creep in, it is difficult not to retaliate.

And obeying "'Vengence is Mine . . . , says the Lord'" is even harder at times like these. Actually practicing leaving the matter with God is not easy. But forgetting the "getting even" and retaliating, and leaving the justice to God is our only hope for reconciliation in family squabbles and hurts.

I've learned an amazing secret. Many years ago during a hurtful Christenson family situation, the Lord relentlessly kept bringing to my mind, "'Vengence is *Mine* . . ., says the Lord.'" Then I found myself *praying* it back to Him over and over and over. In such situations, that repeated prayer almost miraculously changes *my* attitudes and feelings. I no longer need to retaliate—or lick my wounds. And I am able to settle back in peace.

● *Prayer No. 8—"Lord, break the 'victim chain.'"* Everybody is a victim. Every family member is at times the victim of their other family members during various circumstances. Siblings frequently are victims of their brothers and sisters. Children are victims of their parents. Parents also are victims of their children's actions, words, and attitudes. And their parents are victims of their parents—the grandparents. It goes on and on.

As I chatted about this with a best-selling author/psychologist at a

Christian Booksellers Association convention, he remarked, "Everybody is a victim of a victim of a victim of a victim. All the way back to Adam and Eve. We're *all* victims."

Standing one day at my father's grave, I did some mathematics on the dates of those buried around him. His father was buried with his three wives! Quickly, I deduced that my father had been deprived of two mothers very young in life. He had been the victim of a very difficult childhood. After his confession to my mother, it had taken me two years to forgive my father for being unfaithful to her making her (and then me) his victim. But, standing at that grave, I suddenly saw not just myself as *his* victim, but *him* as a victim also. How I wished, too late, that I had understood in my early adulthood when I was so angry with him.

All parents, even though their children may be victims of their sins and inadequacies, also were victims of their parents, who were the victims of their parents.

And more and more we are seeing parents and grandparents becoming a new generation of victims by being blamed by their own "adult children" for their problems.

Since being a victim is inevitable for us all, is it possible for us to break the victim chain? Does everybody have to keep the "victim mentality" forever? Does each consecutive generation pile up all their past hurts and keep them in a seething caldron inside of themselves as "adult children"?

This is where the omniscient, omnipotent God of the universe must take over. His Word, the Bible, has some good advice for us:

> When I was a child, I used to speak as a child, think as a child, reason as a child; when I became a man, I did away with childish things (1 Cor. 13:11).

God deals with us and expects us to deal with problems as adults, if we are. He certainly is not against our past hurts being identified, but never getting to the place of dealing with them as grown-ups is less than God has provided for us. We must come to a place of being accountable to Him and responsible to others for our attitudes. After we grow up, how we eventually handle the hurts is up to us. And how we handle them determines our ultimate healing. We, with the Apostle Paul, can confidently say, "I can do all things through Christ who strengthens me" (Phil. 4:13).

Prayer is essential here. Two kinds of prayer. Much prayer *by* mature Christians brings God's grace and ability to the struggling victim. And time spent *with* God by the victim infuses him or her with the comfort, love, and courage needed to face the problem.

Of course, there are times professional help is absolutely necessary to identify of whom and how they have been victims—especially when the brain protectingly has blocked out the extreme pain and abuse of a childhood trauma. Professional help may be needed to get to the root of a person's current troubles, especially if he or she has been a victim of physical, emotional, mental, or sexual abuse.

Identifying the problem is a necessary step, *but identifying does not heal.* And living and forever wallowing in the newfound information may only compound the problem. So, once that has been established, how does one change into a happy, productive, spiritually healed adult?

The big word in this procedure is *forgive.* Only when genuine forgiveness has taken place can the real healing process take place. The healing process seems to take time in proportion to the hurt. And it is a *process.* There is a grieving process when the loss has been large. But the *turning point* is forgiving.

Judy Rae's (not her real name) process has taken many years. When I wrote her story of horrible child abuse in my book *What Happens When God Answers,* I did not know the complete story. As her memory has returned through years of counseling by professionals and a wise and caring pastor and wife, plus years of intensive prayers for her, the surfaced facts are horrendous. She was the daughter of Satan-worshiping parents who sexually abused her through the years. And as soon as she was old enough, she was forced to have six babies—all of whom were sacrificed to Satan. Once, she was made to plunge the dagger into her own child!

A few months ago I was chatting with that pastor's wife about Judy Rae. She said, "With her master's degree, Judy now is a counselor in our new psychiatric hospital here. They say they could not get along without her, she's so great with these victims."

"When do you feel her turning point came?" I asked.

"Oh, there's no doubt about it. When she forgave!"

I pushed a little further. "Was it the time she called me screaming over the phone asking if what I said Jesus said (in a seminar) was true? When I said that now that she is a Christian, if she doesn't forgive, God won't forgive the sins she commits as a Christian either? (Matt. 6:14-15) And she had bought my *Gaining Through Losing* book, and I told her there was a chapter in there that would show her what would happen to *her* if *she* didn't forgive? And then she called back happily saying she had forgiven them and called again to say she had phoned her family to tell them she had forgiven them—and to ask them to forgive her for her unforgiving spirit so many years?"

"That was the time," the pastor's wife answered. "And the big change came when she called her parents and told them!"

It was good to learn so many years later that forgiving really had worked. There often is just a temporary smoothing over of feelings or even burying them again—but this was real!

Forgiving is not as much for the sake of the one forgiven as for the victim. A recent note from a seminar attendee says it so clearly:

> I was a victim of incest, but when I accepted Jesus, my father persecuted me. When I was an adult, God convicted me of my hatred of my father. When I forgave him, later he was saved. Shortly after that he died.
>
> I have been feeling proud that God had healed me, but today (at the "Lord, Change Me" seminar) I realized I had not forgiven my mother for being a co-contributor, for not protecting me. I have now forgiven her, and Jesus has healed me of this also. Jesus is still the Great Physician!

In India I walked into an amazing home just swarming with happy, polite, loving girls and boys who squeezed and squeezed me as I left. The "parents" of this home currently have 300 drug addict children from the streets and hundreds more they are teaching. Astonished, I asked the "mother" how they all turned out so well. She explained, "They have gone through the most horrible experiences for years with nobody to look after them, begging to eat, sleeping on the train platform and being routinely sexually abused, we pick them up from the train platform. And," she added, *"we never talk about their past.* We just love them, accept them unconditionally into our family, *pray much, introduce them to Jesus—and He heals them!"*

What can help snap that victim chain? Yes, forgetting the past, reach out for the joy that Christ gives. Philippians 3:13-14 wisely tells us: "But one thing I do: *forgetting what lies behind and reaching forward to what lies ahead. I* press on toward the goal for the prize of the upward call of God in Christ Jesus" (italics added).

A woman in California whose face just radiated told me a horror story of family abuse from when she was two years old. "But now I run a home for victims of family abuse," she continued. When I asked her about the transformation in her life, she beamed. "When I accepted Jesus, He made me a new creation in Himself" (see 2 Cor. 5:17).

Yes, this applies even though victims may harbor extreme guilt, feeling the abuse was somehow their fault. But if that victim has come to Christ for salvation, he or she must realize that God has not only forgiven past sins (see Col. 1:13-14) but also is willing to lift all the undeserved feelings of guilt: "In whatever our heart condemns us . . . God is greater than our heart, and knows all things" (1 John 3:20).

SALVATION PRAYER

These eight prayer steps work. They have worked for me and my family; they can work for you. First, however, there may be a prayer you must pray—"Lord, make me one of Your children. Forgive all my sins, and, Jesus, come in as my personal Savior and Lord." All of God's promises for healing were not written to everybody—just to those who have received Jesus as personal Savior and Lord. If you have read this far and have not yet received Him into your life, it is imperative in the healing process to make sure that you, the victim, are a real Christian with Christ living in you. You can "do all things through Christ" only if you truly belong to Him.

Trusting Jesus as Savior does not guarantee all problems will immedi-

*ately disappear, but it does guarantee the emotional, mental, and spiritual
healing process of the Great Physician.*

STEPHEN'S SECRETS

When we are disillusioned, hurt, or even horrified at the words or actions of a family member, we must have the attitude of Stephen who, when he was being stoned to death at the hands of the angry mob, was "full of grace and power." How did he stay so calm in the midst of such an assault? How can we?

The answer is twofold. First, Stephen had supernatural help. He knew Jesus personally as his Savior and certainly as Lord of his life. Then Stephen was full of the Holy Spirit before the attack began. It was not just human grit, heroism, or bravery while they were stoning him to death. It was the omniscient God of the universe having filled Him. And we can have the same.

The second secret of Stephen that can be ours is his seeing Jesus. Today Jesus is looking down at our hurts too. Keeping our eyes on Him, not other humans, will provide that supernatural courage and strength we need so desperately in devastating family times.

When we are disillusioned, hurt, or even horrified at the words or actions of a family member, the greatest lesson we too can learn is to *keep our eyes on Jesus!* He never will let us down or disappoint us. He will never give us wrong advice. And He never will withhold all we need to cope with our family problems.

"What Are You Teaching Us, Lord?"

CHAPTER SIX

"EV, DO YOU REMEMBER the first thing you said when I told you your little seven-month-old Judy was dead?" John Carlson, the chairman of the board of my husband's first pastorate, recently asked me. Whatever, it was I had said had not stayed in my reeling, grieving brain. No, I couldn't remember. John looked at me with a still-lingering slight shock as he reminded me that I had reacted to the death of our baby with, *"I wonder what God is trying to teach us now."*

Judy's seven months of surgeries and being paralyzed from the waist down had ended with our watching her slowly die in the hospital.

It had been Chris who had been taking his turn in the hospital with our little Judy when she went to heaven. And John had come home with him to break to news to me.

Then I had questioned, "God, why teach us *again?*" Hadn't we learned enough through the first miscarriage, then our full-term still-born baby girl, and then another miscarriage? Why another baby's death?

Then John said I had mumbled, more to myself than to him, "I guess if I'm going to be a pastor's wife, I'm going to have to know some of these things."

GOD'S METHOD OF TEACHING

During the summer after Chris graduated from seminary, I had prayed and prayed for God to teach me how to be a pastor's wife. With trepidation in my heart at such a huge task looming in front of me, I sat at the feet of a pastor's wife I deeply respected, gleaning every speck of advice I could get. But God added His divine teaching.

I had been pregnant with Judy in 1952 when Chris went to his first church, but I certainly didn't understand that Judy's death was one of the ways He really was preparing me for the years ahead of that task.

It was over twenty-five years after Judy's death that I was on a California radio talk show and a woman called in from the East Coast. There wasn't a dry eye in the studio after she said to me, "I'm a Christian today because of watching you at my little sister's casket. When I was a little girl my baby sister died, and you and Pastor Chris came home from your vacation to have her funeral. Mrs. Chris, all you did at that mortuary was hold my mother in your arms and cry. And I remember saying to myself, 'If that's what a Christian is, I want to be one.' And I am."

It was March 23, 1971 while studying in John 15:7 about Jesus' promise of astounding prayer power that I prayed, "Lord, I want that power in prayer. *Teach me and break me until I have it.*" Little did I realize that the way I would experience that power was in actually praying. And that it basically would be our family needs and difficulties that would keep this wife, mother, mother-in-law, and grandmother on her knees—wrestling, interceding, releasing.

Yes, I have experienced that tremendous power in prayer in a round-the-world prayer ministry. But I also have experienced the teaching, and the breaking, it has taken for God to answer that prayer for prayer power.

GOD'S METHOD OF ANSWERING FAMILY PRAYERS

Also, when I pray for God to improve some attitude or action in one of my family members, I often am surprised at His method of answering my prayers. Frequently, He accomplishes that for which I have prayed—not by supernaturally sprinkling them with sweetness and goodness from heaven, but by answering through a trial.

My mother, after praying almost thirty years for her son to come back to God, finally prayed, "Lord, do anything you need to to Edward to bring him back to You." But she wasn't prepared for how God answered that prayer. My brother was struck by a car that was traveling fifty miles an hour. Doctors told our gathered family that he would never regain consciousness, but he did—and, as mentioned earlier, he trusted Jesus the two years more of life God gave him!

When our very independent teenager Jan went to college, I prayed that God would teach her everything He wanted her to learn. One surprising answer came in a very hard-to-accept discipline. Majoring in French in high school, she had made the language lab tapes for her college class. Nevertheless, everyone, including Jan, was required to spend a designated amount of time sitting in the lab learning from those tapes. Not seeing why she should comply, she ended up with her only freshman B. She told her friends, "Don't ask my mother to pray for you. She'll pray you right out of all A's." I had to agree with her exasperation and reasoning, but also realized God was answering my prayer by teaching Jan a lesson of following orders that would prove invaluable as she became a medical doctor.

It is dangerous to pray for a family member to lose his or her cockiness and bitterness unless we are ready for God's way of answering. I did, and found God answering with circumstances that humbled that loved one completely.

The same kind of God's answering came when I prayed for Him to soften one of my family members who seemed to be becoming harsh and brusque. And I found myself almost wishing I hadn't prayed that prayer. I much prefer to have God sugarcoat my family. But His methods of getting the desired results usually are different.

> Oh, the depth of the riches both of the wisdom and knowledge of God! How unsearchable are His judgments and unfathomable His ways! (Rom. 11:33)

THE ALL-IMPORTANT FAMILY PRAYER

It is still that well-worn prayer question we should pray when calamity strikes. Not "Lord, *how* can I get out of this?" but "*Lord, what can I get out of this?*"

When there are hurts in my family, that isn't always an easy prayer for me to pray. The wife, mother, and grandmother in me automatically bristles when my family members hurt. My immediate human reaction is to shoot a "Remove it, Lord" prayer up to heaven. And then I want to continue to bombard Him with pleas to "take it away" until He does. But I learned long ago that this frequently is not God's plan for our family.

In my husband's many years of preaching, my constant prayer was for the power of God to come down in that sanctuary while he preached. And when he was sick I'd bombard heaven for God to heal him in time to preach. But God had something more important to teach me. I gradually discovered, however, that it was when he was ill, with no human power of his own to go on, that the power of Christ took over—producing the greatest movings of God (see 2 Cor. 12:9-10).

If God does not change our hurtful circumstances when we pray for Him to do so, it most likely means that He has a very important lesson to teach us.

GOD'S METHOD OF TEACHING WHO HE REALLY IS

I remember over twenty years ago one of the most catastrophic events our family ever has faced suddenly striking us. The prayer I prayed is as vivid as if it had been yesterday. "Dear Father," I beseeched in the depth of that grief, "don't take this circumstance away—until we *all* have learned *all* You want us to from it."

The biggest thing God taught me through the months of that tragedy was to trust him. As the hurts rolled on week after week, I felt more and more like Job in His trials. But it also was with Job that I found my faith in God solidifying until it was immovable and unshakable. It was at Job's lowest point, and mine too, that we both cried out: "I *know* that my Redeemer liveth!" (Job 19:25, italics added)

It has been in these hard things that God has been able to teach me who He really is.

It is in my family trials that He has taught me that He never makes a mistake, that He comes in proportion to my need, that He really does work all things out for my good—because I love Him and seek to please Him.

When things hurt in my family, God has taught me to cling to the promises He gave us in His Word. Promises of His presence, His comfort, His wisdom, His guidance. *Actually, until God has brought us through the hard things of life, we don't really know if those promises are true or not.*

But it is as I have discovered over and over that He really *did keep* His promises, that I am able to accept them unconditionally for the current family trial.

A letter from a mother in North Carolina said it so well. "I just finished reading your *Gaining Through Losing* book, and wept for joy as I read it. The reality of the biblical truth that "fullness of joy" comes through suffering was lost to me until our son Daniel was born without any arms. *The strength, grace, and love the Lord gave me was indeed in proportion to my need. I've known Him in a way that I've never known Him before.* Anything the world has to offer is pale by comparison."

A woman approached me after a seminar recently. "I couldn't *stand* your *Gaining Through Losing* book until my sixteen-year-old daughter committed suicide four weeks ago. I grabbed that book and read it over and over. It got me through!" Well, not the book I reminded her, but the God of that book whose promises she finally had accepted—because for the first time she really needed them.

GOD'S METHOD OF PERFECTING AND MATURING US

When God does not remove painful situations in our families, He has something far better than just taking them away. He is in the business of producing mature, deeply spiritual Christian giants of the faith of our family members. What prayers do we pray in times like these? Pray each thing, in order, according to James 1:2-4:

Consider it all joy, my brethren, when you encounter various trials, knowing that the testing of your faith produces endurance. And let endurance have its perfect result, that you may be perfect and complete, lacking nothing.

Our Kurt was trying to finish graduate school and was deeply frustrated by the malfunctioning of the several million dollar electronic microscope he was working on. Having the lens made and remade several times overseas, often waiting up to six months for delivery, he fretted about all the "wasted time," swinging from impatience to exasperation. And he and his advisor actually ended up making a lens that finally would work. After wearying from persistent prayer for each specific detail, I suddenly found a new prayer attitude emerging in me from God. He showed me that this was not wasted time—but would be one of the most important parts of Kurt's training.

There was a prayer that God would not let me pray for our daughter. She was pregnant while on those thirty-six-hour hospital shifts of her medical residency. My mother's heart bled for her, and I desperately wanted to pray, "O God, please, please remove that nausea. She has more than she can handle!" But God restrained my praying with His question, "How many pregnant women would want her for their doctor if she didn't understand how they felt when they were so sick?"

A military wife in Italy said to me that her husband moved every two years, and each time got a new mistress on that new base. I answered, "Everybody here has been telling me what a fantastic mother you are and what model Christian children you have. God has been teaching and perfecting you through these incredibly hard circumstances, and has made a beautiful spiritual giant out of you. And I believe one of the reasons is so that you can help the many other military wives going through similar trials to find God sufficient like you did" (see 2 Cor. 1:3-4).

It was almost immediately after Dan's firing from his government job that God powerfully gave Hebrews 2:10 for Dan and Nancy to help us understand that His method of perfecting His children is the same He used for His own Son Jesus—through suffering:

For it is fitting for Him [the Father], for whom are all things, and through whom are all things, in bringing many sons to glory, *to perfect the author of their salvation* [Jesus] *through sufferings* (italics added).

HURTS BRING US CLOSER TO GOD

The day after Dan lost his job, I was struggling in prayer with several hard things. My spiritual mentor, Kathy Grant, had cancer. Kurt was in the Twin Cities completing the stressful task of making first job contacts. Jan, our doctor daughter, was facing a very undeserved situation at work. That morning I had prayed first about my critical spirit at what seemed so unfair, and finally was able to pray, "Lord, teach me all I need to know from all of this." But by evening my prayer had progressed to *thanking God for the tribulations which were bringing me closer to Him—* humbly on my face before Him.

It was Jan who learned that wonderful truth in her physical suffering. It was the first night after her very extensive microsurgery which enabled her to conceive Jenna. The pain was excruciating all night. But the next morning she told me, "*I saw Jesus in a way I never saw Him before—in my suffering!*"

Chuck Colson learned this when he was away from all his loved ones the Christmas he spent in prison. I heard him tell how those involved in Watergate as well as several New York Mafia prisoners gathered in John Dean's room in the prison at midnight. Sitting in a small circle on the floor reading aloud from the Scriptures about the birth of Christ, they then prayed quietly for each other—and for their families, most of whom were far away. Although very lonely and cut off from the rest of the world, Chuck added, "*I felt the power of Christ in a way that only comes in times of deepest need.*"

A friend wrote: "We had hoped to be sending you a birth announcement by now. But our darling baby lived just one week before moving on to heaven. She accomplished so much. She opened our lives to God's endless love, and took us more deeply into life than we had ever been and strengthened our love as a couple. *We thank God for making His loving presence known to us in unmistakable ways during the hardest week of our lives.* He was there in the midst of our pain and fear. He was there as we prayed and wept. And He was there to welcome Katherine into heaven."

Far away in Cebu in the Philippines, I suddenly felt helplessness and fear about what Dan and Nancy were going through back in the States. Then I read in Mark 6 about Jesus sending His disciples across the stormy sea and, while they strained at the oars, He walked on the water intending to pass them by. But when He saw they were frightened because they thought He was a ghost, He said to them, "Take courage; it is I, do not be afraid" (Mark 6:50).

And the wind stopped when Jesus got in the boat with them. And I, there in the Philippines, cried, "O Jesus, get in the boat with us!"

God is teaching us through our family trials not only that they bring us closer to God, but also He's teaching us how faithfully and powerfully He responds to our prayers for Him to come closer to us.

"LORD, TEACH US TRUTH"

One of the things that hurt families — and God — the most is deceit. The Bible is full of warnings and the dire results of deceit. For example: "The Lord abhors the man of bloodshed and deceit" (Ps. 5:6).

The Bible lumps a lying lifestyle with some very serious sins:

> But for the cowardly and unbelieving and abominable and murderers and immoral persons and sorcerers and idolaters and all liars, their part will be in the lake that burns with fire and brimstone, which is the second death (Rev. 21:8).

Deceit can be either denial or duplicity. In real *denial,* there has been sufficient trauma to cause the brain to bury the truth in order for the victim to cope. But *duplicity* — knowing the truth but lying to protect one's ego, reputation, or actions — is what devastates families.

It is easy to pray for each other when all the family members are living harmoniously — undergirding, fellowshipping, and rejoicing together. But praying for them when there is suspicion and deceit is quite another thing. How do we pray when we believe someone we love dearly is deliberately deceiving us?

First, we pray to know the truth from God ourselves. In family hurts, all members come into the reconciliation process with differing degrees of bias, prejudice, and incomplete or slanted information. And each thinks he or she is praying correctly, none realizing their prayers might be wrong.

Second, according to 1 Peter 3:16, when slandered we are to "keep a good conscience . . . in the thing in which we are slandered." In other words, we are to pray to make sure *we* are pure before God ourselves and acting accordingly.

Third, it is the "three Ds" of deceit, denial, and duplicity that make it difficult for family members to pray in the light of real truth. But, when we are assured of it without a shadow of a doubt, we are ready to ask God to reprove that person as severely as the situation demands. "O God," we pray, "convict them of their sin of deceitfulness, and show them Your truth."

I, with the Apostle John, "have no greater joy than this, than to hear of my children walking in the truth" (3 John 4). It bubbles up in prayers of joyful thankfulness.

As we drove into their driveway, granddaughters Crista and Jenna were having a heated argument over who got the most magazines in the mail. As Jenna stormed out of the car insisting that one of them had only her name on it, Crista burst into tears. "She's lying, Grandma!"

"You know something, Honey?" I comforted her. "Do you know who's keeping absolutely true records? Yes, God up in heaven. God knows if *everything* said is a lie or the truth — and He hears *everything.* Truth is truth. And no matter what any person says, you or Jenna, it does not change it one bit. Nobody can change truth into a lie or a lie into truth — just because they say so."

It was frightening to listen to Chuck Colson quote statistics relating to truth at a Prison Fellowship banquet. When asked if there was any such thing as absolute truth, 67 percent of Americans said no. But even more alarming was that 52 percent of evangelical Christians also said there isn't any absolute truth!

However, not only does God know the truth and record the real facts, Proverbs 12:22 says: "Lying lips are an abomination to the Lord, but those who deal faithfully are His delight."

Then Psalm 9:8 says that we don't have to worry about the final outcome for "He will execute judgment for the peoples with equity."

Fully grasping these biblical concepts completely changes our praying—and it changes us. It puts our confidence in God's justice—and us at peace while coping with—and praying for—deceitful family members.

SURPRISE LESSONS WHEN WE ARE DOING THINGS RIGHT

Yes, we all know we learn from our mistakes. But when God chooses to teach us when we are doing what we are supposed to be doing, it's hard for us to understand and accept. Chris and I were not being disobedient to God when we lost our four babies, but God used these experiences to teach us so much. When we lost baby number three, Chris had given up a glamorous and lucrative piloting job offer out of Miami to obey God and go back to school to prepare for serving Him full time. And when Judy died, we had just obeyed His call to enter the pastorate.

> By no means let any of you suffer as a murderer, or thief, or evildoer, or a troublesome meddler; but if anyone suffers as a Christian, let him not feel ashamed, but in that name let him glorify God. . . . Therefore, let those also who suffer according to the will of God entrust their souls to a faithful Creator *in doing what is right* (1 Peter 4:15-16, 19, italics added).

Elizabeth and her husband, Zacharias, were doing everything right when God did not "take away her disgrace" of being childless until they were advanced in years. According to the Bible, she and Zacharias were doing everything right. "And they were both righteous in the sight of God, walking blamelessly in all the commandments and requirements of the Lord" (Luke 1:6). But it was after all that sorrowful waiting in barrenness that God sent an angel announcing His intended miracle of the birth of their son John the Baptist (see James 5:10-11).

> For what credit is there if, when you sin and are harshly treated, you endure it with patience? But if when you do what is right and suffer for it you patiently endure it, this finds favor with God (1 Peter 2:20).

God delays His answers to our prayers for many reasons, even while we are doing what's right. In the midst of Dan's trials for standing for honesty, God gave us one of His reasons from Hebrews 12:11 which He taught us first when our Judy died—*training us.*

> All discipline for the moment seems not to be joyful but sorrowful; yet to those who have been *trained* by it, afterward it yields the peaceful fruit of righteousness (italics added).

God is continuously in the business of making His children into what He wants them to be. And He knows when and how to answer our prayers to make it happen. Cutting short that process by answering our prayers too soon or the way we thought He should deprives us of His divine perfecting.

Through Dan's three and a half years of struggling and waiting because of refusing to be part of a deception, thoughts on "What Price Integrity?" kept swirling in his head. But 1 Peter 1:6-7 says it is the *proof* of our faith—whether or not we have seen justice here or rejoicing when Jesus comes back:

> In this you greatly rejoice, even though now for a little while, if necessary, you have been distressed by various trials, *that the proof of your faith,* being more precious than gold which is perishable, even though tested by fire, may be found to result in praise and glory and honor at the revelation of Jesus Christ (italics added).

In God's waiting to give an answer to our prayers, Dan felt strongly that He was teaching him many things. Here's part of a note Dan penned to me one year into the problem:

> I realize when I reach my limits and feel nothing but utter despair, that this problem is inexorably drawing me closer to the Rock. This finding can only be in preparation for a great task ahead. Prayer is changing Nancy's and my hearts. We both are beginning to believe there is light at the end of the tunnel.

WHEN GOD IS SILENT—FROM DAN

Now that the ordeal is over and the verdict of innocent has been returned from the National Merit Board, Dan tells in his own words what God has taught him.

I had questions, so many questions while God was silent those three and a half years. Questions that simmered and sometimes festered in my very being during that long trial.

The question that surfaced first was: *Why me?* Why had I been singled out for all this unfairness and injustice? But God had some powerful Scriptures for me personally to show me why. The first answer was from John 15:18-20: *because the world persecutes Christians.*

"If the world hates you, you know that it has hated Me before it hated you. If you were of the world, the world would love its own; but because you are not of the world, but I chose you out of the world, therefore the world hates you. Remember the word I said to you, 'A slave is not greater than his master.' If they persecuted Me, they will persecute you."

My "why me?" question was also answered by God showing me that *Christians are called to be different.* Not only was I to *oppose* evil deeds, but I was to *expose* those evil deeds I had uncovered:

> Do not participate in the unfruitful deeds of darkness, but instead even expose them (Eph. 5:11).

Another question I asked many, many times as the months dragged into years was: *Why hasn't God answered my prayers yet?*

Assurance from Him that *I was still to wait, patiently,* came from God in Psalm 62:1-2:

> My soul waits in silence for God only; from Him is my salvation. He only is my rock and my salvation, my stronghold; I shall not be greatly shaken.

Becoming desperate at God's silence, I finally agonized over this question: *Am I so stubborn that God must put me through the fire to mold me?*

God's answer to that in John 15:1-2, 8 revealed some "whys"—*that God may be glorified when I bear much fruit and prove myself to be Jesus' disciple.* No question about it, I was being tested—pruned—for the end result.

> I am the true vine, and My Father is the vinedresser. Every branch in Me that does not bear fruit, He takes away; and every branch that bears fruit, He prunes it, that it may bear more fruit. . . . By this My Father is glorified, that you bear much fruit, and so prove to be My disciples.

Another category of God's teaching came when, even without my questions, the Lord taught me incredible lessons throughout those years. One very important one was *the reexamining of my life's priorities.* God sent me back to the Scripture which was the basis of my life and the foundation on which Nancy and I chose to build our marriage.

> Choose for yourselves today whom you will serve . . . but as for me and my house, we will serve the Lord (Josh. 24:15).

And then, after I had gotten the clear picture of whom I was serving, God comforted me with one of the most important lessons of my life: "*If God is for us, who is against us?*" (Rom. 8:31, italics added)

God also taught me that He *demands obedience,* but He *honors righ-*

teousness with a promise. What an affirmation of my refusing to compromise my integrity. Job 8:20-21 says, "God will not reject a man of integrity, nor will He support the evildoers. He will yet fill your mouth with laughter, and your lips with shouting."

Perhaps the most important lesson I learned was to *trust God for all my family's needs—because He is in control.* Financially, it was very grim for us. I spent many sleepless nights wondering how I was going to feed and clothe my little ones. But I learned to trust God—and He never let us down. Every single need was met—in time.

> Do not be anxious then, saying, "What shall we eat?" or, "What shall we drink?" or, "With what shall we clothe ourselves?" For all these things the Gentiles eagerly seek; for your Heavenly Father knows that you need all these things. But seek first His kingdom, and His righteousness; and all these things shall be added to you (Matt. 6:31-33).

The third category of things God taught me was *the importance of living with God's love in my life's personal relationships with others.*

Each day brought challenges and opportunities to let Jesus shine through me to others. And a new *meekness* that God knew I needed to learn was mine from Matthew 5:5, "Blessed are the meek, for they shall inherit the earth."

In my relationship with others, God also taught me that, as a Christian, I personally *cannot afford to be angry about my circumstances.* It was a shock to realize that I opened myself to the devil if I did: "Be angry, and yet do not sin; do not let the sun go down on your anger, and do not give the devil an opportunity" (Eph. 4:26-27).

God forcefully taught me that *I cannot love God and harbor hatred toward others,* even those who have tormented me. I have a higher calling!

> Never pay back evil for evil to anyone. Respect what is right in the sight of all men. . . . But if your enemy is hungry, feed him, and if he is thirsty, give him a drink; for in so doing you will heap burning coals upon his head. Do not be overcome by evil, but overcome evil with good (Rom. 12:17, 20-21).

Finally, through my long hard experience, God taught me *how to live above mediocrity*. As a Christian, I have a higher calling. And God brought it into focus for me through 1 Peter 1:15-16.

But like the Holy One who called you, be holy yourselves also in all your behavior; because it is written, "You shall be holy, for I am holy."

But I could not—did not have to—do it in my own strength. When all human resources within me seemed to fail, I continuously prayed back to God His incredible—and true—promise in Isaiah 40:31.

But they who wait for the Lord shall renew their strength; they shall mount up with wings as eagles; they shall run and not be weary; and they shall walk, and not faint (KJV).

Through it all, my prayers were guided and sometimes almost dictated by God—directly to me through His Word. And they were His day-by-day way of patiently and lovingly teaching me all the fabulous lessons He wanted me to learn by my adversity. And while I waited, sometimes impatiently, for Him to answer our prayers for the trial to be over—He wasn't just silent—He was waiting until I had learned all He was teaching me.

And through the fifty years Chris and I have been married, God has taught our whole family His marvelous lessons also—little by little making us what He, from before the foundation of the earth, planned for us to be. Many, many years ago we as a family learned to pray, not just "Lord, get us out of this adversity," but "Lord, teach us what You want us to get out of it."

Touching Prayers

OUR LITTLE TODDLER granddaughter Crista had a high fever. As I sat holding her on the family room sofa, she slept fitfully with her head on my chest. As I pressed my cheek against her silky hair, soft tears trickled down my cheeks dropping on her little head. What was being interchanged? Whatever it was, it was very real and tangible to this grandmother.

Infants who receive loving touches on a regular basis do much better than those who are neglected, researchers have shown. People alone are prone to more stress, anxiety, and illness. Tests have shown that motherless baby monkeys prefer the warm fuzzy stuffed "mother monkey," even though it gives them shocks, to the cold wire "mother" that provides their milk.

I'm a toucher. I often say that more good is accomplished in my autograph lines than in my teaching because I always reach out to touch the person in some way. Usually it's a quick, sincere hug, but the response to that touch is overwhelming appreciation.

What really does happen when we touch? Do our arms around someone simply tell the person we care—or more? Does a touch actually help an ill person recover more quickly, as some research suggests? Does comfort, love, or even power actually go out through a touch?

JESUS AND TOUCHING

People around Jesus knew that something happened when they touched Him. They saw His physical touch open blind eyes and make the lame walk. The woman who had the issue of blood for twelve years touched the hem of His garment and was healed instantly. Also:

> And wherever He entered villages, or cities, or countryside, they were laying the sick in the market places, and entreating Him that they might just touch the fringe of His cloak; *and as many as touched it were being cured* (Mark 6:56, italics added).

ADDING PRAYER ADDS GOD

Though I have learned through the years that much that is good, helpful, and comforting can be transmitted through touching, there is one additional and powerful ingredient available to Christians in their family touching—*God!* When touching adds God by praying, it brings the God of the universe into that physical encounter.

What happens when grandmas and grandbabies hug? Something very tangible passes between them—a love that is special only to them, a bonding that gets stronger with every hug. One of the greatest places for this to happen is that early morning cuddling when a little one, clutching a worn security blanket, gropes through the predawn darkness and crawls into the expectant arms in Grandma's warm bed. *But when we add prayer, we add God to those happy occasions.*

While Dan and Nancy were going through the depth of their trial, their children, of course, were sensing the tenseness in the insecurity of it all. When I was spending an extra day with them after a D.C. board meeting, Cindy climbed into Grandma's bed to huddle, as we call it, one more time. As she fell back to sleep tightly cradled in my arms, I spent the first minutes just enjoying the love that was flowing from me to her. Then I included God in that precious time. Pouring out my heart for her to my Heavenly Father, I asked for each thing I felt she needed right then. Peace. Security. His love flowing into her. *The prayer added God's arms to Grandma's arms encircling her—*divine arms capable of holding her close with His peace, security, love, plus all the other things He knew she needed. I watched as the facial twitchings of waking played on Cindy's face. Then she saw my face, and shining from her eyes and lips was a little "isn't-this-great?" smile as she snuggled closer. I never miss a day praying for Cindy and every grandchild *long distance,* but this was that awesome touching of my own offspring—while praying.

Another time as we visited Dan and Nancy's family, four-year-old Kathy and I were out of bed whispering so as not to wake up anybody else. At 5 A.M. she had come for her usual huddle. "Do you know what Grandma did while you were in my bed?" I asked.

"Yeah," she said wrinkling up her face in an enthusiastic smile, "you huddled me."

"Right, but *what else* do you think Grandma did?" Her eyes widened, looking intently into mine for an answer.

"Grandma prayed for you, Darling. While I was holding you close I was praying to God for you."

Her little four-year-old mind was trying to put those two things together. "What were you praying for me, Grandma?"

First I asked, "You already have Jesus living in your heart, don't you, Kathy?" With her, "oh, yes" answer, I continued. "Well, I was praying that Jesus would fill you and make you just like Himself."

Straightening, she announced with finality, "It'll never work, Grandma."

"Why not, Honey?"

"Because He's a boy and I'm a girl!"

Struggling momentarily with that theological impasse, I explained, "Oh, I was praying that Jesus would fill you with all the wonderful things He *is*—such as His love, His joy, and things like that."

The puzzled look on Kathy's little face melted into a "that's neat" smile. My eyes never left hers, not wanting to miss a single bit of that new dimension dawning on her.

The same thing had happened the week before when Jan and Skip had an overnight birthday swimming party for me in a motel. After enjoying the pool for hours, we had knelt around one of the beds for a precious prayertime. However, with the children keyed up from the excitement, we played "musical beds" a few times, and Chris and I finished the night sleeping with two-and-a-half-year-old Crista.

Waking early, I cradled her in my arms as she slept; and that special something passed between us as I prayed for her, our faces almost nose to nose. Her little hand reached out and took my cheek, and then, holding Grandma's face, she drifted in and out of sleep. But every time her eyes would just peek open, looking right into mine just inches away, there would be a sweet "I-love-you-Grandma" smile. And my smile would say back to her, "Oh, I love you so much, dear Crista." *Touching and praying!* It was one of those happy family occasions that seemed so complete in itself. But how much more there was for us when God was added—through prayer.

When little granddaughters stay overnight at our house, they don't sleep in our guest bedroom—no way. There's a "cozy" of blankets and pillows on the floor on each side of Chris' and my bed. They start the night in bed with Grandma for their "to be continued bunny stories" and then our prayertime together. Then it's into their cozies for the night. But I know that sooner or later they all will end up back in our big bed.

I'm always awake early spending a couple hours praying in bed. So I already was praying for our family when Jenna crawled into my side of our bed to finish the night. As I held her in my arms, Jenna quickly drifted off to sleep. But I was wide awake—and shifted my praying to only her. I held her close and prayed until dawn broke.

What a difference adding God to the cuddling has made. Whenever any of my dear granddaughters—Cindy, Jenna, Crista, or Kathy—have crawled in for a huddle, I never once have missed the opportunity of adding God—in prayer.

UNHAPPY TIMES

Our doctor daughter Jan was at work in the hospital and ran to meet the stretcher as they wheeled her Jenna into the emergency room the time a dog had bitten her nose almost off. Kneeling beside her, Jan reached her hand under the sheet to hold her child and prayed desperately. And God reached down under that sheet to hold that child close to

Himself. And to heal. Miraculously, as mentioned earlier, there is virtually no visible sign of a scar!

Cindy had several weeks of colic as a newborn. The first time I walked the floor with her, I remember repeating the word *Jesus* hundreds of times as I paced, whispering His name, singing it, sometimes raising my voice above her crying. As I held Cindy close in my arms, I was acutely aware of bringing Jesus into that room with us. Prayer? Oh, yes! Inviting Jesus there with us—to comfort, calm, and relieve the pain.

It was our infant grandson, James, who missed his mummy and daddy so much when they went for a weekend of skiing, leaving him for the very first time. Not knowing his grandmother that much yet, he cried and cried. But it gave me a wonderful excuse to hold him close and walk the floor, whispering over and over in his ear a little "bzzzz" sound that he seemed to love. But I also prayed and prayed while I walked, asking God to provide the security tiny James needed, security that only his parents could really give—security that I as his grandmother could not completely supply. And he settled down, experiencing at that early age God coming in answer to prayer to hold him closely in His supernatural arms.

As you've likely concluded, as a grandmother I snatch every opportunity to include God in my touching experiences with my grandbabies. Then they are not only touched by a caring human, but by the omnipotent God of heaven.

TRANSMITTED THROUGH PRAYER

Jesus was indignant when His disciples rebuked the people who were bringing children to Jesus to touch.

> And He took them in His arms, and began blessing them, and laying His hands on them (Mark 10:16).

In Guatemala busloads of women from the mountains who were brought to my meeting lined up to have me touch their little shiny-eyed babies. As I laid my hand on each one and prayed, the mothers were ecstatic. It was indeed one of the greatest privileges of my life, for I felt something of Jesus flowing through my hands to each of them.

Was Jesus including touching when He said to His followers (today's followers included), "Truly, truly, I say to you, he who believes in Me, the works that I do shall he do also; and greater works than these shall he do; because I go to the Father" (John 14:12). Since touching was one of His most frequent "works," could He have been including what is transmitted in a touch? I do not see why not.

MARRIAGE TOUCHING

In our marriage, Chris and I often have said as we crawled into bed at night, "This is the best time of the day." Why? God knew when He ordained marriage that touching would produce the comfort, assurance, and drawing emotionally from each other so needed by weary mates at the end of a long day.

But the wee hours of the morning are my strongest prayertimes. So as I lie next to Chris praying for him while he still sleeps at 3 or 4 o'clock, it is almost automatic to reach out and lay my hand on the top of his head. When I am communicating with the God of the universe about my husband, it seems so natural to touch Chris. Somehow there seems to be an adding of a physical dimension of God responding to that touching as He pours into Chris the things I am praying for.

A FATHER'S BLESSINGS

As a medical doctor, our son-in-law Skip knows the importance of touching. He also knows the importance of touching family members. But as the spiritual head of his house, he knows the importance of "blessing touching." For many years he has practiced spiritual blessings in their home. Skip tells about it in his own words:

> As parents we are continually being encouraged in our efforts to lovingly nurture our children and spouses. God's Word and some recent writings on the importance of touching and blessing have had an impact on our

family. Our spiritual and secular culture has been rather silent with respect to the importance of the blessing. Occasionally, we are affirmed by parents, teachers, and supervisors; however, touching is known to be vital in healthy social and emotional development.

For several years we have shared together each week in personal blessings after our "special" Sunday breakfast. Our children clamor (usually) to be the first blessed. Seated in our lap, the special person is surrounded by the rest and hugged and kissed by the "blessor." They are blessed in Jesus' name for general or specific requests. Other family members pipe in with particular things in that person they are thankful for and any special spiritual blessing they are led to offer. Frequently we ask for healing blessings. The filling of the sevenfold Spirit of the Lord is sometimes prayed. I like the blessing said about young Jesus, "And Jesus increased in wisdom and stature, and in favor with God and men" (Luke 2:52, KJV). For my wife I am proud to include blessings mentioned in Proverbs: "Her children arise and call her blessed; her husband also, and he praises her" (31:28, KJV).

Recently Crista and Jenna were on my lap as we read from an encyclopedia from "chicken" to "China." Under the word *child* we read that the five- to eight-year-old child is actively forming his self-image based on interactions with his parents and other children. By the preteen years more of that approval begins to come from peers. As a family encouraging and affirming one another with our words, prayers, and affection, we covet God's cement to help us grow together and strong in Him. The family blessing is one of God's tools that helps us accomplish this.

Chris and I were there for one of those Sunday breakfasts, and Skip moved on around the table to place his hands on our heads when finished with his family. What an awesome experience. And what an overwhelming family prayertime! Jan told me that Jenna went to stay over Saturday night at the home of one of her girlfriend's fine Christian home. Aghast, she later told her parents that they didn't do anything on Sunday morning—"they just had breakfast."

The first time I experienced hands blessing a child in Skip and Jan's home was when they brought their firstborn, Jenna, home from the hospital. Although she was less than twenty-four hours old, no hospital could hold the child of those two medical doctors. So Jan called ahead to see if I would get things ready and carry the baby into the house. "Jan, you've waited ten years for this child. Don't you want to carry her over the threshold into your home yourself?"

"No," she replied. "We want you to carry the new baby into the house and sit in the old green chair and pray for her." (The old green chair which had been my "prayer closet" for over twenty years—and was now reupholstered and in their living room.)

Well, I carried that newborn in and sat down in the old green chair. But I couldn't sit there. I laid Jenna on the seat and knelt beside her. As I laid my hands on that soft little bundle and started to pray, I became aware of the new mummy and daddy kneeling down on each side of me—also laying their hands on their first offspring. *Praying*!

Our grandchildren have come in "cousin pairs." Cindy had preceded her little cousin, Jenna, as our first grandchild by just a month. And my first time alone in their home with my first grandchild, I had knelt beside her and prayed. In the awesomeness of laying my hands on that new generation in our family, I had prayed fervently for God to put His arms around her, to protect her, to guard her, and to nurture her, and fill her with Himself. *God's hands touching her with mine!*

TOUCHING HANDS

Jesus must have thought His hands in blessing had special significance, for after a ministry of touching people of all ages, He chose His hands in blessing as His final gesture here on earth. When the risen Savior left this earth, "He lifted up His hands and blessed them. And . . . while He was blessing them, He parted from them" (Luke 24:50-51).

Hands always have been a vital part of blessings and commissionings in Christianity. New missionaries, pastors, and priests are sent into their calling from God with the laying on of hands.

At Antioch . . . while they were ministering to the Lord and fasting, the Holy Spirit said, "Set apart for Me Barnabas and Saul for the work to which I have called them." Then, when they had fasted and prayed *and laid their hands on them,* they sent them away (Acts 13:1-2, italics added).

The Bible certainly implies that something more than symbolic happens when there is laying on of hands.

What they actually received through those hands we are not told. And I used to wonder as I watched commissioning services what, if anything, happened during the commissioning prayer. But now, as the recipient, I know there is something from God. Whenever I go on an overseas trip, launch a new facet of ministry, or begin a new year of my life, my board lays hands on me.

I have been amazed at the difference in what I feel from different hands. Sometimes warmth, sometimes unexpected heat, and frequently something like electricity flowing to me. Friendly hugs from my board members are wonderful, but when prayer is added, God not only is involved, something *from Him* is transmitted.

Our family frequently has "commissioning prayers" too, and not only for our newborn babies. The last time I left for India, Jan and Skip had a family prayertime for me around the old green chair at their own house. As I knelt, the entire family laid hands on me and one by one prayed for God to protect me, guide me, keep me safe. Again that spiritual something passed from them to me. We ended by hugging in a big entwined circle and wiping tears. *Family parting—including God.*

Our little Brett wasn't a month old yet when Jan was leaving him with me to go shopping. As she handed him to me, she asked, "Where do you want to hold him?"

My immediate reply was, "In the old green chair. Then I can do two things at once." Jan paused a minute, sitting down across the room from us, savoring the scene.

As I held that tiny baby close, something just seemed to pour out from my being to him. "Jan, I don't understand what happens when we touch like this, but it does." When I was alone with him, tears trickled down my face as I felt this overwhelming "grandma love" just flowing, even from the palms of my hands as they pressed on his little body. But it was when I began to pray that I included God's divine hands and arms touching that little boy. I don't understand "touching," but I certainly have experienced it—have been the recipient of its results.

MY MOTHER'S HANDS

Years ago whenever I was in a hospital bed or beside a little casket in the mortuary, or facing a crisis in our family, somehow Mother always managed to get the next plane to me. And her work-gnarled hand would soothe my brow or dry my tearstained face. Through the years when I lost babies or my world fell apart, her warm, caring hand would automatically reach out to me. But there always was her praying that accompanied those precious hands.

As Mother got older, we frequently switched roles. After her husband of over twenty-five years (my stepfather) died, I was driving her home one night. I stopped the car on the roadside, and we talked deeply about her loneliness. Then I reached out my hand for hers and held it tightly as we prayed. I'll never know what she felt, but I can still vividly remember the electricity I felt go between our hands.

How often I would take her frail little body, racked with the physical infirmities of old age, into my arms. As I held that little lady close and prayed, I wonder what, if anything, she felt. Did she receive the power, the support, the caring, the love flowing from me—and from God as I prayed? She's in heaven now, so I'll have to wait to ask her.

As I get older and experience those not-so-spry and sometimes painful feelings, I know what I feel when my children hold me tight to their vital, powerful, youthful bodies. And when they add the dimension of prayer, God adds His vitality and power to our hug too.

Most humans, especially married couples, mothers and fathers, children and grandparents, know the importance of touching. But touching *and* praying adds another dimension—*God!*

When We Can't Touch, God Can

AT THE TIME I KNELT at the old green chair and my family prayed as I left for India in 1982, God also had given all four in Jan and Skip's family the same Bible verse for me:

> Have I not commanded you? Be strong and courageous! Do not tremble or be dismayed, for the Lord your God is with you *wherever* you go (Josh. 1:9, italics added).

There was a special need for this promise from God as I traveled that time in India. Political violence escalated day by day. Even in beautiful Bangalore they would not let me step out alone on the street until a car was waiting for me. Spreading government curfews made the planned seminar schedule touch and go, some being lifted just two hours before the start of our meeting. The morning I was to leave for Calcutta, news reports were ominous. As I read Joshua 1:9 once more, God emphasized just one word—*wherever!* God assured me, "*Wherever* you go, I will keep the promise they all prayed for you." And I powerfully experienced God's answers through His protection, power, and victory *wherever* I went all through that rigorous trip in India. God can reach us *wherever* we go!

WHEN YOU CAN'T TOUCH, MAKE A TRIANGLE

Preschooler Kathy was having trouble understanding spatial relations as we talked about her having to leave our family vacation at Lake Michigan and go home. So I assured her I would pray for her even if she was at home a thousand miles away.

"The great part about prayer is that it doesn't matter where you are, Kathy," I assured her. "You see, I just pray up to God in heaven for you; then God reaches down into your heart wherever you are. It doesn't matter if you are in Minnesota or Washington or Michigan. I don't always know where you are, but God *always* knows exactly where you are.

"It's like making a triangle, Kathy. Put the palms of your hands together over your head, Honey. Now that's God at the tip of your fingers. And you and I each have an elbow. When you put your elbows together, that's when we are together like we are now on this vacation. But when you spread your elbows far apart, that's how we are sometimes when you have to go home. But we are still connected through God. So when I pray for you at my elbow, my prayer goes up that arm to God. Then God runs the prayer right down the other arm to you—no matter where you are."

That made going home a lot easier for Kathy.

I learned to use this triangle when Chris had to leave for military duty in England as a B-17 bomber pilot in World War II. I never knew exactly where he was—on a mission, at the base, or in London for a few days. And I had no way of contacting him directly no matter how desperately I needed him. With every bomber raid over Germany, I did not even know if he had returned to his base safely or had been shot down and captured.

But as that young bride, I learned an important lesson: *God could, and would, be there taking the cries of my heart directly to Chris.* My heartcries for his protection, comfort, peace, and even joy in the midst of battle were taken directly by God to Chris' barracks or the cockpit of his plane. No, I could not be there—but God could!

As I was typing this chapter, the phone rang and a weak voice was calling for prayer—once more. The caller was a wife and mother who has scleroderma, the fatal sickness where the skin gradually turns stonelike. She had had to be fed intervenously, but thanked us for praying, for now she was able also to eat to some degree. Together we thanked God for that miracle.

But then she told me about her concern for her ten-year-old son who sometimes has a hard time handling his mother's illness and hospitalization—and she feels so helpless. I assured her that one of the privileges of being in the hospital was having lots of time to pray for her son; and, although she could not reach him, God could—and would—if she would pray. I explained the triangle of her reaching up to God from her hospital bed and then God reaching down to her son. I told her that she was not helpless because her son desperately needed her to pray for him. "But I'm getting so weak," she whispered. I assured her that God understood, that just short sentence prayers would do.

"Your prayers from your hospital bed may be the most important thing you ever could do for your son," I emphasized. "They could turn around the whole direction of his future life—much more than you could just by cooking, doing laundry for him and being with him." *Triangle prayers!*

WHEN WE CAN'T REACH TO TOUCH A FAMILY MEMBER, GOD CAN

Chris and I both have had to travel a lot in our ministries. No matter where our travels have taken us around the world, that triangle praying not only sends God with His answers to the other, but it somehow seems to connect us too.

There is a deep loneliness when Chris or I must be gone from each other. And for at least thirty years I have prayed to God, "O Lord, fill Chris with You in his loneliness—like I feel You filling me when I'm away from him." And no matter whether I have been in Asia, Europe, Australia, or Africa, I have prayed, and God has reached down to wherever Chris has been—and filled the void in Chris' heart.

And when Chris had his cancer surgery, I could not be there every minute while he recovered. But he told me, as mentioned earlier, "I could feel you praying. I felt like my body didn't even touch the bed. I was just upheld by a cradle of prayer."

> Thy loving-kindness, O Lord, extends to the heavens, Thy faithfulness
> reaches to the skies (Ps. 36:5)

There is no limit to how far God can reach. And I am amazed at how
God's arm can swivel at 360 degrees in that prayer triangle. When we
pray up to Him, it doesn't matter where on earth, or even in outer space,
our family members may be, God's arm can find them.

WHEN WE CAN'T FIND LOVED ONES,
GOD'S HAND CAN

There are times we don't even know where a family member is. No
matter what time zone I'm in, I always carry a clock set on "home time."
But, even so, I can't always keep track of where my family members
are—or they where I am.

While I was flying home alone from Bombay, India, the political situation in the Mideast was very tense. My flight included flying over those
deserts in an Air India plane, and my husband was very concerned. Having been trained as a military pilot, he kept track of where my plane was
by keeping in touch with the airlines information system. And he stayed
up all night, not just worrying, but praying. Praying for his wife—
somewhere out over those hostile deserts.

> If I take the wings of the dawn,
> If I dwell in the remotest part of the sea,
> Even there Thy hand will lead me,
> And Thy right hand will lay hold of me (Ps. 139:9-10).

Electronic communications and mail deliveries break down. While I
was in India, it took me several hours and sometimes days to make phone
contact with home while my mother-in-law was not expected to live. One
of the greatest things about prayer is that the God who answers them is
an *omnipresent* God. Even when no telephone or mail delivery is possible,
there is One who still can and does transcend the miles across continents
and oceans—*God.*

SO NEAR, YET SO FAR

The distance between you and your child's school, questionable social event, or just "out with the gang" can be just as devastating as if there
were an ocean in between. But God's hand can reach children in those
places too.

The sting of those early family separations was greatly reduced for
us by our praying for our children. We sent our little ones out into a
cruel world—not alone but with God. At our "front door praying" we
prayed specifically about the bully on the playground, that day's difficult test, a tummy ache, or whatever was looming before them out
there. Our hand could not hold theirs—and should not have. But we
sent our children out with the invisible hand of God tightly holding
theirs.

From the day our Jan entered kindergarten till when our last child,
Kurt, graduated from high school, we never missed a day praying with
each child at the door as they left, as mentioned in an earlier chapter. I'll
admit there were times when our children were adolescents or teens that
they rebelled, verbally, at having to wait at the door. And sometimes the
prayers had to be just a few words "shot up to God on the run." But,
looking back, I know how important those prayertimes were—to
them—and to us. They removed the fear and our possessiveness as God
took over—when we couldn't. When we prayed for them, our children
unknowingly had the same assurance as the psalmist in Psalm 73:23,
"Nevertheless I am continually with Thee [God]; *Thou hast taken hold of
my right hand*" (italics added).

The first time I transported a little grandchild to her preschool, my
daughter Jan warned, "Don't forget to pray in the hall right inside the
door there. She won't go in until you do!"

JUST A PRAYER APART

Although my mother and I experienced a lifetime of "touching
prayers" whenever we were together, the vast majority of our prayers were
when we could not touch. And this is true of most family prayers. The
percentage of times most family members can touch while praying is rel-

atively small. As family members grow up, go to school, move away, or get married, physical touching can be spasmodic at best. So what do we do when we can't touch?

My mother had the answer for that too. Hundreds of times through the years she has reminded me, *"Remember, Evelyn, we're just a prayer apart."* She said it with such finality—no questioning, no wavering. It was just a fact—an indisputable fact!

Living hundreds of miles from my mother in my adult life never broke our incredible closeness. How did we maintain that oneness? It was her quietly reaching for my hand and whispering to me every time we parted, "We're just a prayer apart." It became our shared secret after I married, then while I followed my groom in his military stint, our college and his seminary and pastorates. In later years, the last phone call to Mother as I was leaving for overseas always would include, "Remember, Honey, we're just a prayer apart!"—calming her motherly apprehension—and mine.

So, instead of distance separating my mother and me, our prayers have run like a triangle up to God and down to the other—the connection between us mysteriously, divinely unbroken.

When we can't touch our family member in need, God still can connect us. It was Jan's first night after extensive microsurgery in Mayo Clinic, and we could not be with her. In severe pain, she called my motel across the street in the middle of the night. "Oh, Mother, it hurts so much; *please pray!*" What a struggle to be separated by so few blocks—and yet so completely—while I spent the rest of the night interceding to God for my child in her pain. The next morning as I walked into her hospital room, Jan smiled weakly and said, *"Thanks, Mother. Prayer is just like somebody holding your hand long distance."*

AN ANCHOR AT HOME

It is extremely important for family members who are away to have an anchor back at home. They desperately need the security of the remaining family members, their caring about what has happened—and their unconditional love. They need a phone number or an address that will give them an anchor to hold on to—a place to direct their cries for help.

When families receive calls for help from those far away, a terrifying helplessness can set in. A wanting to run or fly to them immediately—which usually is impossible. Panic can set in as parents and siblings wonder how to help. Or they even may dismiss the problem because they know there is nothing they can do about it anyway.

But how privileged is the distant family member whose family back home *does* know what to do. Whose family knows that, even if they cannot go to their loved one, there is Somebody who *can*—*God*. How privileged if their families know how to *pray*.

It is not our caring or even our loving, as important as they are for the well-being of the absent family member, that will produce results in the difficult circumstances. It is only God who can do that. And God reaches down to intervene in their need in response to our praying.

> The effectual, fervent *prayer* of a righteous person *avails much* (James 5:13, italics added).

Family SOS calls should elicit more than worry, panic, or even ignoring their plight. Fervent and persistent prayer by the family at home should spontaneously explode.

TELEPHONE PRAYER CONNECTION

Our family has kept the long distance phone lines busy since our first child went away to college. We have felt those phone bills were one of the greatest investments we ever could make in our children. Urgent calls of "Please pray—quick!" or "Mother, call the prayer chain" are familiar sounds in our house. Even ordinary calls almost always end up with a verbal promise to pray or a silent resolve to multiply and intensify our praying for them.

When Kurt and Margie were living in New York, they helped avoid an abortion in a young girl by taking her into their home. But they were unprepared for her lifestyle. "Mother, how do you answer when we tell her driving with a gang of teenagers and throwing bottles through car windows isn't right—and she, startled, asks us what *we* do for fun? Please pray, Mother."

As members live away from family, situations frequently arise which they can't handle alone. But they don't have to handle them alone. A phone call or letter to a praying Christian family back home sends the prayer up to God; and, although the family can't help in person, God can—and does. In answer to those prayers!

Just as I was writing about an anchor at home, our phone rang. It was our daughter-in-love Margie, now herself pregnant. "Kurt had stomach flu all night and can't team teach with me in Sunday School this morning. Please pray!" Then she continued, "And I feel so empty this week— with James so sick and me still not feeling well after our bouts of stomach flu. Worse yet, Kurt wrote today's lesson, and he was going to lead today. I have his notes, but have only fifteen minutes to get it together."

My heart reached out to her. "Margie," I replied, "it is in your weakness, like Paul's, that the power of Christ will rest upon you. I know—it is the story of my life and always has been true for me. Don't worry about what you will say. You have lived that Sunday School lesson for many years. So just let the Holy Spirit recall the answers to their questions from what God has done for you. I *know* He will!"

While Margie was teaching, I spent much of the time praying up to God for an outpouring of His power, not only on her, but on the whole class. One of the greatest privileges of my life has been to have my children feel they have an anchor at home where they can call for prayer— any time or under any circumstance.

AN ANCHOR FOR DAN AND NANCY

Of all the prayers phoned to our home, by far the most frequent were from our Nancy during Dan's three and a half years of that job disaster. Living a thousand miles away afforded only brief and scattered visits, but the prayer link never broke. My mother's "We're just a prayer apart" became a way of life for this mother and daughter too. Sometimes I almost think we are much closer *because* she is so far away.

Their needs were endless—and the urgent requests almost continual. Day after day huge mountains loomed before them—from selection of a lawyer, to working with Senator Grassley's office, to appearing before the National Merit Board. They needed prayer!

Then Nancy phoned for prayer because little Kathy had fallen down the stairs and broken her leg. Nancy was getting another degree by extension with constant roadblocks. Cindy's needed surgery was postponed because they found she had a bleeding problem. And on and on the SOS phone calls came home. And over and over we prayed.

You'll recall that phoning prayer requests all started in Rockford back in 1968 when our "What Happens When Women Pray" ladies experimented with using the telephone to communicate the prayer needs resulting in "telephone prayer chains." But it was the call-backs with the answers that convinced them, without my knowing it, that God really does answer when we communicate by phone—if we really take time to pray.

IN NANCY'S OWN WORDS

Here in her own words Nancy tells how much prayer has meant to her:

Many families separated by miles keep in touch by phone or letters. Unfortunately, many of those communications deteriorate from informational to indifference or even gossip.

I grew up understanding that God is a part of everyday activities and decisions. And whenever I call home, the conversation closes with, "We'll pray about that"—and they do. It does not necessarily need to be a crisis. Including God through prayer in the day-to-day activities of marriage, jobs, and raising children keeps our family not only well informed—but close.

Whenever we share, ventilate, or even pray with a friend or a counselor, it can be very beneficial. But when we ventilate or share with a family member, there is an added dimension. The depth and permanence of family love is different. And it creates intensely personal and caring prayers. And that is what I have experienced every time I have called home through these many years.

WHEN THEY PRAY FOR US, GOD'S ARM REACHES US

One of the most important gifts I ever received was a gold cross on a chain. Chris gave it to me when I first started traveling alone extensively. The card read, "Remember when you are out there alone, there is somebody at home loving you and praying for you." How often when things got difficult I would reach up, hold on to that little cross, and feel the assurance of those prayers of my husband.

When I went to Seoul, Korea to teach at the International Prayer Assembly in 1984, Chris gave me a letter to always carry, saying, "I have two reasons to write this letter. First it is my hope that as you carry it, it will be a constant reminder of *my prayers for you*. Prayer that gives a sense of His power, His presence, and His ability to meet every need you will have. He is able. Second, to be a reminder of how much I love you and anxiously await the day of your return."

The prayers from Dan and Nancy have also flowed this way to me. I too share my many needs with them, not just pray for them. When I first asked little Nancy at our "front door prayertime" over thirty years ago to pray for me because Mother had a problem that day, it has borne much fruit. I cherish the freedom to ask for their prayers in my ministry, in my personal life, on boards where I serve, and my relationships. I'm anxious to get to heaven and see all of their prayers stored up in golden bowls up there.

I have had the same kinship in prayer with Kurt through the years and now also his Margie. There is no feeling of superiority or authority over them in our spiritual life together. No, I eagerly admit my needs to them also—coveting their prayers for their mother. It is the "bearing of one another's burdens" of Galatians 6:2 in action in this open and sweet family relationship.

As I have mentioned in this book so often, the prayer support from Jan and Skip has been so wonderful. Many times, in the depth of despair, inadequacy for a task or lack of wisdom, I have poured out my heart to them. And they have fervently and faithfully wrestled at the Throne of Grace for me. Jan and son-in-love Skip have been some of my strongest prayer supporters through the years—at home and around the world.

When overseas, I always rotate the phone calls home among my husband and three children's families. Once in Aberdeen, Scotland, I felt strong spiritual warfare during the committee prayertime the night before my seminar. I phoned Jan and Skip, whose turn it was to get the call—this time for prayer. Jan's reply to me was, "This is for you, Mother, from Romans 8:37: *'more than conquerers!'*" (KJV, italics added) As I read it again at 6 o'clock the next morning, there was a rush of tears—of relief, of complete trust in Jesus, of victory to come. And it did come.

When I returned from my Taiwan prayer seminar tour and the wonderful power of God we experienced, Jan told me that every day while I was gone she had prayed that only God would be seen, and only He would be glorified. And that prayer was answered.

Jan's prayers for overseas trips often have been written to me in notes. My first overseas ministering took me alone to Australia in 1980. I wiped tears from time to time all the way to Australia with her note telling me that every day while I was gone she and Skip would kneel at the old green chair—and pray for me. And Skip's precious notes always are the Scriptures God has given him for me while I am gone.

And her note as I left for South Africa, a country torn by racial terrorism at that time, emphasized that she was praying about my *reason* for going from Luke 24:45-50: "That repentance for forgiveness of sins should be proclaimed in His name to all the nations." God answered that prayer throughout the whole strife-torn trip.

But I don't have to be overseas to receive prayer notes from my family. While I was writing my *Battling the Prince of Darkness* book, I frequently was tempted to soft-pedal some of the harsh biblical truths about Satan and hell. But it was a note from Jan only two miles away that I kept taped by my computer desk the whole time I wrote that book that gave me that godly boldness. It was part of the spiritual armor section from Ephesians 6:19-20 where Paul asked prayer for himself from those wearing the armor of God:

And pray for me also, that whenever I open my mouth, words may be given me so that I will fearlessly make known the mystery of the Gospel for which I am an ambassador in chains. Pray that I may declare it fearlessly, as I should (NIV).

Prayer for boldness!

Also I am deeply indebted to my sister and brother-in-law, Maxine and Rudy, who pray faithfully for me every day while I travel. When they were in the Philippines for a two-year missions stint, we kept their picture on our refrigerator and prayed for them every day. But I was overwhelmed when they told me how much they prayed for me my last trip to India. As members of my Twenty-Four-Hour Prayer Clock, they set their alarm and *got up two hours early every day to pray for me and my ministry there.* Having traveled extensively around the world, they understood the dangers and needs I would have.

Also Maxine went to her Bible every day and wrote down and dated what God had given her to pray for me as she followed my itinerary. Just a few are:

Send angel ahead of her to prepare way (Ex. 23:20) . . .

In Calcutta, that vast city needing Christ—power is in God's hands . . .

"Not by might, nor by power but by My Spirit says the Lord" (Zech. 4:6) . . .

Isaiah 40:31 in that hot climate in Bombay . . .

"The angel of the Lord encamps around those who fear Him" (Ps. 34:7) . . .

Romans 16:20—that God would crush Satan—for her and Operation Mobilization leaders . . .

That, like Stephen from Acts 6:8, she would be God's woman full of grace and power . . .

And on the way home, that He protects the way of His faithful ones—from Proverbs 2:8.

When my mother died there was a deep loss in my life. My ministry calendar, phone calls, and letters always prompted not only her motherly concern but her deep prayer for me. But now I no longer can shoot an SOS to her for prayer. But God has laid on other hearts my mother's mantle of prayer. I have a deep and rare treasure in my family's prayer for me.

WHEN THEY WON'T TOUCH

There are times when family members deliberately cut off touching. A child runs away or a spouse disappears. Also there are times when family members could touch, but are emotionally separated and refuse to communicate. Perhaps they have distanced themselves from the family deliberately because of sin, rebellion, aloofness, an independent lifestyle, or an unforgiving spirit. Our arms ache to hold that dear one close to us—as in years past, but he or she will not allow it.

I recall being told once when longing to feel the healing of a hug from an estranged extended-family member, "The *last* thing she wants you to do is hug her!"

This is a sign loved ones need their distance—but also is a sign they need prayer more than ever. At those times, there is just the standing by, keeping heart and door open to them—interceding. It is a time to hang on without wavering to God's desire and ability to bridge the gap that separates loved ones. It is a time of deep, earnest, persistent prayer—sometimes day and night.

There is no distance too great, and there is no rift too wide, to stop prayer.

"Releasing" Prayers

VERY EARLY NEW YEAR'S morning of 1990 I was lying in bed praying for each child, grandchild, and my husband, not only for a new year but a new decade. I prayed for each one individually—for specific needs and then for God to fill each with Himself. Then an overwhelming feeling swept over me that I should *release* my whole family to God.

I bundled them all up in a package in my mind and gave them to God—for His complete will. "Lord, do anything You need to them to make them what You want them to be. Lord, I release them all to You for whatever You know is best for them—because I know You never make a mistake. Lord, You know every facet and step of the future of each one of them, and You never make a mistake!"

As I picked up a section of our newspaper, my eyes fell on the picture of the first TV newscaster of our area whom we watched every night in the 1940s. Dead. Same age as my husband, Chris. A little apprehension crept into my heart as I wondered, am I releasing Chris for *that* reason? Then I cried out to the Lord, "But *he* is Yours too Lord! And *me* too! I can't release everybody *else* and not myself."

There had been many times before, and have been since, that God has required me to pray releasing a family member to Him for His will—not mine. Just one releasing prayer never has done it. Whenever a new difficult decision has arisen, the releasing prayer has had to be prayed again—and again—and again.

But these are not easy prayers to pray. We all feel that somehow we own our human possessions—the one we married, the ones to whom we gave birth, our parents, our grandparents. It is very difficult to give up those we call "family" to the will of another—even if it is God's.

RELEASED NOT TO ANYBODY—BUT TO *GOD*

Later that year while going through an extended family crisis (which included some family members I had released that New Year's morning), God spoke so powerfully to me out of 2 Timothy:

> For this reason I also suffer these things, but I am not ashamed; for I know *whom* I have believed and am convinced that He is able to guard what I have entrusted to Him until that day (1:12, italics added).

I sank to my knees by my prayer pouf and cried, "Lord, I have completely committed my husband, each child, each grandchild, my service, my will, my body, my health, and my strength to You many times. Now that I'm going through this crisis, I know You *will* keep and guard it all—until that day!"

Released—not to just *anybody*—but to God! I know in *Whom (deity)* not in *whom* (human) I have believed. This is not releasing my family members into the hands of a human leader of a different religion, a human counselor, a peer group with a different set of moral and social values, or a different human mentor to guide them. No, this is releasing them to the omniscient God of the universe! He knows the end from the beginning, knows all the "whys" and "what ifs" of our lives. He alone is capable—and worthy—to have us entrust our human possessions to Him.

> Oh, the depth of the riches both of the wisdom and knowledge of God! How unsearchable are His judgments and unfathomable His ways! (Rom. 11:33)

GOD'S SIDE OF OUR RELEASING

How relieved God must be when we release someone we love for His will. Relieved that He no longer has to wrestle with us as we try to hinder His perfect will in the life of that family member. Relieved that the roadblocks to His dealing with our loved ones we keep throwing up in front of Him finally are removed—and we at last have trusted Him enough not to fight against what He knows is best.

Of course, God is sovereign. And He frequently bypasses us to accomplish His will in a loved one. But in tenaciously holding on to a family member for our will in them, we create a struggle between His will and ours. A battle between divine will and human will.

Jesus, when teaching how to pray in the Lord's Prayer, made it very clear that we are to release *our* wills to the *Father's* will.

> Our Father who art in heaven,
> Hallowed be Thy name.
> Thy kingdom come.
> *Thy* will be done,
> On earth as it is in heaven (Matt. 6:9-10, italics added).

When there was a struggle of wills in heaven as Lucifer (Satan) wanted to be like God, he was violently thrown from heaven. But God deals more kindly with His children on earth. He just expects us to *want* His will—and then to release all our human possessions *for* His will. Then His perfect will can be done in our family on earth—just like it is now in all of heaven.

A woman named Betty called from Texas in late 1990 saying, "I'm beside myself because my two soldier sons are en route to Desert Storm in Saudi Arabia and my daughter-in-law is already there." Together on the phone we prayed, releasing them into God's hands, and then thanking Him for whatever His will would be in their lives. Feeling God's incredible peace, Betty thanked me and hung up. Shortly after that a close friend called me and mentioned that when her son in the armed forces in Saudi Arabia was unable to get a Bible to read and to worship God, he began examining his relationship with Jesus—and for the first time accepted Him as the Savior and Lord of his life. *God's will!*

Releasing frees God to flow unhindered into our family members' lives. Frees Him to reprove and prune instead of our playing God and trying to protect our family members from anything hard. Releasing frees God to call them into His service instead of our wanting our children to be wealthy and succeed by the world's standards. Frees God to open those fabulous doors of ministry we have been trying to hold shut by our stubborn wills.

CAREER RELEASING

God gives each of our children talents and abilities, and it seems so natural for parents to want our children to use them to succeed in life, to become financially secure and to have the comforts that perhaps they missed. But releasing our children to use those talents for God's will, whatever that might entail, is not always easy.

I could relate the series of releasing prayers for the education and career of each of our children, but some of my releasing prayers for Kurt will reflect what was prayed for each of them.

Our praying God's will for Kurt's future started at his birth, but especially came into focus for him at his high school college entrance tests. "Call the prayer chain, Mother. Tomorrow are my SAT tests," he nervously ordered. When I answered that I already had called and asked them to pray for God's will concerning how he would do the next day, Kurt put his hands on his hips and exclaimed, "Oh, boy. It'll be just my luck that it is God's will that I flunk!"

Then I explained to that anxious high-schooler that God, knowing his talents and aptitudes, would open and close doors accordingly. "And God's closed doors may be more important than the open ones, for God knows what is best for you, Kurt."

He did pass, and his reason for wanting to attend Bethel College written in his application brought a thrill to my heart: "I grew up in a church-oriented environment. I accepted Christ as a small child and have recently reaffirmed the decision. I believe that God's will is the most important thing in my life, and going to Bethel is in His will."

Then it was during his entrance tests for his doctoral program in physics that I, not he, struggled so hard with God's will, as I told you about earlier. As I prayed those three hours on two consecutive nights while he took those tests, much of the praying time was about my willingness for God's will in Kurt's career. With deep tearful praying, at 8:20 the first night aloud I emptied myself of every desire I had for Kurt. I released him for God's will, not mine. Then my prayertime turned to worshiping God for who He is in my son's life! The God who knew what talents He put in Kurt at conception—and thus what his career should be!

But when the doctoral training was over, more questions of God's will emerged. As Kurt worked on his first place of employment, I had put an SOS on the telephone prayer chain: "Pray for Kurt that he will know God's *exact* open door for him." Then I had one of the most precious moments I ever have had with my son. As we knelt together at my prayer pouf, Kurt squeezed my hand and put his head next to mine as we wrestled with God—once again giving him over to God for *God's* open door.

Kurt was struggling with finishing his doctoral thesis and getting interviews in areas he wanted to live. One Monday morning Margie, Kurt, and I sat clumped together by the kitchen table, holding hands and praying, "Only Your will, God!"

As he was leaving to give a presentation to a prospective company, Kurt stopped and prayed, "O God, put me where I will be the *most worth to You*. Father, as I go to give this presentation, make me what You want me to be. Lord, if my pride needs them to rub my face in the dirt by their reactions, O Lord, You know I don't want that to happen, but if You know I need that kind of response, OK, Lord."

Kurt's questions were the usual ones through the tedious months of finding God's will. "How can I wait that long, Mother?" "How can I really know what His will is?" And finally, exasperated, he looked at me and said seriously, "Why doesn't God just write it in the sky, Mother?"

During all of this, Kurt and Margie went to the InterVarsity Christian Fellowship Urbana Missions Conference because they were struggling with whether or not it was God's will for them to go to China and share Jesus through their much-needed professions as teachers or to stay in America. They had prayed, but now their praying for God's will escalated. And I prayed continually while they were there, "Lord, keep them from being swayed emotionally in a way You do not want and are not calling." Then, "Lord, lead them to exactly the person or people You want them to talk with. Don't let them miss it if You are calling them to foreign missions. *God, only Your will. No more, no less!*"

Returning from Urbana where several mission executives eagerly had told Kurt and Margie there definitely were openings for them in China teaching English and physics, they prayed and prayed. Then we knelt by the prayer pouf, and I had the deep privilege of praying with and for them once again, "O God, if it is Your will, don't let them miss it. But don't let them go if it is not Your number one will. Don't let them get ahead of Your timing. Prepare them as much and as long as You know is needed." Both Kurt and Margie—after years of urgings of some kind from God to go perhaps to China—were submitting to God to go—or not to go—now or later.

And there was Kurt's wanting to be part of my ministry for years, and now adding Margie, who felt the same. As the three of us sat holding hands on our sofa, we dreamed and chatted about it—and then gave it to God for His will. Kurt just added as I write this, "Even today, the story is not finished. My first position was temporary and far from both families. Looking back, we understand that God knew I had been 'Harold's son' and then 'Evelyn's son' for too long. I needed to follow God through *personal* commitment, not Christian peer pressure."

Parents are tempted to pray for an immediate big salary, important connections in business, and overnight success; but giving up what in our hearts we want them to do is different. However, our omniscient God knows the outcome of each move in our children's lives—and, if we let Him, will direct in the way only He knows best for them. Our family verse, Romans 8:28, says that God will work out everything for good to those who love Him—only if they are called according to *His* purpose—not the parents' wills.

Marked in my Bible is my prayer for my family members (like

Epaphras' prayer): "Always laboring earnestly for you in his prayers, *that you may stand perfect and fully assured in all the will of God*" (Col. 4:12).

JAN'S RELEASING—IN HER OWN WORDS

I asked Jan to tell of her releasing prayer experience. It follows:

When after years of our trying to conceive, God sent us the baby that was to become our Jenna. There are no words to describe our joy. Many times before her birth I thanked God for the privilege of carrying that baby. Then one day it happened. God said, "I want her back."

"What do You mean, You want her back! After all this waiting and surgery, You want me to give her up?" As the depths of my emotions rolled, I heard the still small voice again, "I want her back."

Then I understood. I had to release this baby back to God *for His purposes*. Then I found myself playing a little game. My mind said, "If I give God the baby, then He'll let me keep it." But another part of my brain said, "You foolish one! Do you think God is so stupid He can't see through that?" *I reasoned that if I intended to do what God was asking, I was going to have to do it, knowing that God might take me up on my promise—and that I could accept it if He did.*

The prayer became a lot harder to pray at that point. I knew I had to pray it and that I would pray it, but it still took several days before I was able to say: "God, this child is Yours. If she will never know You (through salvation), and if she is as close to You now as she will ever be, then take her now, before she is born."

It was the hardest prayer I had ever prayed. But I meant it—even if He took me up on it. Since her birth, I have had to give Jenna back on different issues many times since then, but these have been small in comparison, and I keep reminding myself of *whose child she really is.*

In regard to another releasing experience, Jan recalls:

Several years later Mother was preparing to go to South Africa. This was during the peak of their civil unrest, and "necklacing" was not uncommon among warring tribes. This involved having a car tire put around the victim, filled with gasoline and ignited—taking twenty minutes for the person to die. During my mother's preparation, we talked about martyrs and what God had in store for them—and how she had asked God years before for the privilege of being one for Him (see Rev. 6:9-11). Shortly after, I was awakened in the middle of the night by God. "I want you to release your mother to be a martyr." Now, it's one thing to release someone who's sitting home making cookies, and quite another to release someone who is to go speak in a volatile atmosphere to racially mixed audiences about forgiveness. To give her up to go overseas, OK. Maybe even to die. But to give her up to be tortured? God, how could You ask me for that? Then His still small answer came. "For My glory."

After hours of struggling and weeping, it was finally OK. "All right, God, if You want to take her; if my kids lose their grandmother, even if she's tortured for Your sake, that's OK with me." *And I knew from my previous experience that when I said it, I had to mean it—because He might take me up on it.*

I thought I was in for a rest, but the next night I was awake again. Only this time it was over my infant daughter, Crista. "I want her—for a martyr." Just writing that gives me chills. "But, Lord—Crista? She's just a baby." But the still small voice came back. "I want her." So shivering and sobbing, I stood by her crib and gave her up—for whatever the Lord had for her. The thought of my beautiful baby girl being tortured, even for Christ's sake, was and still is very difficult. But I know without a doubt that God is sovereign, and *whatever happens He will be sufficient.*

I hope and pray that God will not take me up on my promises, but I know that He might. And if He does, it will be OK with me.

RELEASING PRAYERS: NOT AN INSURANCE POLICY

Jan and I have talked much about whether God, when He tests us, *just wants us to be willing* to give loved ones up like Abraham and his son Isaac—or whether He really *will take us up on our releasing prayers.* God had said to Abraham in Genesis 22:2, "Take now your son, your only son, whom you love, Isaac, and . . . offer him there [on a Moriah mountain] as a burnt offering." And Abraham, with his heart breaking, had obeyed God right up through binding Issaac, laying him on the altar, and lifting the knife to slay him. (A missionary to Taiwan, Jeanne Swanson, told me to try inserting my own child's name in the place of Isaac.) But then the angel of the Lord called to Abraham from heaven telling him not to slay his son, "for now I know that you fear [reverence] God, since you have not withheld your son" (Gen. 22:13). And then God miraculously provided the ram for the sacrifice. *All God wanted was for Abraham to be willing!*

God has not taken any of the loved ones Jan gave Him either. But this one biblical example is not necessarily what God will do in every instance of releasing a loved one to His will. When God tests us as He did Abraham, He isn't under any obligation to say, "Now that you have obeyed and released your possession to My will, I will let you have your will."

"Mother," Jan warned, "it is important to realize that just because we release someone or something to God for His will, it does not mean He will do it like *we* want. *Releasing is not an insurance policy!*"

THE BLESSING OF OBEYING AND RELEASING

In the Abraham-Isaac story, the angel called to Abraham a second time from heaven and gave him God's *reward* for being willing. "*Because* you have done this thing, and have not withheld your son, your only son [declares the Lord], indeed I will greatly bless you . . . and in your seed all the nations of the earth shall be blessed, *because* you have obeyed My voice" (Gen. 22:16-18, italics added).

When we have released our family members to God, He has poured out His blessings on us too. We have had a new appreciation of each family member's preciousness to us and to God, producing so much sweeter relationships within our family. Thankfulness for each member is so much stronger.

And in releasing prayers, a new realization that they are His, not ours, emerges. As Jan puts it, "Releasing authority and control over your loved ones is liberating because when you release *them, you* are released from the responsibility and worry over what happens to them." Not that it removes our stewardship in taking care of them or our being concerned for them or our intercessory praying for them. No, those are multiplied after we release them to God. *But it is that they are now in the hands of the all-loving, all-powerful God of heaven—who has owned them all along!*

RELEASING REQUIRES FAITH IN WHO GOD IS

But being able to release our loved ones through prayer to God's will and not our own requires an unshakable faith in who God is.

You'll recall earlier mention of Jan's going to Mayo Clinic for extensive microsurgery to correct a problem that had kept her from conceiving a child. Skip and Jan had given the matter of having a baby to God for His will for ten years. The night before Jan was to leave for Mayo, several of us met to pray with her. Kneeling, with all of us laying our hands on her, Jan trembled as she wept and struggled, and again gave the matter of her having a baby to God. But what she said as she stood up showed what she really thought of God. "Oh, Mother," she sobbed as we hugged tightly and wept together, "if God doesn't have a baby for me, I *know* He has something better!"

My hardest prayer while Jan knelt was releasing my privilege of being a grandmother. But I did. And my response through my tears to her was, "Oh, Jan, if God doesn't give you this baby, maybe now that you are a medical doctor He has a million little babies somewhere He wants you to hold in your arms."

WHEN GOD DOES TAKE US UP ON A RELEASING PRAYER—FROM MARGIE

At my request, my daughter-in-love Margie wrote the following tender releasing incident from her own family:

When your hand is clenched tightly around that which you love, it is no easy thing to open that hand and watch the object of your affection fly away. Especially when that object is your child—not holding merely your affection, but all your time, talents, sweat, tears, and your very life invested in a beautiful person you call your child.

Releasing a child, I believe, is one of earth's most difficult trials. That is why God asked Abraham to give up Isaac. And the very God of heaven Himself was willing to be our example, for Romans 8:32 tells us, "He [God] . . . did not spare His own Son, but gave Him up for us all."

I was thirteen when I watched my parents release my older brother, Bob. He was a very bright boy and popular in school. Baseball and football were exciting to him, and he received the all-school sportsmanship award. He and Dad played together on summer teams, and they were as close as any father and son combination I ever have seen. Bob was a serious Christian all through high school, and the coaches and classmates could tell the difference Jesus made in his life.

When Bob graduated from high school, he started his own business at age eighteen, aligning himself with the local big Caterpillar Tractor Company. Life was very good.

I remember the day Bob came home from college registration with new textbooks in hand. The future looked bright, but night sweats had started earlier in the summer. His doctors were stumped and blamed it on stress. Later doctors diagnosed the illness as histoplasmosis, a fungous disease of the lungs that later attacked Bob's brain. He never made it to his first day of college classes.

The next two years were filled with trips to the hospital, the last six months driving four hours each way to a larger metropolitan medical center. My dad, having to work, traveled every weekend to see Mom and Bob. Every day Mom saw her son become worse and go through one nightmarish medical test after another. All this time our parents and we three girls gathered spontaneously to pray. Occasionally, we would pick a day to fast together and pray for Bob—even our eleven-year-old sister joined us. It was these prayertimes and the prayers of our close extended family plus the unsolicited prayers of hundreds of Christians that got us through.

After two years of hospitals, Bob came home, the doctors hoping he might recover somewhat. The healthy football player was a weak man in a wheelchair, unable even to feed himself. I saw the muscles in my mother's arms grow big from lifting her son. Yet who could give up hope?

As Mom struggled through each day, she was praying, "God, not my will but Yours." Dad, however, couldn't pray that way of releasing Bob. He felt praying God's will showed lack of faith or weakness. "Wasn't that giving up hope?" he would ask.

My older sister, Vicki, was being prepared by God first, coming alone to the place of releasing Bob two weeks before Mom and Dad could. Finally, as the burden of Bob's sickness grew greater on the family and on Bob, my dad and mom agreed on a very, very difficult decision. Together they must take Bob to Isaac's altar. They must go to Abraham's "distant place alone" (Gen. 22:4). They must unclench their hands and see the work of God. Finally, they could pray together, "Father, Thy will be done." One week later Bob died in his sleep. Two years of struggle were over.

Releasing—giving God everything—praying "not My will but Thine" permeated all of Jesus' life. Can we do any less?

RELEASING PRAYERS: NOT A DEATH CERTIFICATE

Releasing does not cause death, but it does prepare *us* for that loved one's homegoing. A woman came to me a while after she had attended my prayer seminar. "Did I kill my father? Did I kill my father?" she cried. "My father had been in prison for many years when I released him to God for His will in your seminar. Weeks later I received notification that my father had died in prison and, because they had lost his records, I had not been notified. When I checked the date of his death," she sobbed, "it was the same day I released him! Did I kill him?"

"No, you did not cause his death," I assured her. The releasing just prepared *you* for his death."

When we release a loved one to God for His will, it is we, not the loved one who are prepared for the inevitable death. We don't kill loved ones.

Although I didn't release my miscarriages and stillborn baby to God until after I had gone through the agony of losing them, our Judy was different. Afflicted with spina bifida, she lived paralyzed from the waist down for seven months, and after months our doctor told us to take her directly to the hospital from his office—because she could not live.

That night, in the blackness of my bedroom in Stanchfield, I anguished in prayer on my knees until dawn. I fought and struggled until finally I could release her to God's will—not mine. Until I could release her *for Him to have*—not for Chris and me to have. But I did not kill her by at last being able to give her to God for His will. No, it only prepared me to give her up. And two months later they placed her in that little casket. The grieving was there, but not the battle. I had released Judy into God's loving arms.

FAMILY POWER STRUGGLES

In all families there are conscious, or at least subconscious, power struggles. Toddlers fight to assert their personhood. Kindergartners vie with their parents for control while being model students in school. Grade-schoolers try to substitute peer acceptance for family. Adolescents fight to discover who they are in the family pecking order. Teenagers struggle for independence from the whole family. Mates try to dominate their spouse's time and attention. Wives struggle to become the women God created them to be in a male-dominated society. Husbands try to hold on to their authority over other family members as they go through these various stages. So, how do we resolve this age-old power struggle in families?

Although it may not be easy, there is a simple prayer we can pray that will break the in-family power struggle: every family member releasing in prayer every other member to God's will—not their own.

RELEASING MYSELF

The hardest prayers for me to pray are those when I must decide between family and God. My heart at times seems powerfully pulled in two directions—God and family.

My life's goal has been to be conformed to the image of God's Son

Jesus (Rom. 8:29). And it was said of Him in Hebrews 10:7, "Then I said, 'Behold, I have come to do Thy will, O God.'" This too is my only purpose for living—to do God's will. I have given myself to be a handmaid of the Lord, meaning I am one who has given her will, not just her lifestyle, to the Lord.

God specifically started calling me to win the lost in the world to Jesus in 1980, and from then on has repeatedly called. I was completely broken when God called me again to Jesus' words from Luke 15:4 to forget the ninety-nine and go find the lost sheep. I cried, "O God, take me where *You* want me!" Since going meant leaving my two brand new grandbabies, I sobbed and prayed, "Lord, exchange my empty arms for one sinner finding Jesus in India. No, Lord, many!" And just last year at our "Lord, Change Me" board retreat, I cried to God, "No matter *what the cost,* I will finish what You gave me to do—win the lost!" And that is when the joyous rewards from God come:

> And everyone who has left houses or brothers or sisters or father or mother or children or farms for My name's sake, shall receive many times as much, and shall inherit eternal life (Matt. 19:29).

I have struggled deeply with how I handle what Jesus said clearly to me in Matthew 10:37:

> He who loves father or mother more than Me is not worthy of Me; and he who loves son or daughter more than Me is not worthy of Me.

But the answer is in Jesus' word *more*. It is my priorities—and balance. Doing God's will includes all facets of my life—ministry and family. Balancing the two according to God's perfect will is imperative, but not always easy. Keeping my priorities the same as God's priorities for me takes constant evaluating and committing them over again to God.

I get great joy in serving my family, as I'm sure God wants me to. I am completely happy when surrounded by my entire family, giving myself wholeheartedly to them. However, there have been these deep, deep calls from God and my repeatedly releasing myself to His will. And I have wept before God trying to discern His sovereign balance. But the secret is in the releasing of both my family and myself to God's will.

GOD'S CHOICE, NOT MINE

My husband left his first pastorate after only three and a half years. I had just gotten curtains finally to fit that whole new parsonage, and when we moved into our colonial style house in Rockford, none of the curtains fit! I had torn myself away from all the people I had learned to love deeply in that first pastorate, and I cringed at going through that every three years! *But I knew in my heart the choice was not mine—nor Chris'. It was God's.* Before that first move I had prayed and prayed about every church where Chris had candidated, and felt God had shown me which one was His choice. But I firmly held on to my belief that God had to tell *Chris* where He wanted him as a young pastor to serve Him— not *me*. I was to submit to God's will—and release Chris to follow it.

The next move from Rockford after fourteen and a half years was even harder for me to release my husband, because he was leaving the pastorate and going to work and teach at Bethel College and Seminary. We were at the height of our "What Happens When Women Pray" project in that church, and I wondered if God, for the first time, was making a mistake. It certainly seemed so to me. But my releasing it for God's will— not mine—came. And then I watched as God, who hadn't made a mistake, opened doors beyond anything I ever could have planned or chosen for us in the new place of service.

Although there have been times I have struggled to put in practice my deep belief about releasing, God has given me the grace and strength to live that way with every member of my family.

MY HUSBAND'S RELEASING PRAYER

While I was holding seminars in Japan, a secular newspaper reporter in Tokyo, mirroring his country's male-dominated society, asked me during an interview, "How does your husband handle you being the teacher and speaker?"

Nodding at Chris in another part of the room, I answered, "He's sitting right over there. Why don't you ask him for yourself?"

I was startled and thrilled at my husband's profound answer. Here, in Chris' own words, is what he told that reporter:

"I believe the Christian husband is the spiritual head of his household, God having entrusted him with his wife and children's physical and spiritual care. The Bible says that those to whom something has been entrusted are stewards; thus the husband and father is the steward of the wife and children whom God has entrusted to him. So that also makes him the steward of his wife's and children's gifts and talents from God. As a steward he is *responsible* not only to free them to use their talents from God, he also must encourage and assist them to do so. Also, as the steward of these family members, the husband *will give an account to God* as to whether he has hindered or helped them in the use of their God-given talents."

It is required of stewards that one be found trustworthy (1 Cor. 4:2).

Here are Chris' expanded beliefs about husbands as stewards: "There is a great tragedy occurring in Christian America. Somehow we have come to believe that only men can exercise the God-given talents that He has provided for His children. There is no scriptural basis for only part of God's children receiving and using gifts and talents from God. And if God has entrusted a talent or gift to a household member, then everything about that home ought to encourage it. If not, the steward has failed in his responsibility and falls in the category of Jesus' unfaithful, wicked, slothful servant. (See Matt. 25:26 and Luke 19:22.)

"I'm often asked how I feel about a wife whom God is using outside the home. Shouldn't I be carrying on the ministry that she is—instead of her? Perhaps so, except for one thing—it was she who was called and gifted by God to minister as she does. I didn't decide this—God did. My place, and my joy, is to act as best I can as an encourager and helper in the exercising of her God-given talents and call.

"Years ago I had to humbly release in prayer my wife, my children, and all that I am to the perfect will of God. This has sometimes meant separation and loneliness, but it also has been the place where I am content to know that God does all things well—and rewards me with the sense of knowing that by releasing I too have done all things well and have faithfully exercised my stewardship."

A young pastor recently said to me, "I don't think I ever could release my wife to be away from our children and me. Her place is to take care of us." My answer to him was, "Even if *God* called her?"

When both a husband and wife honestly want God's will for themselves—and for each other—that divine will of God never will make them at odds. God's will never produces conflicting attitudes, beliefs, or actions. When there is conflict, there has to be human will involved—not God's.

THE SECRET OF IT ALL

The secret of harmony in a family is each of the members wanting God's will for the others instead of having their own way.

Almost fifty years of family releasing have taught me that God is not a harsh taskmaster sitting up in heaven rubbing His hands together just waiting to pounce on the one we release to Him. Oh, no! Our releasing our family members to God for His will throws open heaven's gates and allows all the blessings to flow that God has waiting up there for us. And when we decide we will allow them, they don't just trickle down. No, when we release a family member to God, then His perfect, all-knowing, for-our-good blessings will gush uninhibited from heaven—to our loved ones—and to us!

Prayers at Family Births

I HAD BEEN SKEPTICAL about having our almost-three-year-old granddaughter Jenna in the room for the birth of her baby sister. But her mummy and daddy, Jan and Skip, both medical doctors, wanted it, and had prepared Jenna month by month of the pregnancy with her own little "baby book," explaining such details as the "funny stuff" that would be all over the baby, the cutting of the cord, and what that thing (clamp) was that would be sticking out of the umbilical cord. Then Jan's "dry run" two days earlier had given Jenna and me a chance to become thoroughly acquainted with the hospital surroundings and birthing room. But I was not prepared for the deep emotional and spiritual experience that came with the birth of our Crista.

Chris had gotten home from out of town the night before and had joined Jenna and me. The three of us stood waiting "on the alert" outside the birthing room door during Jan's last severe contractions. Suddenly Skip opened the door and motioned us quickly in. I drew in my breath. The room was charged with imminent birth. I picked up Jenna and held her in my arms, but she recognized the steps that had been taught her from her little book and took it all in stride.

But when the little head crowned, I suddenly felt the presence of God just filling the room. The shocking thing to me was the overwhelming

spiritual dimension that permeated, yes almost saturated, the atmosphere. *Birth! God was there—invisible, yet filling that room with His
presence.* Unseen yet so tangible. Powerful yet pleasant. Ethereal yet as
real as the air we were breathing. "God!" my heart silently cried out over
and over.

The oneness of family was awesome. Tears trickled down Jan's face as
they laid Crista, just quickly wiped off and wrapped in a blanket, in her
arms. Jenna had asked if people would cry, and Skip had told her, "Yes,
but they would be tears of joy because we will be so happy—not bad
tears."

So often in the past, and even today, birth has been reduced to just a
medical process with sterile delivery rooms, isolation of the mother—
often even from her own husband—and whisking of the newborn off to
an antiseptically proper nursery. How sad. How much is missed. *Birth is
God starting a new life on earth.*

Jenna had been told about the "blood," and it was the only thing she
didn't like about the birth. And neither did her doctor—nor we. Suddenly, as he worked with the placenta, there was a gush of blood that
soaked his trousers, shirt, shoes, the floor, and even splattered on the wall
behind him. I quickly took Jenna out into the hall, and attendants thrust
that unwashed newborn, still wrapped in her original blanket, into Chris'
arms—and they ran down the hall wheeling Jan into surgery. Jan had
lost half of her blood, and they were fighting to save her life.

Crista appeared shortly before noon, and we had completely ignored
the time. So we decided Chris should take Jenna to the lunchroom, and I
should stay in the birthing room with baby Crista. Everybody else was
completely engrossed in saving Jan's life.

I was totally unprepared for the next hour alone with this new baby.
As I walked the floor with her, the bonding was unbelievable. I pressed
her to me, talked continually, thrilled as she squeezed my finger in her little fist, and helped her suck her little finger when she cried.

But mostly I prayed. I prayed back to God the Scripture He had given
me for Crista—Psalm 22:9:

Yet Thou art He who didst bring me forth from the womb.

All through that long waiting time I had an incredible calmness and peace, praying that assurance from God over and over.

God had given me that verse on Crista's due date, August 6, 1985 after I had been praying a long time before dawn about the timing of the birth and other delivery concerns. When I had opened my Bible that morning, it was at Psalm 22; and immediately my eyes had fallen on verse 9. Instantly, I had known it was for that day—Jan's due date. And the promise to me was that it would be God's divine hands that actually would bring that baby into the world, not the hands of the obstetrician or assisting doctor/husband Skip.

But it was not until August 21 that I knew why I needed that verse from God. While they fought to save Jan's life and I walked the floor with newborn Crista, there was an incredible calmness and peace as I prayed Psalm 22:9. And it came from an unshakable faith in what God had told me fifteen days earlier *that His hands were there, and that He was in control—no matter what happened!*

Yes, God filled that room with Himself as powerfully as I ever have felt Him. But I still needed to communicate with Him—through prayer.

THE HOLY SPIRIT'S ROLE AT BIRTH

The other important prayer I prayed in that birthing room was, "Lord, fill her with You." I put my hand on Crista's tiny, moist hand as I prayed, "O God, fill her with Your Spirit, Your Holy Spirit!" Then I laid my free hand on her little body as I continued to pray for her.

Through the years I have prayed many prayers about the Holy Spirit's role in my family, especially at births. Much of it I have not tried to understand theologically, but just have prayed what God spoke to me from the Bible as I read it.

All four of our granddaughters were conceived sometime before Christmas. For many years I have stayed in the Christmas story for my devotions the weeks before Christmas. Thus many of the things I prayed to God about our coming babies were from the first chapter of Luke. And I have discovered the Christmas story is so charged with the activities of the Holy Spirit.

The Christmas that Jenna and Cindy were beginning to grow as tiny fetuses, God started showing me the Holy Spirit in Luke 1. Reading about the angel promising Zacharias that the son his wife, Elizabeth, was carrying would be filled with the Holy Spirit before birth (1:15) sent me pondering my right to pray that for my grandbabies in their mothers' wombs. I realized that as the future John the Baptist, that fetus had a special calling and role on earth from God; but my heart cried out for God to give all of Himself that He intended for my still fetus grandbabies.

Also the Holy Spirit, not any human, caused the conception of Jesus in Mary. And I knew that miracle was just for Jesus, the preexistent Son of God coming to earth. But when the second pair of cousins, Kathy and Crista, were barely on the way, I prayed, "O God, Holy Spirit, *hover over* our little wee ones like You did over Mary at the Annunciation. Hover over their mothers' bodies in all You are—Your holiness, Your power, Your everything!"

And while those two cousins were being carried in their mothers' wombs at Christmastime, my prayer for them was from Isaiah 44:3: "I will pour out My Spirit on your offspring, and My blessings on your descendants."

And the prayer I continually pray for all of our children and grandchildren is that God will graciously pour out His Holy Spirit upon all of them.

Then it was at that same time that I prayed, "Holy God, fill those wee new ones with the fulness of the Godhead!" based on Paul's prayer from Ephesians 3:19. And I added, "Not for them only but, now since Pentecost, fill *all of us*—parents and grandparents—with the fulness of the Godhead so we too can be all You want us to be."

But I also realized from Luke 1:80 that John the Baptist, although He was filled with the Holy Spirit before birth, still needed to grow and "become strong in spirit." I still am asking, with the crowd at John the Baptist's circumcision and naming (see Luke 1:66), "What then will this child turn out to be?" So it is with all my grandbabies. However God chooses to answer all those prenatal prayers of mine, they still will have to grow in God—and go through the step which will give them eternal salvation—receiving Jesus as their personal Savior and Lord. And so we still are praying that the Holy Spirit will be the implementer of God's will in their lives each day as they grow.

We now are expecting our seventh grandchild. Our Kurt's Margie is due in just three months as I write this chapter. So I have a new prayer project. And just this morning I told Margie that almost every day I pray for God to send His messenger, the Holy Spirit, to hover over, protect, and fill that little unborn one with all God wants him or her to be.

PRAYER ACKNOWLEDGES GOD'S ROLE IN MAKING BABIES

The prayers I prayed during my own pregnancies and those of all of my grandchildren were spawned from God's Words in the Bible. Some of the most meaningful and important were those cementing in my heart *Who* it was at work forming those little ones—right while it was happening.

Just days after we knew Jenna and Cindy were conceived, I read in Psalm 119:73: "Thy hands made me and fashioned me."

And my heart cried out in prayer, "O God, it is *Your* hands making our babies."

While my daughters and daughter-in-love have been pregnant, my almost daily prayer for the little unborn ones has been, "O God, as each little cell multiplies, protect it from incorrect divisions and malformations which would make birth defects." Frequently, I would pray, "Father, today as each cell divides, make it just exactly what You want that child to be. Control the genes. Control the multiplying."

It was when Kathy and Crista had just been conceived that I prayed back to God His assurance to me of His part in forming babies, and the horror of abortions, out of Psalm 139:13 and 16:

> For Thou didst form my inward parts;
> Thou didst weave me in my mother's womb. . . .
> Thine eyes have seen my unformed substance;
> And in Thy book they were all written,

The days that were ordained for me,
When as yet there was not one of them.

SCRIPTURES FROM GOD FOR FAMILY BIRTHS

God has given me many special Scriptures for our grandbabies.

On December 3, 1984 we had a phone call from Jenna. "We're going to have a baby," she shouted happily into the phone. After dashing over to see the new mother and sister-to-be, Chris and I prayed together, "Make that child all You want it to be."

Then the next morning there was my deep prayer of thanksgiving to God. Again, Jan had had to have microsurgery at Mayo Clinic in order to conceive this little one, and I had fretted, almost worried, that if conception didn't happen soon, the surgery would be in vain. So first I had to ask God to forgive my lack of faith. Then I prayed thanking Him, not only for the pregnancy, but that the little blob of cells in Jan's uterus was known unto Him. The potential of that life had been put there by Him, and the future planned and willed by God already.

The Scripture God gave for that future baby Crista was Psalm 78:6-7:

> That the generation to come might know, even the children yet to be born, that they may arise and tell them to their children, *that they should put their confidence in God, and not forget the works of God,* but keep His commandments (italics added).

Yes, the fetus Crista's Scripture from God!

Because Jan had paid such a high price through surgery again for her second pregnancy, newly pregnant Nancy considerately waited for a while to announce her pregnancy to us. She wanted Jan to have the limelight alone for a time. But God, without human communication, had been burdening me to pray for Dan and Nancy's baby for a couple of weeks. So I prayed strictly in obedience to God's prodding. I prayed the same prayers, asking God to fill that little one with Himself and to protect and guide and guard each division as the initial cells were budding—the same way I was praying for Jan's baby. The prayers I prayed about

Psalm 139:13-16 of God forming babies in the womb before they were known were not just for Jan but also for Nancy. Then on January 10 three-year-old Cindy called to tell us they were going to have a baby. "And it's in Mummy's tummy!" she shouted over the phone. When I asked her if she loved the baby and if she was happy they were going to have a baby, I got resounding "Yeah!" answers from her. And I got the confirmation of God's burdening me in prayer—before I even knew about the baby!

On July 14, 1985, just a month or so before Crista and Kathy would be born, the Scripture God gave for them was Psalm 100:3, "It is He [the Lord God] who has made us, and not we ourselves." What an assurance from God to us to know that those almost-ready-to-be-born babies were made, not only by human mothers and fathers, but actually by God!

When it was Jenna and Crista's baby brother Brett's due date, I was thrilled that God answered my prayer for his Scripture, by giving the passage immediately following Crista's in Psalm 22:9:

> Thou didst make me trust when upon my mother's breasts. Upon Thee I was cast from birth; Thou hast been my God from my mother's womb (22:9-10).

But I wept as I pondered why that coming little one would need to trust God. I then rejoiced in the promise of his, with the psalmist, *being God's from his mother's womb*! With joy and assurance I accepted from God that He would keep Brett until that time when he would be old enough to accept Jesus personally.

Grandson James' verse was special too. I had been praying for several days asking God for his verse, and on the morning of his birth September 26, 1990, God led me clearly to Psalm 121:8:

> The Lord will guard your going out and your coming in from this time forth and forever.

It was so definite from God. And tears kept coming as deeper and deeper the words burned into my heart: "From this time"—his birth, "forth"—in his life, "and forever"—to eternity. That's when God would guard him! "O thank You, God," I prayed, "for so much more than I expected. I can't stop the tears from popping in my eyes and down my cheeks."

James' mummy, Margie, had been concerned about and had prayed much for her unborn child's ultimate salvation. What a thrill we both felt at God's verse for him.

RELEASING PRAYERS

Ephesians 3:20 was very special to our Margie. She had the reference engraved in Kurt's wedding ring, and even her father-in-law, Chris, had put it in his square in the quilt all the relatives had put together for a surprise wedding present for Kurt and Margie. But it became doubly significant after trying to have a baby for about a year, and getting a little discouraged when she already was thirty-two. It was then Kurt and Margie prayed Ephesians 3:20 about having a baby:

> Now to Him who is able to do exceeding abundantly beyond all that we ask or think, according to the power that works within us.

"Father," they prayed, "this is our prayer for children—or else Your 'more than we even can think or ask for.'"

Margie explained, "This was our knowing that if God didn't give us a baby, He had something even better for Kurt and me." (It was so much like what Jan had said the night before her surgery they hoped would enable her to conceive Jenna.) "But," continued Margie with a grin, "that prayer was prayed January 9, 1990, and I already was two weeks pregnant with James and didn't know it!"

There have been many difficult releasing birth prayers in my life. After my miscarried baby boy and stillborn girl, I finally released my next miscarriage when God gave me Romans 8:28—God causes all things to work together for good to those who love God, to those who are called according to His purpose." And then there was the releasing of Judy that awful night after we had been told she could not live. But there have been others, just as difficult.

Our doctors Jan and Skip had announced her first pregnancy by knocking on our door and asking us if we wanted to see a picture of their baby. Shocked and thrilled, we said we surely did. And they promptly produced an ultrasound photo of Jan's uterus with a little blob right in the middle. "That's our baby right there!" they beamed. But it was only two weeks later that God called on the father of that baby and me to pray a painful prayer when Jan and Skip were attending my prayer seminar in Calvary Church, St. Paul. During our learning to "pray in God's will," I asked everyone to think of the very most important thing to them, and then in audible prayer to give it to God for His will. I always pray what I ask the participants to pray, and immediately I knew what I had to release to God was that little blob in the ultrasound picture. With my heart breaking, I did. As soon as we finished praying, Skip dashed up to the platform and threw his arms around me. With tears in both his eyes and mine, I sobbed, "Oh, Skip, guess what I just had to give to God!" "I know," he cried, "I did too!" Releasing for God's will—the baby that He would make our Jenna!

In the spring several years later while teaching the same seminar, I came to the place of asking that we all give to God the most important thing in our lives. Immediately, I thought of the grandchildren to be born to Jan and Nancy the next summer. Flashing back into my mind were my own two spina bifida babies (one stillborn child and Judy), the cord wrapped around Cindy's neck during birth, and the possibility of physical problems with these unborn grandbabies too. But, with tears in my eyes, I prayed, "Lord, I give to You two *normal, healthy* babies. Your will, not mine!" Two very precious possessions, released! But God gave us two bouncing baby girls—our Crista and Kathy.

Releasing prayers can, and should, end in praise because we have released that child to our God who never makes a mistake, who knows what will be best in the future, and who does all things for the good of those who love Him and are called according to His purpose. I remember finally not only releasing my second miscarriage but thanking God that He had shown us through Romans 8:28 that He was not off His throne, and this was for our good—for we could not have come back to seven more years of college and seminary with three infants, Chris' father dead, and mine an invalid.

But it was not until after our stillborn and Judy had been born seriously afflicted that I began to see God's "what ifs" in pregnancies. I suddenly was thanking Him for the termination of those two pregnancies by miscarriage—because only God knew what those babies might have been. By that time I had learned to trust God so much that thanks for His possibly avoiding a potential serious situation for Chris and me just rolled from my heart.

Psalm 100:3-5 so well expresses why we praise Him after releasing a child to Him:

> Know that the Lord Himself is God;
> It is He who has made us, and not we ourselves;
> We are His people and the sheep of His pasture.
> Enter His gates with thanksgiving,
> And His courts with praise.
> Give thanks to Him; bless His name.
> For the Lord is good;
> His loving-kindness is everlasting,
> And His faithfulness to all generations.

PRAYERS DURING BIRTH

My secretary Sally's daughter, Sue Moore, has worked for me for several years. She just had her second baby, and I asked if she could share a very special experience she and her husband Jeff had during this baby's delivery. Sue wrote:

> When Jeff would pray aloud during my contractions, he would pray for God to relax me. God answered those prayers. I would feel the tension and fear leave me. I believe that was the major factor in cutting my labor from over sixteen hours with my first child down to less than six hours this time [although Sue delivered a nine pound, one ounce baby girl].

Also as Jeff massaged my aching back, he struggled to reach down far enough on my lower back as I lay on the delivery table. "God, somehow enable me to reach down where it hurts!" he prayed. Soon God answered his prayer, as if giving Jeff a longer arm. I felt Jeff's hand even lower than where it hurt most! This situation made me feel that Jeff and I were not alone. It was like bringing a friend in there with us. I felt loved and cared for by *a big God!*"

Chris and I had our babies during the years fathers basically were excluded from the delivery room during the birth. But Chris' vivid memory is of his pacing the floor outside the door while I gave birth—*praying.* Although he couldn't be there to help, my husband knew well the One who could, and would, be with me—*God.*

Each of the fathers in our family could tell of their own praying for their babies. But our whole family also is involved in praying for each family birth. Developments are phoned to each other, and individually and together as families we uphold the mother, father, and new baby. We pray for God to be in control, pray for Him to ease the pain and possible fear, and at times utter prayers of deep concern. But then as the little one is born, the prayers of praise echo through the family.

A GRANDMOTHER'S PRAYERS AT BIRTH

There have been special prayers that I as the grandmother have prayed during the actual births of our grandchildren too, and the length and intensity of the prayers have been as varied as the circumstances prompting them. But always they were to include and involve the God of heaven in the very special, although sometimes a touch-and-go, event of birth.

At the due date of Nancy's first baby, Cindy, we were on vacation in Michigan. Feeling so helpless and far away, I prayed and prayed that God would let me be near her at delivery. When she started having labor pains, instead of going out fishing on Lake Michigan, I sat by a phone in town—*waiting and praying.* But those contractions, and my prayers, kept up for five days! Finally, I just flew home to be near her. (I've often wondered if that long labor was God's way of granting my prayer request.)

Nancy's Kathy was very late also. I thought I had planned the beginning of my fall seminar schedule late enough to be sure I was there for Kathy's birth, but Nancy's being two and a half weeks overdue wrecked the plans. When Kathy was born, I was on a plane en route to Omaha, Nebraska. How difficult it was for me to board that plane, and then feel it take me ever farther away from the emerging life. But being 30,000 feet in the air and hundreds of miles away did not limit me from praying. I closed my eyes so a stewardess would not bother me with beverages and food—and prayed.

Since it was just a couple of weeks after Jan's losing half of her blood at Crista's birth, I prayed for Nancy's safety. And I prayed about the lack of oxygen to the baby's brain if the cord was wrapped around this baby's neck as it was—three times—around their Cindy's. I think I prayed about everything that a grandmother who had lost four of her own babies thinks about—with anxiety and apprehension steadily growing in me. But suddenly God brought Philippians 4:6 to my mind:

Be anxious for nothing, but in everything by prayer and supplication *with thanksgiving* let your requests be made to God (italics added).

Unsolicited and unformed by me, thanksgiving prayers welled up within me and permeated my whole being. Somehow my focus changed directions, from possible earthly problems to God. Again it was His reminding me that He is the One who takes babies from the womb.

The moment my plane landed, I dashed for the nearest phone, dialed the hospital obstetrics department, and soon I heard Kathy's healthy cry as the nurse held the phone near her! God had answered!

When Jan was due to give birth to her first child, Jenna, I asked God to teach me new dimensions in prayer. And He did. Ten days overdue, Jan had to take two eight-hour days of written internal medicine board exams, as previously mentioned in an earlier chapter. So I asked God to teach me how to pray for her through those two consecutive day's eight-hour sessions.

God started by teaching me how to persevere that long a time in prayer first praying for my own cleansing (so I would have power in prayer) and then asking the Holy Spirit to direct my praying (so my praying would be according to God's will).

Then He taught me the reality of Jesus' hands in an amazing series of prayer events. One prayer was, "Jesus, hold Jan's mind firmly; may there be no fear or confusion." Also, "Fill her mind with Your recall ability— just the amount You know she needs." Then I asked for His hand on her writing hand, steadying, directing, legibility. Next the praying was at the piano as I sang, "Precious Lord, take *her* hand; lift her up, let her stand; she is tired, she is weak, she is worn." The next prayer was asking Jesus to put His hands of authority and power on her back, up by her shoulders. I prayed for Jesus' staying hand on the glands and chemicals that would trigger the birth process until the test was completed—for they only gave the exams once a year, and she would have to study and do it all over again the next year if not finished. As I asked God what she needed next, His answer was, "Her lower back." And then it was the weight on her cervix area. "O Jesus, may Your hands be like a sling under that little one, lifting its weight off Jan as she must sit all these hours." The prayers continued with, "She's cold. Help her, Lord," and praying for the terrible stress on Jan's emotions and thus on the baby.

I recorded each time God told me to pray for those specific needs, and later Jan and I went over those two days. Astounded, she confirmed they were the exact times she had needed those things.

Days later Jan's labor began, and this time I asked God to teach me *how* to travail in prayer with her. And He taught me a new dimension of prayer I never had experienced before. The depth of praying was like I remembered travailing in birth, except it was spiritual. I cannot explain it, but deeply felt it while in prayer.

Brett's birth was exciting with Chris and me watching over two sisters, Jenna and Crista, in the birthing room. I hung on to both girls; but, just as Brett started emerging, I put my hands over my eyes. The nurse in charge smiled and said, "She will be all right. She's fine." But I knew something she did not—how Jan lost half her blood, and almost her life, the last delivery. But God was there again, and the joy of that new life exploded in the room. Two hours later we all celebrated with a Chinese carryout dinner in Jan's room! Again, God answering nine month's of praying.

Prayer for Kurt and Margie's little James started when we received a "For My Grandparents" Valentine card with an ultrasound picture enclosed. Baby Christenson apologized that it wasn't the greatest picture—but he was only six weeks old. Daily I prayed for that picture's little cluster of cells as they divided and grew. And when Margie was in labor with our little James, I prayed all the prayers I had prayed for the four preceding granddaughters. But God added one special prayer for Margie while she was in labor. I'm not sure all the kinds of labor Jesus was talking about in Matthew 11:28, but through those hours of her first labor I prayed Jesus' wonderful words for Margie:

Come to Me, all who are weary and heavy laden, and I will give you rest.

Any woman who has given birth knows what it means to be heavy laden just before the baby comes. And the weariness of being pregnant nine months plus the fatigue experienced at giving birth are very real. But I could pray with confidence that Jesus would be there—and He would give her His rest that she so needed.

What a special time family birth is—and what a wonderful time to pray those special prayers.

BONDING PRAYERS

Bonding of caretaker adults with a newborn happens almost automatically at birth and even before birth with the mother. But bonding is important for other members of the family too. There is a special relationship that should and can develop, giving children a desperately needed sense of being loved and secure in a family relationship.

That first hour I spent with Crista while Jan was in surgery produced a strong bonding. However, bonding came in a different way with Cindy and Jenna. Cindy had just been born, and Jenna was overdue when it was time for me to pack for India. I already had just wept through Jesus' words in Luke 14:33, "So, therefore, no one of you can be My disciple who does not give up all his own possessions." Already I had asked Him if He meant grandbabies too. And His "yes" answer had required my difficult and tearful promise to obey Him no matter what the price—even leaving grandbabies.

Although I knew it was His will, I struggled long with leaving my first tiny grandchild, Cindy, and, even worse, perhaps my being in India when her cousin, Jenna, was born. But one of my deepest concerns was not being able to be bonded to those two little granddaughters. And, adding to my uneasiness, was the fact that their paternal grandmothers, Esther and Ruby, would be taking care of and getting bonded to them—instead of me.

So I prayed and prayed, asking God somehow to miraculously bond us together—while I was half way around the world from them. When I returned home from those six weeks in India, I should have been a total stranger to those two grandbabies. But I was in for a fabulous surprise. God had answered my prayers. We were, and still are, deeply bonded to each other—as grandchildren and grandmothers and grandfathers should be!

But I still had to be away from Cindy and Jenna a lot, and was concerned that we would not be as close as if I stayed near them. But God lifted that burden too. When Cindy was only three months old, at her daddy's birthday party, she wound her legs around me and threw her head back, looked me in the eye, and laughed as if to say, "Oh, Grandma, isn't this great?" And I laughed with her, knowing it—our bonding—*was* great. *My prayers answered by God in relation to Cindy.*

Then when Jenna was eight months old, I took her in my arms after a long trip, and she too wound her legs around my waist and tucked her head into my shoulder. She just clung there—her way of saying, "I love you, Grandma!" And I squeezed her back and whispered in her little ear, "And Grandma loves you too, Jenna!" Bonded with Jenna!

I continually pray for bonding with all six of my grandchildren because we have to be separated by hectic schedules and distance. And I carve out every minute in my busy schedule I can to be with them, sometimes struggling because it's not as much as I would like. But the bonding is there, not from physically communicating, but from God—in answer to a grandmother's prayers.

A GIFT FROM GOD

Chris' and my praying for our family developed gradually. First we always dedicated the child of each of our seven pregnancies the moment we knew I was expecting. Then we came to the place of praying much about having babies who would be healthy and live. We also prayed for each of them throughout the pregnancy. But it was at their actual births that we especially dedicated them in prayer to God. They were His—for His will. They were His gift to us for as long as they would live. We knew well that they were the Lord's gifts to us. "Behold, children are a gift from the Lord" (Ps. 127:3). That psalm is often quoted at birth celebrations, christenings, baby showers, and on birth announcements. And it is believed by most Christians.

But I wonder how often we actually practice what it says. Yes, children are a gift—but not from any human source. They are a gift from the Lord. So God deserves, and expects, to be included in every aspect of conception and birth.

And how do we include Him? Through prayer. Prayers of asking Him for a baby, then prayers of releasing our wills for His, prayers of protection while the baby is developing, and prayers of thanksgiving. And sometimes, when all has not gone well at the birth, there may be prayers of anger toward God, prayers telling Him of our heartache, but then eventually prayers of thanksgiving—because we know He does all things well.

Praying When Loved Ones Die

SOMETIMES GOD DOESN'T answer our prayers about the death of a loved one the way we expect. For example, over many years I prayed asking God to let me be with my mother when she died. She had lived so close to the Lord all her life, and I wanted to see how God would usher her into His presence. Yet, always having at least 400 miles between us, deep down in my heart I knew it was unlikely I'd be near her if she died suddenly.

As we sat eating breakfast while we were vacationing in August 1986 on the shores of Lake Michigan twenty minutes drive from Mother's home, a car raced up the driveway. "Come right away, Evelyn," the driver shouted. "Your mother is sick. Very sick!" Instinctively, I knew she was gone—knew I had missed her final moments on earth.

As the car seemed to crawl down the resort road toward town, questions whirled in my head. "Why wasn't I there when I was only minutes away?" "Why hadn't God answered my prayers by letting me be in town instead of at that cottage?" "Why didn't that rented cottage have a phone so they could have summoned me immediately?"

I sat stunned. Had God deliberately allowed me to miss what I had prayed for all those years? Had He intentionally *not answered* my persistent prayers?

When I arrived at her house, my instincts were confirmed. Mother had died of a massive stroke. Paramedics and family had wisely decided against CPR. There was no way they, nor I, would want to keep Mother alive mechanically. For years she had asked her prayer partners to pray that she would go fast when she died. Well, at least God had answered *their* prayers!

My sister, Maxine, and her family were standing in a silent knot in the living room, searching my eyes for answers. They motioned to the sunporch, and I walked hurriedly by them, dreading what was waiting for me. I sat down beside Mother on the couch where they had laid her and put my arms around her frail body. Holding her close, I pressed my cheek against her silver hair. And then it happened. . . .

I felt something like electricity coming from her body. I didn't understand it, but it was there. Very real and very powerful. Almost tangible. I was acutely aware of her spirit exiting this world and entering heaven—and Mother not only hearing angels sing but singing with them. Those standing by confirmed that all I kept saying was, "Mother, you're singing with the angels! Mother, you're singing with the angels!"

I always had thought that, no matter how strong I had been in previous disasters, I would fall apart at Mother's death. I knew deep down it would be one loss I couldn't handle. We had been too close. But there was no uncontrollable sobbing, no horrible grief, just an undeniable awareness of her entering heaven. Instead of my expected collapse, I was included in that unspeakable earth-to-heaven scene. My spiritual senses were unbelievably aware of a fantastic celestial drama.

That night as I lay in bed in the blackness, my mind raced. The angels singing. Mother singing with them. My being part of the scene. Then I began to worry. Was it all wishful thinking on my part? Did my desperate longing to be with her make me *think* I was present in the fleeting moments while life was making its final exit from her body? Was the experience really my imagination running wild?

I began to struggle with the questions again, but this time praying to the Lord about them. I inquired of Him why He hadn't given us time to say our good-byes. I questioned how He could deny a prayer request so important to me. Hadn't He understood, or even heard, all of my years of praying?

But a shock came with God's answer. Distinctly He said to my troubled soul, *"But I did answer your prayer. She waited for you!"*

Although God didn't answer it my way, He answered in a way beyond anything I ever could have imagined. God's answer was that *He let her wait for me so I could be a part of her entering heaven!*

DEATHS NOT ALL THE SAME

The next morning when I called my prayer board president to tell her Mother had died, still not understanding it, I recounted my experience at her death. "Oh," she replied, "that's very much like I just read in Catherine Marshall's book about her knowing her husband, Peter, wasn't gone yet when the paramedics pronounced him dead after his fatal heart attack." It helped some to know somebody I trusted as much as Catherine Marshall had had the same experience.

But I still wasn't satisfied. I still wondered if it all could have been just my imagination running wild—because I so wanted to be with Mother when she died. Hesitatingly, I approached our daughter Jan and recounted the story. "Oh, that doesn't surprise me, Mother," she responded. "In my experience I have found that people don't all die the same. But medical science does not have the tools to measure that. As a medical doctor working a lot in cardiology, I have to sign many, many death certificates. But when I step into that room, it is not always the same. Sometimes there is absolutely nothing—just a body. But other times it is different. There is still something there. I can feel it. I know it."

Then Jan added, "Mother, that's the difference in resuscitation and just keeping a body going on pumps. Medical science can support the body's basic functions, but the person isn't alive. If you can resuscitate, bring a person back to life, then that person was not really dead. The soul had not departed."

Jesus dealt with this at the deaths of Jairus' daughter and Lazarus. He said of Jairus' daughter, "She has not died, but is just asleep"—and the mourners laughed at Jesus, knowing she was dead. But then Luke 8:55 says that "her spirit returned." Then also Jesus said to His disciples when they thought He had meant that Lazarus was just slumbering, "Lazarus *is* dead." And he had been dead in the tomb four days (John 11:11-14). Whatever their conditions, Jesus had power over both. And He had power to have Mother wait for me.

LISTENING PRAYERS

The most important prayers we pray during family death situations are listening prayers. Death is a time we need to *receive from God*, when we need to hear what He has to say to us.

The night my mother died, I had asked God a myriad of questions. But it was in my lying still—listening—that I received answers. It was then God, in His part of the prayer conversation, could bring His divine answers into my reeling brain, divinely settling my questions.

When we receive the news that a family member's death is inevitable (the illness is terminal), or is imminent (any moment they will go) or has occurred (too late to avoid), it is normal to bombard God with questions. Questions of why like this? Why now? Questions of disbelief. Confused and bewildered questions. Angry questions asking God why He allowed it. Asking why He hadn't performed that miracle He was capable of doing when we had prayed for it so long. *But usually we stop at the asking, not taking time to wait on God for His answers.*

The only way we can find out how all-sufficient God can be at times like this, is to *stop talking at Him* and let Him show us who He really is—the omnipotent God of heaven. Psalm 46:10 says, "Be still, and know that I am God!" (KJV)

ANSWERS FROM GOD'S WRITTEN WORD

There are times in my grief that I go directly to the Bible for the comfort and explanations I need. But many times my sorrowing brain isn't yet capable of reading. This is when God's Holy Spirit performs one of His most important tasks—recalling what Jesus has taught us previously (see John 14:25-26). This is what happened the night my mother died, and "We do not sorrow as those with no hope" ran through my mind like a ticker tape. It was the third member of the Trinity recalling what I had stored in my mind years before from God's Word—and needed right then.

That is one of the reasons it is so important for us to stay in God's Word—reading, studying, memorizing, hiding *His* words in our hearts. It was why when my stepfather, Rollie, died and I didn't have time to rush to my Bible for comfort on the way to the mortuary, that the Holy Spirit recalled to me, "Why seek ye the living among the dead? He is not here, but is risen" (Luke 24:5-6, KJV) as the angels spoke to the women seeking Jesus on Jesus' own resurrection morning that first Easter.

Also, if we recall Scriptures, we are sure the thoughts come from God. In times of grief our minds can play tricks on us. And we can fantasize, picturing in our imagination what we so desperately want to be true. See that loved one still alive. Or coming back to earth—perfect. That's what I found myself fleetingly doing after our little Judy died. The picture was of her decending down through the roof of the crowded church sanctuary, smiling—not paralyzed anymore—into our waiting arms. *Whole!*

But that fantasy was not from God. It was my mind helping me temporarily escape the shock. But God gently brought His truth to me, day after day and week after week, both from His continually recalling memorized Scripture to me and speaking to me directly from the Bible as I searched for His answers. It was His way of producing the real healing He knew I needed so badly. How wise for us to immerse ourselves thoroughly in His Word now, making it part of our unshakable beliefs—so that it will be ready for the Holy Spirit to use to help us when grief strikes.

PRAYERS WITHOUT WORDS

But sometimes the grief is so deep that no words will come, and there is a numbness over our whole being, making praying impossible. It is then that God comes, not with words either, but with Himself. God did this for me after our baby girl was born dead. World War II was raging, and adequate medical treatment was scarce for civilians at home. My horrible labor ordeal left me barely alive. An ambulance brought me to Mother's home, where I struggled with my baby's death for two days in the blackness that seemed to surround me. No words went from me to God—nor from Him to me. Just His loving filling the void with Himself. With His love, His comfort, His assurance—and His healing.

WHAT THEY SEE

When a loved one is dying, it is a time for us to see what they see. It is time for us to lift our eyes heavenward, as they so frequently do. A time for the things of this earth actually to grow dim—while the past with all its pain and heartaches fades as the glow of heaven's gates grow brighter.

In our own family deaths, that experience has been so real. My father had been in a coma for weeks, but suddenly he rallied, looked heavenward, lifted his hands upward, as if reaching for something, and cried out, "Jesus!" Then he fell back on his pillow—dead. Our own tiny Judy, also in a deep coma, raised the little hand that had been lifeless so long, reached toward heaven as if grasping something—and fell back—gone. I've often wondered about the angels Mother and I heard and with whom she seemed to join in singing. I did not see them. But did she— while that spark of life was fleeting from her body?

My stepfather, Rollie, spent his last day gazing intently into an upper corner of his hospital room, detached from the people and events around him. And then he went to be with the Jesus whom he had served so faithfully all his life. Our daughter Nancy told me that when she is working in the hospital with patients shortly before they die, they frequently gaze up at a corner of the ceiling. However, they are not focused on *it*—but, looking past it, their eyes are focused on *something*.

But there is a word of caution necessary here. We must not expect our loved ones to be welcomed into heaven at death if they have not received Jesus as their Savior and Lord. When Jesus in John 14 told His disciples

He was going to prepare a place for them (who believed on Him), Thomas said, "Lord, we do not know where You are going, how do we know the way?" Then Jesus so clearly but definitely answered with:

> I am the way, and the truth and the life; no one comes to the Father but through Me (John 14:6, italics added).

What do believers see? Is it the place Jesus said He was going to prepare for His followers? The many dwelling places, mansions, Jesus told them were in His Father's house? They certainly see more than the tunnel so many unbelievers see at death. More than even the bright light at the end of that tunnel. No, if they really have their names written in the Lamb's Book of Life (see Rev. 21:27) by truly receiving Jesus as their Savior, they are seeing the glories of their new home in heaven.

Our family had gathered for a private visitation at the mortuary that summer Sunday morning before my mother's afternoon funeral. The windows of a neighboring church were open, and suddenly their trumpet ensemble triumphantly filled the air with the song "We Shall Behold Him." Our Nancy told me that she had the overwhelming feeling of the heavens opening up and the song being fulfilled—as she *knew* Grandma was beholding her Savior.

GOD'S VIEW OF DEATH

When I left Minnesota for India in 1990, all my family members were healthy. Death was far from my thinking. But a phone call that finally got through to me in Calcutta changed all that. My husband's mother was in a coma—and none of the doctors expected her to live. I had to leave immediately for Hyderabad, struggling whether to go on with the just-started national tour or fly home immediately. My seminar coordinator, Juliet Thomas, slipped me a little note just before the seminar which I hadn't had time to read. In the wings of that auditorium in Hyderabad, I was trying to collect my composure as my heart was reeling over the news I had just received. Facing all day of teaching that large crowd, I sat on a stool staring at the floor, trying to switch my thinking from Grandma Chris to what I was to teach. Remembering Juliet's note, I opened it and read, "Psalm 116. Evelyn, this psalm is so precious to me." As I hurriedly turned to the psalm in my Bible and began reading, my eyes immediately fell on verse 15:

Precious in the sight of the Lord is the death of His godly ones.

Suddenly my heart focused not on Minnesota, nor India, but on heaven. And on God—sitting up there with a smile on His face, so happy that one of His choice servants was close to coming to Him. And all my feelings turned upside down. I saw God's view of death, not the human side of losing a loved one we all were feeling. God's side of joyously and anxiously awaiting His beloved's homecoming.

THANKFUL PRAYERS AT DEATH
As the death of a family member comes closer, often there is pleading in prayer with God to let the loved one stay just one more day, or week, or month. And often drastic medical procedures are put in operation to fulfill this desire. And then, when that dear one has departed, comes the many kinds of grieving prayers. God expects us to grieve, and knows our emotional well-being depends on it. But sooner or later in these steps, there should come one more step in the death praying—*thankfulness!* Thankfulness? For what?

My telephone prayer chain chairman, Jeanne, had been taking care of her dying ninety-five-year-old mother. But when she died and the funeral was over, Jeanne said to me, "I miss her so terribly. But, amazingly, I have a tremendous sense of *thankfulness* engulfing me. Thankfulness for her just slipping into another phase of her life. Mother has not died but is just in a continuation of her life in another place. Oh, I'm so thankful."

Going back to visit my mother's home two years after her death, I was surprised at a spirit of thankfulness that kept sweeping over me—still missing her so much, but engulfed by an attitude of thankfulness. Why? Revelation 21:4 once again was real to me:

And He shall wipe away every tear from their eyes; and there shall no longer be any death; there shall no longer be any mourning, or crying, or pain.

I think of three loved ones especially in that connection. My mother, as I have mentioned, had a very hard life. My dad was an invalid for years. Our little Judy's partially paralyzed body gradually could not handle the escalating fever that turned her from red to the final deep purple. And many, many times I have prayed thanking God that they now are experiencing life without the hassles and pain of that reassuring Bible verse.

When my loved ones have died, I have uttered prayers of thankfulness to Jesus because He, by His death and resurrection, put an end to the agony of death (Acts 2:24). I have thanked Him that through death He rendered powerless the devil who had the power of death (Heb. 2:14). And I have breathed prayers of thankfulness because Jesus delivered those who through fear of death were subject to slavery all their lives (Heb. 2:15). "Thank You, Jesus!"

O death, where is thy sting? O grave, where is thy victory? (1 Cor. 15:55, KJV)

Another surprising thankfulness came when my mother was just in the middle of reading my then just-released book *What Happens When God Answers*—and suddenly died. Immediately, I was so sorry that she had not finished the book because I had so wanted her to read in the final pages about where all of her lifelong prayers were preserved and enhanced in golden bowls in heaven. Then I stopped short. "O Lord," I prayed, "thank You that she doesn't have to read it in a book. *Thank You that now she sees those prayers of hers You have preserved until the final day.* (See Rev. 5:8 and 8:3-4.)

Also, when a loved one who faithfully has supported us in prayer dies, we feel a terrible loss. How can we thank God in prayer for that? Mother was our family's powerful prayer supporter, and that loss flooded over me—until I focused on how God actually handles answering prayers. He never stamps "case closed" after He initially answers, but He continues answering and answering as long as is needed. Although there is nothing in the Bible about Mother praying new prayers now, I was able to pray, *thanking God that I would still be the recipient of all those years of Mother's prayers for me.*

One day in her latter years I lovingly told her, "Mother, you can't die!" Startled, she asked why not. "Because I need you to pray that prayer you pray for me every day—that I won't get proud." But God is still using that prayer in my life to this day.

When Nancy, still in her deep grief, wondered if Grandma, now that she was up in heaven, could see her, I answered, "I don't know that, Nancy; but I do know that all of those prayers she prayed for you will follow you throughout your life."

Reunion in heaven is another reason for my prayers of thankfulness. Is my mother holding Judy in her arms now? Oh, how she loved Judy! And holding our stillborn baby girl? Mother was the one who stayed with me the two full days of terrible labor—and then picked out Judy's prettiest dress to bury her in. And then that first miscarriage when Mother so carefully put that little boy fetus in a blue velvet jewelry box and buried it in the shade of the tree in our garden. Are they all together in heaven—singing and shouting together? I believe they are. "O Father, *thank You!*"

WHAT MY MOTHER LEFT BEHIND

One of my deepest prayers of thanks at Mother's death was for what she left behind. When we went through her possessions, everything we found was about one of two things—Jesus or her family. All of her books, magazines, songbooks, letters, notes, pictures, and even her checkbook were exclusively either of family or her Lord.

Her personal belongings reflected the Apostle Peter's words about what he had taught them when he knew "the laying aside of [his] earthly dwelling" (death) was imminent: "And I will also be diligent that at any time after my departure you may be able to call these things to mind" (2 Peter 1:14-15). Mother truly left us the heritage Steve Green sings about in Jon Mohr's song "Find Us Faithful."

After all our hopes and dreams have come and gone,
   And our children sift through all we've left behind;
May the clues that they discover,
   And the memories they uncover,
Become the light that leads them
   To the road we each must find.*

Discovering at Mother's death all these godly personal things made my heart swell with thankfulness to God for her. And it multiplied my resolve to be and do the same for my children and all who come behind me.

In much the way I remember my mother, my husband, Chris, has special memories of his father, Rudolph, an unusually godly man and a man of prayer. When Chris was almost three years of age, the Christenson family moved into a brand new home, and one day before the large lawn and sidewalks were in, Rudolph came in for lunch. Behind him came little Chris, struggling to put each foot where his father had made tracks. Triumphantly, he announced, "Look, Mummy, I came all the way home in Daddy's footprints!" And my prayer still is, "O thank You, God, for giving Chris and me such godly examples. May we always be the people of deep devotion and prayer as were my mother and Chris' father and mother."

VICTORY PRAYERS AT DEATH

Several hours later in that sleepless night after Mother died, I prayed a lot more "death prayers." Prayers that many Christians have prayed when a loved one has gone to heaven.

Experiencing a strange peace and lack of wrenching grief, I prayed,

**"Find Us Faithful" written my Jon Mohr. © 1987 Birdwing Music (A Div. of The Sparrow Corp.) / Jonathan Mark Music (Admin. by Gaither Copyright Mgt.). From the album "Find Us Faithful" by Steve Green, © 1988 The Sparrow Corp. All rights reserved. International copyright secured. Used by permission.

"Lord, I'm supposed to be devastated. But the terrible void is filled with something so positive." Then apprehension filled my heart as I remembered that one of the steps of grief is not facing reality. "O God," I cried out in the darkness, "am I not facing reality? Is my mind playing tricks on me?" But God lifted my fears by gently, yet very clearly, bringing to my mind Scripture I had used so many times as a pastor's wife to comfort a loved one left behind. The Scripture that also was to be mine when I had been left without her. From God Himself was the explanation for my lack of devastating grief:

> But we do not want you to be uninformed, brethren, about those who are asleep [have died], that you may not grieve, as do the rest who have no hope (1 Thes. 4:13).

Why no deep grieving? Because we have hope—hope in Jesus that those without Him do not have. And we not only have the hope of being together again with them for eternity, but the awesome scene that Paul described next to use to comfort each other—when Jesus comes back:

> For if we believe that Jesus died and rose again, even so God will bring with Him those who have fallen asleep in Jesus. . . . For the Lord Himself will descend from heaven with a shout, with the voice of the archangel, and with the trumpet of God; and the dead in Christ shall rise first. Then we who are alive and remain shall be caught up together with them in the clouds to meet the Lord in the air, and thus we shall always be with the Lord (1 Thes. 4:14, 16-17).

AN EXPERIENCE MARGIE RECALLS

Kurt's wife, Margie, at first hesitated sharing the extraordinary experience she and her family had at her brother Bob's death (see chap. 9) because, she said, "It seems like such a special gift given personally to my family who needed extra encouragement from a very loving, personal Heavenly Father." But she decided to recount the experience because "it illustrates how much hope and joy there can be in mourning. They can coexist," she pointed out, "but mourning must rest on the foundation of the hope that we have in Jesus—or despair will become too great." She recounts the experience as follows:

> Even in death, the hand of God can reach down to the true believer in comfort and compassion hard to comprehend. The night my brother Bob died, none of us wanted to go to bed and be alone. So we pushed two double beds together. But before my parents and we three sisters lay our heads down, we knelt and prayed as we had done so often during my brother's illness. We prayed for peace and the ability to sleep. And peace came—almost like a thick, heavy blanket laying across the room. God's peace—safe, warm, secure, the kind that "surpasses all comprehension" (Phil. 4:7).
>
> But God had more for us. The night of my brother Bob's funeral, two high school friends of my older sister were walking in the park. Rich was a good friend of the family, but Kevin only knew of our struggle with Bob's illness; he never had seen Bob. As they walked and talked of the day's events, Rich suddenly stopped, seemingly frozen and unable to move. They both felt a strange presence. Kevin grabbed Rich's arm and explained a vision he was seeing. Two people, he said, were in the clear, late summer sky, both bright and shining. One seemed to be Jesus and the other was a boy with blond, shining hair. His young face was bright and full of light; it was hard to see detailed features, but the shape and hair were distinct.
>
> Rich and Kevin ran to our house and Dad opened the door. I saw them standing there still quite wide-eyed and shaken, telling us what they had seen. Dad grabbed Bob's graduation picture, and Kevin said yes, that *was* the boy with Jesus in the night sky!
>
> We were filled with awe and wonderment at the vision. Why was God so kind as to send the vision to a hurting, grieving family? I don't know why, but we know that God did—and He is sovereign. I'm also sure, although we already knew it from Scripture, that God wanted us to be assured that in death the righteous have a refuge (see Prov. 14:32). He wanted us to know we don't travel through death's door alone as if it were an uncharted journey. *No, Jesus is there!*

CORONATION, NOT CULMINATION

Death periodically has stalked our family. Two miscarriages and a stillbirth in between, the later occurring just five weeks after my husband's father's death. A few years later while attending a convention in Amsterdam, Holland, I felt an overwhelming urge to call home. My cheery "Hello" turned to chilling silence as Mother related the horrifying details of my nephew's murder. He was the only son of my only brother. Mother rehearsed for me how a large object had been deliberately dropped on him while he was inspecting a construction site after hours. My thoughts had raced across the Atlantic to his pregnant wife, Stephanie. What was the shock doing to her? To the unborn baby? Two weeks later the baby was born to Stephanie, and they called to tell Mother of the birth. But it was the last phone call my mother received. Minutes later she was dead.

But through it all there was victory. As my husband preached Mother's funeral service, he had us all pick up the obituary we had been handed as we came in, and said, "You are not holding in your hand an obituary. You are holding a *ticket to a coronation*. This is not the culmination of Edna Moss' life, but rather a coronation—a victory celebration as one of God's choice servants enters His presence. Our victory prayer: Coronation—not culmination!

> And the righteous will shine forth as the sun in the kingdom of their Father (Matt. 13:43).

Special Prayers for Special Times

GREETING CARD STORES bulge with cards of best wishes, good cheer, good luck, and blessings for every conceivable occasion and for every taste. People spend large amounts of time and money reaching other people on their special days. Being remembered at special times of our lives is extremely important. It can cheer us up, make us grateful for friends, appreciative of their thoughtfulness, and even raise our self-esteem because we were important to someone. All of this is good. But the source of all of these wishes is human, and has little or no power actually to produce what was wished for them in the greeting.

But there is a communication on special days that is beyond the human sphere. It really can bring to the recipient what was desired by the sender. It is called prayer.

Prayer for special people on their special days brings God's input into their lives. Our "best wishes" actually turn into divine influence, divine favor, and divine blessings—*when we pray.*

FAMILY MEMBERS' SPECIAL DAYS

Through the years I have prayed special prayers for each family member on his or her special days. It is that individual's "intercessory prayer day." I set aside a special time for each family member when it is his or her birthday, wedding day, graduation day, or any other important day that comes along. That loved one gets the bulk of my intercessory prayertime that day.

However, these are not just my human wishes for them. No. Before I start praying for them, I stay in prayer asking God to direct me to a special Scripture *He has for them for that special occasion.* Sometimes this takes several days. And, when God either calls a Scripture to my mind for the person or stops me in my devotional reading on a verse for the individual, that is what I pray for that family member. Special day prayers are very precious to me.

FAMILY BIRTHDAY PRAYERS

God has given me inumerable birthday prayers for my husband, children, grandchildren, mother, father, sister, and brother. Some birthday prayers God has given me have been quite special.

It was the summer of 1988, and Jenna was the first granddaughter for whom God gave me a very special birthday verse. All my granddaughters were having birthdays within a few weeks, and I had been praying for their birthday verses for quite a while. Jenna's came July 18, two months before I would need it to include in my intercessory prayer for her—and give to her on her birthday card.

The summer before Cindy and Jenna each had given me a feather very important to them. Jenna's was a multicolored peacock feather which I had randomly tucked in my Bible at the thirty-first chapter of Proverbs. Many times I had seen that feather as I turned to something else in my Bible, and always had stopped to pray at least a short prayer for Jenna, frequently stroking the silky feather while I prayed.

But on that early summer day as I sat praying on the empty Lake Michigan beach, I felt compelled to pray for Jenna's birthday verse. So I turned to Proverbs 31 and Jenna's feather, and immediately my eyes fell on the last half of verse 30:

A woman who fears [reverences] the Lord, she shall be praised.

I tried to read and apply the first part of that verse, "Charm is deceitful and beauty is vain," but somehow it didn't fit. It was not what God was giving me for Jenna. Later her mother, Jan, became almost alarmed thinking that God might have been saying that negative side too. But I assured her that, no matter how hard I tried to read the whole verse, God definitely said it was the last half about the woman who reverences the Lord being praised.

What a wonderful verse for a precious little girl just beginning to grow into womanhood. What a promise for the future from God— that if she would reverence Him, she would be praised. Not praised for her charm or beauty which are only deceitful and vain, but praised for her beautiful life of reverencing the Lord! *My birthday prayer for Jenna!*

Cindy's special feather came the summer of 1987 too. We were walking on the Lake Michigan beach, and she became fascinated by the sea gull feathers and started a collection of them. She gave me one of her prize feathers which I put in my Bible, and every time the next year I saw that feather as I opened my Bible, I would pray for Cindy. While away from her in the middle of the next winter, I found myself gently running my fingers over that soft feather, remembering doing the same over her soft little face as I had prayed for her that summer.

Amazingly, the place I had tucked Cindy's feather that previous summer was also where God had her 1988 birthday verse waiting. Again as I walked that same beach, the sea gull feathers strewn in my path were a reminder to pray for Cindy, which I did. When I sat down to read my Bible, I instinctively turned to Cindy's feather. And there it was, positively, from the Lord. Almost jumping off the page at me. Cindy's next birthday promise:

For you will go out with joy (Isa. 55:12).

But little did I understand how important God knew that verse would be to Cindy. It was not until several months later that an upset Cindy called and announced firmly, "Grandma, I have a new name. My name is 'Rebecca' now. I wanted a Bible name, but my parents didn't name me a

Bible name. And I don't like my name 'Cynthia Joy' because it isn't in the Bible. So I just changed it."

"Oh, Darling," I replied, thrilled at her wanting a Bible name but also sensing the urgency of the situation, "don't you remember your feather and birthday verse from Isaiah 55:12, 'For you will go out with *joy*'? You *do* have a Bible name. 'Joy' is mentioned more times in the Bible than any name given to anybody. Look at that picture on your wall spelling J-O-Y from the Bible that Grandma gave you. And remember how the angel said to the shepherds that first Christmas that he was bringing good news of great 'joy' for all people—the Baby Jesus. And, Honey, the second fruit of God's Holy Spirit in us is 'joy.' The Bible is full of the word *joy*."

Year after year I pray for that joy for Cindy. And just last summer (1991) God gave me another dimension of her birthday joy for now nine-year-old Cindy. Whose joy would be hers? Jesus' joy that He left for us on earth! And, amazingly, it was His joy when He was ready to go to the cross (John 15:11). When I told Cindy about the new dimension of her birthday verse and explained that it was Jesus' joy during a sad time when He was ready to go to the cross, Cindy thoughtfully replied, "Grandma, Jesus gave them His joy because He wouldn't need it any-more in heaven!"

No, Jesus wouldn't need that kind of joy in a perfect heaven, but He knew Cindy would down here on earth. Many, many times I have prayed that prayer for Cindy, and many times, too, when things were difficult, I've reminded her of her precious name and birthday gift from Jesus—*joy*.

TWO MORE BIRTHDAY PRAYERS

Crista and Kathy were just turning three that summer of 1988 when God gave me those special birthday verses for Jenna and Cindy. And He had one for Crista and Kathy too.

Crista's verse puzzled me at first because it seemed so mature and ad-vanced for such a little girl. But I knew it was from God, and I wrote on her birthday card: "Dear Crista: I prayed and asked God for a birthday

Bible verse for you. Then I turned to the page where I was ready to read my Bible that day, and immediately my eyes fell on these words for you:

> Blessed are those who hear the Word of God, and observe it (Luke 11:28).

"Crista, that means that God wants you to listen to His words in the Bible, and then do what they say. Darling, that will make you a strong Christian and make God very happy. I love you, Darling, with all my heart. Grandma."

The "On the contrary" that starts Crista's verse shows Jesus is answering the woman who, in the preceding verse, had said, "Blessed is the womb that bore You, and the breasts at which You nursed." But Jesus said, "No, it is those who hear the Word of God and obey it who are blessed."

As Crista has gotten older, the "why" of this verse is becoming more clear. Not only is it quite difficult for a child to screen out all the sources of wisdom vying for their little minds (see James 3:15), but really obeying God's Word isn't taught much any more, even in many Christian circles. Somehow we have taken 2 Timothy 3:16 to read, "All Scripture is inspired by God and is profitable for teaching" and have stopped there. We have forgotten that it says that teaching ("doctrine," KJV) must be applied because Scripture also is good "for reproof," "for correction," and "for training in righteousness." For Crista, God was saying that as she grows up He wants her to listen to His words in the Bible, for correct doctrine to be sure, but then also to obey what it said. Then she will be blessed in His sight. What a tall order for a little girl. But what a precious privilege to have God tell her what will make her blessed! *What a birthday prayer for Crista.*

On Kathy's birthday in 1988 I was very concerned that God had given me a Scripture verse for all the other granddaughters, but nothing definite for her. On her birthday in her special prayertime, for some reason I had kept praying claiming the blood of Jesus against Satan harming her. Then I prayed and prayed for God to send His angels to protect her. Then I prayed for His angels to surround her. The day after her birthday it was still the same kind of praying, even asking God to give it only when it was *His* time. God even had rebuked me out of Luke 12:26 about being anxious as I kept asking about it. However, the third day after her birthday while praying for her, I suddenly realized that *God had given me Kathy's birthday Scripture*. I had been praying it all those three days!

> He will give His angels charge concerning you, to guard you in all your ways (Ps. 91:11).

Kathy's birthday verse actually was two verses. God first brought to my mind Hebrews 1:14, "Are they [the angels] not all ministering spirits, sent out to render service for the sake of those who will inherit salvation?" But that was only to remind me of the explanation of God's task for angels. Psalm 91:11 was Kathy's special verse.

Kathy's birthday verse came vividly into focus for that little girl, and us, two years after God gave it in 1988. After a meeting in Washington, D.C., I had stayed two extra days to be with their family for Monday the Fourth of July. On the way home from church, I sat between the girls in the back seat of the car, and we read in the Bible and discussed their individual birthday verses—joy and angels. Kathy had asked, "What do angels do, Grandma?" And we talked how they protect us from harm.

The next morning Dan, Nancy, the girls, and I drove through the Blue Ridge Mountains to Luray Caverns for our holiday outing. Driving up a narrow mountain road with almost no shoulders, we rounded a blind curve. To our horror a truck straddling the yellow line appeared right in front of our car. Suddenly the truck swerved several feet in our direction—facing us head on. Dan furiously jerked the steering wheel, violently tossing us all about—and the truck narrowly missed us. After getting settled and catching our breath, we talked about and thanked God for the angels protecting us *right then*.

After seeing the cavern, we drove out into the mountain country to eat dinner in a 200-year-old farm house, now a restaurant. After playing with their beautiful horses and kittens, we got in the car to go home. Pulling out onto that mountain back road, Dan and Nancy both had looked carefully both ways, and there were no cars. But just as we got across the road while turning left up the hill, a car shot over and down that hill traveling at least sixty miles an hour. As the driver slammed on the brakes, the car fishtailed several times, barely missing us twice. As Dan jammed our car into reverse, the other car came to a stop right in front of ours. When the shock subsided a little, we remembered the angels. This time their reality and thanks for them were much more vivid in our minds. It had become obvious to all of us that we really did need—and had had—*God's angels protecting us.*

God has given me many more Scriptures about the angels protecting us through these many years; and, because God knew we would need them, I have prayed them for all of us.

BIRTHDAY PRAYERS FOR BOYS

James and Brett were yet unborn when God gave me those special birthday verses for our four granddaughters. But it was at the births of these grandsons that God so clearly showed me their verses.

On Brett's due date, I was reading devotionally in Psalm 51, and read, "The sacrifices of God are a broken spirit; a broken and a contrite heart, O God, Thou wilt not despise" (v. 17). Remembering Jan's near-death experience while giving birth to her last child, Crista, I wept over this Scripture. But then I prayed, "O God, if this is not the Scripture for this new baby, please give it to me."

And it wasn't! He firmly guided me to Psalm 22; and, surprisingly, to the words immediately following the assurance of "Yet Thou art He who didst bring me forth from the womb" (v. 9a) that had taken me through that first hour after Crista's birth while they were fighting to save our Jan's life. I wept again, only a different kind of tears, as God clearly gave me the words (vv. 9b-10) for our soon-to-be baby Brett Jezreel Johnson.

> Thou didst make me trust when upon my mother's breasts. Upon Thee was I cast from birth; Thou hast been my God from my mother's womb.

My apprehension as to why that baby would have to trust while an in-

fant, and why it would be cast upon God at birth, soon turned to the
wonderful promise that God would be its God from its mother's womb!
And the day Brett was born, I prayed with joy and victory in my heart—
knowing that God was his God.

James' verse came from God also after I prayed several days over and
over for God to give it to me. On September 26, 1990, God finally said
"Psalms," and I turned to Psalm 121 where He seemed to be leading. I
recorded in my Bible, "Strong tears. Very definite at verse 8."

> The Lord will guard your going out and your coming in from this time
> forth and forever.

The tears just kept coming and coming as these words went deeper
and deeper into my heart. My question of "When will the Lord guard his
going out and coming in?" was answered: "From this time"—at his birth,
"forth"—on into his life, and "forever"—to eternity. I wrote it in capital
letters with three exclamation points. God's assurance in my heart for
James' eternity! The promise engulfed my whole body as I wept before
God. "Oh, thank You, Lord," I prayed with overwhelming and surprised
thankfulness. This verse was so much more than had been expected, I
couldn't stop the tears from flowing down my cheeks.

As I write, baby boy/girl Christenson is due soon. Kurt and Margie's
second baby, our seventh grandchild, is on the way. And I can't wait to
see what Scripture God has for that little one at birth!

BIRTHDAY CELEBRATIONS

Birthdays always have been very special at our house. Every birthday person gets breakfast in bed, and is king or queen for that day. We
decorate the house with balloons and streamers, and brightly decorate
the pile of gifts. We either use the best china and silver or a carefully se-
lected theme of birthday plates, napkins, and tablecloth. Then we let the
birthday person choose his or her very favorite menu and birthday dessert, and gather together as many members of the family who possibly
can be there to celebrate. I can recall many times of feeling overwhelmed

at the expressions of love and being loved—in the warmth of the glow of those birthday candles.

But amidst all that, there is something much more important that we do. We always include the *birthday prayer.* This is giving thanks to God for giving us that special person, and then evoking God's special blessing on him or her for the coming year. This usually is prayed by an "elder" of the family—dad, mom, grandfather, grandmother, or great grandmother.

Grandma Chris is the one we call on to pray for her children. Now that she's ninety-two, she has prayed these blessings on her own children up to a seventieth birthday for her son, Chris. An especially meaningful one was when he turned sixty-five, and Grandma Chris thanked God for His bountiful mercy and guidance through all those years, and then evoked God's blessing and direction for Chris in his retirement years.

One of the most meaningful birthday prayers of our family was prayed in July 1986 by my mother, Grandma Moss. All of her great grandchildren had gathered at a cottage on Lake Michigan for a rare combined big birthday party. Those great grandchildren were very precious to Grandma Moss, and she had lived sacrificially for them and her grandchildren and her children all of her life. So we were thrilled to have her there at age ninety-one to pray for that collection of her great grandchildren, captured for us all on video tape.

Holding baby Crista on one hip, she surveyed her rich family possessions, and raised her voice to the God she knew so well. "As we look to Thee at this time, God, we have so many things to thank You for." Then, flowing from the depths of her being came, "We begin, Lord, by thanking Thee that Thou hast privileged us to be together today. So many of our family are here. . . ." Next came her deep lifelong goal for herself and goal for all her family line. "And we want to make Thee first in our lives, and we want to please Thee in everything we do and everything we say."

And, before thanking God for the wonderful food and all the hands that had prepared it, Grandma Moss prayed the last thing she ever prayed in public for anyone. *Her blessing for her offspring.*

"And, God, we just ask Thee to bless each one and bless these, especially these that are having their birthdays. God, we ask Thee to come and bless their lives, and help them to grow up to be wonderful Christian men and women. And we'll give Thee the praise and the glory. Amen." At the end of that week Grandma Moss dropped dead of a massive stroke. That birthday prayer was her final blessing!

JESUS' BIRTHDAY

The first celebration a child seems to become aware of is his or her own birthday with blowing out of candles and family members singing "Happy Birthday." Sensing our first child Jan's grasping of the specialness of birthdays, we decided to help her understand Christmas by having a birthday cake with candles for Jesus.

Through the years that has been a part of our family Christmas celebration—the birthday cake or fancy dessert for Jesus, candles to blow out for Jesus, the singing of "Happy Birthday Dear Jesus" and the *birthday prayer* we prayed about Jesus just as we prayed for them on their birthday. At first the prayer was just thanking Jesus for being born on earth, then it progressively got deeper as the children matured spiritually—until they could understand thanking Him for being our Savior and for saving us from our sins.

This celebration taught our little ones so much. Early in life it made them aware of Jesus being a real person, and that Jesus' birthday was just as important to Him as ours was to us. They learned to give Jesus the love we received on our birthdays. It cemented in their little minds that Christmas was about Jesus' birth and not Santa Claus or presents. And it made Jesus that extra special Person, King for a day—and then eventually King of every day of their lives.

MAKING CHRISTMAS SPECIAL—FROM JAN

All of our family homes have special day observances that have become a tradition. And Chris, as a pastor much of his adult life, kept our whole family deeply aware of the spiritual significance of each holiday through his preaching and emphasis in the church's entire calendar. But since fifty years of marriage have produced far too many celebration prayers to put in one book, I have touched on only a few.

Our daughter Jan comments as follows:

Special days are wonderful. Holidays cause us to focus on concepts that are lost in the turmoil of day to day family life. When our children were very small, Santa Claus and the Easter Bunny were major figures in their lives. But I felt a deep desire to explore with them the fundamentals of our faith through the Christian truths of these holidays.

It amazes me the depth with which children think and their ability to understand profound spiritual concepts. So much time and energy is rightly spent on intellectual stimulation for our children. But they need adequate spiritual stimulation so as not to stunt their God-ordained growth, and develop into spiritually underprivileged kids.

However, children often understand ideas better when they are graphically displayed. Jesus knew this and so He spoke in parables to all of us. Special days give us a chance to translate concepts into "visual parables" so that, before we try to pray in abstract terms with our children, they already will understand the concepts of our special-day praying.

Christmas is one of those wonderful, special times—a time of family gatherings. I'm struck, however, by how much we lose when we leave Jesus in the manger. Christmas is not about a baby. It is the beginning of the unfolding of God's plan for redemption, the opening scene of His Passion Play. To focus only on the Babe in the manger and the surrounding events, as miraculous as they are, is to lose sight of *who* that Baby was. He was not a sweet little baby boy; He was the omnipotent, victorious Savior of the universe. Only when we understand this can we begin to comprehend the truly incredible nature of what happened in Bethlehem.

Weeks before Christmas, rather than using the usual advent calendar and candles, our family begins our journey through the four times we feel Christ comes to the believer. His "advents" if you will, and we light each week's candle at our special Sunday morning breakfast.

The first morning of our "advents" we light the pink candle as one child says, "Jesus came in the flesh." Then we pray thanking the Son of

God for His coming in the flesh and giving up heaven to take on the pain of humanity for us.

The second time Christ comes is to a person in salvation when he or she actually receives Him as Savior. After lighting the red candle on those mornings, another child says, "Jesus comes to us with His blood." Then we pray thanking Him for His saving blood. We have had many good discussions among all of us about what that means to us personally and what Jesus did to make that possible.

Christ also comes for the believer he or she dies—our third week's topic. Jenna chose a light blue candle for us to light this day. A child then says, "Jesus comes for us when we die." The concept of death has fascinated our children, and this has given us opportunities to talk about what death is—and what it isn't. We then pray together thanking God for His provision for eternal life with Him.

The last time Christ comes to the believer is when He returns to earth in final judgment. As we light this white candle, a child repeats, "Jesus comes for us at the final judgment." What a great picture we can, and do, paint of a victorious Christ coming in all His glory for us, and Satan forever defeated. *Now we are ready for Christmas.*

On Christmas Eve our whole extended family gets together, and after dinner we read in unison the Christmas story from Luke 2. Then we discuss what Jesus would like for a birthday present. The children decide (sometimes with help) that He wants our hearts. But our hearts are dirty, and we can't give someone a dirty birthday present. So, under each plate is a red heart with a black sticker on it. We have a quiet time when people ask God for forgiveness for the "black spot." Then they peel it off, throw it into the blazing fireplace, and then put their clean heart in a box wrapped like a birthday present. When everyone is finished, the children put the box under the Christmas tree and sing "Happy Birthday, Dear Jesus." It's a sweet, introspective time that I treasure and the girls love to set up.

MY FIRST GRANDMOTHERING CHRISTMAS

The first Christmas Eve we had grandbabies, the joy and love flowing was incredible. The thrill of soft cuddly toys and clothes, and the babies having more fun with the pretty wrappings than with their gifts, made that Christmas truly special. But when the festivities died down, I had the wonderful privilege as a new grandmother of putting each of our new wee ones to bed. But on such a special night as that, I didn't waste it on Santa and reindeer stories or even on singing Christmas carols as lullabies. No, this was the time for *special Christmas prayers.*

As Jenna snuggled, burrowing herself into my arms, I laid my hand on her and prayed out loud. First it was "Happy Birthday, Jesus." Then I thanked God for Jenna, asked Him again to fill her with His Holy Spirit, and kissed her long on that forehead I loved so much.

How precious it was to rock baby Cindy to sleep that night while she snuggled. I held her close and thanked her for all the hugs and pats she had given me that evening. And then I laid my hand on her too and prayed that God would fill her and make her exactly the girl He has planned for her to be. Again it was that special time of prayer for that special night in her life. Christmas praying!

EASTER AT SKIP AND JAN'S HOUSE
Jan tells of Easter in the Johnson home:

Of all the holidays Easter is the pivotal point of our faith. Somehow, though, it can get lost in bunnies, eggs, and new dresses. Not to say that those things are all bad—we have bunnies and eggs, and sometimes new dresses. But I felt the emphasis needed to be refocused on the real issues of Easter.

Easter without the risen Christ exploding out of the tomb is an impotent holiday. Our preparation for this special day begins several weeks before Easter when Skip brings the hand-hewn six-foot cross into our large front hall and we hang our purple "veil" on the wall near it. That hall connects all the areas of our house, and sometimes when I catch just a glimpse of one of these Easter reminders, it brings a whole flood of thoughts about the price our Lord paid for my sin. And I offer up a prayer of grateful adoration through my tears.

Our eating table holds our crown of thorns with four candles signify-
ing the concepts of redemption. Every year as I work the candles into this
centerpiece, I invariably prick my fingers. And, as I wipe off the blood,
my mind drifts back to Jesus' bleeding head.

The Sunday we light the first candle, we thank God for His plan for
redemption. How awesome it is to realize that I am important enough to
Him to die for. And He never gives up on us. On Palm Sunday we light a
purple candle reminding us of Jesus' triumphal entry, and together hail
the King of Kings, Jesus.

Good Friday is always a powerful time for us as we light the blood red
candle and ask God for the outpouring of Jesus' blood on our family.
There is power in the blood, and it hangs heavy in the air as we proceed.
Standing before the cross with four-inch spikes and hammer, we nail red
ribbons symbolizing our sins to the cross. It seems almost unbearable as
we listen to the blows of the hammer. What must it have been like the
first time! I have no response but to kneel at the foot of the cross and
plead for the blood to keep covering my sins.

Then we have Communion as a family seated on the floor between the
cross and the purple veil. What tender times we have had discussing forgiveness and the meaning of the veil being rent in two like the veil
of the temple was supernaturally torn from top to bottom when Christ
died. It was at this time that three-year-old Crista prayed, "I'm sorry,
God, for breaking Your rules." Together we pray, thanking God for His
almost unbelievable act of love. Then we rip our veil in two from top to
bottom.

Easter morning dawns, and our white candle in the crown of thorns
reminds us of the white-hot power of the Resurrection. Somehow
in my mind I have this picture of Christ exploding out of the top of the
tomb in a flash of nuclearlike energy. Talk about alternative power
sources—Christ is the ultimate, inexhaustible, alternative energy
source.

While this whole observance was designed for our children, I have discovered that I have gained perhaps more than they. Even those of us who
think we know the true meaning of Easter need to stand at the foot of the
cross with a hammer—and feel the blows.

THANKSGIVING DAY PRAYERS AT THE THOMPSONS'

Nancy gives a glimpse of how she and her family celebrate Thanksgiving:

Our most special Thanksgiving prayers came from a surprising source. We always thought we knew what it meant to be thankful when our large extended family of aunts, uncles, cousins, and grandmothers would gather with our immediate family for a sumptuous Thanksgiving dinner. And we heartily agreed with whichever elder of the family led in the Thanksgiving table prayer, thanking God for all the blessings we all had experienced the past year. Then we would gather at the piano and sing together the "Hallelujah Chorus" from Handel's *Messiah* to usher in the Christmas season. Yes, life was good, and we were thankful.

But during our difficult years because of Dan's wrongful unemployment situation, we learned what true thankfulness really was. Our prayer at our Thanksgiving dinner was an unbelievably sincere thanksgiving.

It was interesting to listen to our Cindy and Kathy pray their Thanksgiving prayers. It no longer was the usual list of thanks for Daddy and Mummy and Grandpa and Grandma. During really difficult times, children understand what real thankfulness is. Suddenly in our children's prayers, and in ours, there was a sincere appreciation for the bountiful dinner that was on our table—and deep thanks to God that He really had been the One who had supplied all our needs.

A "THANKSGIVING TREE"

At Jan's house they begin every November 1 to focus on being thankful by getting out their "Thanksgiving Tree." It is a branch set in plaster of paris on which each of them daily hangs a leaf, praying thanks to God for the thing or person whose name they have written on the leaves. "But," says Jan, "the thing that makes us really thankful is keeping the leaves in a baggie, and getting them out the next year and seeing what God has done in answer to those prayers."

WEDDING PRAYING FROM KURT
Kurt writes about special prayers relating to weddings:

There are many reasons to pray before and during a wedding. A wedding is the culmination of months of work, and we often pray that the day's events will occur as we have planned. Also we pray for safety in travel for the many friends and relatives who will attend. But there are two much more pressing issues to bring before the Lord in prayer.

First, a wedding may be the only time that our unsaved friends enter a church. Though we often fail to witness in our workplace or school, a wedding provides an excellent opportunity to publicly state our faith in God. We must be sure that the Gospel is clearly portrayed during the ceremony, and we should pray for the Spirit to work in the hearts of our unsaved guests. We must pray as if they had accepted an invitation to an evangelistic meeting, for so they have. A wedding is an example of an earthly groom awaiting His bride, and this can help the unsaved understand that Jesus, the Heavenly Groom, is waiting for them.

But the primary focus of our prayers is requesting God's blessings in the creation of a new entity, the marriage. When we ask for God's blessing on the marriage, we are not asking to receive health or riches or fame. We are asking for God's best for our lives, for His will. As the two should have sought His will individually, so now the couple, as one, should seek His will together. Just as Jacob wrestled with God in the night seeking as blessing, so a couple should wrestle in prayer—wrestle to turn over their preconceived plans, their selfish expectations, and their wills to the God who is all-knowing and never makes a mistake. No other preparation does so much to guarantee a successful marriage in God's eyes.

Margie and I can look back at the beginning of our life together and know that these are the prayers that we prayed—and that God is at the foundation of our union.

Kurt had been the photographer at many weddings and knew well the turmoil that precedes most ceremonies. So as he and Margie planned the preparation hours in the church leading up to their wedding, they carved out a one-half hour period for prayer. They asked all the close family, wedding party members, and officiating pastors to save that time to meet with them in a room for prayer. It was deep, moving prayer as we each prayed for the bride and groom and the ceremony. And the scheduling of that quiet time with God drew us aside from the hectic pre-wedding chaos; it quieted our hearts and invited God not only to be there but to be in control. That half hour also produced a special atmosphere of God's presence for the ceremony itself as we walked from prayer into the sanctuary. Even many guests commented on it. It was one of the most meaningful prayer times of my whole life.

WEDDINGS PRAYERS FROM CHRIS

In all of our children's marriages—Jan to Skip, Nancy to Dan, and Kurt to Margie—their father, Chris, has had the wonderful privilege of performing their ceremonies. And with that came the opportunity to pray the first prayer for each emerging couple as "the two became one in God" in one of the most special days of their lives. *Their wedding day!*

In the thrill of adding another child to our family, and yet also in the reality of giving our child to another, Chris remembers praying this kind of prayer, from his father heart, for our children as each couple was being married:

> Dear Father, I wish I had the pen of a psalmist or the tongue of an angel that I might thank You for what You are doing. But, Father, in a very human voice I would pray that You would add the unction of Your blessing on these two. I don't pray that they would go through life without trials. Please give them enough to keep them at the foot of the cross. I do not pray that they would go through life without sorrows, but that Your presence might be their everyday companion through them. I do not pray that You would give them great wealth, but would give them enough that they might enjoy life together.
>
> Father, as they walk down through life, I pray that not only those around them but the two of them together honestly can say that they are walking hand in hand with their Savior, Jesus, and because they are, all things have become more precious.

So, God, I commit them unto You, and ask that You would make out of them the kind of people that You have planned for them to be as this new couple—now one in You. In Jesus' name. Amen.

It was at our own wedding on Valentine's Day 1942 that Chris and I knelt and prayed a very special prayer. We were very aware that many of our loved ones had not received Christ as their personal Savior yet, so we wanted to be a witness to them during our wedding ceremony as we committed ourselves to serving God throughout our marriage.

Chris' dad made a three-foot high cross with soft lights on it; we covered the cross with lilies and hung it in front of our church choir loft. As we knelt under it, our soloist sang, "Beneath the cross of Jesus, I fain would take my stand." Although it was to declare to those present that we were taking our stand beneath the cross of Jesus, while we knelt there Chris and I prayed our own marriage commitment—to stay at the foot of Jesus' cross for the whole of our marriage.

Then fifty years later on Valentine's Day 1992, while celebrating with our whole family that special day in our lives, Chris and I once more knelt—while our family sang, "Beneath the cross of Jesus, I fain would take my stand."

And this is where we have been in our entire marriage—beneath the cross of Jesus. Relying on God through prayer for all our special days—and ordinary days too. *And it has worked!*

The Supernatural Reason for Prayer

CHAPTER THIRTEEN

THE ONLY REASON families need prayer is because there is a supernatural battle raging on earth, and human resources, wisdom, and power are not sufficient to win in this battle.

All the things that make family prayer necessary—rebellion, dissension, unforgiveness, abuse, infidelity, sickness, pain, sorrow, and eternal damnation—were brought to earth by Satan. God's world was created perfect by Him, but when Satan tempted Eve to sin in the Garden of Eden, Adam and Eve fell. This opened the door for Satan to bring all this evil to Planet Earth. And he still is the source of all of it on earth—and thus in our families.

PRAYER IS OUR SUPERNATURAL WEAPON

Since the source of all that plagues our families is supernatural, we need supernatural weapons to combat it. This is so clearly emphasized in 2 Corinthians 10:3-4:

> For though we walk in the flesh, we do not war according to the flesh, for the weapons of our warfare are not of the flesh, but divinely powerful for the destruction of fortresses.

The only One who can bring victory over all this evil that plagues our families is God. And the way we enlist His help for our families in this supernatural battle is prayer. When we pray, God enters the supernatural problem with His supernatural wisdom and power. So our supernatural weapon is prayer (see Eph. 2:18-20).

Now it is true that God is sovereign, and He does intervene in our families' problems as He chooses, *but the only way we can enlist His help is through prayer.* Prayer is the supernatural communication to a supernatural God who then supernaturally reaches down to our families and supernaturally brings the reconciliation, healing, peace, and love our family members need.

CAN FAMILIES ESCAPE THESE EVIL ATTACKS?

Shouldn't a husband and wife who have put Christ as the head of their home be free from Satan's attacks? If they read the Bible and pray faithfully and bring up their children "in the way they should go," shouldn't they escape being the target of evil supernatural attacks? Not at all.

A seminary professor and his wife shared with me about their daughter who rebelled against God for two years. At times they all but lost hope of her ever coming back to God and home. "But," they said, "we recognized the *source* of her temptation and rebellion—and *prayed and prayed spiritual warfare prayers.* And now she has come back to us, is studying at a Christian college—and has a deep relationship with the Lord!"

When Jan and Skip were first married, they were spending the night in the apartment upstairs at Grandma Moss' (my mother's) house. In the middle of the night our phone rang. "Mother, pray! We know we are not alone up here!" I told them to claim the name and the blood of Jesus. "We already did!" Then I said to go downstairs and get Grandma and Grandpa to pray because their prayers had tremendous spiritual power. "We already did that too!"

Jan and Skip had done everything right and prayed everything they should. So I told them to go to bed claiming Jesus' victory over Satan.

"And," I added, "when you wake up in the morning, you will be amazed at the sweet peace from Jesus you will be experiencing. There will even be tears of joy in your eyes!"

The next morning Jan called again. "You're right, Mother! There is incredible peace. If I didn't still have my robe on in which I slept all night, I wouldn't believe anything bad even happened last night!"

No one is immune from Satan's attacks. He even entered the heart of Ananias, a member of the first Christian church on earth, tempting Ananias to lie to the Holy Spirit. And he did. Also Jesus' disciple Peter, who was to become the spokesman for the early church, was sifted by Satan resulting in his denying his Lord. Also our serving the Lord seems to make Satan more anxious to make us ineffective and defeated; or he seeks to cause us to lose our credibility if he can—because of family problems.

(A word of caution—don't blame Satan if you have brought your problems upon yourself by you or your family breaking God's laws. You then have opened yourselves up to Satan.)

WHY SPIRITUAL WARFARE SINCE THE CROSS?

Since Jesus came to defeat the works of the devil (1 John 3:8) and said on the cross, "It is finished" (John 19:30), why are our families still plagued by the evil Satan brought to earth? Didn't Jesus fight the final battle with Satan on the cross—and didn't Jesus win? Absolutely He did! So why is there still such a huge battle with evil in our families?

The following true story illustrates clearly why the battle continues in the time era in which we are living since the Cross. It is a story about a python, a huge snake which grows up to twenty feet long in India and can swallow rather large animals such as a goat or sheep. It is so strong it winds itself around its live victim and squeezes to break its bones to make it easier to swallow and digest. (I brought home a newspaper article from India about a python that had swallowed a mother and her baby but spit out the mother.)

The man who told me this story is P.K. Das, the husband of my Bangalore, India, hostess. For many years Mr. Das had been the United

Nation's chief Asian advisor assessing their technology levels, energy systems, and productivity. I was fascinated as he told me a python experience his father had told him.

Mr. Das' father had been a senior officer for the British government during British colonial rule of India early this century, traveling extensively with his entourage of servants. The British, Mr. Das explained to me, had built forest houses in the jungles for their administrators to stay overnight. At one of the forest houses just south of Calcutta, a servant readying the house rushed to his father, white as a sheet and mumbling incoherently. Following him to the living room, the caretaker pointed in great agitation at a huge python coiled under a table.

So they quietly closed all the doors and windows, and his father went to check his ammunition box. He found he had just one bullet powerful enough to kill a python of that size, provided it was hit squarely in the head. So he took very careful aim, fired—and hit it right in the head. But, to his amazement, the snake did not die. Instead, it became crazed with that bullet in its head. Mr. Das and his servants stood terrified outside for an hour and a half as the python violently coiled and uncoiled itself in powerful convulsions, completely smashing every piece of furniture and light fixture in the room.

Then suddenly, after that hour and a half of terror, the python crumpled to the floor and died.

"My father was quite a preacher," Mr. Das told me, "becoming the chancellor of the Serampore Theological University upon retirement. He explained the python story like this:

> Just as we had only one bullet to kill the snake, so God also had just one bullet to kill the snake, Satan. God's single bullet was His own Son Jesus Christ. Satan's head was crushed when Christ conquered him on the cross.

> And the Lord God said to the serpent, "Because you have done this, cursed are you more than all cattle. . . . And I will put enmity between you and the woman, and between your seed and her seed [Jesus]; He shall bruise you on the head" (Gen. 3:14-15).

The fatal blow, said Mr. Das' father, has been dealt to the snake Satan. He has been mortally wounded already, and all the havoc and sorrow Satan now is causing on earth are only his convulsive death throes. The final end of Satan will come when Jesus comes back. It will take the second advent of Jesus for us to see the final end of Satan. The First Advent accomplished all God intended. The fatal blow was struck. But not until Jesus comes back will all of Satan's thrashing and attacking cease!

So this explains why our families still are being attacked by Satan after Jesus' victory over him on the cross. We are living in God's "hour and a half" between the cross and Jesus' return. And Satan, crazed by the fatal wound, is violently thrashing and attacking us in the time he has left.

USING SCRIPTURE IS IMPERATIVE

Twenty-five years ago I discovered the source of so many of the problems in our family, and since then have kept up a running battle against Satan through prayer. But I have learned that it is Scripture in my praying that is so powerful against Satan. I have hurled Scripture at him as part of the Christian's armor.

Therefore, take up the full armor of God . . . and the sword of the Spirit, which is the Word of God (Eph. 6:13, 17).

I have dug in my heels as I have resisted his attacks against my family.

Submit . . . to God. Resist the devil, and he will flee from you (James 4:7).

I angrily have hissed through my teeth at Satan to get out when he was causing hurt and pain in my loved one.

Be of sober spirit, be on the alert. Your adversary, the devil, prowls about like a roaring lion, seeking someone to devour. But resist him, firm in your faith (1 Peter 5:8-9).

I have enlisted the prayer support of my prayer chains and other family members according to the last item of God's armor.

With all prayer and petition pray at all times in the Spirit, and with this in view, be on the alert with all perseverance and petition for all the saints (Eph. 6:18).

Even the Lord Jesus Himself, the actual Son of God, quoted Scripture in His Mount of Temptation forty-day battle with Satan (see Matt. 4:1-11).

CLAIMING THE NAME AND BLOOD OF JESUS

But I also learned through the years that my own name, our family name, or the name of my church or denomination had no effect on Satan. There is no power in them to fight this supernatural battle. So I have claimed the victorious name of Jesus:

Therefore also God highly exalted Him, and bestowed on Him the name which is above every name, that at the name of Jesus every knee should bow, of those who are in heaven, and on earth, and under the earth, and that every tongue should confess that Jesus Christ is Lord, to the glory of God the Father. (Phil. 2:9-11).

I also have claimed the irresistible power of Jesus' shed blood on Calvary against Satan:

And the great dragon was thrown down, the serpent of old who is called the devil and Satan, who deceives the whole world; he was thrown down to the earth. . . . And they overcame him because of the blood of the Lamb and because of the word of their testimony (Rev. 12:9, 11).

One day Nancy called saying, "Mother, Cindy has developed the most horrible personality, and no matter what we do—love her more, scold her, give her more attention, or discipline her—nothing works. If we send her to her room she cries hysterically until she just about throws up. We're tried everything we can think of. *Please* pray for her!"

Five days later when calling to say good-bye as I was leaving for Italy, Nancy said, "Mother, right after I asked you to pray for Cindy, she abruptly changed. She's the sweetest, nicest girl you ever could ask for. Absolutely opposite of what she was. What did you pray for Cindy?"

"Nancy," I answered, "I went to prayer immediately. And as I was praying, God said 'Satan.' So I did battle with Satan, claiming the blood of Jesus in the name of Jesus."

The next day in Italy, during my devotional Bible reading I read this reassuring verse about Jesus' power over evil in Luke 4:36:

> For with authority and power He [Jesus] commands the unclean spirits, and they come out.

After returning from Italy, I said to Nancy, "I won't always be available to pray, so it's imperative that you learn what to pray in these situations." Sensing her hesitancy, I said, "Honey, I don't like this subject either. In fact, I hate it. But it's extremely important that the family's elder members know how to pray scripturally claiming the blood and name of Jesus, and to experientially know the power Christians have over Satan and his cohorts. With the victorious Jesus living in you, you can have an unshakable attitude of authority over Satan—lived in front of your children in all the hassles of Satan."

CLEANSING OUR HOME

Satan attacks our family by bringing confusion, defensiveness, oppression, and a heavy negative feeling into the atmosphere of our home. Frequently, I struggle under these attacks for a period of time before I wake up to the source. Then I immediately address Satan, telling him in the name of Jesus to get out of our house. Then, after asking God to cleanse the house with the blood of Jesus, I ask Him to fill it with Himself—all His purity and positive qualities. And it works. But it is amazing how often this happens, especially when I am working on material that threatens Satan. But I know the source—and what to do about it!

A few days ago while writing this chapter, I began feeling many of those things. Just then Skip called, and he prayed over the phone asking God to cleanse our house, claiming the blood and name of Jesus. It is hard to describe what I felt, but it was as if something lifted, and the air seemed to be so clear—like water after impurities have been removed.

SKIP'S SPIRITUAL WARFARE

Our son-in-law Skip has discovered God's power over Satan's influence in their own home. Here are some of his own thoughts:

We came across a liturgical church protocol several years ago which was inspiring to use as various members in our church "Agape Group" moved into new residences. We would all walk through the various rooms in the house, even stopping in the furnace room, and in each room give a short Bible reading or Bible verse and pray. As we cleansed each room with God's Word and prayer, we believe we made a declaration in the heavenlies that only God's purposes, presence, and Spirit were permitted in this new house.

Last year as we made preparations for Easter, I decided to construct a cross for our home. The chain saw hummed, and soon a six-foot cross lay before me. Hammering nails to erect it, I was overcome by emotion at the thought that my sin required a cross to be constructed for Jesus to be crucified. With tears in my eyes and the cross I had made on my shoulder, I brought it into the house. I was greeted by an outburst of crying by my three children, even including three-month-old Brett. We sensed an evil source to the cries, and were able to pray, allowing God to remove the foreign influence from our Easter and restore peace to them.

Our bedtime ritual with our children is a high point of our day. Drawing our children into our arms, we ask for prayer requests or items of praise. As we deal with the specific requests, we make a point to enclose our children in *God's cocoon of protection*. We ask for *His angels* to be present in their protective role. We ask for *God's hedge of protection* to be established around us and the *blood of Jesus* to be applied to us. Standing in His might, as believers in Jesus Christ, we *take authority over Satan and his kingdom* and *rebuke it in Jesus' name*. We ask that *Satan's purposes and plan* for us be canceled and rebuked, and in its place *God's purposes and plan* be allowed to happen.

Occasionally, perhaps about 2 A.M., we hear a thud and the staccato patter of little feet. One of our children announces a "scary dream" and cuddles up to us, asking "Daddy, please pray that my scary dream will go away." It is a father's richest blessing to sense the tenseness and fear dissolve as God always answers that pray.

STAYING ON THE VICTORY SIDE

Always stay on the victory side in your praying. Never question who is stronger, Jesus or Satan. Jesus always has been God, Satan just a created being. And never succumb to the lie that Satan might win. There is nothing in the Ephesians 6 "armor" section that even hints at falling, only standing—*if* we follow God's rules and wear His spiritual armor.

The first time I recall praying a very important spiritual warfare prayer was for my teenage Nancy in the early 1970s. She finally told me that for years she had had dreams of a terrifying face in a mirror telling her that in some way she was the heir of England's Bloody Mary. Feeling like a mother whose child had been attacked by a mad dog, I rushed into the battle without really knowing too much about what I was doing. But I seated us both by our dining room table, and then prayed claiming the blood of Jesus in the name of Jesus until we felt the victory come. I used every Scripture I could think of, swinging away with the "sword of the Spirit." I was too furious to be afraid. Too incensed to be cautious.

But it worked. After that praying, Nancy told me that face appeared in her mirror only once more—pale and indistinct and as if in a cracked mirror. It told her it could not come back anymore. And it didn't!

The greatest thing of all is that God not only delivered from those horrible attacks, but now has erased it completely from Nancy's mind. And I too never have been haunted by it, and had to refer to my notes I wrote at the time to make sure of the correct details for this book. *Victory in Jesus!*

Another thing that routs Satan is praise music. I frequently rock in a chair on my deck singing "In the name of Jesus, In the name of Jesus, I have the victory—and Satan will have to flee!" And I love to sit at my piano playing with gusto and finality, "There's power in the blood—of the Lamb." When in the midst of the battle, I find myself singing—in the car, in the kitchen, at the office, or wherever I am—the chorus based on the Scripture on which I firmly stand—1 John 4:4:

> Greater is He [Jesus] that is in you, than he [Satan] that is in the world (KJV).

Skip told me of their use of praise tapes. "Our home has been said by many to be 'so peaceful.' We do believe that God 'inhabits the praises of His people' (Ps. 22:3, NKJV). We have a large collection of praise music which frequently is playing. For several years Jenna had a special praise tape which she went to sleep listening to. Singing praises with our children in the car," says Skip, "the miles are shorter and our lives are enriched by the unity of His Spirit."

Many times I have stepped into Skip and Jan's house with praise music charging the atmosphere with God's presence. Satan cannot stand against songs of God's praise and Jesus' victory.

MINISTRY-RELATED ATTACKS OF SATAN

In 1972 I started teaching in youth groups, schools, and colleges on the dangers of the occult experimenting our young people were practicing; and I experienced wonderful protection and peace from God because of the praying of my "occult prayer chain." However, a local pastor who found Jesus after coming out of a childhood home with incredible occult power, said to me, "Evelyn, I believe you will be strong enough to stand up to Satan, but where he will get to you is through attacking your children. You as a mother will find it very difficult to battle him at the expense of your own children." And I have found this to be very true.

Our Nancy says she always knows when the Lord is moving with special effectiveness in my ministry, because at that time she and husband, Dan, always experience unusual hassles in their family. For years, she told me, they mentally kept track of this, and finally were convinced it was more than coincidence. "It usually isn't one big thing," Nancy said, "although at times it is, but a series of extremely upsetting things you just know never will happen—but they do. Most are not life-threatening but are beyond the normal hassles of life. But their sheer numbers necessitate expending so much time on them, and focuses my energy away from the important things in my life. And they contribute significantly to anxiety, and sometimes just routine life becomes a challenge.

"Also," Nancy continued, "they seem to have a pattern, always coming when God is blessing your prayer ministry. Dan and I now believe strongly that they are not from God, but from Satan because he wants to dilute your ministry's effectiveness. So I have named them 'hassle demons.'"

"But," said Nancy, "those hassles produced an incredible benefit at our house. Whichever child was being affected, we would pray and pray together. When one of us parents would feel at the end of our rope, we learned to trust God in a new way in those very difficult situations."

Yes, it is very hard on my mother-heart even to surmise that my ministry could cause spiritual hassles in my children. And I have prayed much about this through the years. Many times I have discussed this with Dan and Nancy, and over and over have asked them if they wanted me to give up my ministry. But I am overwhelmed and humbled at their unselfishness and the sacrifice they are willing to make for God's will to be done. Their resounding answer to this question always is, "No! We will pay any price we need to pay!"

My board and I have noticed the correlation also. Whenever I am going to a new continent, publishing a new book, or some other first related to my ministry, not only do my family and I feel the unusually strong attacks from Satan, but they do too. They even report their families falling apart at the same time. And our families' hassles take up so much of our time, energy, and praying that our time of praying for our ministry is drastically diminished. It is like the thwarting of Satan that Paul experienced when he wanted to go once to Thessalonica (see 1 Thes. 2:18).

When my first prayer tape was published, our junior high-schooler, Kurt, sighed a big sigh of relief. "Now maybe I'll be able to sleep nights, Mother." And Jan, away at college, frequently would call and say, "I know what you spoke on tonight, Mother!" And she always was right—spiritual warfare. The last time I returned from India, Nancy said, "Mother, lots of souls were being won in India, weren't they?" I said yes, why? "Because of the hassle we have been going through here!"

Reading James 1:1-4 on February 14, 1990, about trials believers experience, I recorded, "Finished writing *Battling the Prince of Darkness* book today. I have had complete joy through the whole writing since July '89. But the hassles from Satan have come from attacks on my family, keeping me off balance and consumed by praying for them." Satan's attacking my family has been the hardest of all spiritual battles for me.

BOXING WINDMILLS?

One night Jenna and Crista were each sleeping in their favorite "cozy" of blankets and pillows on the floor on either side of Chris' and my bed. Suddenly in the middle of the night Chris reared up in bed and bellowed, "Get out of here, you . . . you . . . you. . . !" While he boxed wildly at a white object seemingly floating in the air in the darkened room, two sleepy heads popped up over the sides of the bed and gaped in bewilderment.

But when we turned on the light we saw it was only a white terrycloth robe somebody had hung by its hood like a head over the closet door—with its sleeves at a rakish angle like arms. We all had a good laugh, and settled in for the rest of the night's sleep.

I wish all battles in our home were only like Don Quixote boxing windmills. I wish they all were with an imaginary enemy like that. But, unfortunately, they are real battles with a real supernatural being—who has chosen our families as one of his main, and most productive, battle-grounds for his evil, diabolical plans.

***

A CONCLUDING WORD—PONDERING OR PRAYING?

Much of what we think is prayer actually is only pondering. Even when we are on our knees in our prayer closets, it is easy just to roll our own thoughts and our own answers around in our minds, not really including God at all. This is not prayer; it is only pondering.

My dictionary defines "ponder" like this: "To consider something deeply and thoroughly; to meditate over or upon, to weigh carefully in the mind; to consider thoughtfully; to reflect, cogitate, deliberate, ruminate." This is a healthy process as it helps us sort out whys, unravel perplexing puzzles, come to conclusions, and even put to rest hurtful events. But people frequently think they have prayed when they have spent time pondering. *Pondering is not prayer.* Only when we involve God in this process does it turn into prayer.

In the supernatural battle for our families, pondering is inadequate. It is powerless to change the family problem about which we are deliberating.

In pondering we only wallow in our own reactions and feelings with all of our human biases and misunderstandings in control. At best pondering can give us human answers to our dilemmas which may or may not be right. There is no divine guidance or wisdom introduced into the family need.

But when we include God, our pondering suddenly involves the omniscient, all-wise, God of the universe. The God who never makes a mistake. The God who knows all the whys, all the outcomes, all the perfecting He intends through everything that happens to our families. When God becomes personally involved in our pondering, there are accurate conclusions and correct attitudes in and for our families—supplied by a loving, caring, all-knowing God.

When our pondering turns to praying, we also have the divine input of the omnipotent, all-powerful, God of heaven who has the power to intervene supernaturally into our family problems. And He also desires to supply us with all the power we need to cope with, handle, and solve our family needs.

Only when we include God in our ponderings, we are praying.

Examine carefully what you have been calling your "prayertime." How much of it is really praying? Have you learned to address God deliberately—and then listen to His responses? Or are you basically just pondering? Make sure!

Draw near to God, and He will draw near to you (James 4:8).

Then heaven will open up to you, and God on His throne will attune His ear to you—eager to provide all of Himself to you and your family. Because you prayed!

What Happens When God Answers Prayer

CONTENTS

Through the long difficult months of living through and writing this book, my four precious granddaughters have filled my life with sparkle and joy. God's timing in sending them to us was incredible, as their hugs and affection have charged my whole being with new life and motivation.

So this happy grandmother dedicates this book to those four little girls:

Cynthia Joy Thompson
Jennifer Diane Johnson
Crista Alisse Johnson
Kathleen Mae Thompson

And now I would like to add the newest members of my family, three delightful little boys:

James Karl Christenson
Brett Jezreel Johnson
Jonathan David Christenson

"Our ultimate goal is to be engulfed by an attitude of gratitude," Evelyn Christenson writes toward the end of this splendid book. She is writing about an attitude of thanksgiving toward the Lord that should mark everything we do. But I don't mind saying that Evelyn herself fills me with an attitude of gratitude. I am grateful for the privilege of being able to know her well over these years, grateful for her ministry, and grateful to the Lord for giving us the opportunity to work together as board members of Prison Fellowship.

This is one of those rare books that tells us something of what God is like. Mrs. Christenson begins with a simple question: What happens when God answers our prayers? She doesn't say *if* God answers our prayers; she assumes He answers them, as indeed He does. Neither does she have in mind a crude cause-and-effect relationship: we ask for something, God gives it to us—or He doesn't. For her, prayer is something more subtle and complex. It opens a door; it shows us a way. When she asks, "What happens when God answers?" she is asking a basic and somewhat frightening question. What happens when we walk in the door and discover that the Master of the universe is speaking to us, directing us, making demands of us?

He tells us many things—that we need to pray more, that we've been praying the wrong prayer, that we need to search the Scriptures, that we need to grow in holiness, or even that our prayer has already been answered.

Very often—and this is where I find Evelyn Christenson's book most challenging—God answers our prayers by telling us to change the way we relate to Him and to the people we love. Do we pray for grace to overcome an area of weakness? The Lord will tell us to get on our knees and repent. Do we pray for a wayward spouse or an unbelieving child? The Lord might tell us to serve that person to the limit of our strength. Do we pray for grace and wisdom? The Lord will give it—and then commission us to spill out our lives in the work of sharing the Good News with the unsaved.

It can be a fearsome thing to pray. We might fall into the hands of the living God. Evelyn Christenson has no illusions about how difficult it is to follow Him.

Yet, as I read this book, I kept thinking to myself, "Hard as it is, who would want to live any other way?" So often we go through our days and weeks and months with our heads filled with *our* plans; instead, we need to live *His* way, with *His* way to love, *His* way to serve, *His* way to think. His ways are not our ways—and that is a relief. Our Father in heaven has revealed a better way to live. How good it is to be freed from the burden of our own ideas.

The gateway to this freedom is prayer. Evelyn Christenson has tirelessly devoted her life to showing us how to open this door to freedom. Because of her ministry—and because of the prayer support of many of her friends and associates—thousands of people all over the world know how to pray. In this book, they will learn what happens when God answers prayer.

That is enough reason to read this book. But there is another reason. By reading it, you will get to know my friend Evelyn Christenson—a woman who embodies the lifestyle of prayer in her own life. Evelyn herself has discovered what happens when God answers prayer. She willingly shares this discovery with us, just as she has willingly spent her whole life serving the God she loves.

CHARLES W. COLSON

PREFACE

Because twenty-five years have passed since our original experimentation in prayer which produced the book *What Happens When Women Pray,* it seems only right to take a good, honest look at what really *did* happen. The magnitude of what we have seen God do in answer to those years of praying is in this book.

Starting with a committee of eight women in Rockford, Illinois in 1968, God has exploded this ministry across America and overseas. I personally have taught hundreds of thousands in all denominations how to pray both here in the United States and around the world. And millions have read that book, studied it, and taught it. Prayer groups and chains have formed in all kinds of churches, organizations, in whole cities, and even in some entire countries.

Through the years, we have concentrated on the *human perspective* of prayer — learning to obey the scriptural prerequisites to power in prayer and then discovering the power of our prayers. Now, this book contains what we have learned about *God's perspective* of prayer. What He expects to happen *with* His answers. What happens to us and through us *after* He answers.

We have learned that an answer to prayer is not an end in itself, but it is always God's opening of the next door of our lives and ushering us into the next era He has for us.

Prayer is one of God's chief means of accomplishing His will on Planet Earth. Here is the way we have discovered He does it!

1

When God answers...

Here Is My Perspective

When God answers a prayer, it is not the final closing curtain on an episode in our lives. Rather, it is the opening of the curtain to the next act. The most important part of prayer is what we do with God's answers and how His answers affect us.

God never intends that an answer to prayer be an end in itself. He expects much more than an emotional response—joy, disappointment, or anger—to His answer. He expects us to be prepared to act or to be acted upon by His answer to our prayers.

God's answer to a prayer is His means of accomplishing His will here on Earth. The way He answers reveals to us His sovereign will, His plan, His reasoning, and His perspective on the subject. We must ask, "What does God expect to accomplish *with* this answer?"

God's Intentions

We seem to place so much emphasis on our prayer requests, and then on God's answers, that we forget what He intends us to do *with* His answers. Most of us pray a specific prayer, receive an answer—whether or not it is to our liking—and consider the case closed. In our prayer notebooks, we write down the request, and then opposite it—with joyous or resigned finality—record the answer when it comes. But God does not consider the case closed. He opens a whole new arena of action by the answer He gives. Our response to His answer should be, "What next, Lord?"

According to Jeremiah 33:3, there is another step, something *after* the prayer and *after* the answer:

Call unto Me, and I will answer thee, and show thee great and mighty things, which thou knowest not.

God's time-tested promise to Jeremiah is in three parts, not our usual two-part approach of "our calling" and "His answering."

Rarely does God stamp "case closed" when He answers one of our prayers. Rather, it is often what happens after God answers that is life-changing.

"Which Thou Knowest Not"

Have you ever wished that you could get a glimpse into God's mind? The God who ordained all the physical laws of space and time? The God who designed all the minute details of an incredibly complex universe? The God in whom all things consist and operate? There is a way. It is possible to perceive what is in the mind of the omniscient God of the universe. How? By examining His answers to your prayers!

In our prayer ministry, we have been continuously surprised at God's "things we did not know." As we have experimented for twenty-one years with ever-enlarging amounts and methods of prayer, God has surprised us with so much more than that for which we asked. I am constantly amazed that God does not limit answering our prayers because of our inability to ask.

The exciting thing is that the last phrase of Jeremiah 33:3 refers to things we know nothing about—not ideas we dreamed up or plans we devised. As I look back over my life of prayer, this pattern becomes so obvious. I ask God for just one thing, and He keeps on answering long after I even recognize it as His response to my prayer.

Months before my first prayer seminar in war-torn Belfast, Northern Ireland in June of 1981, our prayer chains "called unto God" in prayer for my safety, for those whom He wanted to attend, and for His power in the seminar. Then when He started answering, we praised Him that, after the registrations were filled to the capacity of 1,000 people, others called, crying and pleading over the phone, "We must come to learn to pray, for the only hope for our country is prayer."

As God continued to answer prayer at the seminar, the prayers thanked Him that the large downtown Presbyterian Hall had been engaged and was filled—by both Catholics and Protestants who were at war! In awe, we praised Him as members of these opposing factions held hands in their groups and asked God to forgive them as they forgave each other. Many actually trembled as they prayed together. And the pray-ers almost burst with praise when at the close they all held hands and sang, "Blest be the tie that binds our hearts in Christian love." How thrilled we were that 700 from both sides signed up for combined telephone prayer chains in Northern Ireland. And then with prayers of relief and thanksgiving, my husband, Chris, and I were whisked out of Ireland safely after the seminar. We called unto God and He certainly did answer.

But I wonder how many of those pray-ers then turned to the "Belfast Prayer Seminar" page, dated June 9, 1981 in their prayer request notebook and mentally stamped "case closed" on that page?

God's Continued Involvement

God, however, did not stamp the case "closed." He continued to work after those initial answers and accomplished "great and mighty things, which [we knew] not."

God left the situation open-ended so that He could expand those 700 pray-ers into prayer chains and groups all over Northern Ireland—so that He could use those Irish pray-ers—along with others—to reach Liam and Jimmy, two imprisoned terrorists from opposite sides of the Irish "religious war"—so that two years later, I could sit and listen spellbound, as I interviewed Liam during our Prison Fellowship International Symposium in Belfast, a part of Charles Colson's ministry.

Liam was a boyish-looking Catholic inmate furloughed from prison for a few days to attend our symposium. How privileged I felt that he had saved a couple of hours just to talk with me. As I sat with my mind riveted on his incredible story, Liam told me that as an IRA terrorist he had been arrested and imprisoned for ten years. He spoke of the "blanket" protests when IRA inmates refused to wear the British clothing issued to them. He shuddered as he recounted their "dirty" protests when they refused to wash and threw their own excrement against the walls of their cells. Then, quietly, he spoke of his own hunger strike. The limp in his walk was a painful reminder of its devastation on his muscles.

Liam told me that as the last person on the Bobby Sands' hunger strike in the Maze Prison, near Belfast, he was blind and dying after fifty-six days without food and had slipped into a coma. It was his mother who then insisted on his being fed intravenously, thus ending the series of ten young prisoners who had starved themselves to death for their cause. (Later, I squeezed that dear, brave Irish mother as she stood beaming at her son's side at our symposium.)

After recovering from his horrible experience of being just hours from death, Liam found himself in a solitary confinement cell. "All they would let me have," he told me, "was a Bible. And while I read that Bible and . . ." He paused, slowly and deliberately enunciating his next words, *"because all those people were praying for me—*I accepted Jesus as my Savior."

Also attending that symposium was a Protestant prisoner named Jimmy, who, although on the opposite side of the conflict, had watched Liam's transformed life. And Jimmy, wanting what Liam had, also accepted Christ. Now the two are in Magilligan Prison, studying the Bible together in the same study group and meeting on a regular basis to pray together. Liam told me that if he had seen Jimmy before finding Christ, he would have "shot him dead" (not a stretch of the truth). "But now," said Liam, "I would die for Jimmy."

Our final Prison Fellowship rally at Queens University in Belfast was open to the public—both Catholics and Protestants, who were still at war. As Liam and Jimmy stood together on the platform radiating and sharing their mutual love for Jesus, the whole crowd erupted in a thunderous standing ovation, weeping together and hugging each other throughout the huge auditorium.

God had used the prayers for a seminar, perhaps in a small way, to help accomplish some of His will for that war-torn country. And He will continue to answer, fulfilling Liam's words to me, "My hope is to believe that God is changing the hearts of men like myself and Jimmy. And that's the only hope I have for peace in my country, Northern Ireland."

Yes, each answer to prayer is God's opening of the door to

what He intends to accomplish next in this world. With the answer to the initial prayer comes the continuation of God's involvement. But we may not recognize it as such; we may even forget that we prayed, or even worse, take for granted that what is happening is just the natural course of events. "Great and mighty things, which thou knowest not."

God's Surprises

My prayer ministry has been full of God's surprises—great and mighty things He did over and above that for which we prayed. In fact, I have experienced a continuing shock in my prayer seminars. God has been showing me what I call His *hidden mission field*. And no matter how frequently I see it, I am still surprised. I did not seek to find it; in fact, I really did not know the extent to which it existed. But God has shown me a *hidden mission field* existing right inside Christian churches around the world. This mission field is made up of church members who are not sure whether they know Jesus personally as Savior and Lord.

I first experienced this shock when I started my overseas ministry. Teaching my first prayer seminars in Australia in 1980, I found that most of the attendees already belonged to well-respected churches and were regularly studying the Bible with my sponsors, an international women's Bible study organization. However, when I asked all who were not sure of their personal relationship with Jesus to pray aloud together in their groups of four—to my utter amazement—approximately a fourth of them prayed, accepting Jesus for the first time or making sure of their salvation.

This pattern has continued wherever I have gone: in the audience of Protestants and Catholics in Ireland, in Scotland, and all across England; next in Taiwan, Japan, India, and back through the British Isles. Then back home in America, to my amazement, the percentage began to rise.

The usual 5 percent and then 10 percent praying the prayer of commitment in my seminars hadn't surprised me too much, but when the percentage suddenly soared to 25 percent and above, I was stunned. It seemed incomprehensible that so large a portion of those coming to learn to pray were not sure whether they had a personal relationship with Jesus. And most incredible was the fact that almost everyone who attends my seminars here and abroad is already a member of a respectable church.

In the past two years, the statistics have risen to 50 percent quite frequently, and even as high as 75 percent several times, making the average almost one half of our audiences praying this prayer.

Wondering if I was exaggerating these statistics, after my last seminar I shared my concern with the host pastor who had been on the platform with me. "How many would you estimate prayed aloud today, making sure they knew Jesus as Savior and Lord?" I asked.

"Oh, well over half!" he exclaimed with profound joy. God's surprises us with "things which thou knowest not"!

God's Perspective of Answers to Prayer

But there are other kinds of surprises from God when He answers our prayers. I have discovered how "unhuman" God's ways of thinking really are. Things that seem so right, so good, so timely, so logical, so obvious to us frequently are refused, replaced, and even reversed by God as He—without ever making a mistake, missing the mark, being too early or too late—fields the answers out of His omniscient mind.

We need to see prayer from God's perspective. We should try to see the big picture of what God's overall plan might be and how each little and big request with His answer fits into His sovereign purpose. How often we question when God doesn't answer the way we wanted. How we grumble when we think He has not answered, when actually we have not recognized His answer. Or, when in rebellion, we decide that if this is how God is going to answer, we are never going to pray again.

But God has told us the "great and mighty things" He would do after His answer were "things we know not." God's omniscient thought process determines His answer to the prayers His earthly children pray, as well as all things those answers initiate.

Also, God's answer usually precipitates expanded and more fervent prayers from us. With His answer, we find ourselves on the next plateau from which we then launch our next endeavor through prayer.

How often we hear, "God always answers, but His answers are

yes, no, or wait." In my own experience, I have not found God's answers to be that simplistic. His interaction with me in prayer is much more complex and far-reaching. His answer always includes, "Keep interacting with Me, My child. I have much I want to accomplish through your prayers."

Our Response to God's Answers

People respond in various ways to God's answers to their prayers. Many different responses to prayer are recorded in the New Testament. There is the choice of *witnessing*. Anna prayed for many years to see the Messiah, and when God answered her prayers at Baby Jesus' circumcision, she went out and told everyone she had seen the Messiah. But Simeon's response was quite different. After praying the same prayer for a similar time period, he too saw the Messiah. His response? "Now I am ready to die."

There is the reaction of *disbelief*. As the early Christians prayed for Peter's release from prison, they could not believe that God had answered their prayers, thinking it was his ghost knocking at the gate. There is the response of *obedience*. Peter's prayers on the rooftop were answered by God in a vision he did not understand at the time. But even so, when God did explain it, Peter obeyed immediately and brought the Gospel to the Gentiles.

We have to make a *choice*. Paul and Silas prayed and sang in the prison, and God answered by sending an earthquake that opened all the doors and broke the prisoners' chains. But Paul chose to forego immediate freedom in order to win the jailer to Christ. Perhaps one of the most difficult responses to God's answer to prayer was Paul's response of *acceptance*. Paul prayed three times for his thorn in the flesh to be removed, but accepted God's answer—no—relying at last on God's strength.

The Bible reveals myriads of different responses to God when He answered prayer—some good, some bad, some rebellious, some submissive, some joyous, some thankful, some angry. Our responses to God's answers to our prayers can be many and varied also. The decision is up to us.

Ushered Into

The decision as to our response will determine the next state of our spiritual condition, attitude, relationship with God, or arena of activity. Every prayer request, no matter how large or small, always ushers us into our next state. We pray, God answers, and then we decide what to do with His answer.

Through all His answers, God's desires are always that we step into the next room of forgiveness, joy, Christlikeness, peace, power, and fruit-bearing. And, if necessary, His answer includes our being restored to this state. But we must accept His answer.

But God's answer may have to include the steps He knows are necessary to answer our original prayer. So, rather than looking at a once-for-all answer to a prayer, we must look to what must happen after God answers to produce His ultimate answer. We usually can expect a series of more prayers and more answers that are generated by our first prayer, and then each subsequent prayer.

Since God's answer is always that which ultimately will produce what is absolutely best for the pray-er, we must be willing for His intermediary answers. They are the steppingstones He knows are essential to His ushering us into that eventual end state He desires for us.

Opening the Curtain

Jesus said in Matthew 7:7, "Knock, and it shall be opened unto you." What will be opened? Whatever God has for you! His next open door. A better life with Him. God is using the prayers you are praying today to open the curtain to the rest of your life.

Closing Prayer

Oh, God, I deeply desire to understand Your perspective of prayer. Please teach me how I should respond to Your answers to my prayers so that You can direct my life through them.

In Jesus' name, **Amen.**

2

When God answers...

I Am Not Able

How do we handle God's answers to a prayer when He says, "I am not able. Capable? Yes. Able? No."

How shocking it is when, although we are praying for something we know is His will, God answers, "My child, I am not able!" Then He explains, "It is true that I am capable of everything. It is true that I have more power than the combined power of all the things I have created. Yes, it is true that I am capable of doing 'exceeding abundantly above all [you] ask or think' [see Eph. 3:20], but as to answering that prayer, I am not able!"

Even while longing to answer yes to our prayer requests and when eager to usher us into that next open door or condition, there are times He must answer: "I am not able."

God taught me this as I stopped in California for a prayer seminar en route home from Taiwan. After spending much time in deep intercessory prayer that morning, I had asked God to bring to my mind the Scripture He had for me for that day's seminar. Ephesians 3:20 instantly flashed across my mind. I silently recited it over and over:

> Now unto Him that is able to do exceeding abundantly above all that we ask or think, according to the power that worketh in us.

According To

But as I repeated the verse over and over, only two words kept standing out: *according to, according to.* I puzzled over what God was trying to teach me. The verse suddenly seemed so complicated; I decided to break it down. I lumped the words "exceeding abundantly above all that we ask or think" into a simple "all that." God can do "all that." Then it read, "Now unto Him that is able to do . . . all that . . . according to the power that worketh in us." I had it! God is able to do "all that" *only* according to the power that works in us!

Then I really began to ponder this in my heart. I asked myself, "Don't I have God's power in me all the time?" I must have, for as a Christian, all three persons of the Trinity dwell in me. I have Christ in me, "the hope of glory" (Col. 1:27); the Father will come and dwell in us (1 John 4:12-15); and Jesus promised that the Holy Spirit would be in us (John 14:17). In fact, just before Paul's doxology in Ephesians 3, which includes verse 20, he prayed that the Christians at Ephesus would "be filled with all the fullness of God" (Eph. 3:19).

The next question loomed, But do I always have the same amount of God's power working in me? From years of experience, I knew automatically that the answer was no. I do not have the same proportion of God's power all of the time. And He is able to do only in accordance with, in proportion to, the measure of that power which is working in me!

God Limits Himself

Slowly, I saw it. God has the ability to *limit* the amount of power He releases in me. Although I have within me that divine force, the Triune God, who is capable of anything and everything, He chooses the amount of power that He will unleash in me. Yes, God can do all He wants to do, but He sets limits as to how much power He will "work in us."

I couldn't wait to get home to check the accuracy of this theology in my reference books. And there it was in many places, including this quote in the old Cambridge Bible commentary: "In the saint [true believer] . . . resides already a Divine force capable in itself of the mightiest developments. To attain these, not a new force, but a fuller application of *this* force, is required."[1] According to!

Augustus Strong wrote, "God can do all He will, but He will not do all He can. Else His power is mere force acting necessarily, and God [would be] the slave of His own omnipotence. God is not compelled to do all He can do, but uses as much of His power as He pleases. Just because He is omnipotent, He does not have to do all He can do."[2]

Still not satisfied, I phoned Berkley Mickelsen, a professor of New Testament Greek at Bethel Seminary, and asked him if my thinking was correct. "Evelyn," he replied, "that seemingly unimportant prepositional phrase 'according to' is the crux of that time-tested doxology of Paul's prayer in Ephesians. You have discovered the most crucial phrase in that verse. Most people never see it." Well, I hadn't seen it either. It was God who showed it to me so clearly that morning in California as I was returning from Taiwan.

Yes, the extent of what God is able to do in us in answer to our prayers depends on, is according to, the measure of power that is working in us. God is capable of all things—but is able to do only according to the amount of power working in us!

We Limit God

What is it, then, that releases greater amounts of God's power? Our prayers, of course! God sends His power in response to adequate praying.

God, through His answers, accomplishes what He has wanted to do all along but has been hindered by our lack of prayer. And although He is sovereign and can and does do as He chooses without the help of believers' prayers, He has chosen to operate extensively in response to them.

In 1973, I was one of eleven people who organized 6,000 prayer groups in the Minneapolis–St. Paul area for the upcoming Billy Graham Crusade in August of that year. We were expecting—and had—50,000 people in attendance. Before leaving my home to train the St. Paul pray-ers one Saturday morning, I noticed that our local newspaper carried the headline, "Billy Graham Has 500,000 First Night in Korea." Shocked, I reported this to our pray-ers and asked why we were aiming at only 50,000. But I knew the reason for the difference and gave them the answer. It was all the prayer that the Korean Christians consistently practice. Since the early part of this century, thousands have been going to their churches to pray daily before breakfast;

every Friday night, all night, finds tens of thousands in several different prayer meetings, and they solve their problems and intercede in cubicles on their prayer mountains.

At the National Religious Broadcasters Convention in 1985, I was overwhelmed at the display of electronic equipment. Later in the day, in the workshop I was conducting, I asked the people this question: "Are you depending on this tremendous wattage from your transmitters *for* power, or are you sending your message of Jesus *with* power? With all your super transmitting power, are your broadcasts still powerless because of lack of prayer for them?"

Then I had to ask myself the same question. In our daily broadcasts to all of China, are we depending on Trans World Radio's unbelievably powerful transmitters to get our prayer message *to* that one fourth of the world, or are we sending it *with* God's power—through prayer?

People frequently ask me how much time they should spend in personal closet praying. I reply, "That depends on how much power you want." E.M. Bounds in his book *Power through Prayer* explained, "Our short prayers owe their point and efficiency to the long ones that have preceded them. The short, prevailing prayer cannot be prayed by one who has not prevailed with God in a mightier struggle of long continuance."[3] So, even though God can do anything He wants, He has chosen to permit us to limit many of His actions by our lack of faithfulness in prayer. Conversely, our sufficient praying will enable Him to give the answers we both desire.

God with all the power of the universe, is sitting on His throne in glory, even today, waiting and longing to release that power on Planet Earth. With absolute unlimited power at His disposal (in fact, He *is* unlimited power), He is ready to pull aside the curtain and let us step into a new era of that power in our lives— appropriated by and released through prayer!

Since I found Jesus Christ personally at age nine, I've diligently prayed for others and myself. And I have depended on God's power through prayer in my whole life of ministry. What I have felt all of these years was summed up in January 1982, when I wrote in the margin of my Bible beside 1 Corinthians 2:4, "This is what I want for my ministry: '*And my message and my preaching were not in persuasive words of wisdom, but in demonstration of the Spirit and of power' "* (NASB, emphasis mine). God has been faithful in sending that power in answer to the prayers of thousands of faithful pray-ers.

Released by Prayer

As I reflected on my trip to Taiwan after receiving God's "according to," I realized the whole thing had been an "Ephesians 3:20 experience." Throughout it all, we had seen an unusual demonstration of God's power released in answer to a tremendous amount of prayer.

Thousands were praying individually, in telephone prayer chains, in groups, and on my twenty-four-hour prayer clock. When I minister overseas, my prayer clock operates continuously. Faithful pray-ers across the United States sign up for specific prayer periods, with the result that many people are on their knees around the clock, day and night, in uninterrupted prayer for my ministry.

There had been just one day between Christmas and my departure for Taiwan. On Christmas night, the last of our guests left at 11:00, and in one day, I had to put away the stacks of gifts and wrappings and the best dishes and silver, store all the leftover food, and get my husband ready for his trip to Florida and myself ready for the flight to Taiwan. In addition, the clothes dryer repairman had come just as our family was about to open gifts on Christmas Eve, leaving the clothes we needed for our trips heaped in the laundry room baskets!

With all the preparations, by the middle of that afternoon I couldn't go on. Emotionally and physically exhausted, I went into my bathroom, shut the door, and cried. "Lord, I can't go to Taiwan. Look at me. I'm a basket case!" I didn't have to tell the Lord that—He already knew it! But I knew I had to go to Taiwan. So I stoically ironed Chris' shirts and packed.

With sheer determined obedience, I went to the airport the next day. As I slowly trudged down the ramp to the airplane, reluctantly dragging my tote bag behind me, I kept complaining inwardly, "I can't go. I can't go to Taiwan." But just a few feet from the plane, something happened. It was just as if something came right down from heaven and enwrapped me like a blanket.

And suddenly, I was filled with excitement, anticipation, strength—and power!

I stopped dead still on the ramp and exclaimed under my breath, "What happened?" And then I remembered. "Oh, this is the day the twenty-four-hour clock starts praying for me!" And, had there not been an airplane at the end of that ramp, I felt as if I could have flown all the way to Taiwan—on my own power!

When God Answers: "I Am Able"
When there is enough prayer, God is able!

Was the only power He relased on that Taiwan trip for my personal strength? Oh, no. In Taipei alone, we had participants from forty-three different Christian organizations and church affiliations, a "first" on that island for this kind of unity in women's ministry. A missionary there told me, "Statistically, Taiwan is the most idolatrous nation in the world. The seminars were a light in that dark and pagan country. Such love was manifested there. The women even held hands and prayed together." "The non-Christians," she continued, "brought by Christian friends and family members were overwhelmed by the love shown." So God's answer to much praying began to break a barrier that had been there for many years.

Then God began to melt away the centuries-old Asian tradition of "saving face." Jeanne Swanson, the missionary responsible for my coming, had said to me, "Evelyn, if you can get them to admit their sins, your whole trip will be worth it." In the seminar, when I was ready to ask them to confess their sins aloud, I panicked at the possibility of nobody daring to pray. But God suddenly brought to my mind the words *all together*. After getting a whispered confirmation from my interpreter, I stood amazed as the whole room erupted in audible prayers—sounding like 10,000 swarming bees—from women confessing their sins and asking God for forgiveness in front of each other. And they confessed their sins so fervently and so long that the interpreter finally asked them to stop so we could go on with the seminar. Prayer power—breaking the ice!

Then there was the thrill of seeing God overcome Satan's power in his incredible stronghold in South Taiwan. On the first night of the seminar, I felt almost as if there were chains binding me as I spoke. It took almost a whole night of wrestling in prayer by my missionary hostess and myself to bring victory over that evil power. But it broke and was gone, and God poured out His power on us all. We saw God vividly demonstrate the use of the last and often neglected piece of armor listed in Ephesians 6 with which to fight Satan—prayer (v. 18).

But this power in Taiwan was not the only result of the praying being done in America. God was answering prayers from both sides of the Pacific Ocean. Four women in Taiwan had been burdened for their island and were meeting regularly to pray. Then their number grew to thirty-five, and they prayed together for more than a year. Then in faith, they stepped out to invite me to come for prayer seminars there. These were the women God used to bring about the display of His power and the beginning of the binding together of the body of Christ in Taiwan.

God's power didn't stop working when I flew back to America either. The original group of 35 women in Taiwan has now been multiplied by Him to more than 10,000 praying women on this small island. It was God *"able* to do exceeding abundantly above all that we [could] ask or think" in answer to thousands of prayers.

I had called my mother from California to say good-bye on my way to Taiwan. Her last words to me were: "Evelyn, don't forget Ephesians 3:20!" Mother, I shall never forget Ephesians 3:20!

Corporate Praying

Although there are many biblical promises of prayer power from one person's prayers, in Ephesians 3:20 the promise is addressed to many. It is plural—*"we* ask or think." And "according to the power that works in *us"* might well read "according to the amount of prayer for *us*—and by *us."*

In my thank-you letter to my pray-ers about God's power at work in my trip to Japan in 1981, I included these words: "I'm contemplating writing a book about the tangible evidences of *your prayers* in my life." This is the book! Who prayed? The secret of this power from God for ministry is corporate prayer with thousands of pray-ers releasing it.

Since 1968, we have been developing and practicing methods in my ministry of intercessory prayer that have produced His exceeding, abundant power. (See *What Happens When Women Pray.*[4]) And corporate prayer for serving the Lord has been an indispensable part of my life since 1964, when Signe, Lorna, and I started our four years of praying together every Thusday afternoon. This praying was the forerunner of the "What Happens When Women Pray" project of 1968, which has expanded around the world through our United Prayer Ministries, Inc. It has produced an astonishing series of lessons about what God is able to do when there is enough prayer. So prayer is not just a theory in my head of what should happen or might happen. I have seen it happen.

At the publisher's million-copy party for my book *What Happens When Women Pray,* I was asked to speak on the subject, "What produces a million-copy book?" My answer was simply, "Prayer." God literally produced the book. It was conceived in prayer, is about prayer, and was continuously prayed for through the writing, production, distribution, and its use—to this day.

But the book, published in 1975, was just another step in the prayer ministry God was able to open up because of prayer. After leaving our "What Happens When Women Pray" church in Rockford, Illinois in 1970, God chided me to "stir up the gift . . . which is in [you]" (2 Tim. 1:6). Which gift? "Prayer! Start teaching what I taught you in all the prayer experimentation!" God replied.

These are the methods He taughts us. **Just three**—Gloria Davidson, Jan Mudge, and I—started out. And we prayed through every step and every decision in our fledgling prayer seminar movement, knowing well that we didn't know how to do it, but we just had a tremendous burden to teach people to pray. We enlisted many faithful pray-ers to support us.

Then it was our praying about getting the seminar material on audio cassettes that led the three of us bravely to order 1,000 sets from Bethany Fellowship, only to creep back like three timid mice to cut our order in half. Then we all prayed diligently and fervently that they would sell—which they did—immediately. In shock, I called Dave Anthony to tell him to put into production the other 500 sets. I could almost feel him smiling over the phone as he answered, "I knew they would sell so I just went ahead and made the 1,000 sets. Just come out and pick them up."

Next came praying for the book Victor Books asked me to write after hearing those tapes. In the meantime, we three had incorporated into United Prayer Ministries, Inc., praying through every unexplored step; and the board members had multipled. It was my **Personal Telephone Prayer Chain** of about thirty women that upheld me during the writing of every word all those long months. For more than ten years, I have been sharing my physical, emotional, mental, and spiritual needs with this chain. And they have upheld me with their powerful prayers, sacrificially giving of their time and effort daily. Frequently, it was their deep striving and wrestling in prayer that enabled God to send forth our ministry.

Other corporate prayer, enabling God to produce that book and its subsequent ministry, came from my **Personal Prayer Group** of nine women, organized in 1971. How we agonized in prayer over each concept and word, titles, time in my schedule to work on it, guidance for those publishing it at Victor Books—and even a printers' strike! Also, the intercession for these needs by faculty wives at Bethel College and Seminary during our weekly prayer meetings—as well as by relatives, friends, and fellow church members—all corporately enabled God to release enough wisdom and power for that book on prayer.

But when I saw the first copy of *What Happens When Women Pray* and realized that I had promised to pray for each person reading the book, I panicked. How could I do that? So we devised a **Prayer Calendar** with each day assigned to an "intercessor" whose job it was to pray for those reading the book or teaching it that day (while the rest of us prayed for the intercessor). Now, more than ten years later, the calendar is still in operation, including daily prayer for everyone reading and teaching my books, those using the tapes, and for my daily schedule.

I pass our experiences of answered prayer on to the interdenominational **Steering Committees** planning my seminar and request that they meet regularly for up to six months to pray. (They hardly need me after all of their unity and power in prayer!) But when I step into a seminar, I can feel the amount and quality of prayer that has been offered. God's power in my seminars is always directly proportional to the amount and kind of praying done by the committee.

Running Our Organization on Prayer

In our United Prayer Ministries (UPM), we depend completely on God's direction. When asking God for guidance, wisdom, or the opening of doors, we literally follow the advice in my first book—to "pray first and plan afterward." About half of each **Board Meeting** is actual praying. We usually open the meeting with an hour of prayer and then close with all taking part in extended praying, with prayer for present and future ministry after the business session. Then, while discussing business, we have found a fantastic secret for wisdom. When we do not know what decision to make, we just stop and pray. Between monthly board meetings, the praying continues with requests communicated through our UPM telephone prayer chains.

God taught us early that "prayer *is* the answer." And it has worked. We have no superstars, only "God's fellow-workers" (1 Cor. 3:9, NASB). Together with us, He has taken this prayer ministry around the world.

In addition to our own board telephone prayer chains, we organized an area-wide **Metropolitan Prayer Chain** in the Twin Cities of St. Paul and Minneapolis, consisting of several hundred members from all denominations. It has been the pilot project for similar ones in many countries around the world.

Our most active prayer chain is the **Government Telephone Prayer Chain,** praying for local, national, and world governments, leaders, and legislation. The participants research, pray diligently, and enlist further praying from other Christians.

Recently, after a debate that lasted past midnight, the full Minnesota Senate passed, by a preliminary vote of 32–27, a bill that gave state approval to a lifestyle which the Bible calls abhorrent to the Lord. Supporters expected certain victory at the final vote the next evening. However, Christians across the state went to prayer. Heavy phone responses caused five legislators to withdraw their support of the bill. Five others who had been absent during the preliminary vote also decided to oppose the measure. The bill's author knew it was futile to even present it again. He threw it on the floor and cursed "those Christians."

But success is not always visible and immediate. Someone once asked me, "Since there is all of this prayer, why is America's drug scene, abortions, pornography, child abuse, and so on getting worse?" My answer was, "What would America be like by now if we hadn't had all that prayer?" I shudder to think!

Telephone prayer chains have no power in themselves, but they enable many people to pray simultaneously and immediately for a need without having to wait for mailed prayer lists or group prayer meetings.

Another use of the telephone for prayer is **Conference Calls.** I just hung up the phone after praying in a powerful prayer session with two others for revival in our nation's capital. Again, the time and effort spent in getting together physically is avoided, and the call is an effective "two or three together" method. A pastor in California told me he spends the first two hours of each day, starting at 5 A.M., in conference calls with his board members, prayer supporters, and even his mother-in-law!

The **Twenty-Four-Hour Prayer Clock** is one of the most powerful forces in our ministry, operating only when I am overseas. Each person signs up for a specific period of time during which they promise to pray daily, and the time of day or night they will pray, thus making an unbroken circle of intercession all the time I am gone.

This prayer clock usually stops praying for me when my plane touches down in Minneapolis–St. Paul. But when I returned from India in the fall of 1983, without telling me, they decided to add two days of prayer to get me through jet lag. After three weeks of an extremely intense schedule, excessive heat, intestinal problems, and conducting the whole National Prayer Assembly without my husband (who had flown home because of severe intestinal problems), I arrived home exhausted. To greet me were two new grandbabies and a son home from graduate school to celebrate his birthday. But, to my amazement, I had no jet lag. Kathy Grant, a twenty-four-hour prayer clock member from Washington, D.C. called me with a startling story: "Evelyn, as I prayed, I actually suffered *with* you in your jet lag."

"No, Kathy," I assured her, "you did not suffer *with* me, you suffered *for* me. I didn't have any jet lag!"

Feeling the Power
I learned quite by accident that feeling God's power is one of the experiences of people for whom we pray. Back in 1968, when we

did our "What Happens When Women Pray" experimentation, I interviewed the people for whom we had prayed. Their most common response was, "Oh, I could *feel* you praying." What could they feel? The power of God released through prayer!

The President of the United States, Ronald Reagan, at the annual Presidential Prayer Breakfast held after he had been shot, said to us, "Nancy and I want to thank you for praying. It is true that you can feel and sense that power!"

It was what our United Prayer Ministries board member, Dorothy, felt this weekend after receiving the shocking news that her only son had just been burned to death in Arizona. As I put my arms around her at the memorial service, I told her that we had been praying for her almost constantly. "I know," she said, smiling through her grief. "I could *feel* it. Thanks."

In Adelaide, Australia when those 500 out of 1,000 women prayed aloud, making sure they knew Christ personally, I was so overwhelmed at feeling God's power in that room that I could not speak. I just stood there with tears streaming down my face. A large women's Bible study movement had invited me, and their international president had come down from the Philippines to attend the seminar. Afterward, she said, "When that happened it felt as if a surge of power ran down my back—almost like an electric shock."

Then the local president chimed in, "I felt the same thing. Did you feel it, Evelyn?"

"No," I replied, "I just stood there—unable to speak in the presence of that awesome power." Again, God was able to release His power because of all the prayer.

Power released through prayer was the difference Jeanne, our current board president, reported that she and her surgeon husband, Dr. Bill Scott, felt in Bangladesh. After finishing their missionary work in India, they returned to America where Bill was practicing surgery in a large Minneapolis hospital. Then they went to Bangladesh to complete a hospital in Parbatipur. After returning home, Jeanne told of the difference in what they *felt* from the prayer support of our board, our prayer chains, and other prayer-support groups. Of course, there had been fine missionary support the first time, but this time was different. She told me, "With the increased prayer support, God opened doors in remarkable ways, mobilizing resources and help so that in twenty months a hospital was dedicated and opened, as well as a chapel."

It was God's power released by corporate prayer that I felt in Central Hall, Westminster, London where the first session of the General Assembly of the United Nations took place in 1946. As I mounted the huge marble staircase on the way to the speaker's platform, my back gave way due to a recurring lower back spasm, causing excruciating pain. But I was able to stand and speak all that day with God's strength literally being mine. Later, the president of the British Bible Society, learning of my almost unbelievable experience, said I must have sent word to my prayer chains back in America. "No," I answered, "they already were praying and God knows my needs and how to answer." And He did!

On my first morning in Perth, Australia last March, I wrote in my diary: "Feel great! No jet lag. Woke at 4:30 Perth time. Lord, it's right on *the* dot! It was my usual waking time in America, but Australia is halfway around the world. This was in spite of fifty-three hours from my bed in St. Paul to the bed in Perth—caused by the second-worst snowstorm in our history which hit Minnesota the day I was to leave, the airline going on strike just as I was about to depart, and an eight-hour delay in Los Angeles. Then our pilot on Qantas Airlines quipped while we were still seeing only the Pacific Ocean below us that we were running out of gas (because of an unusually strong headwind), and we would be making an emergency landing in Brisbane. *"This is the strongest I've ever felt the pray-ers."* I underlined in amazement as I continued to write.

This morning in the predawn darkness while reviewing all the corporate prayer offered for me since 1964, my eyes suddenly filled with tears—tears of thanksgiving—as I realized the magnitude of all this combined prayer for me. My heart just exploded with thanks to God for the indescribable privilege of all those years of unbroken prayer support by so many.

I repeated in my mind the thanks I wrote to my pray-ers after I returned from the seminar series in England: "You also join in helping us through your prayers, that thanks may be given by many persons on our behalf for the favor bestowed upon us through *the prayers of many"* (2 Cor. 1:11, NASB, emphasis mine). And I, with Paul, "do not cease giving thanks for you, while making mention of you in *my* prayers" (Eph. 1:16, NASB, emphasis mine). At the beginning of my prayer ministry, our then high schooler son, Kurt, said to me, "How can you miss, Mom, with all that prayer?" How very true, Kurt!

Above All That We Ask or Think
What Jeremiah said in the Old Testament of God showing us "things . . . thou knowest not" (Jer. 33:3), Paul said in the New Testament with his "above all that we ask or think" (Eph. 3:20).

No matter how much I expect from God, He always gives more. No matter how much faith I have, I never seem to have enough to equal the fabulous amount of whatever God is ready, willing, and anxious to do—when there is enough prayer. God's intention is to exceed by His answer even the far-reaching petitions of His pray-ers and the aspirations that prompted them.

While doing the first arm of "Mission: England" in 1983, one of my privileges was to sign up people for "triplets." In this method, three Christians each choose three people who do not know Christ and then promise to get together weekly to pray for those nine people until they find Christ as their Savior. Altogether, 30,000 Christians signed up for the triplet groups prior to Billy Graham's six crusades comprising "Mission: England." These were in addition to the people in seventy-five countries who signed up to pray for his "Mission: England." And the outcome was phenomenal! Billy Graham reports that he had by far the greatest results in people finding Christ of any other crusade in his history. George Wilson, executive vice-president of the Billy Graham Evangelistic Association, excitedly reporting this to us, said, "And, Evelyn, we know why, don't we? It was all that prayer!" Yes, the prayers of all those dear people in England, who, in turn, had been prayed for by us as they signed up and prayed.

The Lausanne Committee for World Evangelization, sponsoring our first International Prayer Assembly in Seoul, Korea in 1985, was anxious for us to emphasize Pentecost Sunday and scheduled the assembly to include this date. As head of the women's workshops, I had prayed repeatedly for six months, "Oh,

God, send something of Pentecost to us at this Assembly." (Occasionally, while praying, I smilingly wondered, *If God would really decide to send some of what happened at Pentecost, how many of our international participants would flee for home? Were we really ready for that?*)

The women's workshops met in the sanctuary of the Young Nak Church with simultaneous translators for each language being broadcast in booths. The people listened in their own language over their own radios with earphones; but, the first day, we did not have a Chinese translator along with the others. One of the reporters interviewing participants after each session was an American missionary who spoke fluent Chinese. Asking the Chinese delegation about the session, she was told how meaningful my lessons on the "cleansed life" and "forgiven as we forgive" and the praying afterward had been. "But," the reporter said, "you don't speak English."

"No," was their reply.

"And you didn't have a Chinese translator today," said the missionary.

"Oh," exclaimed the surprised Chinese women, "it must have been the Holy Spirit!"

I certainly had not asked for—nor even thought of—something that close to Pentecost, and I was reluctant to report it until I could validate it. But this had come from Faye Leung, the Chinese woman responsible for my Trans World Radio broadcasts into China, who also speaks fluent English. At dinner in Hong Kong after the Prayer Assembly, I asked Faye's opinion about it. She said, "Oh, that doesn't surprise me at all. I was praying that day with a Chinese woman who, although she doesn't understand a word of English, prayed each prayer you asked us to pray!" I'm sure the pray-ers before Pentecost hadn't asked or thought of what God had sent them either.

Exceeding Abundantly

I have not always expected most of the dramatic answers from God in this prayer ministry. When we started in 1968, I didn't even know if my church women would pray with me; and, if they did, if God would do anything. But now, with God's overwhelming responses, I know! But I also have become painfully aware of all the good things God desires to pour out on Planet Earth, which I limit Him from doing because I do not pray enough.

Over the crib for our grandbabies in our spare bedroom, I have hung a small needlepoint wallhanging. It says, "Prayer IS the answer!"

Dr. Paul Yonggi Cho, pastor of a now 500,000-member church in Seoul, Korea, said to us while explaining the power for that kind of church growth, "Americans stay after church and eat. We stay after church and pray." I mentioned this at a recent pastors' conference. We then went to prayer, and one pastor blurted out, "Oh, God, I don't pray enough. Forgive my lack of prayer—my personal prayer, prayer with my family, prayer for my church. Oh, God, forgive me!" Surprisingly, almost no American seminaries teach for credit the subject of prayer and its power. But prayer is the key that unlocks God's omnipotent throne room.

In Ephesians 3:20, Paul gives us a tremendous look into God's mind. And I have found that life bathed in, saturated by, and directed through prayer has been exhilarating and exciting. I feel as if I'm continuously standing on tiptoe, straining to peer into God's mind, wondering how and what He is going to do this time. Yes, I have learned about His "exceeding abundantly above all that [any of us could] ask or think" when we prayed.

Capable, yes. And able too—when there is enough prayer! How much power is God releasing because of *your* prayers? Then again, how much power is God waiting for you to unlock with your key of prayer?

Closing Prayer

Oh, God, I confess that there is not enough prayer in my life. Father, You are not able to do many of the things You desire to do here on Earth because of my lack of praying. I long to see Your exceeding, abundant answers over and above anything I could ask or think. Lord, I commit myself to spend more time in prayer daily. Help me to discipline myself to more actual praying.

In Jesus' name, **Amen.**

3
When God answers...

You Prayed the Wrong Prayer

That God *will not* answer prayer under certain conditions is just as clearly taught in the Bible as is the fact that He *will* answer the prayers of His children at other times. Even though they had prayed, James said: "Ye ask and do not receive, because ye ask amiss, to consume it upon your lusts" (see James 4:3).

There are two kinds of prayer to which God answers, "You prayed the wrong prayer." First, there is the prayer that asks for the wrong thing—which God in His holiness never would grant. But then, there is the prayer to which God would have answered yes, except that it was for the wrong reason.

Wrong Motives

The reason God sometimes answers no to our prayers is that we prayed with the wrong *motives*. Although the things for which we ask may be good in themselves, we want them for the wrong reasons. So, even though we do ask, we do not receive.

Motives are the *reasons* for praying as we do. The reason for praying for a certain thing can in itself make it a "wrong prayer." What are wrong prayers? Those prayed to *"consume them upon our lusts."*

The word *lusts* in James 4:3 has been translated more recently as "pleasures," and accurately so. But to us today, the word *pleasures* basically means something that is good and positive. Then there are things that are good for Christians that also are translated "pleasures" in the Bible. However, this particular biblical word *pleasures* always is negative and off-limits for Christians.

The literal definition of the Greek word translated "pleasures" in James 4:3 is, "The gratification of natural desire or sinful desires." This word is much better understood today when translated "lusts."

The word, of course, is much broader in meaning than just sexual lusts. How shocking to realize that the prayers we ourselves are praying frequently are prayed with a wrong motive — to consume upon our lusts. And God must answer, "You prayed the wrong prayer."

Here are some of the common, everyday motives that creep into our praying: praise, fame, love of power, love of display, love of preeminence, status over others, ease, comfort, personal satisfaction, self-pleasing, self-vindication, gratification of sinful desires, and revenge.

While most of us are careful basically to pray for things we believe are good and which God wants to grant us, we usually are completely unaware of the wrong motives that can be inspiring these prayers. And praying with wrong motives for things to which God usually answers yes spells failure in prayer.

For Whose Glory?

Wanting something for our own glory, not God's, is one reason why a prayer, although scripturally accurate and acceptable to God, is ruined by our reason for praying it.

I am astounded in my ministry at some of the motives that surface when people or groups are praying about having a prayer seminar. Several years ago, I had a severe leg problem and my doctor insisted that I miss a scheduled prayer seminar on the West Coast and stay in bed another week. But then at the end of that week, he decided I was well enough to travel, so I could conduct the seminar in a city near the one where the seminar had been canceled. I received a phone call from the very irate pastor of the church I missed; he was absolutely furious with me for not appearing in *his* church and then having all those people come to his competitor's church the next week.

I wondered what his reason really had been for wanting my seminar. Was it actually to teach people to pray? Was it really to bind the different churches together in unity? Or was it to attract people from all denominations of the area into *his* church? Was it basically to bring glory to *his* church—and to *him?* Although praying to have a seminar to teach people to pray certainly is a good prayer, the motive can be so wrong. And God answers, "You prayed the wrong prayer."

In 1979, as I prayed my birthday prayer for the coming year, my words simply were these: "God, You be glorified, not me!" And when the year ended, my praying for only His glory did not end. Praying the "right prayer" about God getting all the glory has been a learning process for me for a long time.

Through the years, I have prayed before speaking that I will not be seen as I speak—only Jesus. After the sometimes flowery introduction is all over, I pray that what I am wearing, my hair-do, and so on will all fade from the audience's consciousness and be replaced by Jesus. The greatest compliment I ever receive is when someone steps up to me and quietly says, "I saw Jesus standing there instead of you all day today." For *His* glory!

Also, before a seminar, I always pray, "Lord, remove every illustration and point that will bring glory to me instead of You." The illustration or point may be very good in itself, but if my motive for bringing it is for *my* glory, God will not use it to move in the lives of those in my audience. It has to be for His glory.

We can even have the wrong motive in praying to win others to Christ. For whose glory do we want to bear spiritual fruit? Jesus in John 15:7-8 tells us that if we fulfill His conditions, we shall ask what we will and it shall be done unto us. But why? So that we can be glorified? Oh, no. It is so that we can bear much fruit—not for our glory but for the Father's. Are we trying to win another to Jesus to get credit ourselves? For whose glory?

A subtle motive of our receiving the glory instead of God slips in when we have discovered something exciting and shared it with someone, only to have that person come out with it later in a discussion, in a sermon, or in a book! How it hurts when another gets the credit instead of us. But then we must examine the reason for feeling this way. God can get a lot done if we don't care who gets the credit—and the glory!

To Consume It on Our Lust of Pride

So many of our prayers are prayed with another wrong motive: *to be seen by people,* not God—so we will get the credit and glory.

But Jesus, in Matthew 6:5, said our motive for praying is not to be as that of the hypocrites standing in the synagogues and on the street corners "in order to be seen by men" (NASB). This is a wrong motive; no matter how good the content of these prayers might be, the Lord is displeased.

This is the lust of display—one of the major reasons we ask and have not because we are asking to consume it upon this lust. How proud we can become by being known as "one who never skips a prayer meeting" or "one who prays such beautiful prayers in public." Things good in themselves but done with the wrong motive. The lust of pride! God told Solomon that it was only when His people would *humble themselves* and pray" that He would answer and "heal their land" (2 Chron. 7:14, NASB, emphasis mine).

There also can be the motive of pride in our private devotional praying. I find that I must be constantly on the alert for wrong motives in my own prayer life, and usually, I am surprised when they surface.

While our Kurt was taking his entrance exams for a doctoral program in physics, I spent the three hours in prayer. Not knowing how to pray for three whole hours on the same subject, I asked God to teach me. One of the amazing things He showed me was that, although I sincerely was praying for God's will, some of my motives for wanting Kurt to pass those tests were wrong. It was God waving His yellow caution flag, "Watch it!"

Creeping into what I thought were only pure motives about God's will for my son's future was a wrong motive—pride. I found myself praying a seemingly normal, motherly prayer: "Oh, God, what if Kurt's cousin Paul passes his tests and gets into his biomedical engineering program and our son flunks?" God's rebuke set me praying for forgiveness for the wrong motive in my praying.

Four years later, I found it much easier to heed God's yellow caution flag. I was deeply in prayer as Kurt feverishly wrote to get a report of a discovery of his published before a "competitor" in another university. He had been told inadvertently what Kurt was doing, and if he published before Kurt, he would receive the credit for Kurt's discovery. As I prayed, I suddenly became aware that God was waving His caution flag. Immediately, I changed my prayer to, "Oh, God, You know who deserves to get the credit for this discovery. You know what Kurt's needs are—and also what he deserves."

In the whole section of James 4:1-3, one of the reasons for not receiving is that "you are envious" (v. 2, NASB). We always want immediate success, victory, and credit when praying for someone we love, but our motives can be to consume it upon our own lust—our pride.

James 4:6 tells us that "God is opposed to the proud" (NASB), so He certainly won't grant our requests that are prayed to be consumed on our lust of pride. A wrong motive makes it a wrong prayer—which, of course, God won't answer.

Your Kingdom, Not Mine

How many Christian leaders are building their own kingdoms, not God's? Here again, what they are praying for may be good and scriptural—a growing congregation, a larger church building, better headquarters for their organization or campus—but their *reason* for praying is for praise, fame, and glory for themselves.

But Jesus in His model prayer in Matthew 6, as He taught His followers to pray, was very explicit about whose kingdom must be built: "Our Father . . . *Thy* kingdom come . . . On Earth as it is in heaven" (vv. 9-10, NASB, emphasis mine).

In a large, seemingly successful church in which I held a recent seminar, several members commented sadly to me, "But there is no power." Why? Perhaps it was because their very talented pastor might have been building not the kingdom of God and His glory but his own kingdom and his own reputation.

This love of preeminence, status over others, and building one's own kingdom instead of God's seemed already to be a problem in the first century. In 3 John, the Apostle John said that he needed to expose Diotrephes because he loved to be first among people. Diotrephes refused to acknowledge the Apostle John, lest his own position of authority should be challenged.

We tend to think this wrong motive exists only in the large, splashy ministries; however, in actuality, it may be as true or even more true in the small, struggling churches and organizations. In a desperate attempt to prove their importance in a community or in their denomination, such churches resort to building their own kingdom instead of God's.

It is possible that we are deceiving ourselves, as well as other people, about our motives in prayer—but never God. He is aware of all our hidden attitudes and motives—many times unrecognized even by ourselves.

It is not only our words that ascend to God in prayer but our motives as well. God looks within—and our motives are just as obvious to Him as our spoken words. "And all the churches will know that I am He who searches the minds and hearts" (Rev. 2:23, NASB).

Praying with the wrong motive, then, is praying anything to which God must answer no because, although perhaps good in itself, the reason for praying is "to consume it upon our own lusts."

Asking Amiss

Praying with wrong motives actually is the cause of asking amiss which, of course, is praying wrong prayers.

We like to think that the "to ask amiss" of James 4:3 is just slightly missing the right content in our prayer. However, it means wicked, evil asking. To ask amiss literally means: "*to ask evilly.*" It is praying for the satisfaction of those things that God explicitly calls on the true Christian to suppress. Thus, it is not a prayer than can be answered by God. A prayer that asks amiss must be answered by Him, "You prayed the wrong prayer."

But in John 15:7 (NASB), didn't Jesus promise that we could ask for "*whatever* [we] wish"? And then in this chapter's sixteenth verse, didn't He say that "*whatever* you ask of the Father in My name, He may give to you"? How, then, could anything we pray for be asking amiss and a "wrong prayer"?

Well, Jesus also gave us innumerable rules by which to live; and His promise for answers to our prayers did not, and could not, negate all His rules and commands. Jesus is truth (John 14:6). He cannot lie. How could He teach and demand purity, holiness, and righteousness and then imply in His prayer promises that we could ask for—and receive—just the opposite?

Again, Jesus said in John 14:14, "If you ask Me *anything* in My name, I will do it" (NASB, emphasis mine)—seemingly giving us a blank check to request any amount of anything we choose. However, in His preceding words, He clearly says why He will do whatever we ask in His name—"that the Father may be glorified in the Son" (John 14:13, NASB). So, obviously, Jesus would never promise anything in answer to prayer that would not glorify the Father. And certainly, those things that God calls on us to suppress because they are sin would not be granted—even if prayed "in the name of Jesus."

No—all of our prayers must conform to and adhere to God's rules and laws as set forth for us in the Bible. They must be based on scriptural guidelines. They must be in the confines of God's will as set forth in Scripture. Proverbs 28:9 actually says, "He that turneth away his ear from hearing the law [literally, the Word of God], *even his prayer shall be abomination*" (emphasis mine).

A young wife and mother kept calling me from Hawaii about her husband and his girlfriend. One day, she asked, "Is it all right for me to ask God, if it is His will, to allow my husband to leave me and marry her, because God wants him to be happy?"

"No," I retorted, "don't ever pray that prayer. God's answer to that prayer already is in the Bible. God explicitly said that it is not His will for a marriage to break up." I explained to her that, in Matthew 19:6, God clearly said, "Consequently they are no more two, but one flesh. What therefore God has joined together, let no man separate" (NASB). Then I told her God's words in Malachi 2:16 as He almost thundered, "I hate divorce" (NASB). You do not pray for the fulfillment of your husband's sexual lusts—but for him to suppress them.

Resentment and refusal to submit ourselves to any kind of scripturally required restraint is sin. And praying for things in opposition to what God's Word teaches certainly is "wrong praying."

Here, again, the word *pleasures* in James 4:3 is the same word Jesus used in the Parable of the Soils in Luke 8:14: "The seed which fell among the thorns ... are choked with worries and riches and *pleasures* of this life, and bring no fruit to maturity" (NASB, emphasis mine). Writing to Titus, Paul used the same word: "For we also once were foolish ourselves, disobedient, deceived, enslaved to various lusts and *pleasures*" (Titus 3:3, NASB, emphasis mine). So asking for something that would choke and enslave us certainly is praying "wrong prayers."

Peter put it this way: "Beloved, I urge you as aliens and strangers to abstain from fleshly lusts, which wage war against the soul" (1 Peter 2:11, NASB). Our bodies and minds are the camping ground and battlefield of these lusts. So how could God grant us our wishes when those things for which we pray wage spiritual war within us? Praying for them is grossly "asking amiss."

The history of Christendom reveals many parallels of asking for God's blessing on something evil—slave-traders piously asking God's blessing on their wicked traffic, and Italian outlaws propitiating their patron saint before attacking bands of travelers. Today, how many of us piously lift our voices to the holy God of heaven and then ask for something He calls an abomination?

God never promised, "Delight yourself in your neighbor's wife, and I will give you the desires of your heart." No! The psalmist told us God's way: "Delight yourself *in the Lord;* and He will give you the desires of your heart" (Ps. 37:4, NASB, emphasis mine).

God rebukes us for delighting in the wrong thing. But Paul gives us an example of praying "the right prayer" in his prayer for those in the church at Thessalonica. "To this end also we pray for you always that our God may count you worthy of your calling, *and fulfill every desire for goodness and the work of faith with power;* in order that the name of our Lord Jesus may be glorified in you, and you in Him, according to the grace of our God and the Lord Jesus Christ" (2 Thes. 1:11-12, NASB, emphasis mine).

Every prayer, in order to be the "right prayer" which can be answered by God, must pass the test of His omniscience, His sovereignty, and His holiness.

Good—but Still Wrong—Prayers

There are many other prayers to which God must also answer, "You prayed the wrong prayer." They are not evil in themselves at all or even petitioned with a wrong motive. In fact, they are just the opposite. The pray-er may be sincerely seeking to do what is scriptural and what seems to be God's will. To these pray-ers, God *lovingly* must say, "You prayed the wrong prayer." It seems as if He kindly is saying, "Thanks anyway, but. . . ."

" 'For My thoughts are not your thoughts, neither are your ways My ways,' declares the Lord. 'For *as* the heavens are higher than the earth, so are My ways higher than your ways, and My thoughts than your thoughts' " (Isa. 55:8-9, NASB). These are not evil prayers—but God knows something we don't.

You Are Not Ready Yet

God tenderly must explain to us at times that "your timing is not My timing." In our zeal, we often get ahead of God's timing for us. Not that the prayer in itself isn't good—it just may not be for us at that time. This reponse from God to prayer, of course, seems like a no answer. And God may or may not explain at the time that it is just a "Wait, I have more to do *in* you before I can answer yes."

This answer to my call to foreign missions at the end of our schooling was an especially hard one for me to handle. After I had prayed, submitting my whole life to God's will, I was sure God was giving this call—to which I had answered in prayer a deep, final yes. But then I thought God had decisively slammed shut the door to foreign missions once and for all.

I was absolutely devastated when our denomination's Foreign Mission Board's examining doctor decided that Chris' war-related ulcers would not allow him to serve where finding milk and cream could be a problem—the standard treatment for ulcers in those days. At the next foreign missions commissioning service, I sobbed as all the others went off—except us. In fact, for several years, I avoided that part of our denomination's annual meeting, for I could not face the hurt and bitterness in my soul when God's call to India had seemed so definite.

Chris had been a World War II bomber pilot and, in a burning B-17 plane over Germany, had promised God that if He would bring him safely to neutral territory he would serve Him the rest of his life. He even instructed pilots in the early Missionary Aviation Fellowship program. Then at the end of the preparation years at college and seminary, together we accepted God's call to foreign missions in Assam, India. Chris was to be the first flying evangelist in that country, and we were ecstatic.

However, being the secretary to our college president for four years hardly had prepared me for the mission field. Even the difficult war years, three miscarriages, and other family tragedies hardly had either. And certainly, a liberal arts college education hadn't done all that much. But nobody had seemed very concerned about what I would do once I got there. So I was as excited and committed as any missionary candidate could be.

But God's door to India for us stayed tightly shut for thirty whole years. However, God's answer really was not no but just His *"I have much preparing to do in you."* And the steps of preparation have been long and slow. But in 1982, Chris and I finally went to India.

As I was speaking for the first time in New Delhi, I was so choked up that I could hardly speak. Tears kept filling my eyes as I told these women of my devastating disappointment in 1952—and now my overwhelming joy thirty years later.

Our omniscient God has reasons for His timing in fulfilling calls. I'm sure He knew I was not ready to go to India in 1952. But these thirty years have prepared me through eighteen years in my husband's pastorates, the "What Happens When Women Pray" experimenting, my books, tapes, and the privilege of personally training hundreds of thousands to pray in seminars in the United States, Canada, and overseas.

As we did leave for India, included in the Scripture our Jan gave us were these words about God's sovereign timing from Psalm 31:15, *"My times are in thy hand."*

In our impatience, we try to tell God *when* we want our prayers answered. But how good God is to control the timing of His answers to our prayers. However, our prayers do start a process in our lives that prepares us for the answer—only to emerge years later as the answer to what we desired so long before.

Is the World Ready?

It is also possible that God knows that not only are we not ready, but the world is not yet ready for what He has called us to do. For years before the printing of my book, *What Happens When Women Pray,* people at my prayer retreats and seminars would say that they thought the ideas about what produces power in prayer should be in print. "If you think so," I would always answer, "then you pray about it."

But when God did say, almost miraculously, "Write it!" I realized that something new was happening in our country. There was a turning of Christians to a dependence on God not known for many years. We had been an "I can do it myself, God" generation. But Watergate had humbled us, and we became "the ugly Americans" in many places overseas. Christians were ready and yes, eager to learn more about prayer. I believe that had the book been published sooner it would not have sold as many copies. But when it did come out, people were ready to pray. God's timing, not mine!

I have learned that God's timing is not my timing in the big and little things about which I pray. Sometimes God keeps me persisting in prayer, becoming more fervent in my wrestling with Him, through days, months, and even years. And then there are times when I know He is directing me to release the request back to Him after praying, and I just wait for His answer to come— when He decides it is time to send it.

But He always answers. In my life, there are what I call "answer times," which come suddenly—when God knows it is time, and multiple answers just start flowing. And I struggle to grasp them all, like feverishly plucking dandelion seeds scattering in the wind.

You Are Not Spiritually Ready to Handle That

God is too loving to answer our prayers before we are spiritually mature enough to handle them. Many times, He must withhold the answers He wants to give us because He knows we have not matured enough spiritually. Then, He answers our prayer with "I love you too much to give you that."

Our Jan had six-hour microsurgery at the Mayo Clinic to enable her to become pregnant with her first child, our little granddaughter, Jennifer. Last fall, Jan and Skip felt God was telling them it was time to have another child; but tests showed the surgery would have to be repeated if there was to be any chance of pregnancy. Jan was more than willing, but we all shuddered at such a high price to pay for little ones.

So for months we literally bombarded heaven with a barrage of prayers for God to perform a miracle. There was no lack of faith that the God who created Jan could perform what was humanly impossible—but so simple for Him. As the time drew near for her last date to become pregnant before the scheduled surgery, I felt almost a little tingly in my whole being as I was anticipating God's answer.

But then I questioned whether my attitude might not be from God at all and earnestly sought His face. Suddenly, I admitted to myself that I was not in condition spiritually for what He might answer. If the last chance for Jan to become pregnant passed, how disappointed would I be? Could I handle it? Was it really God speaking? If not, who? "Oh, God," I cried, "prepare *me* for Your answer!"

Then I wondered, "What if He does answer by giving a baby without surgery?" How would I handle that? Would I remember all the prayer? Would I be able to give *Him* all the glory? What would I become if I received the answer I wanted? Would it do me harm? "Lord, *am I ready* for Your answer? Oh, God, prepare *me!*"

Then came the phone call from Jan that her last possible test before surgery was negative. I cried. "Lord, which one, or ones, of us was not prepared for Your miracle? Was it I? Which one of us would not have given You all the glory? Which one would have thought it was *our* power in prayer rather than *Your* power in answering? Which one would have become arrogant or prideful at our special place in Your plans? Which one, or ones, of us did not deserve a miracle? All of us?"

The motive of spiritual superiority is a lust covered in James 4:3. What would we have done with a miraculous answer of "no surgery necessary for this pregnancy"? And what would it have done to us?

God will never bestow upon us anything above our capacity to receive and exercise, even when we ask in prayer. He will do as much *for* us and *through* us as we have let Him do *in* us.

Alone in the house after Jan's call, I spent most of the day in contemplative prayer. "My God, my heart is weeping—and so are my eyes. Oh, God, prepare me for Your answers to all my prayers that You are just waiting to give!"

In a letter from Tasmania, Australia, a Christian woman wrote, "I had to go to hospital for an operation. I had prayer for healing a month before that, but the operation was still necessary. I can now see why. The Lord had a lot to teach me, the first thing being trust—and it had to be complete trust. The next thing was joy in my circumstances. While I was in hospital, the Lord gave me peace and joy and many prayers to pray for others in my ward—and then to see those prayers answered in front of my own eyes!"

No, God's love will never bestow anything on us above our spiritual capacity to handle it—even when we ask in prayer.

"My Purpose, Not Yours"

There are also times when God must answer, "You prayed the wrong prayer," because His purpose for our lives is not the same as ours might be—even though our purpose in itself may not be wrong.

In Bristol, England in May 1983, God had to jog my memory that my feelings and the purpose for which He had called me might not be the same. My husband had become ill the first days of my "Mission: England" seminar tour in the British Isles. The day after he left to return to America, I did some deep heart-searching in prayer about completing that five-week mission.

From the time I was twenty-three years of age, my philosophy of life had been based on Romans 8:28 that "all things work together for good to them that love God, to them who are the called according to *His* purpose."

I struggled long in agonizing prayer for an answer. True, Chris had returned to the home of our daughter, Jan, and her husband, both physicians, and our other daughter and Chris' brother, also a doctor, were in the same city. But what was my first responsibility—as a wife or as a servant of God? I felt as if I was being torn in two parts: half of me longing to go home with him, and the other half facing my responsibility to the thousands who had signed up for seminars in the first arm of "Mission: England."

Then God gently directed me back to Romans 8:28, and I turned to read it once again in my Bible. But this time, God's emphasis was not on the usual, "all things" or "good" or "who love Him," but was reinforcing that He had called me "according to *His* purpose," not mine.

Since 1968, my "Lord, change me" prayer has been, "Lord, make me the *wife* You want me to be." And through the years, I have tried to live this prayer. But as I agonized over it once again, God gently changed the emphasis to a different word. It then was, "Lord, make me the wife *You* want me to be."

His purpose? Tossing to and fro with the wind as the circum-

stances fluctuate? Oh, no. God always had known what His purpose would be for me for different times of my life. As the writer
of the Book of Hebrews explained in 6:17, "the unchangeableness
of His purpose" (NASB).

Our deep prayer of submission is always what God expects
when He has called us "according to His purpose." While I was
reading Galatians 5 in a "Lord, Change Me" seminar in Stockton,
California, God stopped me at verse 17, "For the flesh sets its
desire against the Spirit, and the Spirit against the flesh; for these
are in opposition to one another, so that you may not do the
things that *you* please" (NASB, emphasis mine).

After reading this, my submission prayer to God, the Author of
these words, was, "Lord, I see that I cannot do the things that *I*
please. Whatever the next steps are, they are Your decision, not
mine." "Lord," I continued praying, "I submit to *all* You please! I
do not hold back because of a chance of being misunderstood. I
want what You want only. No more. But, oh, God, *no less*. I love
You, Lord!"

Jeremiah said it so well in 29:11, " 'For I know the plans that *I*
have for you,' " declares the Lord, 'plans for welfare and not for
calamity to give you a future and a hope' " (NASB). His purpose,
not mine! And I stayed to complete my mission.

"That Is Not for You"

At times we may pray for something good and even scriptural
that God has decided is not for us. For other people perhaps—
but not for us. And our persistence in this prayer does no good
for this can be one of God's "you prayed the wrong prayer"
answers.

While in my thirties, I prayed repeatedly for the "gift of administration," which, of course, is one of the gifts mentioned in
1 Corinthians 12:28 in the list of spiritual gifts. I had watched my
husband's secretary, Carolyn Carlson, with her tremendous gift
of administration and longed for it too. I kept thinking of all the
wonderful things I could organize for God—if He just would
give me the gift of administration.

So I begged and pleaded with God to give me this gift. But this
was the wrong prayer—God never gave me the gift of administration. However, it was not until I finally realized that God

withholds gifts just as deliberately as He gives them that I realized He knew what He was doing, and I accepted His no answer.

But this was not God being mean and withholding a good scriptural gift. It was God answering me that He had called me "according to His purpose" and not according to what I thought I should be and do. God knew that I would have just twenty-four hours each day, and He had decided before the foundation of the world how He wanted me to spend them. I had been praying the wrong prayer.

I still occasionally wish I had that wonderful gift, but God's plan for me from the beginning was that I should study and teach, not spend time organizing everybody and everything.

So, praying for a gift God absolutely did not intend for me to have was spending all that time praying the wrong prayer. And through the years, He graciously has provided my Sally, whose gift *is* that wonderful gift of administration, to run my ministry while I do those things He *did* equip me to do.

"Not for Them Either"
Another time God answers "that is not for you" is when He firmly and with finality says, "That is not for you—but only for My children." Without having accepted Christ, many people are praying for the things God has promised only to His children. If people do not know Christ as Savior and Lord, there is no promise in the New Testament that God will grant them their wishes.

The promises of God's peace, that He will work all things together for their good, and give His direction in their lives—and His joy, strength, and grace—are not mentioned any place in the Bible as being for those outside the body of Christ. God did not give these promises to those who have rejected His Son, Jesus, and thus do not have Him as their Savior and Lord.

"My Will, Not Yours"
Sometimes, we try to thwart God's will by the prayers we pray. But God then answers, "You are praying the wrong prayer." We must never forget that God is sovereign.

A pastor's wife told me that her husband was so enamored with his mistress (a woman in their church) that he always walked the long way to and from church just to walk by her house. Living in this sin and guilt, he was on the verge of an emotional collapse. But his wife told me she was trying to protect him from God's wrath and was continually praying: "Oh, God, he's so close to a nervous breakdown—don't convict him of his sin. He won't be able to handle it. He'll collapse emotionally."

"What a desperately wrong prayer to pray," I told her. "The only hope for your husband is for God to show him that what he is doing is a grievous sin—and then to so convict him that he will repent, straighten out, and turn from his wicked ways."

God's will is never to coddle a sinner and just ignore the sin because we ask Him to. No, this is praying strictly against His will—and praying the wrong prayer.

Then there are those times when what we are praying for really is God's will too, but His overriding rule is that He has given each person on Earth a free will and will not coerce them. Woo them, yes. Coerce them, no.

A wife, whose husband had abandoned her, had asked God to send him back home by Christmas. But she called the day after Christmas and just yelled over the phone at me, "I'm so angry at God! I even screamed at Him. I just asked Him to send my husband home by Christmas. All I wanted was one little miracle." Spewing out her venomous feelings, she shouted, "I just told God I hated Him because He is capable of performing this miracle and bringing my husband back—but He didn't! God is able to do it—but He won't!"

"Don't be angry with God," I replied. "Of course, He is able. But God also has given everyone, including your husband, a free will. God's will is definitely for your husband to come back to his family. Your husband knows that is right too, but if he absolutely refuses to do it, God will still allow him his freedom of choice.

"But," I assured her, "God will woo and work on your husband in proportion to your praying. However, don't blame God for your husband's rebellion. That is praying the wrong prayer."

When another woman shared her story with me at a weekend "Lord, Change Me" retreat, I questioned whether her praying "to be single and serve the Lord full time" was a right prayer. "I came here today to get out of the house. I've been married eighteen years to an unsaved, unfaithful, critical husband whom I'm in the process of planning to divorce," she said.

"My sixteen-year-old daughter has run away five times and has torn our family apart. She's done drugs since the sixth grade," she continued. "I have a thirteen-year-old girl and a five-year-old girl. I'm thirty-nine, have been saved since age seven, and have been a good, godly wife and mother. I want to be single and serve the Lord full time. I know God will guide and direct me. Plese pray for me."

Where did God really want her to "serve Him full time"? What was His will about her being a mother to those children? I asked her if she had considered these aspects. Her no answer made me see—she had been praying the wrong prayer.

We must be careful not to pray these wrong prayers, for the outcome may not be as great as we expected it to be. The Bible tells us that God sometimes actually will give us our request, but it will not be with His blessing, but with His judgment. When the Children of Israel left Egypt and journeyed to the Promised Land, Psalm 106:14-15 tells us that they "lusted exceedingly in the wilderness, and tempted God in the desert. And He gave them their request; but sent leanness into their soul."

But at the same retreat, a young, abused wife for whom we had been praying in our prayer chains in Minnesota told me a different story. "My husband who has been abusing me has now left our child and me—and I don't want him back. It's so much better this way!"

Of course, God's will is for these marriage partners to be reunited. But only He knows if her prayers that he not come back—at least not until he changes his lifestyle—are wrong.

However, there is one prayer that never is "the wrong prayer." When we pray what Jesus taught us to pray in His model Lord's Prayer, it always is the "right prayer." And this prayer is, "Our Father. . . . *Thy* will be done" (Matt. 6:9-10).

How can we be sure we are not "praying the wrong prayer"? First, we must stay in the Bible to become aware of what is right and what is wrong in God's eyes. This will enable us to identify those prayer requests that are innately evil in themselves. Then, after praying a request, we wait in God's presence, letting Him examine our motives for praying what we did. And God will bring these wrong motives to our minds and guard us from praying "wrong prayers."

Then God never will have to rebuke us with "You prayed the wrong prayer!"

Closing Prayer

Dear Father, show me the wrong prayers I have been praying. Please forgive me for not reading the Bible enough to find Your right things for which I ought to pray. And please search my heart for my wrong motives in even the good things I pray for. Cleanse me, O God, from all evil desires.

In Jesus' name, **Amen.**

4

When God answers...

I Prerecorded That Answer

God frequently answers our prayer inquiries with, "I already told you that." Then He adds, "I prerecorded that answer for you!" How? Where? In the Bible. God has prerecorded in His Holy Word most of the instructions we will ever need in our whole lifetime. Then He leads us to them in direct answer to our prayers.

This is an amazing procedure in which God does not give the answer during our prayer, as He frequently does, but rather leads us to the Scripture that contains the answer to our request. When we pray, asking Him for something specific, He replies with a specific prerecorded answer from the Bible.

God communicates with us through the Bible in many different ways. While reading or studying His Word we may or may not know our need, but God does. And He takes the initiative to rebuke, comfort, or instruct us as we are reading. However, this method is different. Being acutely aware of a need or some instruction, we seek His answer in prayer, then God brings to our minds the place where He already has recorded the answer in the Bible.

The Author Is Always Present
Why can we get specific answers from a book whose closing words were written almost 2,000 years ago? Because the Bible is the only book on Planet Earth where the Author is always present while it is being read.

I am always surprised at people's reaction to having the actual author of a book in their midst. Some stand in awe, wondering if they might touch us, while others question if we are really human. Yet, the very God of the universe is present with us every time we read His book. But how few of us treat the Bible that way! How little awe or excitement we display at having its Author, the very God of heaven, actually speaking to us about our personal needs and desires. In fact, many people seem to ignore Him completely while reading and studying the Bible.

Ways God Answers from the Bible

How does God answer us by His Word? There are four basic ways. Sometimes when I've been asking God in prayer for an answer, He just shows me in the portion of Scripture I'm currently reading devotionally. Then there are times when He brings to mind a thought or word that will be a clue as to where I should look. Occasionally, He will remind me of a book of the Bible or a chapter or a place on a page where He has my answer. And, occasionally, I'm startled to find the answer staring at me from the page to which I have randomly turned. Let me illustrate ways in which He has answered from the Bible.

1. It was the night before my first prayer seminar in Japan when *God used where I was reading devotionally* to influence not only me but all my audiences throughout the Japanese prayer seminar tour.

Chiko Templeman was dedicated, winsome, and beautiful, and seemed to be the ideal interpreter for me on this tour. She was an excellent Bible study teacher in Washington, D.C., and had taught my prayer material in Japanese several times. After Chiko and her church raised her expenses, she joined me in Tokyo.

But I suddenly found myself almost panicking the night before my first seminar. Doubts overwhelmed me. Twenty years had passed since Chiko had married an American soldier and moved to the United States. I fretted, "Has the Japanese language so changed in that period of time to make the understanding of her interpreting difficult?" Even worse, I had just been told that the Japanese language was spoken differently in three levels of their society. I agonized, "As the granddaughter of a former Prime Minister of Japan, does she speak only that exclusive formal Japanese which will make our audiences uncomfortable or even unable to grasp what she is saying?"

Almost physically trembling at the thought of being unable to communicate with our Japanese audience, I prayed desperately. I felt as if I were actually shaking on the inside as I begged God for an answer.

Picking up my Bible, I turned to where I was reading devotionally, ready to start Psalm 16. And there it was—verse 8: "Because He is at my right hand, I *will not be shaken*"! (NASB) I relaxed in God's answer. The psalmist's confidence in God became mine.

The next morning as I stood before a huge Japanese audience with Chiko at my left side, I opened with, "You can see only two people on this platform, but actually there are three. Last night, the God of the universe promised me that He would be on my right hand. You cannot see Him, because He is Spirit. But He is here. And He will tell me what to say to you. I will say it in English, then Chiko will say it to you in Japanese." Their response was overwhelming. We were communicating! And never once did we lose rapport that day—or throughout the five-week tour.

At our farewell, our missionary hosts asked how I ever understood the Asian mind like that. I explained that I really had not. It was God's prerecorded answer in Psalm 16:8 that did it when He said that, because He was at my right hand, I should not be shaken.

2. Then there are those times when *God brings words to my mind that direct me to His answer.* However, this method necessitates having spent time in the Bible. Unlike reading devotionally until He speaks, which requires no previous knowledge of the Bible, God can only bring Scriptures to our minds with which we are already acquainted. And the better we know the Bible, the more He can direct us to it for answers.

I learned this lesson vividly in Taiwan. As we flew to southern Taiwan to our second prayer seminar series, I was warned that this was one of Satan's most powerful strongholds in the world. Spirit worship was everywhere. Shrines dotted the fields and were even in the homes of the Christian wives attending our seminar who had pagan husbands. Evil seemed to permeate the very air we breathed. I felt I could almost reach out and touch it.

A great spirit of oppression was on my body and my mind as I spoke the first night. Back in my room, I struggled in prayer for many, many hours. My missionary hostess, who was used to such spiritual battles, fasted and prayed most of the night.

Early the next morning, I implored God for the Scripture that would break this oppression. All He brought to my mind were two words: *Psalms* and *delight*. *Delight* to me meant Psalm 37:4. So I turned to it and read it once again, "Fret not yourself because of evildoers. . . . Delight yourself in the Lord; and He will give you the desires of your heart" (Ps. 37:1, 4, NASB).

"Oh, Lord," I prayed, "my *desire* is that You would break this oppression and pour out Your power on this prayer seminar and on those dear ones living in the midst of this awful oppression of the enemy, Satan." Then I read verse 5, and I had God's method. First, "Commit your way to the Lord." This I had done thoroughly when coming all alone to Taiwan, never having even met anyone from there. Second, "Trust also in Him." "Oh, God," I cried, "I am trusting this morning. You know I am." Then, third, His answer, "And He will do it" (Ps. 37:5, NASB).

I claimed the victory. I recorded in the margin of my Bible, "This morning great power in prayer!!" I thanked Him and praised Him as I prayed. *He* was going to do it. I threw on my robe and, beaming, dashed across the hall to my missionary hostess, and exploded, "It's OK. The victory is here!"

My hostess rose from her knees, her eyes shining. "I know, I know," she exclaimed. God had just given her the *same Scripture*—with the same answer. *He* had broken the oppression. Together, we shed tears of joy, rejoicing over what God was going to do that day—which He did! From that time on, there was not one moment of oppression or lack of great power sweeping through our "What Happens When Women Pray" seminar!

In the times when you do not have within yourself the power to do something God has given you to do, have you learned that His wonderful prerecorded answer is already available to you?

3. *Bringing to my mind a book of the Bible, a chapter, a verse, or a place on the page.* Once in a while, God gives me His prerecorded answer. This is not an everyday experience, but it happens occasionally when I am deeply in prayer, asking God for an answer.

One such instance occurred right after the Presidential Prayer Breakfast on January 31, 1985, in Washington, D.C. I was exhausted from a strenuous schedule, including Prison Fellowship's board meeting and an annual international banquet the night before, and rising for that breakfast with only a few hours of sleep. After the breakfast, I crawled back into my bed at the Washington Hilton, telling myself I deserved to spend time alone in prayer with the Lord for, after all, it was my birthday!

I always wait on the Lord for His specific birthday prayer for me for the coming year, so I lifted my heart to Him and said, "God I really need something for *myself* for this year." I continued praying, "I'm exhausted from digging up all the old hurts to write them in this book. It's bad enough to experience them once, but to live through them over and over to get them written in a book is so hard. Lord, I'm drained emotionally and physically."

Immediately, God brought to my mind the lower left-hand page in my Bible. Then the word *Psalms* and the number 4 came to my mind. I picked up my Bible, and there it was—Psalm 4— starting on the lower left side of the page.

As I read the psalm, there were many promises; but nothing specific came. Then I read it once again, and there it was: Psalm 4:7a. It almost jumped off the page at me. "Thou hast put gladness in my heart." I wrote in my Bible, "Amazing certainty! I felt the heaviness melt away—replaced with actual gladness."

Then I became aware of a big grin on my face and was surprised by a spontaneous, audible laugh. The gladness was there—replacing the misery. And God had given me my 1985 birthday prayer, which He had prepared and prerecorded for me from before the foundation of the world—and presented it to me on my birthday!

4. Then there are those very rare instances where His prerecorded answer is *on the page of the Bible to which I randomly turn.*

It was our daughter Jan's due date for her second baby, and I had been praying for an hour and a half that morning at the cottage about the delivery of her baby. Extensive microsurgery had been required once again to make conception possible, so this day was especially important to all of us. I prayed, claiming the blood of Jesus against Satan in the possibility of the cord being around the baby's neck, lack of oxygen to the brain, our daughter's body, and so on. Then I asked God for the peace and assurance I needed at this critical time.

After praying, I decided to look up a verse of Scripture I needed for the section I was working on in the writing of this book. But as I picked up my Bible and opened it, my eyes immediately fell on a verse. There was no scanning or searching for something appropriate. In fact, I was actually looking for something completely different. But the verse on which my eyes fell was an incredible answer to my morning's prayer. Psalm 22:9, "Yet Thou art He who didst bring me forth from the womb" (NASB).

The thought engulfed me. God's hands would be lifting that little one from the womb to breathe the air of that birthing room. It would be His omnipotent hands, not just the doctor's, that would securely hold that tiny body. It was His sovereign will that would decide on every bit of timing and condition of mother and baby! My heart soared at the security I felt. The assurance!

God had the answer there for me all along, but He had waited to give it to me when I needed it specifically that morning. Also, God guided my thumbs as I opened my Bible. God directed my eyes to fall on that uniquely appropriate verse. God directed my heart to Him instead of the possible problems in that birth. And God lifted my apprehension and turned it into a granitelike faith in Him—with His prerecorded answer to my prayer.

Two weeks later, this same answer also kept me serene and trusting when Jan, with us watching the delivery, suddenly lost one half of her blood. The peace never left. God was in control, engulfing us with His presence in that birthing room at the hospital.

We read in 1 Samuel 3:1 that, when the boy Samuel was ministering to the Lord before Eli, "word from the Lord was rare in those days" (NASB). But today we do not live in a period of such leanness. We have the Word of the Lord all prerecorded and waiting for us to seek answers from it.

Different Tones of Voice

Sometimes I can almost hear the different tones in God's voice when He gives us His prerecorded answers. He doesn't chant in the monotone with which we tend to read the Scripture. Sometimes, He uses a chiding tone with us for not remembering what He has already told us or a scolding tone when we ask, but already know His answer. Then sometimes, it seems as though

He sighs in relief that we have finally asked. Here are some of the many kinds of responses God uses in answering the questions we ask in our prayers.

"Don't insult Me," God declares in an indignant voice when we whine, "God is it all right if I do so and so?" "Father, is it OK if I tell it this way? You know it's just a little white lie." "Could I have just a 'little friendly time' with him or her?" "Is it permissible for me to spend just this one little check without reporting it for taxes?"

Outraged, God answers, "If you have to ask *if,* you already know My answer. Don't insult Me by asking!"

Hebrews 1:1-2 tells us that God had communicated with us in two ways—through the prophets of long ago and then through the manifestation of His Son, Jesus. But since Jesus returned to heaven at His ascension, how does the Father now communicate with us? One way is by answering our prayers. And a large percentage of these answers were recorded by "holy men of God" (2 Peter 1:21) for us in the Bible.

So, let us not insult God by asking again when we already know what He has prerecorded for us. These are prayers we do not pray because He already has answered them for us in the Bible.

"I already told you that," God impatiently reminds us when He has prerecorded specific instructions about the matter we are questioning.

People frequently question me about asking God if it is His will that they pray for salvation of another person. God must sigh patiently—or more likely, impatiently—at these prayers as He leads them once again to His prerecorded will in 2 Peter 3:9, telling them that He is not willing for *any* to perish. Or to 1 Timothy 2:1-4 where He tells us that praying for others is good and acceptable in His sight, because He desires *all* to be saved. So His prerecorded answer once again is "I already told you that."

But they also ask another question of God, "God, since it is Your will that none should perish, why don't You answer my prayer and make them accept Christ?" And God replies that He also has a law that He will not break—that every person has been given a free will. He will not allow any person to usurp the inalienable right of every human being—the right of free choice.

Otherwise, Jesus would have declared that every inhabitant in Jerusalem had to be saved; but instead, He wept over them wanting to gather them as a hen gathers her chicks, but they were unwilling (Matt. 23:37).

"So the reason you should pray for them," God replies, "is that I will woo them and move in their lives in proportion to your prayers." It is not enough just to desire the salvation of the lost. Paul not only desired that the lost be saved but prayed to that end, "Brethren, my heart's desire and my prayer to God for them is for *their* salvation" (Rom. 10:1, NASB, emphasis mine).

"Don't blame Me," God frequently retorts when things go wrong in our lives.

I was reading some Scripture passages in Galatians with a person who had sinned grievously in a sexual way and was struggling to work through confessing it. Suddenly, a question burst forth in prayer, "God, are You punishing me?" Together, we read God's prerecorded answer in Galatians 6:7-8, "Do not be deceived, God is not mocked; for whatever a man sows, this he will also reap. For the one who sows to his own flesh shall from the flesh reap corruption" (NASB).

God's answer resounded in our minds with unmistakable clarity, "Don't blame Me. I already told you not to do what you did. I prerecorded My warning of what would happen if you did. But you did it anyway!"

"That's no excuse," God thunders at our whimpering excuse-making. How often we pray, "Oh, God, I didn't know!" and God answers in disgust, "That's no excuse!"

Then He adds, "Especially you theologians, you pastors, you Bible study leaders, You Sunday School teachers, you who read My Bible devotionally, don't feign ignorance! You have the whole Bible in your own language, and I have prerecorded all that information for you." And God reminds us of His recorded warning, "For unto whomsoever much is given, of him shall be much required" (Luke 12:48).

"I didn't change My command just because you live in the twentieth century," God declares, "with its humanism and 'whatever-feels-good-do-it' philosophy creeping into and, yes, almost overgrowing today's Christian church."

Today, one of God's commands that is most distorted is, "Let none deal treacherously against the wife of his youth" (Mal. 2:15).

An acquaintance of ours has had affair after affair because his wife "is getting old and fat." Continuously brainwashed by this concept in every conceivable media, he has asked himself, "What is wrong with being satisfied with younger, firmer flesh?" And, worst of all, his wife is taking all the blame on herself because he has convinced her that she is the guilty one for being this way. But God has not rescinded His command, "Be ye holy; for I am holy" (1 Peter 1:16) just because we live in the twentieth century!

Today, we have the opposite problem of wives out in the marketplace and, as they grow older, associating with men with fresh minds and younger bodies. And this situation can be pleasant to them also. It is therefore just as important for a wife to obey God and not "deal treacherously against the [husband] of [her] youth."

One of the most common complaints I hear from aging wives confirms what a medical doctor told me years ago. "As the husband grows older," he said, "he tends to settle down, pull back from the action, while the wife still feels full of vigor, vision, and plans for the future." But this seemingly common problem does not give her the right to gravitate toward, and be fulfilled by, younger men.

"Enjoy life with the woman whom you love all the days of your fleeting life," says the author of Ecclesiastes (9:9, NASB). Enjoy! Don't stoically "put up with" each other because God commanded it, but in love and fellowship enjoy each other!

"But I promised My peace," God's voice so often consoles me. Frequently, it is not His scolding voice, but it is God's reassuring voice calming and soothing my anxious spirit.

I had just one week to get ready for my first trip to Japan and was frantically trying to get everything done. When I prayed about and shopped for the raincoat and the dress I would need for speaking, God explicitly directed my thinking to a familiar passage in Matthew 6:25. Turning to it, I read again Jesus' words, "For this reason I say to you, do not be anxious for your life, *as to* what you shall eat, or what you shall drink; nor for your body, *as to* what you shall put on. Is not life more than food, and the body than clothing?" (NASB, emphsis added)

I had His answer! Breathing a heartfelt prayer of "Thank You,

Lord!" I relaxed in His prerecorded answer to my anxiety and decided to make my old raincoat do. (It never rained once while I was there.) Then I trusted Him to lead me to just the dress I needed—which He did—almost miraculously.

Recorded in my Bible's margin by Matthew 6:25 are these words, "I awoke early the day before going to Japan with a smile on my face and complete peace in my whole being. Anxious for nothing!"

The next year God reinforced this prerecorded answer to me at the Mukti Ramabai Mission in India. My husband and I had parted the day before at the Bombay Airport, where he boarded a plane to return to America because of illness. As I sat alone outside the mission gate watching the dawn break, apprehension filled my heart as I was praying about being left without him to do all the speaking that week at the National Prayer Assembly of India. The air was filled with the noise of a thousand birds as a pale sliver of moon gave way to the pink dawn.

Again God directed my mind back to that Scripture about anxiety in Matthew 6, and I turned to read it. His answer, "Look at the birds of the air," sharpened my awareness and intensified the cacophony of bird sounds while I continued listening to Jesus. "They do not sow, neither do they reap, nor gather into barns, and *yet* your heavenly Father feeds them. Are *you* not worth much more than they?" (v. 26, NASB, emphasis mine) Oh, yes, He would take care of me! His answers about anxiety had been there all the time. I had even claimed them myriads of times before. But when I needed them again—and asked—God guided me to His prerecorded answer, fresh for that day.

"*Just trust Me,*" came God's reassuring voice after we had prayed many months for our daughter Jan to be able to conceive after ten years of a childless marriage. He guided me to read once again the faith chapter, Hebrews 11. I was surprised as the list of males of faith suddenly changed to a female of faith, "Sarah herself received ability to conceive [literally, the power for the laying down of seed], even beyond the proper time of life, since *she* considered Him faithful who had promised; therefore, also, there was born" (vv. 11-12, NASB).

Therefore, because of their faith, God gave Sarah and her husband, Abraham, a child. God had kept His promise. And to our

Jan, because of her faith and the faith of her husband, Skip, God gave our Jennifer.

"Oh, I have just the advice you need," God said as He gently led me to 2 Corinthians 2:14 the morning of the seminar in London during my second British Isles tour. The night before, the committee had been concerned and prayed much that the peace marchers, who had a reputation for disrupting vocally and lying down in the aisles, had secured tickets for the seminar. Slightly unnerved, all I could pray that morning was, "Oh, God, make me what You want me to *be."*

And His prerecorded answer as I reached for my Bible was, "But thanks be to God, who always leads us in His triumph in Christ, and *manifests through us the sweet aroma of the knowledge of Him in every place"* (2 Cor. 2:14, NASB, emphasis mine).

"Oh, God, please make me just a sweet aroma of Jesus," I cried. And He answered my prayer. There was not one disruption all day, even though all the seats were taken, indicating to us that the peace marchers were there. The sweet aroma of Jesus! Prerecorded for me!

I prayed this same verse before every secular interview of the tour. It was the first leg of "Mission: England," and whole days were filled with interviews by the secular press, radio, and TV. I knew I wasn't smart enough to answer their questions about President Reagan's Central American policy or the nuclear arms race; so before each interview I prayed a simple prayer, "Oh, God, let them see only Jesus in me. Only Jesus!" And He answered. The deep spiritual questions they asked astounded me. Never once did they expect me to solve America's foreign policy.

Not knowing why, our daughter Jan had given me this same verse—because God had given it to her to give me—as I left for that speaking tour. The sweet aroma of Jesus—prerecorded for us both to find!

I struggle to close this section because of the hundreds of illustrations I have to leave out; but here are a few more of the different tones of voice God uses when answering my prayers with His prerecorded answers.

"I knew you were going to hurt," God tenderly answers our anguished cry for help, "so I wrote these tender words of comfort to heal your broken heart." Then He sends us to some of His

prerecorded words, which almost seem to enfold us in His loving arms.

"Let Me explain that," God calmly instructs my befuddled mind with His voice of omniscience. Then He directs me to His prerecorded answer that clears up the puzzle and enlightens my confused mind.

"Speak with My authority," God firmly commanded in June of 1981. It was my first seminar in London, and the night before, a "scary awe" had come over me as I looked over Westminster Hall, where the seminar was to be held for those 2,500 women. A tremendous reluctance swept over me at the thought of my having the audacity to tell these lovely ladies they needed to change.

The next morning, I asked God for His Word for me. While I was reading in Titus 2, He firmly assured me with His prerecorded answer: "These things speak and exhort and reprove with all authority. Let no one disregard you" (v. 15, NASB).

From the time I started teaching, there was no sense of anything but God doing His great work in our midst; and I had indescribable freedom to speak and exhort and reprove all that day because God had assured me of His authority with His prerecorded answer!

"I've just been waiting to share that secret with you," God eagerly answers my searching mind. And then my heart burns within me, as with the two on the Emmaus Road that first Easter (Luke 24:32), while He opens His treasure of wisdom and knowledge and pulls back the curtain on deep and exciting mysteries from His Word—mysteries that have been there since the foundation of the world but are just now mine—because I asked.

"I thought you'd never ask." Of all the ways God answers, this probably is the one He most often repeats. God almost sighs in relief as we finally get around to including Him in our search for advice and instruction. "But why did you wait so long," He sighs wearily, "when I had the prerecorded answers ready for you all along?"

Yes, God's voices in answering me are as varied as my needs, frequently surprising me, but always giving me just what I need or deserve. God is not remote, speaking from somewhere up in the sky, but is always present with me while I turn to His Word for His answers.

Hindrances to Accepting God's Prerecorded Answers

Unfortunately, there are hindrances to receiving God's prerecorded answers which we have built up within ourselves.

Disbelief in the authenticity of the Bible frequently keeps people from believing God's prerecorded answers. Disbelief in the authority of God's Word also can be a stumbling block to accepting His prerecorded answers.

Theological hang-ups can also hinder our acceptance of God's answers to our prayers. Most of us are hemmed in by a theological system either from the denomination into which we were born, the church we chose as an adult, or from gullibly accepting what others have taught us. We have put God in our little theological boxes; and when His answer in the Bible doesn't quite fit our well-worked-out doctrinal system, we have difficulty accepting it.

Rebellion. Even though we agree theologically with God's answer and know we should accept it, many times we rebel against His will for us and are too stubborn to accept His prerecorded answer.

Not applying it personally is also a hindrance to the effectiveness in our lives of God's prerecorded answers. It is far easier to apply that reproof, correction, or instruction to the ones we are teaching, our congregation, or even our mates, children, or acquaintances. But it is only as we are willing to accept His answer for us personally that it can accomplish that which God intended it to do when He recorded it. "Blessed are those who hear the word of God and observe it" (Luke 11:28, NASB).

Interact with the Author

Since God is personally present when we receive His prerecorded answer from the Bible, it is logical that He expects us to interact with Him about what He has said. And since this is the only book in which the author is always present while it is being read, it also is true that this is the only book where a personal interaction with the Author, God, is necessary.

The Bible differs from all other books ever written in that it is alive. Hebrews 4:12 says "The Word of God is quick and powerful and sharper than any two-edged sword . . . and is a discerner of the thoughts and intents of the heart." This is only possible because God Himself, its Author, is active in its convicting, enlightening, and instructing process. Thus, the Bible can be applied practically only through spiritual involvement with God Himself. And this interaction is prayer.

This is not true of any other book. When we obey the traffic rule book and stop our car when the light turns red, there is no personal involvement with the person who at some time decided we "stop on red" and "go on green." Also, with textbooks, it is not necessary to become personally involved with the author in order to put into practice the laws, information, rules, or suggestions he or she is teaching. Learning and using a mathematical formula is not dependent upon a personal relationship with its originator. Not so with the Bible. There must be the reader's spiritual response to the Author to ensure adequate and meaningful application of its precepts.

Three steps are necessary in using God's prerecorded answer effectively: (1) accept it, (2) respond to its Author, and (3) live it. We frequently want to bypass number 2 and resolutely set our jaws and grit our teeth declaring, "I will not," or stoically set out to obey its commands. But it is only when we involve the Author of these rules and instructions that we receive the wisdom, grace, strength, power, and, most important, the desire to apply them.

But one difficulty today is that we are basically teaching our children, Sunday School pupils, Bible study groups, and church members only numbers 1 and 3. We are trying to impose the application of the Bible's laws and rules on others and ourselves without a relationship with and a response to the Author, God.

Then we wonder why God's Word is a seemingly dead set of do's and do nots, why its precepts are compared with the teachings of other books, why we rationalize away its truths in the light of what other books say, and why we test its veracity in the light of other writings.

We must respond personally to God about what He has said to us—asking forgiveness for that specific sin, staying quietly in His presence while He cleanses us, seeing ourselves in contrast to His holiness, imploring Him to make us more like the Jesus He just showed us. Or remaining in silence until we feel the love for which we asked come from Him. Or waiting for His filling with power to accomplish what His answer just directed us to do.

There is no other author who discerns and judges the thoughts and the intents of our hearts and scrutinizes the spiritual, emotional, and intellectual aspects of our lives. Nor do we stand before any other author stripped and bare and fully exposed, with nothing concealed (Heb. 4:13). Thus, no other book consistently and without fail can have prerecorded answers for the immediate and specific needs of the reader, for no other author is actively involved in the inmost and hidden self of the reader.

To be confronted by God's prerecorded answers in the Bible is to be confronted by God Himself.

Closing Prayer

Father, thank You for prerecording most of the answers I shall ever need. Forgive me for neglecting to read the Bible for Your prerecorded answers to my prayers. Teach me to submerge myself in Your prerecorded instructions and commands for me and then to interact with You about them. Lord, I now promise You I will seek, accept, and obey Your prerecorded answers for me.

In Jesus' name, **Amen**

5
When God answers...

You Have Not Fulfilled My Requirements

Have you ever wondered why God answers no to some of your prayers? He may be saying, "You have not fulfilled My requirements. You do not qualify for My answer!" This is the greatest secret of unanswered prayer.

Many Christians sincerely desire to have power in prayer, prayer that produces changed people and circumstances here on Earth, but they are bewildered when nothing happens. They pray earnest, fervent prayers; but God does not seem to answer. However, when His answer is no, He may be saying, "There are some missing qualifiers in your life."

God decreed these "if," "when," and "because" conditions in our lives before the foundation of the world, and His no answer may actually be, "When you do, then I will."

Because You Do, Then I Will

First John 3:22 gives us one of God the Father's basic rules for answering or not answering our prayers. It is the Father's "then":

> And whatsoever we ask, we receive of Him, *because* we keep His commandments, and do those things that are pleasing in His sight.

The Father's approval or disapproval of our actions determines whether or not He will grant our prayer requests. Since both words *keep* and *do* in this verse of Scripture are in the continuous present tense in the Greek, power in prayer is conditioned not by an occasional burst of obedience but by lives that consistently please Him. *Then* He promises that we will receive that for which we ask.

One of the numerous "thens" in Scripture that determines answered prayer is in 2 Chronicles 7:14. God told Solomon that if His people would "humble themselves, pray, seek [His] face, and turn from their wicked ways; *then* [He would] hear from heaven, and [would] forgive their sin, and [would] heal their land." When they did, He would.

David, after his deep sin with Bathsheba, knew and prayed God's *then* principle for the return of fruitfulness in his life. He was aware of the order God required. When he acknowledged his sin, deeply repented, begged God to create in him a clean heart, and asked God to restore the joy of His salvation—only *then* could he again teach transgressors of God's ways and sinners would be converted (Ps. 51).

We seem to be unaware of God's "thens" when we pray. But the Bible clearly tells us that God can answer our prayers only when we have been willing to be and to do what He requires. "When you keep My commandments and do the things which are pleasing in My sight," says the Lord, "only then will you receive that for which you have asked" (see 1 John 3:22).

If You Do, Then I Will

Recently, I have been basing our "What Happens When We Pray" seminars on Jesus' words in John 15:7, in which He gives His two all-inclusive *if* conditions for answered prayer: "If ye abide in Me, and [if] My words abide in you, ye shall ask what ye will, and it shall be done unto you."

These words, "shall be done unto you," contain the most powerful prayer promise in the New Testament, according to G. Campbell Morgan. They actually involve God's creative power, and they are equivalent in power to the account of God's creation of the universe in the Book of Genesis.

In March 1971, as I was studying this verse, I became overwhelmed at the thought of the power Jesus was promising His followers—and us. "Lord, how much power did it take to create the universe?" I prayed. Then my mind boggled as I tried to envision the tiny percentage of the universe we have explored or even measured. And His power had to be greater than the combined power of all He created. I tried in vain to comprehend the power it took to create it by the word of His mouth. I wept as I prayed, "Father, I want that power in prayer." Slowly, I implored, "Teach me—and break me—until I have it!"

This promised power is not a deep, dark, unobtainable mystery available only to a privileged few. It is there for all Christians today. However, Jesus did say that there are conditions for obtaining it. There are things that must be evident in our lives in order for God to answer our prayers.

What are these qualifiers? In John 15:7, Jesus clearly identifies them for us. Jesus' first condition for this prayer power is: "*If* ye abide in Me." Just before He was crucified, He spoke these words to His disciples in His discourse on the vine and the branches. So abiding in Jesus is first being intrinsically, organically connected to Him, the vine. Of course, only true Christians qualify as those who are abiding in Him. And nowhere in the New Testament is there a promise of intercessory prayer power to any but those who are true Christians—who can pray "in the name of Jesus."

In addition, to abide in Jesus is to receive sustenance, strength, and power from Him as branches from a vine. It is resting securely in Him not only when all is going well but also in those dark times when we are being pruned—this is abiding in Jesus.

The second *if* qualifier from Jesus in John 15:7 is "[If] My words abide in you." If we want this prayer power, all His words must abide in us, take up residence in us. And we must obey them and live by them.

What are Jesus' words? First, when Jesus was praying to His Father at the close of His life here on Earth, He told God that He had given to us all the words the Father had given Him (John 17:8). Second, "But the Comforter, which is the Holy [Spirit], whom the Father will send in My name, He shall teach you all things, and bring all things to your remembrance, whatsoever I have said unto you" (John 14:26). These things recalled and taught by the Holy Spirit were written down as the rest of the New Testament. Third, between His resurrection and ascension, Jesus opened the Old Testament to His followers in the light of His life, death, and resurrection. In other words, the Holy Scripture is the word of Jesus.

All of this is summed up in 1 John 3:24: "And the one who *keeps* His commandments abides in Him" (NASB, emphasis mine). It is obedience to all His commandments that proves we are abiding in Him—Jesus' first requirement for prayer power.

A few years ago, I had a too-close-for-comfort brush with someone who, although knowing full well what Jesus' words on infidelity are, certainly was not letting them abide in him, nor was he obeying them.

I learned of this when our son, Kurt, then a college freshman, phoned and with an unusual urgency in his voice asked, "Mom, can you bring the car to me?"

When I pulled up at the college, he got in, slammed the door, and blurted, "Do the prayer chains pray at night, Mom?"

Fearing the worse, I assured him, "They do if you need them. Why? What's wrong?"

"Well, this freshman girl in my class is having an affair with a local pastor. I told her it is wrong, and she has to break it off. Well, she's afraid to go alone. So I'm going to take her to see him and help her."

My heart sank. "Honey," I promised, "the prayer chains *will* pray for you tonight!" Which they did—and his daddy and I—all the time they were gone.

Finally, they came back to our house, and we sat around the kitchen table listening to Kurt's recounting of the evening. Suddenly he said, "I told the pastor, 'She's only a college freshman and may not have known better, but you—you have a theological education. Boy,' " Kurt swung his fist in the air to make his point, " 'I wouldn't want to be in *your* shoes when you meet God!' "

All of the teaching in the Bible on infidelity was being absolutely disregarded by this teacher of the Word. I wonder how many of the pastor's prayers were being answered by God.

In our prayer seminars, we call Jesus' second "if" condition— His words abiding in us—"prerequisites to power in prayer." We include His words about being forgiven, forgiving one another, praying in God's will, making sure it is God to whom we have drawn nigh, personal prayer life of the pray-er, and actual praying of intercessory prayers. I teach all my personal prayer chain, twenty-four-hour clock, and metro prayer chain people these prerequisites either in a seminar or require them to study and apply them from the book, *What Happens When Women Pray*. For without obeying Jesus' words, there is no power in their prayers—and their praying is futile.

Of course, Jesus' words include His declaration in John 3:3 of the necessity of being born again. Without this first step, there is no obedience to Jesus' words, thus no abiding, and thus no power in prayer. Jesus also said, "No man cometh unto the Father, but by Me" (John 14:6). Without this required step, none of the promises in the Bible pertaining to answered prayer apply.

Lord, Is It I?

I was in for a surprise last September at my board's fall kickoff "Lord, Change Me" retreat. As we all sat around sharing our experiences of the latter part of the summer with its struggles, words like *desert, dearth,* and *dry* kept coming up. They expressed exactly the way I had felt in August, even to the point of toying with the idea of giving up my ministry. But I had been unaware of what had caused this unusual response in me.

We began our retreat by taking our Bibles, going apart by ourselves, and each reading the same portion of Scripture silently until God stopped us on a particular thought. As we came together to share what God had said to us individually, all but one board member had been reproved by God's Word (1 Tim. 3:16). Mentioned were sins of commission, omission, attitudes toward a splitting church, and a critical spirit that had crept into my board members' lives which they, weeping, confessed. And I joined my board members, confessing the sin that God had shown me of thinking I had the right to shut Jesus' door on my life as I chose—which I had been thinking about doing that last difficult month.

Just before leaving the retreat early to go to Chattanooga for a seminar, I told them I now understood why the summer had been so difficult for them and me. It was sin in their lives and mine. Not those big "dirty dozen" sins—just those everyday attitudes and actions that had closed heaven's door, and thus its power, to us. In the words of Peter to the Christians of his day, we were reminded that "the eyes of the Lord *are* over the righteous, and his ears *are open* unto their prayers: but the face of the

Lord *is* against them that do evil" (1 Peter 3:12, emphasis mine).

Now, these board members are the main prayer supporters of my ministry. And even if they had prayed for me, God would not have answered—because they weren't fulfilling His condition in Psalm 66:18 that He will not even hear us if we regard iniquity in our hearts.

Once again, we had learned the truth of David's Psalm 24:3-4, "Who may ascend into the hill of the Lord? And who may stand in His holy place? He who has clean hands and a pure heart" (NASB). But because we confessed our failures openly and honestly as sin before God, I went to Chattanooga to minister with great joy, freedom, *and God's power*—while they prayed. Yes, God has His requirements in our lives for prayer power.

At my board's next executive committee meeting, we were struggling with a financial need for our newsletter. We opened with a period of prayer for about an hour and, as each one prayed, the theme seemed to be: Is it *my* attitude, *my* sin, *my* prayerlessness, *my* lack of faith that is keeping You from answering our prayers about our financial need? Lord, is it *I?*

Isaiah clearly explained God's response to the prayers of His people who were living in sin and rebellion: "So when you spread out your hands in prayer, I will hide My eyes from you, yes, even though you multiply prayers, I will not listen. Your hands are full of bloodshed" (Isa. 1:15, NASB).

Are you lacking God's power in your life? Could it be unidentified and unconfessed sin?

The Holy Spirit Thwarted

All three Persons of the Trinity work in accordance with certain principles when answering our prayers. Most of these principles are the qualifiers in our lives, which God expects us to meet.

The Person of the Trinity about whom Paul is writing in Ephesians 3:20 is, of course, God the Holy Spirit. He is working in response to, according to, our praying, but He is only able to work to the extent that we do not hinder Him by the sins in our lives.

According to the Bible, there are ways we can offend the Holy Spirit that will keep our prayers from being answered because, of course, these are all sin.

We can *grieve* the Holy Spirit. As Paul in Ephesians 4:25-32 lists the sins that must be banished from the Christian's life, he says abruptly in the middle of the list, "And do not grieve the Holy Spirit" (v. 30, NASB). Do not cause Him pain, distress, or grief by denying in practice His indwelling, holy presence. This is what we do when we commit this and other sins.

A pastor called one Saturday night and said, "We're studying your book *Lord, Change Me!* and are having a great time learning so much. But," he paused, "I have a question for you. Are you Superwoman? Do you ever have any struggles? Are you perfect?"

Shocked, I explained, "Oh, no! I confess my sins daily! Many times a day! I do strive to be holy, but the more I do the more God shows me my sin."

Every morning before teaching or speaking, I spend as much time as necessary waiting on God in silence after praying, "Search me, O God . . . and see if there be any wicked way in me" (Ps. 139:23-24). This searching is not morbid introspection, but one of the jobs of the Holy Spirit. It gives God a chance to bring to our attention those little attitudes, thoughts, or motives that slip by so easily without our recognizing them.

If I am living with any known sin—pride, wrong attitudes or priorities, or disobedience to where He is sending me—I am going to be ministering in my own strength, and there will be no moving of God's Spirit in power in my seminar. Oh, I can mouth the right words and give the correct illustrations, but the power to move lives isn't there.

In another country, a young evangelist, whose wife is physically handicapped, came to me for prayer. While traveling away from home, he was having a difficult time working with the active young women on his committees. He shared the constant temptation he was experiencing. My answer to him was simply, "You have a tremendously bright future, but there is no way God will play games with you. He will not tolerate sin in your life. And if it is there, He absolutely will not hear and answer your prayers."

Speaking at a Successful Living convention in Canada in 1978, I suddenly felt a lack of God's power. Then I became aware of an attitude in me that was sin. I recorded in my diary, "It is good for me to be aware that I cannot entertain any un-Christlike attitudes and still have the power essential for God's moving in my ministry." The greatest deterrent to my sinning or allowing unconfessed sin in my life is knowing that there will be no power in my ministry. This is my responsibility.

Whenever there has been any lack of His power in a seminar or on my board, my first question always is, "Lord, is it I? Do You mean that the exceeding abundant things I asked You to do, You cannot do because of me?" And He again reminds me that He is able to do only according to the capacity I permit Him by my cleansed lifestyle.

In addition to grieving the Holy Spirit, we also can *quench* Him. In 1 Thessalonians 5:12-22, Paul lists instructions for living for Christians in that day and for us today. In the middle of this list of admonitions, he abruptly states, "Do not quench the Spirit" (v. 19, NASB).

What does it mean to quench? It is to put out a fire. How often I have agonized in prayer before a convention for the Holy Spirit to descend in power, then felt Him beginning to come—only to have someone piously "move the order of the day." And the quenching successfully has taken place. I would go home heartbroken because I so desperately wanted God to set us on fire— with His fire. He tried so many times to answer this prayer, but people just would not let Him.

Or, who of us has not been in a church service when God really started to move, only to have the order of the service proceed as usual—or dismiss on time? The Holy Spirit quenched. And that is sin, which must break God's heart.

Surprisingly, Peter tells us in 1 Peter 3:7, that a husband's prayers can be *hindered* if he does not have the right attitude toward his wife. To hinder means to impede a person by putting an obstacle in his path or breaking up the road in front of him as he travels, detaining him unnecessarily. So a wrong attitude, which in God's eyes is sin, can impede our answers to prayer.

The night before a prayer seminar in Texas, I spent a half hour asking God to bring to my mind every attitude, thought, and action that would hinder His working in the seminar. Then, any attitudes, thoughts, or action against anybody whom I needed to forgive. I then asked for forgiveness from God and forgave those who had sinned against me. I experienced a tremendous sense of being completely clean on the inside!

The next day as I was teaching about keeping our pipeline to God clean so as not to hinder our prayers, I actually felt as if the inside of my "pipeline" was like highly polished mirrorlike metal. Nothing was hindering His power—which was very evident as at least half of the participants prayed aloud making sure that they had a personal relationship with Jesus (including a prominent local pastor). The difference is whether I provide a clear channel—or one with hindering friction.

Yes, the Holy Spirit is a Person, the third Member of the Trinity, who can be quenched, grieved, hindered, vexed, resisted, ignored, blasphemed against, lied to, and offended. Even His work of trying to rescue the sinner can be despised and rejected. And all of these are sins which will stop God's power from working in us through answers to our prayers. This, of course, is just the opposite of being filled with, and walking in, the Spirit.

God's Spirit is sorrowful and sore-troubled at the ignoring, resisting, and despising of His work on the part of those He is trying to rescue from sin and lead into a joyous Christian life. But, amazingly, no matter how hurt He is at our sinning against Him, instead of retaliating or withdrawing, the Holy Spirit constantly reproves and woos us back. How opposite to the way we humans respond to each other when we are offended!

Holiness

If we expect God to answer our prayers, we must meet His requirement of holiness. The Triune God expects this of us. God the Father commands, "Be ye holy; for I am holy" (1 Peter 1:16). Paul writes in Romans 8:29 that we are predestined "to be conformed to the image of His Son"—Jesus, who, although tempted in all things as we are, yet was without sin—to be holy (Heb. 4:15). Then, "Be filled with the [Holy] Spirit" (Eph. 5:18). Holiness is the fundamental attribute of God and His requirement for us.

At a seminar in Perth, Australia, as I sent us all to read Galatians 5 and 6 until God spoke to each of us, I prayed, "Oh, God, give me something very personal—just for me today." And He directed my eyes across the page to Ephesians, chapter 1. There it was—His word for me. "Just as He chose us in Him before the foundation of the world, *that* we should be holy and blameless before Him" (1:4, NASB, emphasis mine). His requirement for me!

Yes, holiness. Anything less in my life is sin. And "if I regard iniquity in my heart, the Lord will not hear me" (Ps. 66:18). So, here is the reason for many of God's seemingly no answers.

"Is it all hopeless?" you ask. Oh, no! Identifying and confessing our sins does produce the holy life that is necessary for God to hear and answer our prayers.

Lists of Sins

Perhaps you have difficulty identifying the things in your life that really are sin. Well, the Bible has the answer for you. The most powerful tool I use in my prayer seminars is a list of twenty-three portions of Scripture which, as with all Scripture, if not obeyed, is sin. I explain that according to James 4:17, "To him [or her] that knoweth to do good, and doeth it not, to him [or her] it is sin."

In my thirteen years of full-time seminar ministry, I have seen a consistent pattern in at least 99 percent of the participants praying aloud in their groups of four, asking God to forgive specific sins. This, by the way, is the first prayer I ask to be prayed aloud; and we estimate that approximately half of those who attend our seminars have never prayed in public before. The secret is the Bible's power to reprove sin (2 Tim. 3:15).

The Bible abounds in the things we should do, but don't, and those things we should not do, but do—thus, we are found guilty of the sins of omission and commission.

Colossians 3:5-9 covers these two categories of sin. The first is the list of things we should not do. And if we do any of them, we sin before God. Take time right now to read them slowly, pausing to consider each sin as it may apply to you personally:

> Therefore consider the members of your earthly body as dead to immorality, impurity, passion, evil desire, and greed, which amounts to idolatry. For it is on account of these things that the wrath of God will come, and in them you also once walked, when you were living in them. But *now* you also, put them all aside: anger, wrath, malice, slander, and abusive speech from your mouth. Do not lie to one

another, since you laid aside the old self with its evil prac-
tices (NASB, emphasis mine).

Then Paul goes on at verse 12 to list those things that we
should do; and, if we fail to do them, we sin:

> And so, as those who have been chosen of God, holy and
> beloved, put on . . . compassion, kindness, humility, gentle-
> ness and patience; bearing with one another, and forgiving
> each other, whoever has a complaint against any one; just
> as the Lord forgave you, so also should you. And beyond all
> these things put on love, which is the perfect bond of unity.
> And let the peace of Christ rule in your hearts, to which
> indeed you were called in one body; and be thankful. Let
> the word of Christ richly dwell within you, with all wisdom
> teaching and admonishing one another with psalms and
> hymns and spiritual songs, singing with thankfulness in
> your hearts to God. And whatever you do in word or deed,
> do all in the name of the Lord Jesus, giving thanks through
> Him to God the Father (Col. 3:12-17, NASB).

Now that we have considered these scriptural requirements,
we are responsible for living up to them. It is awesome to realize
that failing to do any of the above constitutes sin in God's eyes.

Jesus, in Mark 7:21-22, gave to us His very revealing list of
things that come forth from us and defile us. He included: "evil
thoughts and fornications, thefts, murders, adulteries, deeds of
coveting and wickedness, as well as deceit, sensuality, envy, slander, pride and foolishness" (NASB). What a combination of the
"big," blatant sins and the "everyday" sins of the Christian!

Paul gave us an unnervingly specific list of sins in Galatians:

> Now the deeds of the flesh are evident, which are: immoral-
> ity, impurity, sensuality, idolatry, sorcery, enmities, strife,
> jealousy, outbursts of anger, disputes, dissensions, factions,
> envyings, drunkenness, carousings, and things like these, of
> which I forewarn you just as I have forewarned you that
> those who practice such things shall not inherit the king-
> dom of God (Gal. 5:19-21, NASB).

Yes, James 4:17 clearly tells us that now that we know to do good, when we don't do it—to us, it is sin. Not shortcomings. Not personality quirks. Sin!

Did you find your "pet" sin in those verses of Scripture? Was your "secret" sin, or sins, exposed by one of them? *If so, you have one of the reasons for God not answering your prayers—you do not qualify!*

But the great fact is that we don't have to stay in the condition where God answers our prayers with no because there is sin in our lives. The Bible emphatically states that "if we confess our sins, He is faithful and just to forgive us our sins, and to cleanse us from all unrighteousness" (1 John 1:9).

While I was on vacation in 1983, God showed me this tremendous verse, "Therefore, having these promises, beloved, let us cleanse ourselves from all defilement of flesh and spirit, perfecting holiness in the fear of God" (2 Cor. 7:1, NASB).

The required order is God's: identify, admit, confess, ask God to forgive—and forgiveness!

Of course, God has His requirements for our power in prayer. But He also has the answer—forgiveness—when we ask!

Closing Prayer

Father, You seem to be answering no to my prayer requests—or not answering at all. Could it be unidentified and unconfessed sin, or sins, in my life that is keeping You from answering my prayers? Lord, please show me which ones. Oh, God, I do confess all my sins! Please forgive me! Cleanse me!

In Jesus' name, **Amen.**

6

When God answers...

Repent

When we have prayed, "Father, I have sinned," how does God answer us? Does He say, "Now that you have confessed the fact that you have sinned, it will be all right"? Oh, no. God then commands us to "Repent!"

A bewildered wife called me asking for prayer. She said that her husband was sleeping with another woman, then getting up the next morning and asking God to forgive him. He told his wife it was OK because God always forgives us when we ask Him to. "Is this true?" the wife questioned. "Does he have a right as a Christian to live this way?"

"No," I replied, and then shared a part of Romans 6 with her: "Are we to continue in sin that grace might increase? May it never be!" (vv. 1-2) "Therefore do not let sin reign in your mortal body that you should obey its lusts, and do not go on presenting the members of your body to sin as instruments of unrighteousness; but present yourselves to God as those alive from the dead, and your members as instruments of righteousness to God" (vv. 12-13, NASB).

After we have identified a specific sin in our lives as sin and have admitted it to God in prayer, we humans are prone to say to ourselves, "Now, just forget it," or "Oh, that's really not a sin." Or we may say, "You really didn't mean to hurt anybody," or "That's not such a bad sin." But God says, "Repent!"

When we have admitted a sin, God never says, "Oh, that's all right, My child. Let's just forget it now, and you get on with your life." Oh, no. He doesn't say, "That's that," and close the curtain on the whole thing. He expects continued action on both our part and His. Our part in the next act is to repent.

Jesus and Repentance

Why repent? Because Jesus said so—to both Christians and non-Christians.

Jesus had been back in heaven after His ascension for approximately sixty years when He sent messages to His churches on earth to repent. The Apostle John, recording these messages in Revelation 2 and 3, startles us with the force and frequency of Jesus' command, "Repent!"

When the Son of God began His ministry on earth, He proclaimed the same message, "Repent!" He came into Galilee preaching, "The time is fulfilled, and the kingdom of God is at hand: repent ye, and believe the Gospel" (Mark 1:15).

Even His forerunner, John the Baptist, prepared the way for Jesus by calling the religious leaders of the day to repentance. He cried, "Repent ye: for the kingdom of heaven is at hand" (Matt. 3:2).

Jesus, also, seeing sinful men in contrast to His Father's holiness and His own sinlessness, commanded them to repent throughout His earthly ministry. He was so disturbed by the sin He saw on earth that, in His Sermon on the Mount, He actually said it was better to cut off the offending member of our body than for the whole body to perish in hell (Matt. 5:29).

Then, after dying and paying the price for all sin, some of the final words the resurrected Jesus gave to His followers are recorded in Luke 24:46-47, where He admonishes them to keep on preaching repentance to all nations:

> And He said to them, "Thus it is written, that the Christ should suffer and rise again from the dead the third day; and that repentance for forgiveness of sins should be proclaimed in His name to all the nations, beginning at Jerusalem" (NASB).

Then Peter, so fresh from his own repentance, immediately obeyed Jesus' command in his very first sermon, admonishing the nonbelieving men of Israel, "Repent, and let each of you be baptized in the name of Jesus Christ for the forgiveness of your sins" (Acts 2:38, NASB; see also Acts 3:18-19).

So the purpose of Jesus' coming, His preaching, and His death and resurrection was that repentance for forgiveness of sins could be proclaimed in His name to everyone, everywhere. And it is still His concern as He lives back in heaven with His Father.

Right now, Jesus is at the right hand of the Father interceding for us. For what is He praying? Only for our strength, power, grace, and guidance? I think not. For, since He had to send instructions to the young churches to repent, what might He be praying for us today? Is He interceding for me, for you, for our churches—right now—that we will repent?

"What Do You Mean, Repent?"

What is repentance? It is much more than a quick "forgive me" prayer. It involves three things: being truly sorrowful for the sin, actively turning away from that sin, and bringing forth fruit in keeping with repentance.

Being really sorry for the sin is to be absolutely devastated by the thought of it. It was when the men of Israel heard Peter raise his voice and recount their sins that they were "pierced to the heart" and cried out, asking the apostle what to do. Peter's reply was, "Repent!"

True repentance is not being afraid of the consequences of sin, but horrified at the sin itself. In my childhood home, repentance was my own father literally hitting his head against the wall because of what he had done to my mother. After years of being untrue to her when he traveled as a state highway contractor, he finally confessed his sin to her. Why did he confess? Because he saw his sin in contrast to my dear mother's holy life before God. When he came home from his week on the road, he told her he could almost see an angel hovering over her. It was her godlike holiness in contrast to his lustful wickedness that led him to confess—and change his lifestyle.

A Christian leader, who had an affair with his secretary for several years, shared that it had been his wife's constant quest for holiness too that had made his life so unbearable that he finally confessed his sin to her. But rather than confess, at first, he frequently had contemplated suicide and did attempt it, but failed when stopped by the police. Writhing in agony on his bed, he confessed the filthy, lurid details of his sin.

Yes, after acknowledging our sin as sin comes the step of repentance—being horrified and devastated by the sinning and begging God for a clean heart once again.

I have watched this pattern of repentance in thirteen years of "What Happens When We Pray" seminars. The first prerequisite for prayer power in our lives that we study is "no known unconfessed sin in the life of the pray-er." Before we begin our first audible prayer time in small groups, I read a list of commonly practiced sins from the Bible—such as pride, lying, lust, wasting time, bitterness, money as our god, corrupt communication, and being a fake. As the Holy Spirit convicts us through God's Word, there almost always is deep repentance, with all confessing and many weeping. Frequently, this prayer of repentance goes on far into our scheduled morning break time.

Although seeing our sin may make us uncomfortable or even embarrassed, Paul tells us that this process is good for us. After sending a letter to the Christians in Corinth condemning their sins, Paul wrote a second time, rejoicing in the fact that it was godly sorrow that had produced repentance in them: "For I see that that letter caused you sorrow, though only for a while—I now rejoice, not that you [Christians] were made sorrowful, but that you were made sorrowful to the point of repentance; for you were made sorrowful according to the will of God . . . For the sorrow that is according to the will of God produces a repentance without regret" (2 Cor. 7:8-10, NASB).

Turning away from the sin is the second step in true repentance. There is no real repentance without this step. For years, I have asked God daily to search my heart and show me my sins. And I find it relatively easy to admit that these un-Christlike attitudes and actions are sin and to ask for forgiveness. And I truly do regret having said, done, or thought certain things, but I do not actually repent until I turn away from them. Proverbs 28:13 says, "He who conceals his transgressions will not prosper, but he who confesses *and forsakes* them will find compassion" (NASB, emphasis mine).

The husband who thought he could sleep with another woman every night and then be forgiven the next day did not understand God's requirements. The only words God had for him were "Repent—and prove your repentance by a change of actions!"

Third, *true repentance is bringing "forth fruit in keeping with . . . repentance"* (Matt. 3:8, NASB). It is not only turning *from* something, but also it is turning *to* something.

Before getting up early one summer morning at our cottage, I was praying, asking God to forgive an attitude I had shown the night before. I was truly sorry and repented of my un-Christlike reaction to another person. As I walked down to the beach to read my Bible, I asked God to give me what I needed from Him. And as I was reading in Matthew 3, He showed me so clearly, "Therefore bring forth fruit in keeping with your repentance" (3:8, NASB). God firmly was saying to me, "Evelyn, do deeds—don't just repent in prayer!"

The word *repent* in Greek literally means to change one's mind and to turn *from* sin and *to* God. As Jesus told the woman taken in adultery to "go, and sin no more" (John 8:11), it means a drastic turnabout in thinking and lifestyle.

This expected, drastic change in action applies to both the Christian and the non-Christian when they repent—the Christian reestablishing a God-pleasing lifestyle and the non-Christian embarking on one. Second Corinthians 7:8-10 shows us the Christian turning *back* to God, and Acts 26:20 shows the unbeliever turning *to* God.

There is a striking contrast in behavior when there is true repentance. A lifestyle just the opposite of the old one of sin emerges. Repentance produces real changes in behavior. The contrast is clearly described in Romans 6:12-13, "Therefore do not let sin reign in your mortal body that you should obey its lusts, and do not go on presenting the members of your body to sin as instruments of unrighteousness; *but* present yourselves to God as those alive from the dead, and your members as instruments of righteousness to God" (NASB, emphasis mine). Repentance demands action. Don't just repent and repent. Get up from your knees and do something about it!

As I shared with my secretary the phone call from the bewildered wife whose husband was daily seeking forgiveness for sleeping with another woman, she said, "Wait until you hear this one. A call I just took was for prayer from a woman whose pastor-husband was sleeping all night, every night, with another woman, then coming home to the parsonage every morning, taking a shower, putting on clean clothes, and then going to work at the church." I wondered aloud if that pastor had ever read 2 Corinthians 6:3, "Giving no cause for offense in anything, in order that the ministry be not discredited" (NASB).

Yes, God's Word tells us that true repentance is being truly sorrowful for the sin, actively turning away from that sin, and bringing "forth fruit in keeping with repentance." Not just the big, brazen sins, but all sins! Oh, how far from this we have fallen in our modern-day understanding and handling of sin.

As you prayed the closing prayer on God's requirements at the end of the last chapter, did you pray a quickie "forgive me" prayer? If you did, were you really sorry for that sin? Did you really abhor it—enough to make you turn away from it? Or are you already back thinking about it, or perhaps even doing it? If so, you did not repent.

Why Repent?

Why repent? Because I've seen myself as God sees me.

Seeing ourselves as God sees us reveals our need to repent. This came forcefully to me when we first arrived at the cottage after Chris had surgery in 1982. Completely exhausted and frazzled, I had dashed from my last speaking engagement at a convention to drive our car, with our boat in tow, to our vacation spot. I struggled hour after hour, pushing harder and harder to catch the car ferry we were to take across Lake Michigan.

My husband, propped up on foam pillows next to me in the car, kept giving me every little direction for slowing down, turning, speeding up, and parking. I found myself getting more and more edgy, responding with short and sometimes rather unkind answers. Our son and my husband's sister were along, and I suddenly became aware of how I must look in their eyes—and was not at all pleased.

However, the very next day as I took my Bible down to the beach for my early morning devotions, I saw something much more important than how they saw me. I was reading in the first chapter of 2 Peter, carefully observing the wonderful list of Christian attributes. While reading "applying all diligence, in your faith supply moral excellence . . . godliness . . . brotherly kindness . . . Christian love" (1:5-7, NASB), suddenly, the word *kindness* almost jumped out at me.

Then these words in the next two verses horrified me: "If these qualities are yours and increasing, they render you neither useless nor unfruitful in the true knowledge of our Lord Jesus Christ. For he who lacks these qualities is blind or shortsighted . . . for as long as you practice these things, you will never stumble" (2 Peter 1:8-10, NASB).

Suddenly, I saw myself as God saw me. Oh, how much more important this was than how other people saw me—even those dear to me! Weeping, I repented there alone on the deserted beach.

Peter must have felt like this when, after he had denied Jesus three times following His arrest, the Lord turned and looked at him. Peter too must have seen himself as the Son of God saw him—a deserter. The hurt that must have been in Jesus' eyes sent Peter out, weeping bitterly in deep remorse and repentance (Matt. 26:75).

In another instance, the song leader of one of our seminars shared a difficult situation which her husband, as chairman of their church, had to handle. Their pastor and his secretary were having an affair. The board kept the matter just within the board; and, after the pastor had confessed his sin and was deeply repentant, they sent him to a Christian counseling center for psychological restoration because they felt he needed the help. However, they knew his usefulness in *that* church was over. But he, forgiven by God and the church board, is now pastoring another church.

However, the secretary's reaction was not the same. To this day, she has not seen, or at least admitted, that what she did was sin. The church board, of course, fired her. She now has a job in another church but constantly complains that she just isn't accepted any more, and people don't seem to like her.

How does God see a woman like this? As a "Potiphar's wife." When we read in the Bible how the wife of Potiphar repeatedly attempted to seduce God-fearing Joseph, we become incensed at her. But what is our attitude toward the modern-day "Potiphar's wives" in our neighborhoods, places of employment, and, yes, even in our churches? Do we see them as God sees them? And do they see themselves as God sees them?

And the one being seduced? How many who are enjoying the flattery, attention, the ego trip, and sexual stimulation from such a person actually see her as God sees her? (See Jesus' warning in Revelation 2:20.) What would happen to our moral standards if, every time there was a seduction to any degree, we would cry out as Joseph did, "How then could I do this great evil, and sin against God?" (Gen. 39:9, NASB) Joseph saw himself as God saw him. Do we?

Somehow, we feel that if we can deceive those around us, no one will know of our sin. Also, we think we can fool those against whom we are sinning, although this usually is not true either. However, we never deceive God. David, before praying his famous "search me, O God" at the close of Psalm 139, opens it with "O Lord, Thou hast searched me and known me. . . . Even before there is a word on my tongue, behold, O Lord, Thou dost know it all" (vv. 1-4, NASB). The writer of Hebrews expresses the same thought, "And there is no creature hidden from His sight, but all things are open and laid bare to the eyes of Him with whom we have to do" (Heb. 4:13, NASB).

Denial of our sin sometimes is a protective shield we build around ourselves to keep from getting hurt. In the self-protection of the denial, we justify the self-preservation instead of seeing the denial as God sees it—as sin. But denial actually produces the sin of "deceit," found in so many lists of sins in the Bible. Denial, of course, is lying (itself a biblical sin). Then one lie demands another, and then another, to keep covering up the original lie—until there is a hopeless web of deceit which we have spun around ourselves.

When we stop denying and start admitting to ourselves that what we are doing or have done is sin, then we are able to admit it to others—who most likely knew it anyway—and to God—who positively did know it anyway. Paul was addressing Christians when he wrote, "Do not be deceived, God is not mocked; for whatever a man sows, this he will also reap. For the one who sows to his own flesh shall from the flesh reap corruption, but the one who sows to the Spirit shall from the Spirit reap eternal life" (Gal. 6:7-8, NASB).

Why Repent? More Reasons

Three verses in Galatians also give us one more reason for re-penting—*the consequences* if we don't. Romans 2:4-6 contains frightening words about this, "Or do you think lightly of the riches of His kindness and forbearance and patience, not know-ing that the kindness of God leads you to repentance? But be-cause of your stubbornness and unrepentant heart you are stor-ing up wrath for yourself in the day of wrath and revelation of the righteous judgment of God, who will render to every man according to his deeds" (NASB).

Then Paul, addressing the people in Athens who were not Christians, used these clear words, "Therefore having overlooked the times of ignorance, God is now declaring to men that all everywhere should repent, because He has fixed a day in which He will judge the world in righteousness" (Acts 17:30-31, NASB).

God does not ask, "Would you like to repent?" or say, "It would be nice if you did." No, rather, He is saying in His word that we must repent—or else face His consequences.

Another surprising reason for repenting is found in Psalm 38:3—David's prayer as a suffering penitent: "there is no *health* in my bones because of my sin" (NASB). And he goes on to describe his physical problems that he is suffering because of God's indig-nation. James echoes this same thought in his epistle, chapter 5, verses 14-16, where he links the confession of sins one to another and prayer for one another—so that there may be healing.

This is illustrated in the life of a pastor, who was afflicted with many physical problems. Crying out in anguish over a personal sin in which he had been living, he asked, "God, are You punish-ing me?" God answered by showing this pastor from Psalm 32:3-4 that, by living in his sin while he preached for several years, he had broken God's moral laws. "When I kept silent about my sin, my body wasted away," lamented the pastor with the psalmist.

In effect, God was answering, "I have decreed My moral law from before the foundation of the world. My answer is already recorded in My Holy Word. You are reaping the already known results of breaking My moral law."

But how wonderful that God added verse 5: "I acknowleged my sin to Thee, and my iniquity I did not hide; I said, 'I will confess my transgressions to the Lord'; and Thou didst forgive the guilt of my sin" (NASB). And this pastor, with David, rejoiced at God's forgiveness when he admitted his sin and repented.

This same thought is found in Christ's message to the church in Thyatira in the Book of Revelation where the Son of God is described to this church as having "eyes like a flame of fire" (2:18, NASB). And He was seeing this church tolerating the woman Jezebel—leading His bond servants into immorality. And then He gave the *dire results* if there was no repentance (Rev. 2:18-22).

In fact, all but two of the seven churches given messages by the Lord in the Book of Revelation were told to repent. After commending the church at Ephesus for the good things they were doing, He told them He had something against them. They had left their first love. And, as inconsequential as this may seem to be, Jesus said, "Repent . . . or else I am coming to you, and *will remove your lampstand out of its place*" (Rev. 2:5, NASB, emphasis mine). Unless they repented, Jesus was going to remove their church from their midst.

Source of the Temptation

While we recognize that the originator of all temptation since Adam and Eve's fall is Satan himself, we are witnessing his fresh frontal attack today. At our metropolitan prayer chain's recent brunch, it was reported to us that a Christian woman was seated next to another woman who refused a meal during a luncheon and explained that she was fasting.

"Oh, are you a Christian?"

"No," she replied angrily, "I'm fasting and praying to Satan to break up the marriages and ministries of Christian pastors by infidelity."

There was also a report of a Christian man who sat beside a person on a plane who had refused a meal. He was also asked if he was a Christian. He replied, "No, I'm fasting and praying to Satan to bring other men into the lives of the spouses of Christian pastors."

My prayer time this morning was interrupted by a telephone call from England. It was from a wife and mother of two children who was struggling to be the wife that God and her husband wanted her to be. "But," she wept, "although he has been a fine Christian, he is leaving tomorrow for America, is getting a divorce, and planning to marry another woman." I find myself getting very angry at this kind of sin.

Repentance Produces Revival

What do you think God answers when you as a Christian pray, "Lord, send revival"? Surprisingly, He doesn't send showers of blessings or bring others to Himself as Savior and Lord, but He first tells *us* to repent. Then the outcome of our being revived will be that others will find Christ.

Our National Prayer Committee discovered firsthand what history tells us about every revival. We were burdened for revival in our nation and had our first national meeting to pray for it in November 1982 in Washington, D.C. But we were in for a surprise. After calling prayer leaders from across the United States to participate, thinking we would be praying for *revival,* as it turned out, we spent the first half of the convention *repenting* for ourselves.

I was to bring a message on the cleansed life first; but, as our committee met the day before the conference, I knew we needed to know the reason for praying through the cleansed life. So we asked Joy Dawson, of Youth with a Mission, to speak on what revival really is. Joy asked us two questions: "What is revival?" and "Now that you know what it is, do you really want it?"

Here is her definition: "Revival is the sovereign outpouring of the Holy Spirit in God's way and in God's time *first of all upon God's people,* where the revelation of God's holiness is greatly amplified and, as a result, God's viewpoint of sin is revealed. . . . Revival is God greatly stirring, shaking, and changing His people from apathy, selfishness, and self-promotion to desperate praying, humble, open, and broken people with a passion only for God Himself and His glory."

As I asked God what I should speak on after Joy Dawson's message, He laid 2 Chronicles 7:14 heavily on my heart. I was hoping for something newer and fresher as we have almost worn out this one, using it as our "American Christian" theme verse for several years. Yet, we may have been missing its message. God said to me, "Put the emphasis on *My* emphasis of this verse." Here it is: "If *My* people, which are called by *My* name, shall humble *themselves,* and pray, and seek *My* face, and turn from *their* wicked ways: then will I hear from heaven, and will forgive *their* sin, and will heal their land" (emphasis mine).

We have been blaming our national problems on and pointing our fingers at humanists, abortionists, pornography kings, and atheists; but God in His Word points His finger at us—His people—and lays the responsibility squarely at our feet.

Following the message on the cleansed life, we started confessing our own sins at about 4:30 in the afternoon of that first day. With just a short break for dinner, we were back praying and weeping over the sins God was bringing to our minds until midnight. And the next day, it kept up until the afternoon. We were shocked at the seemingly inconsequential attitudes and deeds God kept expecting these national leaders to confess.

I remember being called on late in the night to come to the front to lead in prayer, but I was weeping so hard I could barely speak. Why? Because God had reproved me of previously unrecognized sin. To me, it was such a trivial thing that I had not realized it was a sin until God started reproving me. It was just a tiny speck of satisfaction, unseen, deep within me, of a competitor recognizing the scope of my ministry. "Repent first, you leaders!"

At times, we weren't too sure ourselves that we wanted revival either, but the power we felt as God finally led us to pray for others was one of the greatest joys of my life. Real revival is always characterized by true repentance. In fact, without it, there is no revival.

Evangelism versus Revival

America is long overdue for a revival. Since early in the 1600s, we have had a revival somewhere in our country on the average of every twenty years. But in the twentieth century, we have had "brush fires" here and there, but not one major revival. We have had much evangelism, but no real revival.

What is the difference? Evangelism, while scripturally accurate and commanded, is man-initiated; but revival is strictly God-initiated. Evangelism, hopefully, is inspired and empowered by the Holy Spirit; but revival is God taking the initiative and sending His outpouring in response to extraordinary prayer.

Differing from evangelism, revival always produces repentance first in the Christians who are praying for it. Evangelism centers on the one who does not know Christ as Savior and Lord; but revival, after Christians have been revived through repentance, then results in people who do not know Christ repenting and receiving Him.

I have prayed for revival for forty years; but three years ago, I prayed for it specifically in my birthday prayer for the next year in my life. It was when the urgency of praying for revival was breaking in America that my heart was more and more burdened for this revival. Since I already knew it always started with Christians seeing God's holiness first, I prayed a two-pronged birthday prayer, "Lord, show me Your holiness—and send revival."

As I waited in the stillness of my prayer closet for His answer, He directed my thinking to that time-worn Scripture portion on holiness in Isaiah 6. As I turned to it and read, my heart almost exploded within me, just as it had that morning more than three years earlier on the beach at Lake Michigan when I recorded in my Bible, "Explosion of worship and adoration! Spontaneous! Slowly drew in my breath at *who God is.*"

Also in the margin of my Bible at Isaiah 6:1-4 were the words I had recorded the year before at Deerfield Beach in Florida, "At Isaiah's words, 'lofty and exalted,' tears popped into my eyes. I shut my eyes and lifted my face to the morning sun—streaming in through the deck's open window with ocean roaring below. The tears slowly trickled down my cheeks as my heart soared up to Him—lofty and exalted. Oh," I continued writing, "how weak those English words are. What must God *really* be? There are no words! Only—'Holy, holy, holy.' "

No words ever did come for my prayer that morning in Florida. I was just engulfed, enwrapped by who God is. Soaking into my whole being—just like the sun warming my body—was God. Holy!

Again, on that birthday morning, I saw His unique, awesome purity. I saw with Isaiah the seraphim above Him, calling to one another the only attribute of God recorded in triplicate: "Holy, holy, holy!" (Isa. 6:3) I had glimpsed a speck of His holiness!

But at this birthday time, I had asked for more—revival. And when I saw His holiness, I cried with Isaiah, "Woe is me" (Isa. 6:5). All I too could see was my sinfulness, my unworthiness to be in His holy presence. For two weeks, it continued as I was letting God search me and cleanse me—preparing *me* for revival.

So, when Christians earnestly start praying for revival, God always shows them His holiness and answers them with, "You must repent first!"

Recently, I was asked to conduct a noon staff prayer meeting of a large Christian television organization. They were to begin eight days of revival on their campus in a few days and asked me to lead them in preparatory prayer for it. Defining the difference between revival and evangelism, I then talked about seeing God's holiness and seeing ourselves as Isaiah did—as sinners.

Before confessing aloud our sins, I asked how many of them who had just lifted their hands as we sang songs of praise had actually lifted up hands full of sin. Hands that had turned the pages of a pornographic magazine, dialed to an X-rated TV movie, touched forbidden fruit—when the Bible says explicitly that we are to hold up *"holy* hands" (1 Tim. 2:8). Shocked, many of them wept as they prayed for forgiveness.

Forgiven!

Since there are two classes of sin—the singular state of sin into which all humans are born and the plural sins that we commit after we become Christians—there are also two classes of repentance. And God's Word calls on both categories of sinners to repent.

What happens when we have gone through the steps of admitting to God that we have sinned, God has answered that we must repent, and we have truly repented? What then?

It is like the missionary surgeon in Ethiopia who invited my husband and me to watch an operation. The surgeon adjusted a coat hanger so that the lamp it supported focused on the abdomen of a tiny, frail woman lying on the makeshift operating table, a woman whose family had discarded her on a trash heap to die. As the surgeon tenderly reached into the gaping cavity, he scooped out a huge tumor with both hands. Looking around the tiny, ill-equipped room, he muttered, "Where'll I put this thing?" Then, stepping over to me, he said, "Here." I recoiled as he thrust that football-sized, cancerous tumor into my reluctant, bare hands.

How like that surgeon God is. A year ago, I had a particularly trying day, releasing the wounds of many years with a person who had hurt me deeply. Weeping, I afterward slumped into a chair. I was filled with self-pity and physical and emotional exhaustion. The next morning at prayer, I repented of my human reaction and asked God to remove all my un-Christlike attitudes. And suddenly, it felt as if His holy, loving hands were reaching down inside me, scooping out my cancerous attitudes.

No, God doesn't leave us on the trash heap to suffer and die when we sin. He says, "Repent!" And when we do and ask Him to forgive us, He gently yet firmly reaches down into our hearts. Then, sliding His holy hands underneath our cancerous skin, as did that surgeon at the operating table, He lifts it out completely!

When we truly repent and turn from the sin we have confessed, God answers by pulling aside the curtain; and we find ourselves stepping into a beautiful condition called *"forgiven!"*

Closing Prayer

Oh, God, I realize that my "quickie," "I-admit-I-have-sinned" prayers are not enough. I now truly repent of my sins. I abhor them, Father. I'm so sorry. And, dear Lord, I realize that my real repenting includes my turning completely away from committing these sins again. Since I have done my part, thank You for doing Your part in forgiving me.

In Jesus' name, **Amen**

7

When God answers...

Be Reconciled to Me

When we pray, "I have sinned," God not only answers, "Repent," but He also includes in His answer, "Be reconciled to Me."

Reconciliation is necessary only because a relationship has been broken. And all human sin breaks the relationship between God and the one who has sinned.

While this reconciliation to God actually comes simultaneously with true repentance and forgiveness, there are two sides to the transaction. Repentance is man's action; reconciliation to God is God's action. So this is why God's forgiveness as we repent must include our reconciliation to Him.

Only when there have been broken vows, shattered commitments, or violated persons do we need to be reconciled. It is a necessity when someone is grieved, wounded, angry—or all three.

The night before a seminar, I was having dinner in a parsonage with my hostess, the minister's wife, when the phone rang. She walked to the phone and started to greet an obviously good friend, but she stopped midword. The apparently rapid-firing voice on the other end kept clipping off her responses, limiting them to "No," "Really?" "What?" My hostess's expression kept swinging from one of surprise, to a twisted grin, then to wide-eyed shock, and finally exploded into an incredible, "You didn't!"

It seems the caller had known all about her husband's girlfriend and was calling to tell the pastor's wife what she had just done. Her husband, she exploded, had just bought two new Cadillac cars—one for himself and one for his girlfriend. So incensed was the wife that she jumped into her husband's shiny new car, drove furiously to the girlfriend's house, took careful aim at the shiny new Cadillac in her driveway, slammed the gas pedal to the floor—and smashed them both.

The pastor's wife sank trembling in her chair in a state of shock. As the reality and magnitude of the deed unfolded, our responses vacillated between "Oh, no," and "That's illegal"; then, "she shouldn't have—but I don't blame her"; and finally, with the wry smile we were unable to control, we exclaimed, "Good for her!"

Who could honestly blame the wife for such uncontrolled anger? Hadn't her marriage vows, rights, and very person been violated? I inwardly breathed a sigh of relief that, if there were to be a jury, I would not have to be on it.

"Who's Angry?"

Since reconciliation is necessary only when there is enmity and hostility between people or groups, we must ask, "Who's angry?" The surprising answer is "God!"

Why does God insist on reconciliation? Because He too is angry at our sinning.

The Bible never speaks of God being reconciled to man, only of people being reconciled to God. Although people are frequently angry with God, He never has to be reconciled to us because we are angry. God never sins or errs in His relationship with us, thus necessitating reconciliation back to us. Only we sin against Him.

I once heard a pastor ask his Sunday School class, "Are we still, as in Jonathan Edward's day, 'sinners in the hands of an angry God'?" Somehow this biblical view of God has been neglected or rationalized away in recent years. But the preaching of this unpopular truth by that spiritual giant in the 1700s precipitated the Great Awakening in the early years of our country. And that revival changed the course of American history. Yes, God still demands that we be reconciled to Him because He was, and still is, angry with those who sin.

God was so grieved and angry at sin that He was ready to blot out all mankind from the Earth—with the exception of righteous Noah (Gen. 6:5-8). Also, God was angry with the sinning Children of Israel as Moses led them toward the Promised Land for forty years. And, because of their sin, God did not permit them to enter that land (Heb. 3:17). David too knew all about God's wrath when he cried in Psalm 6:1, "O Lord, do not rebuke me in Thine anger, nor chasten me in Thy wrath" (NASB).

The same truth is carried over into New Testament teaching. John the Baptist, almost echoing Jesus' words to Nicodemus in John 3:18, explained to his disciples that "he who believes in the Son has eternal life; but he who does not obey the Son shall not see life, but the wrath of God abides in him" (John 3:26, NASB).

Then after the death of Christ, Paul in Romans 1:18 warns, "For the wrath of God is revealed from heaven against all ungodliness and unrighteousness of men" (NASB). And again, "What shall we say? The God who inflicts wrath is not unrighteous, is He?" (3:5, NASB) Then Paul says to us, "Because of your stubbornness and unrepentant heart you are storing up wrath for yourself in the day of wrath and revelation of the righteous judgment of God" (Rom. 2:5, NASB).

Again, I was at a dinner the night before a seminar where a fine young woman told me her story. Although she had been deeply into the drug scene, she had wanted cassette tapes of the Bible. Her hippie friends later chided her, saying, "What are you listening to *that* for?" And she, high on drugs, would giggle and say flippantly, "Oh, it's just the Bible!"

But one day while taking a drag on a joint of marijuana, she heard on the tape, "It is a fearful thing to fall into the hands of the living God" (Heb. 10:31).

"Oh," she cried out in fright, "I don't want that to happen to me!" And she immediately accepted Christ.

Why Is God Angry?

God is angry because His holiness has been violated by our human sinning. Holiness? Yes—the attribute of God which is His own moral purity. This is not just the absence of sin in Him, but it is that God is the source and the standard of moral purity. So God not only is repulsed by our sin, He recoils in horror at it.

Yes, holiness is the only attribute of God given in triplicate in the Bible. We never read of Him as "love, love, love" or "truth, truth, truth," but the seraphim that Isaiah saw standing above God's throne in his vision were calling out to one another: "Holy,

holy, holy, is the Lord of hosts" (Isa. 6:3).

So real repenting must include knowing what we have done, not only to the other people involved, but to God. We must realize that in sinning we have violated His holiness, thus causing His anger. And it is only through our repenting and His forgiving that reconciliation between Him and us can take place.

With Whom Is God Angry?
Since there are two classes of sin, there are two classes of sinners with whom God is angry. Thus, there are two categories of sinners who need to repent and be reconciled to God—reconciled to Him either for *the first time* or *back* to Him.

The first class of sin is that state of sin into which all humans are born.

Paul in Romans 5:18 told us why we are already judged while explaining how all have sinned through the sin of Adam and Eve: "So then as through one transgression there resulted condemnation to all men" (NASB). Then he so clearly shows us the process of reconciliation to God in Romans 5:8-11:

> But God demonstrates His own love toward us, in that while we were yet sinners, Christ died for us. Much more then, having now been justified by His blood, we shall be saved from the *wrath of God* through Him. For if while we were enemies, we were reconciled to God through the death of His Son, much more, having been reconciled, we shall be saved by His life. And not only this, but we also exult in God through our Lord Jesus Christ, through whom we have now received the reconciliation (NASB, emphasis mine).

So, since we all were born in a state of sin, if Jesus' blood has not cleansed us at salvation, we are still living in that state of sin under the wrath of God. And we still need to be reconciled to Him.

When we pray, accepting Christ as Savior, we must first recognize that we need to be reconciled to God and repent before Him because He is angry that His holiness has been violated. Jesus said it so bluntly in Luke 13:3 and 5, "Unless you repent, you will all likewise perish" (NASB), and in John 3:18, "He who does not believe has been judged already" (NASB).

This class of sinners is made up of those who are either deliberately refusing salvation in Jesus, those who are just indifferent, not realizing they are lost without believing in Him, or those of the hidden mission field in our churches who are trusting in church membership but never have had a personal relationship with Jesus.

A member of our church in Rockford was one of our neighborhood Bible study teachers. She astounded us one Sunday by announcing that she had discovered during her own Bible study that she really did not know Jesus. "After twenty-nine years of prenatal care," she said, "I was born."

In my prayer seminars after reading my list of twenty-three scriptural sins and questions, which include "Are you a fake, just pretending to be a real Christian?" God powerfully breaks down cultural inhibitions, reservations, and their "we never do it that way" excuses. Sometimes, everyone just seems to explode, all praying aloud in their groups at once; and at other times, they continue one by one all over the room, as they did once for twelve minutes in Bristol, England. In a recent seminar of 2,700 people, it sounded as if two thirds prayed aloud simultaneously, making sure they had a personal relationship with Jesus.

It is likely that some of those praying may already be real Christians but are just not sure about their personal relationship with Jesus. The Bible tells us we can be sure. With a prayer of repentance and by accepting Jesus, we can join the ranks of those assured of their reconciliation with God from that state of sin into which we were all born, "These things I have written to you who believe in the name of the Son of God, in order that you may *know* that you have eternal life" (1 John 5:13, NASB, emphasis mine).

In Australia in 1980, almost all those attending my prayer seminars were already members of a large Bible study movement, yet never less than 25 percent of these people prayed aloud making sure they knew Jesus as Savior and Lord. As I left, the leaders of the international Bible study organization said to me, "The most important thing you taught us as Bible study authors and leaders is that we have not included in our material an opportunity to make a personal commitment to Christ. We have just taken it for granted that all who study the Bible already are saved." And I have found that the most surprising part of all is that these people in the churches are just waiting for someone to ask them.

This morning, I received a phone call from a pastor's wife who told me that the day after I had a prayer seminar in their church a man came forward to join the church. When asked by the membership committee when he had accepted Christ as Savior and Lord, he replied, "Yesterday, in Evelyn's seminar."

In Japan, nonbelievers frequently attend Christian churches for several years as seekers, without making a commitment. But I observed after conducting several prayer seminars there that many people had come to Christ. I learned why from a missionary who said, "The reason there were so many decisions for Christ is that Evelyn laid it on the line and came right out and asked them to make a decision." Reconciled to God through Jesus! "God is now declaring to men that all everywhere should repent, because He has fixed a day in which He will judge the world in righteousness" (Acts 17:30-31, NASB).

When you ask Jesus, on the final Judgment Day, "Lord, when did I not visit You in prison, feed You, and so on?"—how will you handle it if Jesus answers, "Depart from Me ye cursed"? (Matt. 25:41) What a horrifying answer this will be for those who have only been cultural Christians, who belonged to fine churches or thought they were God's grandchildren because they had believing parents.

God's Incredible Provision
But there is another side to our God. While God's holiness demands reconciliation by a sacrifice for our sin, His love provided it!

God loved us enough to send the means of reconciliation—His own Son, Jesus. Romans 5:8 says, "But God commendeth His love toward us, in that, while we were yet sinners, Christ died for us." Jesus was the sacrifice that satisfied the demands of God's violated holiness. And this—God's own love—has saved us from His own wrath.

Christ came not only to preach the Gospel but so that there would be a Gospel to be preached! "For He hath made Him

[Jesus] to be sin for us, who knew no sin; that we might be made the righteousness of God in Him" (2 Cor. 5:21). Overwhelmed, my heart cries, "How could He not spare His own Son but deliver Him up for us, and do it while we were still His enemies?"

Reconciliation is the removal of God's wrath toward man by the shedding of Jesus' blood on the cross. Through Jesus, our status with God is changed. We stand in the presence of the Holy God of heaven, justified—just as if we never had sinned, and reconciled—with God's wrath toward us eradicated, erased. "Not imputing their trespasses unto them" (2 Cor. 5:19). Reconciled!

Charles Colson, in a college commencement address, put it this way: "The Gospel of Jesus Christ must be the bad news of the conviction of sin before it can be the Good News of redemption."

In May of 1983, while on my way to a British Broadcasting interview, my taxi was following a bus with a sign on the back that read, "Therefore having been justified by faith, we have peace with God through our Lord Jesus Christ" (Rom. 5:1, NASB). After looking at it for many minutes, I suddenly realized the importance of the preposition "with." When we are justified at salvation, we don't receive the peace *of* God but peace *with* God.

During the same British Isles seminar tour, I was reading my Bible in Belfast and underlined Romans 8:1, "There is therefore now no condemnation for those who are in Christ Jesus" (NASB). With tears and deep gratitude welling up within me, I prayed: "Thank You, God, that You took away my condemnation when I was nine years old!" Reconciled to God! "He who believes in the Son has eternal life; but he who does not obey the Son shall not see life, but the wrath of God abides on him" (John 3:36, NASB).

Are you sure that you have been reconciled to God by accepting Jesus as your Savior and Lord? If not, have you ever considered that God is angry since you are still living in the state of sin into which you were born? And that He is angry because you are violating His holiness? But—have you also considered that He loves you so much that He is just waiting and longing to change His relationship with You? Be reconciled to God!

Ministry of Reconciliation
Those who are already real Christians have been given the ministry of reconciliation by God. Once we have been reconciled to

God through Jesus, He immediately gives us the job of reconciling others to Him. "Therefore if any man is in Christ, he is a new creature; the old things passed away; behold, new things have come. Now all these things are from God, who reconciled *us* to Himself through Christ, and gave *us* the ministry of reconciliation" (2 Cor. 5:17-18, NASB).

For the first annual symposium of Charles Colson's Prison Fellowship in Belfast in 1983, we had chosen the theme "In Christ—Reconciliation" from 2 Corinthians 5:17-20. As I spoke, I reminded the justice officials, prison workers, ex-offenders, and international board members that we must identify what this ministry of reconciliation is. Then I explained that Paul did this with his little word *namely* in the very next verse. "Namely, that God was in Christ reconciling the world to Himself" (2 Cor. 5:19, NASB). The world—always those not of the body of Jesus.

There will always be other subsequent valid and necessary teachings, but it is this word and ministry of reconciliation give to us by God that must come first. While speaking at the symposium I reminded those present that we must see every prison inmate as condemned by God, no matter what his or her status with their country's judicial system may be—unless they have been reconciled to God through faith in Christ. Even if pardoned, paroled, or freed from prison, they are still condemned to death by God unless they are reconciled to Him.

At our last U.S.A. Prison Fellowship board meeting we reemphasized the importance of all our material, stating, and members of the field staff recognizing, that real rehabilitation begins in the prisoner only when he or she has been reconciled to God through Jesus. All other teaching is subsequent to this.

On a blustery March morning during my devotions, I was "praying through" God's removing of all sin from me. Then, knowing He never leaves me as a fragile, empty shell from which He has removed these sins but that He then fills me, I started to tell Him all the things I knew I needed from Him. But suddenly, I changed my mind. "No, Lord, not what I think I need. This morning, would You please fill me with what's burdening You? Lord, what is Your number one priority for me today?" And immediately, before my mind's eye were two huge words, almost as if written in capital letters: WIN SOULS!

I often question why we spend so much time in our church prayer meetings praying for sick Christians who, if they die—and they will eventually—will go to be with Jesus, but we spend almost no time praying for the sinners who, when they die, will go to a Christless eternity.

Speaking at the Wednesday night prayer meeting in a famous church known for its deep spirituality, I mentioned in passing the appalling content of our church prayer lists. When the time came for group prayer, the interim pastor stood, holding a stack of mimeographed church prayer sheets in his hands. Then, blushing, he stammered, "I'm ashamed to hand these out." And for good reason. All but one request was for sick people. Please don't stop praying for your sick members but *add* all those who are dying without Christ—lost—unreconciled to God.

God, in giving us the ministry of reconciliation, has made us ambassadors for Christ. It is "as though God were entreating *through* us; we beg you on behalf of Christ, be reconciled to God" (2 Cor. 5:20, NASB, emphasis mine).

In the Apostle Paul's day, ambassadors were envoys responsible for bringing vanquished people into the family of the Roman Empire. Today, the Christian ambassador for Christ brings God's terms to others whereby they can become citizens of His kingdom and members of His family. Also, the honor of the Roman Empire was in the ambassador's hands; and today, the honor of Christ is in our hands. And by our lives, we cause people to think more—or less—of Christ as we seek to bring them into God's family. To have the honor of Christ and the church in our hands is a tremendous privilege but also an almost terrifying responsibility.

I learned the privilege—and responsibility—of being an ambassador for Christ during my last British Isles tour. With whole days of interviews with the secular press, before each one I prayed, "Oh, God, only let them see Jesus in me."

"The press is waiting for you in the bar." I cringed. Everything inside me rebelled as I heard the Belfast hotel clerk's words. On my one day to get over jet lag and after a four-hour picture-taking tour of the riot-torn part of Belfast, I was exhausted. Pictures in front of graffiti walls, pictures with soldiers, pictures with the mother of the first young man murdered in the Irish war—all out in the cold, windy rain—left me wanting only a bowl of hot soup and a bed. Was this what the Bible meant by being an ambassador for Christ? I gritted my teeth and breathed a desperate prayer as I marched in to meet them. "Oh, Lord, may they only see Jesus in me!"

The last interview that day was by a woman reporter who wiped away tears as she struggled to concentrate on her interviewing. Our press agent had whispered to me, "She learned just two days ago that her brother, an international rugby player, has cancer. The doctors have given him two weeks to live." Her questions turned to the ones we all ask at such times. Questions about God, eternity, healing. I longed to pray with her right then, but I knew she was not ready for that yet. I squeezed her hands in mine as I asked, "Would you like me to pray for you when I get back to my room?" Tears spilled over on her notepad as she gratefully accepted my offer.

The next week when I arrived in Birmingham, England and was facing another one of those whole days with the secular press, I expanded my prayer: "Oh, God, keep me a pure, Christlike ambassador, only saying Your words and radiating Christ— His reactions, His love, tolerance, patience, joys, His burden for the world."

As the four to eight hours of newspaper, radio, and TV interviews and phone-in programs every day between seminars stretched into a month, I began seeing an amazing pattern. Not one derogatory, unkind, or embarrassing question was being asked. Not one unanswerable question about President Reagan's position on the nuclear arms race. Then questions like "Isn't Reagan embarrassed that you Americans think he needs prayer?" and "Could we pray for Margaret Thatcher that way?" began to surface. Eagerness to learn more about what I believed began filling the interviews. The media people were hungry for the Jesus they saw in me.

Then, at the committee's pre-prayer meeting the night before one of our last seminars, an ecstatic press reporter almost exploded with the news. "That Belfast reporter accepted Christ the day after your interview, and the doctors found her brother's cancer miraculously gone!" An ambassador for Christ! The position to which God calls all who have been reconciled to Him. A reconciler. The privilege—and the responsibility.

This responsibility is explained by Paul. Immediately after the call to be ambassadors, he gives the conduct expected of one charged with the ministry of reconciliation, "And working together with Him . . . giving no cause for offense in anything, in order that the ministry be not discredited, but in everything commending ourselves as servants of God" (2 Cor. 6:1-4, NASB).

The specific examples of the awesome lifestyle expectations for an ambassador who is reconciling the world to God goes on:

> In much endurance, in afflictions, in hardships, in distresses, in beatings, in imprisonments, in tumults, in labors, in sleeplessness, in hunger, in purity, in knowledge, in patience, in kindness, in the Holy Spirit, in genuine love, in the word of truth, in the power of God; by the weapons of righteousness for the right hand and the left, by glory and dishonor, by evil report and good report; regarded as deceivers and yet true; as unknown yet well-known, as dying yet behold, we live; as punished yet not put to death, as sorrowful yet always rejoicing, as poor yet making many rich, as having nothing yet possessing all things (2 Cor. 6:4-10, NASB).

While God is calling us to be reconcilers, He at times must say to us that we have to be reconciled back to Him ourselves. Anything that gives cause for offense in our ministry is sin in God's eyes. As Christians reconciling others to God, we must be alert for anything in our lives that God considers sin.

The second class of sin is the sins that Christians commit. They are "sins," not the singular state of sin into which we all were born. These are committed after the original reconciliation with God at salvation. And this sinning also requires reconciliation with God—because He is also angry at our sinning as Christians.

Why shouldn't God be angry? After all, He has entrusted to us the honor of our Christ and of our church, but our sin has made a mockery of the sinless Christ we are representing as ambassadors.

After we are washed clean by repenting and accepting Jesus as Savior and Lord—reconciled to God—we still create enmity beween Him and ourselves when we sin. This does not mean that we have broken our initial relationship of reconciliation to Him obtained at salvation, but we have created a gulf between God and ourselves by our sins. Our sinning has broken our formerly established communication and fellowship with God. Thus, reconciliation is necessary.

Peter, writing to Christians, said, "The eyes of the Lord are upon the righteous, and His ears attend to their prayer, but the face of the Lord is against those who do evil" (1 Peter 3:12, NASB). The Apostle John, writing to Christians, tells us that "the blood of Jesus keeps on cleansing us from all sin"—if we confess it. And then "[God] is faithful and righteous to forgive *us* our sins and to cleanse *us* [not those still in their original state of sin] from all unrighteousness" (1 John 1:9, NASB, emphasis mine).

So again we ask, who's angry? God! It is not important that we may be angry at God but that God is angry with us. Even as Christians, we can violate His holiness over and over again.

In Romans, chapter 1, God gives a sickening picture of the sins of those He finally gave over to a depraved mind—women and men exchanging "the natural function for that which is unnatural" (v. 26, NASB), full of "all unrighteousness, wickedness, greed, malice; full of envy, murder, strife, deceit, malice; they are gossips, slanderers, haters of God, insolent, arrogant, boastful, inventors of evil, disobedient to parents, without understanding, untrustworthy, unloving, unmerciful" (vv. 29-31, NASB). But in chapter 2, he switches from the world's sins and directly addresses the Christians to whom he is writing. Paul says this to them:

> Therefore *you* are without excuse, every man *of you* who passes judgment, for in that you judge another, you condemn yourself; for you who judge practice the same things. And we know that the judgment of God rightly falls upon those who practice such things. And do you suppose this, O man, when you pass judgment upon those who practice such things and do the same yourself, that you will escape the judgment of God? . . . But because of your stubbornness and unrepentant heart *you* are storing up wrath for yourself in the day of wrath and revelation of the righteous judgment of God, who will render to every man according to his deeds (vv. 1-3, 5-6, NASB, emphasis mine).

With what sins of Christians is God angry? All of them! Paul explained to the Christians in Colossae: "Therefore consider the members of your earthly body as dead to immorality, impurity, passion, evil desire, and greed, which amounts to idolatry. For it is on account of these things that the *wrath of God* will come" (Col. 3:5-6, NASB). Not on the sin but on the sinner. God doesn't punish sin, He punishes the sinners.

While a pastor's wife, I remember walking into our empty church time and time again and finding one of the members, who had deserted his wife and child for another woman, grieving in the darkened sanctuary. Holding his head in his hands, he would shudder repeatedly, not only over what he had done to his family but at what he had done to God. He had violated God's holiness.

What an awesome thought this is to me. All of my sins violate God's holiness! Me, His child! All of my pride, touchiness, unkindness, anxiety, lack of faith—the list seems so endless—violate my Heavenly Father's holiness!

The Bible contains many lists of sins God's children are to avoid. Jesus' list in Mark 7:21-22 covers a large number of the glossed-over "common" sins Christians commit as well as those horrible ones found *even* in our families and churches. Scripture is God's source of reproof for us. "Oh that my ways may be established / To keep Thy statutes! / Then I shall not be ashamed / When I look upon all Thy commandments" (Ps. 119:5-6, NASB).

As I read this, my heart cried out with the psalmist, "Oh, to come to the place where I need no reproof from the Scripture and am not ashamed when I look in it—because I am keeping all His statutes!"

His Holy Presence

So few people, Christians and non-Christians, are even aware that they are not reconciled to God. It comes as a complete shock that while they are living in sin, although He still loves them, God certainly doesn't like them.

When I feel far from God and pray, "Father, I long for a deeper, closer walk with You," God answers me with "My child, you have broken our fellowship with your sin. You must be reconciled to Me first."

"Therefore I want the men [people] in every place to pray, lifting up holy hands, *without wrath and dissension*" (1 Tim. 2:8, NASB).

Although we are carnivorous beings, one thing that distinguishes us from most other meat-eating creatures is that we do not devour one another. However, there are times when this is not true in the body of Christ.

I can recall more than ten years ago when two large national organizations were vying for the potential prayer power of our Twin Cities. Both had fine fruit-bearing ministries, but they were almost pushing and shoving to persuade our local pray-ers to sign up with them. In the midst of the controversy, I called out to God, "Oh, Father, solve this ugly competition for me. What is Your answer?" And He shocked me with His oh-so-relevant reply from Galatians 5:15, "If you bite and devour one another, take care lest you be consumed by one another" (NASB).

No Reconciliation to God without It

At the end of His earthly life, Jesus prayed to the Father in His High-Priestly Prayer about this requirement that we Christians be reconciled to one another. And as long as we are not reconciled to each other, we are sinning because we are disobeying this recorded desire of Jesus. And, of course, as long as there is sin in our lives, we are not reconciled to God. Jesus prayed:

> I do not ask in behalf of these [whom the Father gave Him] alone, but for those also who believe in Me through their word; *that* they may all be one; even as Thou, Father, art in Me, and I in Thee, *that* they also may be in Us; *that* the world may believe that Thou didst send Me. And the glory which Thou hast given Me I have given to them; *that* they may be one, just as We are One; I in them, and Thou in Me, *that* they may be perfected in unity, *that* the world may know that Thou didst send Me, and didst love them, even as Thou didst love Me (John 17:20-23, NASB, emphasis mine).

Contrary to popular thought, Jesus did not ask His children to be reconciled so that they *could become one,* but because they *were* one! So, whenever we pray asking God with which Christians we should pray, He answers, "But you *are* one!" "There is neither

Jew nor Greek, there is neither slave nor free man, there is neither male nor female; for you are all one in Christ Jesus" (Gal.
3:28, NASB).

But God's requirement for reconciliation is broader than just
within the body of Christ. It includes *individual* reconciliation to
mates, parents, in-laws, children, brothers, sisters, pastors, neighbors, employees, employers, competitors, and our enemies—all of
whom may or may not be Christians. So, as long as we are not
reconciled to even one of them, we are not obeying Jesus' plan
for us. "Forgiving each other, whoever has a complaint against
any one; just as the Lord forgave you, so also should you" (Col.
3:13, NASB).

This "any one" includes *societal* reconciliation—encompassing
people of every race, color, sex, denomination, political party,
capital and labor, youth and the aged. First John 2:9 clearly states,
"The one who says he is in the light and yet hates his brother is
in the darkness until now" (NASB).

Thus, being unwilling to be reconciled to other people is a sin,
which must be confessed, repented of, forgiven, and turned from
if we are to be reconciled back to God.

In 1983, just before leaving war-torn Belfast for America after
the Prison Fellowship's powerful International Symposium on
"Reconciliation," I was interviewed on a local television station.
"What is your parting word for the TV audiences in Ireland?" the
interviewer asked.

Looking directly into the camera, I said, "Be reconciled. Forgive—and ask God to forgive you!"

Horrified, my sweet Christian hostess retorted, "After what *they*
did?" Then she flushed with embarrassment, remembering the
words of God—and the theme of our symposium: "Be ye
reconciled!"

So, Who's Angry?

On a human level, it really doesn't matter who is angry. Whether
we are angry with someone, or they are angry with us, or if the
feeling is mutual—the answer from God is the same: "Be
reconciled!"

When it was God who was angry at our sinning because we
had violated His holiness, we had to be reconciled to Him. But

When my efforts as a reconciler of the world to God are ineffective and in frustration I ask God why, He frequently insists, "You must be reconciled to Me first!"

When I pray, "Lord, give me power in prayer," He sometimes answers literally, "Since you are regarding iniquity in your heart, I cannot hear you" (see Ps. 66:18). "Repent and let Me reconcile you once again to Myself—and reestablish our powerful relationship."

The only reason God convicts us of sin and demands repentance is so that we can be reconciled to Him and once again experience fellowship with Him. It is so that we can step into that room marked *His holy presence.* "Who may ascend into the hill of the Lord? And who may stand in His holy place? He who has clean hands and a pure heart" (Ps. 24:3-4, NASB).

Yes, when we have sinned, our part is to repent—and God's part is to reconcile us to Himself.

When God answers, "I forgive you and have reconciled you back to Myself," we step into the rare privilege of being, uninhibited and unrestrained, in the very presence of the Holy God of the universe. All hindrances to His presence are swept away, and we walk hand in hand with Him—just as if we never had sinned! "Yet He has now reconciled you in His fleshly body through death, in order to present you before Him holy and blameless and beyond reproach" (Col. 1:22, NASB).

Closing Prayer

Oh, God, I confess that I have violated Your holiness and, thus, our relationship is broken. Please, God, cleanse me from all known and unknown sin. And thank You, Father, for being holy enough to be angry at my sin—but loving enough to forgive me and to reconcile me to Yourself.

In Jesus' name, **Amen**

8

When God answers . . .

Be Reconciled to Others

Complete reconciliation to God is not possible without a willingness to be reconciled to others as well. Why? Because one of the clear commands in the Bible is that we be reconciled to others. And as long as we are not obeying God's scriptural commands, we are sinning—and thus not reconciled to Him. "If someone says, 'I love God,' and hates his brother, he is a liar; for the one who does not love his brother whom he has seen, cannot love God whom he has not seen" (1 John 4:20, NASB).

Frequently, I am asked, "Do you mean you pray with *them?*" Aghast, they are wondering aloud how I could stoop to, and even defile myself by, praying together with Christians of different denominations or forms of worship.

At the International Prayer Assembly in Seoul, Korea, in June 1984, I was asked to be on the committee writing the "International Call to Prayer" for the sponsoring Lausanne Committee on World Evangelization. While discussing which Christians around the world we should call to prayer, the representative of a European country said, "If we include *them*, those praying in my country will throw this out."

Acting as secretary for this section, I became exasperated and inwardly horrified at such a discussion. Finally, facetiously yet firmly, I asked, "As I word this for the printer, should I include all those with whom we are going to spend eternity in heaven, or. . . ." There was a long, shocked silence. Then all agreed with emphatic oneness that worldwide prayer is for *all* Christians. Blushing in shame, the European delegate apologized profusely.

whenever there are broken relationships here on Earth, His instructions to us are equally clear: "Be reconciled to each other!"

Jesus, in Matthew 5:22-24, gives us extremely hard admonitions: "But I say to *you* that every one *who is angry with his brother* shall be guilty before the court; and whoever shall say to his brother, 'Raca,' shall be guilty before the supreme court; and whoever shall say 'You fool,' shall be guilty enough to go into the hell of fire" (NASB, emphasis mine).

Then Jesus looks at the other side—anger against you. "If therefore you are presenting your offering at the altar, and there remember that *your brother has something against you,* leave your offering there before the altar, and go your way; first be reconciled to your brother, and then come and present your offering" (vv. 23-24). No anger at others or by others is tolerated by Jesus.

How Is Reconciliation Possible?

In this world of such diverse desires, goals, and dogmas, is it realistic to believe the real body of Christ can be reconciled? As members of the human race, our answer has to be "No, it never can work." However, this answer is wrong because the reconciliation has already been accomplished on the cross of Christ.

Jesus *was* the answer to this question. Paul tells us in Ephesians 2 that the blood of Christ broke down the dividing wall between the Gentiles and the Jews of the Old Testament, "Who made both groups into one . . . that in Himself He . . . might *reconcile them both in one body* to God through the cross, by it having put to death the enmity" (vv. 14-16, NASB).

He also tells us that those who were united in the body of Christ "have put on the new self who is being renewed . . . a renewal in which there is no distinction between Greek and Jew, circumcised and uncircumcised, barbarian, Scythian, slave and freeman, but Christ is all, and in all" (Col. 3:10-11, NASB). Therefore, our responsibility is to live out in our daily lives what has already been accomplished for us by Jesus. Reconciliation is the application of Christ's work on the cross.

Jesus Is the Answer

A letter from Charles Colson included a story which, he said, so beautifully demonstrates the reconciling power of Jesus Christ. (I have changed the names of the inmates.) He wrote:

"It is about two inmates. One is Steve, a muscular forty-year-old man currently serving a five-year sentence for his involvement in pornography. He entered prison already a tough, hot-tempered man; prison life hardened him even further, making him bitter and resentful.

"During Steve's trial the key witness against him was an older man, John, a respected member of a special task force against pornography. But four years later John himself was convicted — ironically — on a morals charge. He was sentenced to the very institution where Steve was imprisoned.

"As soon as Steve learned from the inmate grapevine that his old accuser was in prison with him, he became obsessed with finding ways to get even. It started with harassment and an attempt at blackmail. Still Steve's hatred was unsatisfied, and finally the inevitable happened: Steve let it be known he was out to kill John.

"As I can testify from my own time in prison," wrote Colson, "behind the walls there is no one more universally hated than an informant or government witness; and John, a small, frail man, feared it was only a matter of time before he would be beaten or stabbed.

"However, during the weekend of May 3–5, 1985, we conducted one of our in-prison evangelism seminars at that prison. Incredibly, both Steve and John signed up to attend. Although Steve probably viewed it as an opportunity to stalk his prey, God had other plans. After the weekend of clear teaching on the forgiveness available through Jesus Christ, instructor Lorraine Williams closed with a special challenge.

" 'If there is anyone here who needs to forgive another person, I challenge you to do something about it — right now.'

"After a minute of heavy silence, Steve stood up. Would this be his time to strike? Or had this 'religious stuff' become too irritating for his bitter spirit to bear? No one was quite sure as he began walking toward John. Shaking, John sat with his head bowed.

"Finally, Steve stopped square in front of the man he wanted to murder. John lifted his head, and the two enemies faced each other in front of the entire seminar group.

" 'I'm sorry,' Steve said timidly. 'Will you forgive me?' Shocked,

John paused a moment, then nodded slowly. 'I will,' he said, and as Steve sat down next to him, the two pledged to work out their differences as *Christian* brothers."

Not retaliation, not retribution, but reconciliation in Jesus!

Reconciliation in Prayer Seminars

In our prayer seminars through the years, we too have seen innumerable instances of striking reconciliations. The struggles and then the joy that bursts forth is astounding. Weeping, hugging, dashing for a phone, or turning to a friend for forgiveness or to forgive—these fill every seminar with life-changing experiences. Seeing the real body of Christ praying with and for each other during a prayer seminar is one of our great joys. We see political, cultural, racial, and personal differences resolved and the oneness of the body of Christ emerging—sometimes slowly and haltingly, but nevertheless beginning.

A scene of cultural reconciliation that moved me deeply took place in Madras, India. The committee there had wisely scheduled the prayer seminar in the gorgeous cathedral in that city, attracting many elite ladies. So they came, wearing their shimmering, pure silk saris decorated with designs made of gold and silver threads. And the poor, some in rags, came too. The leaders of the city told me that, with the caste system still very much a part of their culture, this was the first time these two groups had ever come together, much less repeatedly prayed together all day, holding hands in their small groups.

When the seminar was over, I had to leave for another appointment. But they did not want to go. They said they had not finished praying together. As I reluctantly walked out the front door of that huge cathedral, I turned to see—reconciliation. I caught my breath as I saw the women kneeling in circles all over the cathedral, with their foreheads touching the floor and their saris pulled up over their heads in a sweeping kaleidoscopic effect. A beautiful step in breaking down a centuries-old division which humans had built.

Much of this unity is the result of the ground rules we insist be followed in our seminars. First, before I accept an invitation to conduct a prayer seminar, we request that the *organizing committee* find one born-again Christian from each participating church in the community to be on the steering committee. The shocked response usually goes something like this, "You mean there is a real Christian in *that* church?" (Of course, we are careful to explain the difference between real members of the body of Christ and just church members.) Then they are pleasantly surprised to find real sisters and brothers in Christ in *all* the churches.

However, the reason for this composition of steering committees is not so much for the work that needs to be done, but to fulfill the requirement that there be concentrated prayer at their regular meetings six months prior to the seminar. Then I have the unspeakable privilege of stepping into their committee dinner and prayer meeting the night before the seminar and feeling myself surrounded by their mutual love and engulfed by their power in corporate prayer.

I tell them that after they have learned to pray together like this, they hardly need me to come for a seminar! They have already discovered, usually for the first time, the oneness of the body of Christ in their area—an absolute necessity for the large metropolitan telephone prayer chains or other joint community-wide ventures they are planning to organize after our seminar.

I shall never forget praying with the committee in Glasgow, Scotland the night before our prayer seminar there in 1981. The committee was made up of outstanding women leaders, and in spite of some doctrinal differences, there was a unique and powerful oneness in Christ which had grown through the months of their praying together. But that night, they had invited their husbands and pastors. Some of the women even had to get permission to pray in the presence of those men (which in some instances was rather reluctantly granted). But as we knelt to pray together, my husband and I became acutely aware of a beautiful oneness in Jesus emerging. Finally, exploding with the wonder of the presence of God there, my Chris burst out in song, leading us all in singing on our knees, "*He* is Lord, He is Lord!" And we were all one—bound together in Him!

Another seminar rule that has produced this amazing reconciliation is to *invite all*—races, colors, denominations, political parties. One area of our country seemed almost to be still fighting the Civil War as they asked me to hold a prayer seminar. When they noted that one of the prerequisites for a seminar was that all the churches of the community had to be welcome, they said, "But never in our history have we done it that way."

"Then I don't come."

"Oh, Evelyn," lamented their godly leader, "I feel just horrible about this; but I know which of our members will get up and walk out if a black person comes to our church."

With great trepidation, but also with determined courage, this lovely woman president called on the women's leader of the neighboring black church. When she issued her invitation to come to their church, the black leader stammered, "But we aren't welcome in your church."

"I know you're not," came the chagrined reply. "But I'm inviting you anyway."

And they came. Hesitantly, cautiously, they sat there, furtively glancing from side to side to see how "they" were reacting. But before we knew it, God was at His work of reconciliation, and the age-old barriers began to melt away. Joy started taking over. By the end of the day, I wiped away tears as I watched them holding hands in prayer circles, with the love of Jesus radiating from so many of their faces. Reconciled? It surely was a start!

The problem was reversed when the auxiliary of the black ministerial association sponsored my prayer seminar in a southern state. It was an exciting time with great fellowship. And all of their pastors came, taking notes all through the day. I had a delightful time of warmth and acceptance by all—except a few women who were furious that their pastor would stoop to be taught by a white woman. But there's another invitation on my desk right now—from *these* same women!

In our recent seminars in Guam and Western Australia, a familiar pattern surfaced. For the first time, Christians of all persuasions came together to learn to pray. And in Taiwan, for the first time, both political sides came together to learn to pray with representatives from forty-three different Christian organizations and church affiliations, with the result that there are now more than 10,000 organized pray-ers from both sides on that island.

It was during our 1981 prayer seminar in Belfast, Northern Ireland which produced so much prayer for Liam and other prisoners, that we saw amazing reconciliation. I had the audience form prayer groups of four, with a strange mixture of Protestants and Catholics—at war—in each. My Scripture Press hosts and my husband watched from a high balcony. And for the first time, for them, and for me, we witnessed actual physical trembling in prayer as people forgave someone. Forgave the ones who had bombed their home or place of business, killed or maimed their loved ones. There it was—at least a little glimmer of hope for future reconciliation.

Closing reconciliation. The last praying we do in our seminars is an active step toward reconciliation. At the close, those who have been praying together all day in groups of four are given a final assignment. I ask one group member to name his or her church and the pastor or priest. Then the one on that person's right will pray for them by name while all the other members are praying silently. As we go around our little circles, each church and pastor or priest represented in the seminar will be the recipient of intercessory prayer. Frequently, this is the first time many of them have ever prayed for another church, especially if it is considered a competitor or has even a slightly different way of worshiping God.

Then to close the prayer seminar, we all join hands across the whole auditorium—those who have had a personal relationship with Christ for years and those who just that day made sure of their membership in the real body. And we sing together:

> Blest be the tie that binds
>   Our hearts in Christian love;
> The fellowship of kindred minds
>   Is like to that above.[1]

Then, while they all are still holding hands, I say, "Now squeeze!" And the final burst of unity comes in this parting hand-squeeze as big smiles spread across faces—sometimes surprising even themselves. And many turn to embrace their new-found friends in Christ. Or to weep. Or both. Reconciled in the real body of Christ!

I believe God has given me a ministry of reconciliation—not only of the sinner to God, but of brother and sister to brother and sister. And it works! But I also know that this unity is one of God's astounding answers to thousands of prayers through the years for these seminars by my prayers and the local seminar committees.

Secrets of Reconciliation

There are many secrets of reconciliation that we teach and practice, but the most important one seems to be *forgive*.

I received a phone call from a woman who had been at my prayer seminar the day before, but had left without forgiving her family. As I listened over the phone to this distraught and screaming woman, it occurred to me that I was probably receiving her "suicide call." (I learned later she actually had tried to take her own life twice before.)

"Mrs. Christenson," she screamed, "did you mean what you said Jesus said yesterday?" Asking her what it was, she literally screeched over the phone, "You said that Jesus said that if I don't forgive others now that I've become a Christian, God won't forgive me the sins I've committed as a Christian either."

Assuring her that Jesus really did say that both in Matthew 6 and Mark 11, I queried, "Why, what's wrong?"

"If you knew about my childhood," she shrieked, "you would never teach that again!" Then describing its horror, she continued, "My older brother raped me almost every night from the time I was seven. And my father, with my mother standing there consenting, would tie me to the bed and abuse my body. Then one day, he stripped me naked, tied me to a tree outside, and mutilated my body so badly that I never can have children. I'm going in for my second corrective surgery at the end of this week."

Oh, how I wanted to tell her Jesus really didn't say that and that I had just made it all up. But I could not lie. Jesus did say those words. So I kept her on the phone, talking and praying with her, striving desperately for a long time to change her mind. Then abruptly, she said, "I just bought a copy of your book *Gaining through Losing*. Will this do any good?"

Relieved at her abrupt change of attitude, I replied, "Yes. In the seminar, we only learned about your responsibility to forgive, but there is more to it than that. There is a chapter in that book about what will happen to you if you don't forgive them."

She ended the phone call by promising to read the chapter;

and it was just two days later that she called back. Her happy-sounding voice exclaimed, "Well, I did it. I forgave them!" We rejoiced together, and I called the prayer chains to tell them the good news and thank them for praying.

But two days later, she called again. "Well," she announced victoriously, "I did the whole thing! My family is 1,000 miles away, but I called to tell them I'd forgiven them and"—she soberly added—"to ask them to forgive my unforgiving attitude toward them."

Her pastor had been out of the country during that week, and I asked if he had returned. He, along with other professional counselors, had tried to help her for more than two years. When I asked what he had said when he saw her, she proudly reported, "Judy Rae, that's the fastest transformation I've ever seen!" Reconciled by forgiving.

Time magazine of January 9, 1984, in an article about Pope John Paul spending minutes in prison with his would-be assassin, Mehmet Ali Agca, recorded these startling words: "As Pope John Paul tenderly held the hand that had held the gun that was meant to kill him—it was a startling drama of forgiveness and reconciliation."

Isn't it amazing how the admonition in Ephesians 4:31-32 really does work? "Let all bitterness and wrath and anger and clamor and slander be put away from you, along with all malice. And be kind to one another, tender-hearted, forgiving each other, just as God in Christ also has forgiven you" (NASB).

In addition to forgiving, another secret of reconciliation is *love*. In our "What Happens When We Pray" seminars, we have practiced the scriptural reconciliation formula in 2 Corinthians 2:5-11 for years with truly remarkable results. After forgiving someone, we ask God for all the love He want us to have for that person, wait in prayer to feel it come, and then go home to confirm that new love.

A letter from a seminar participant shares the miracle God performed in her life:

> Dearest Evelyn:
> I can't tell you how much your life and message have affected mine! I lost my dear mother five years ago and she

was such a godly, loving woman and mother as you are.

My father remarried three years ago . . . a woman who just couldn't seem to love me. The hurt was deep and intense as she took many opportunities, where love could have been shared, to express rejection and bitter dislike . . . maybe even bordering on hate.

I have prayed much about this but a root of bitterness began to develop which also spread into other relationships, making me very touchy and emotionally unstable.

At your prayer seminar in Reno, Nevada, I had three people placed on my heart whom I had a lot of bitterness toward. I forgave them during the seminar (with many tears), and within the next two weeks the Lord beautifully brought about true forgiveness between all three persons and myself and also brought about opportunities for sincere and true reconciliation.

I received the first letter I have ever received from my stepmother, and it was a sincere attempt to express love to me. The Lord also freed me to express love to her by allowing her to be in a great need!

I can't express the freedom, joy and new fruitfulness which has come into my life because of this forgiveness and release from bitterness.

Thank you so much for being the Lord's willing and anointed handmaiden. I love you so much in Him! God bless you *so much!*

Tressa

The night Jesus was betrayed, He gave these words to His disciples, "A new comandment I give to you, that you love one another. . . . By this all men will know that you are My disciples, if you have love for one another" (John 13:34-35, NASB).

I watched a beautiful Christian mother whose son was deeply involved in organized crime live out this Scripture. Loving unconditionally, forgiving and forgiving again—although certainly not condoning—she kept her arms and home open to him through the years of agonized waiting and praying. How much easier it would have been for her to kick him out of her home or to disown him, as is done so frequently by embarrassed or angry parents. But it all paid off. He has come back to the Lord; and now he, his wife, and mother are living as inseparable friends.

Marriage Oneness

So often we hear, "My marriage has been over for a long time." No, this is not true. Incompatibility, cooled love, or conflicting interests do not dissolve the "one flesh" God created at the time of the marriage. What the couple needs most is reconciliation.

My autograph lines are full of people with shining eyes, joyously explaining how their marriages have been saved as they followed the instructions in our seminars or in the book, *What Happens When Women Pray*, to forgive, love, and confirm their love.

In a beautiful letter to me, a woman apologized for not telling me about her reconciliation with her husband six years ago. She said they were on the verge of divorce, fighting continuously, emotionally separated. "All it would have taken was for one of us to say two words, 'I'm leaving.' But in your prayer seminar you said we needed to ask forgiveness from those we hurt and forgive those who have hurt us." She recalled that she and her husband turned to each other, asked forgiveness of one another, and then forgave each other. "At that instant the Lord healed our marriage. We had come to the seminar as two independent married people and left as one in mind and heart. Praise God. We have two sons who would have been devastated by divorce."

Someone once told me, "A good marriage is made up not of two good lovers—but of two good forgivers!"

But family rifts and bad marriages are not always mended by forgiveness and love. My heart broke as we were asked to pray for a thirty-five-year-old Christian woman who was bringing up alone the baby she had as an unwed young teenager. Ostracized by family and friends, she was almost breaking emotionally under the strain. Even her mother had refused to speak to her since it happened.

When They Won't Be Reconciled

No matter how hard we try, there are those who refuse to be reconciled to us—the marriage partner who files for divorce and marries another, the parent who never again accepts the disowned child, the runaway child who severs all ties, the family member who refuses to break the angry silence of many years.

What do we do now? Romans 12:18 spells out our responsibility in these situations. "If possible, *so far as it depends on you*, be at peace with all men" (NASB, emphasis mine). In other words, we must do absolutely everything possible to bring about reconciliation with that person. But in real life, this is not always possible. However, whether others will or will not be at peace with us, God says we must be at peace with them.

A promising young seminary graduate just starting to serve his first church was devastated when his bride left him for her career, and she now admits to being deeply in love with another man. His dreams, his hopes, and, he is afraid, his career are lying shattered at his feet. In agony of soul, he has searched for reasons—and solutions. He has exhausted every avenue of wooing and begging, only to be repulsed time and time again.

What then? There comes a time when there is nothing left but prayer—two kinds. First, *a prayer of relinquishment.* Just before I spoke at a church luncheon, I couldn't understand why so many were weeping as a lovely articulate woman gave a short devotional on Catherine Marshall's "Prayer of Relinquishment." But the wife of the pastor of this beautiful church whispered the reason: "She was the wife of the former pastor, who ran away with his secretary and has just married her." Yes, when the one God joined in one flesh with you is married to another, it is time for the prayer of relinquishment.

A pastor at the National Prayer Assembly of India wept openly as he shared with us how he, just that day, had forgiven a member of his church who had twice put a knife to his throat to kill him. Then he wrote to me: "That rich man has closed the doors of my preaching there . . . but I prayed with broken heart in tears, 'Oh, Lord, forgive that man's mistakes and sins. Help me, Lord, to accept him as my own brother.' " Then he told me how he went to him and said, "Please, my dear brother, forgive me; I love you very much and I pray for you." But the offender just said, "You do not come to my house. Go away from here."

But this pastor in India also discovered the other kind of prayer to use when all seems hopeless—intercessory prayer *for* them. Jesus said, "Pray for them which despitefully use you" (Matt. 5:44).

I am continuously amazed at the flood of phone calls I receive from Christian wives whose husbands have found other women. Over and over, they tell me how they had remained faithful and prayed for years for their unfaithful mates; and even now, they are continuing to pray for them—no matter how despitefully they have been used. And the calls and letters from those who have been despitefully used at work, at school, in their neighborhood, even in Christian organizations—still praying *for* those who have wronged them—astounds me. They are following Jesus' admonition to pray for those who despitefully use them!

Amazing Results of Oneness

Jesus knew why He demanded reconciliation and oneness. He knew the fantastic results of being reconciled to each other. In His High-Priestly Prayer recorded in John 17, He gave us His reasons for praying that we might be one (John 17:20-23). Jesus knew that so many of the things we need and hope for are the results of being reconciled. They are *that* in our oneness we can have the same relationship as the Father and Son have. *That* we can have the privileged position of actually being *in* that Father-Son relationship of oneness. Our unity will prove *that* God sent Jesus. And Jesus gave us the glory God gave Him that we may also be one. *That* we may be perfected in unity so *that* the world will know God sent Jesus, and *that* He loves the world just as He loves His Son, Jesus. For what more could we ask?

But even more amazingly, the credibility of Jesus in the world hangs on our unity! So, when we are tempted to pray, "God, with whom should I be reconciled?" He will unhesitatingly answer, "Everybody!"

Closing Prayer

Father, I'm sorry for living as if my broken relationships with people did not matter to You. Please forgive me. Help me to make reconciliation as far as it is possible for me to do. I promise to pray for those who have despitefully used me. Thank You that Jesus insisted on the reconciliation

of members of His body, not so that we could become one, but because
*we are one. And I promise to seek out the real body of Your Son, Jesus,
and practice the oneness He died to give us.*

In Jesus' name, **Amen.**

9
When God answers...

Make Restitution

Although God no longer holds us accountable to Himself for the sins He has forgiven, we still are responsible to the human beings we have hurt.

After praying, "God, I have sinned," and taking the steps of repenting and being reconciled to Him and others, are we absolved of all further responsibility and action? No. We still have a responsibility to the one against whom we have sinned.

This is the step of restitution. It is making amends, making good for a loss or damage. It is giving back to the rightful owner something that has been taken away. When we have sinned, it is our duty to make amends to the one victimized by our sinning.

While we must be reconciled to God when we sin, restitution is only made to the persons against whom we have sinned. There is no way we can repay God for violating His holiness. All we can do is repent because we have hurt Him so deeply and love Him so much that we will do everything in our power to restore our relationships with Him. Then we can serve Him with a new passion, making up for the lost days or opportunities. But our human relationships are different. Reconciliation to people against whom we have sinned or committed a crime usually includes making restitution of some kind.

Thinking of Our Victim
As we study and teach the biblical accounts of David's sin, we tend to ignore Bathsheba's side. But David did not; he finally got around to thinking about her.

When the Lord sent Nathan to David to rebuke him for his sin with Bathsheba and for having her husband killed, Nathan told David a story. It concerned a rich man who killed the only lamb of a poor neighbor to feed his guests instead of one from his own large flock. David burned with anger and cried, "As the Lord lives, surely the man who has done this deserves to die. And he must *make restitution* for the lamb fourfold, because he did this thing and had not compassion" (2 Sam. 12:5-6, NASB, emphasis mine). Then, as Nathan said, "You are the man!" David was devastated and repented of his horrendous sins.

But the results of his sin extended to his victim, Bathsheba. When David recognized himself as the sinner and repented, Nathan said, "The Lord also has taken away your sin; you shall not die. However, because by this deed you have given occasion to the enemies of the Lord to blaspheme, the child also that is born to you shall surely die" (2 Sam. 12:13-14, NASB) So, although God did forgive David's sins, because of his sin, the innocent victim, Bathsheba, lost in death the two humans closest to her—her husband and her child.

David finally realized that repenting before God was not the end of his responsibility. As king, he had said that the rich man who had killed the poor man's lamb had to make restitution. And now he realized that he, being the man Nathan was talking about, also had to make restitution. So he turned to the one he had hurt—Bathsheba. Second Samuel 12:24 tells us that after the child died, "Then David comforted his wife Bathsheba" (NASB).

There was a point after the child's death that David stopped having a "pity party." He stopped looking only at what had happened to himself—because he got caught. David saw that his lust for Bathsheba had twice caused deep sorrow in her. When he had her husband killed on the front lines, Bathsheba was in deep anguish and mourning, like any other bereaved widow. David's sin not only caused her to be widowed, but it also caused the death of her child conceived in his sin.

The Victim's Hurt

My phone rings many, many times with calls for the devastated victims of sinning children, mates, or others begging for prayer support. I wait silently as the grief so wells up within the caller that words are unutterable. Or I listen with my heart aching as they sob uncontrollably, trying to ask for prayer. Their lives have been shattered; and, while I understand that no child or parent or mate is perfect, there usually seems to be one who is grievously sinning and causing the heartache. There *are* innocent people being hurt.

I held a grieving mother in my arms after a seminar as she related how her seemingly fine Christian daughter had turned her back on God and was trying every conceivable thrill of the world on the streets of one of our large cities. Then I felt this mother's whole body shudder violently at the repulsive mental picture of all that filthy sin in her darling child. She was a teenager fulfilling her own evil desires but was completely oblivious, or at least insensitive, to what she was doing to her parents.

I remember the chagrined agony of a mother as I sat in the local police station with her and her ninth-grade son as he was given jobs in the community to make restitution for stealing "just little things" from his employer. "Where have I gone wrong?" she moaned. "Where did I fail? I have tried so hard to live and teach biblical values in our home." Here was a parent giving her very lifeblood to her child—only to have him repay with a lifestyle producing anguish and even guilt in her.

The sinning son or daughter must see the devastating hurt they are causing their heartbroken parents. The untrustworthy employee must face the ruptured trust of the employer's faith; the sinning spouse must admit the pain of broken marriage vows; the sinning pastor must see the hurt to his congregation. The sinning parent must be aware of the deep hurts he or she is causing in the children, and the criminal the loss of possessions, dignity, or life he has inflicted upon his victim.

For more than a year, I have prayed on the phone with Kaye, whose husband fell in love with another woman in their church. And, while Kaye watched from her seat in the choir loft, the situation progressed from that of girlfriend to a lover, then to the divorce, and now with the new wife all but snuggling with Kaye's former husband during church services. The pastor had watched it all from his vantage point in the pulpit and later performed the marriage ceremony with his blessing—evidently without questioning whether it was God's will that the already-married couple stay married. And evidently, the pastor did so without remembering Jesus' teaching in Matthew 19:6, where He said, "What therefore God has joined together, let no man separate" (NASB), and the words in Malachi 2:16, " 'For I hate divorce,' says the Lord" (NASB).

Those agonizing months of seeing the romance progress were times of deep self-examination for Kaye—as with most with whom I pray. She constantly kept asking me what she had done wrong, where she had failed, how could she improve so as to mend the rift. One of the most difficult things to deal with in these phone calls is the victims' search for answers from God on how to change themselves, when the sinning mates seem oblivious to any problem in themselves.

The women I talk with not only are working to become better mates, but are struggling to keep the children together and care for their physical and emotional needs—all this while pouring out their hearts in prayer for their wayward partners.

My own saintly mother told me her feelings when my father confessed to her his unfaithfulness. "I always had said that my husband would never do anything like that. I believed he could do nothing wrong. I had complete trust in him, my bridegroom," she wept. "The thing that hurt the most was lost trust. Being betrayed by the one I had absolute, complete faith in. My bridegroom! I wanted to die—to jump off a bridge—to kill myself."

Welling up within me as she talked were God's words in Malachi 2:15, where He almost thunders, "Let no one deal treacherously against the wife of your youth" (NASB). Marriage vows are shattered, bodily purity is desecrated, and lifetime promises are broken for the mate still believing in the sanctity of marriage as one of life's most valuable possessions!

Frequently, the victim remains skeptical, unable ever to trust again. But not so with my Christlike mother. Although my father was not a Christian, I watched in amazement as she forgave him and little by little restored him and their marriage with her astonishingly selfless love.

What Do You Expect?
Prisoners often expect to be pardoned or paroled early after being sentenced regardless of the injury to their victims. But a

pastor speaking at a recent National Religious Broadcasters convention made an important point when he said, "The criminal should stay in prison as long as the victim has to stay in the hospital."

A story I am told so frequently is that a husband leaves home, lives with another woman for a while, then comes back and acts as if nothing had happened. He feels as if he has a perfect right to expect all the comforts of home—just the way it was before. One woman told me that her husband comes and goes like this and becomes absolutely incensed if she so much as suggests that it may not be right and is hurting her.

Jesus told of a much more realistic expectation by the prodigal son who, after squandering his estate from his father in riotous living in a far country, came to his senses and went back home—*expecting* to be made just a hired hand. Even though his father embraced him and kissed him, the son cried, "Father, I have sinned against heaven and in your sight; I am no longer worthy to be called your son" (Luke 15:21, NASB).

We too should not *expect* to be welcomed back with open arms when we have caused grief and anxiety in someone. We should understand that the human response from our victim is more apt to be like that of the prodigal's elder brother who was angry and unwilling for a restored relationship. We should be extremely grateful when the victim is willing to forgive, accept us back, and restore our relationship.

Accept Responsibility

When I teach the biblical responsibility of the one sinned against to forgive (*What Happens When Women Pray*) and what the serious consequences are to us if we don't forgive (*Gaining through Losing*), people say to me, "But what about *them?*" Well, this chapter is about "them"—the responsibility of the sinner who has caused the hurt.

Basically, it is the selfishness of the one sinning that causes the hurt the victim must endure. The current popular philosophy even among some Christians is to think only of being fulfilled themselves, doing what feels good, with little or no concern for those they may be hurting. It is the philosophy of humanism which is rampant or so-called Christian humanism, by which these Christians are living diametrically opposed to God's biblical rules.

I recall the depth of our prayers for a pregnant wife who was on the verge of collapsing emotionally because her husband was having an affair. The girlfriend decided to have a baby shower for the coming baby—but didn't invite the mother-to-be! Then, when all the guests had left, she and the husband lay down in the midst of the baby gifts and had sex. The strain of the pregnancy plus this unbelievably inhuman treatment made many fear for the wife's health as she was almost breaking emotionally. This was fatherhood—without the least concern or responsibility for the emotional harm he was causing to his wife and unborn child!

Sinners must see themselves as the wrongdoers. They must accept the fact that they are guilty of having hurt another person or perhaps many others. The one who has caused the emotional, mental, and perhaps physical suffering must accept responsibility for the one he or she has devastated—realizing that this person needs to be healed and that restitution is imperative.

Have you sinned by stealing someone else's reputation by passing on false or only partially true rumors about them? Have you undermined a minister God has called because of your vicious criticism of him? Have you destroyed somebody else's self-worth because this was the only way you could feed and satisfy your own pride and ego? Have you gotten ahead and succeeded by trampling a coworker? Is your sin with someone of the opposite sex, in thought or deed, devastating your mate? Is your child's emotional well-being shattered because you are selfishly living in sin? Are you causing anguish and undeserved guilt in your parents because of your lifestyle? Is stepping on somebody else the only way you can get what you want and what fulfills you? Then restitution to that person is in order.

Make Restitution

In Colonial America, Jonathan Edwards considered restitution an ongoing obligation and failure to make it an ongoing sin. He said, "I exhort those who are conscious in themselves that they have wronged their neighbor to make restitution. This is a duty the obligation to which is exceedingly plain. . . . A man who hath gotten anything from another wrongfully, goes on to wrong him every day that he neglects to restore it, when he has opportunity to do it."[1]

After acknowledging responsibility for our victim's hurts, it is time to take active steps to make amends. And there are those sinners and criminals who have accepted this responsibility and have courageously acted upon it, making restitution.

Prison Fellowship is sponsoring successful Community Service Projects in which Christian prisoners are released into communities for a couple of weeks to repair homes of needy citizens and to participate in other helpful projects—to make restitution.

The Reverend Sam Hines, a powerful pastor in Washington, D.C., whose church already provides foster care for homeless children and breakfast five days a week for hundreds of the neighborhood's homeless, hosted a Prison Fellowship Community Service project. Five Christian inmates spent two weeks repairing the home of a needy, nine-member family on the block. The response from the community was overwhelming, and even the mayor of the District of Columbia commended Prison Fellowship's community service.

When the project was over, Pastor Hines said, "People see convicts negatively—but this project exploded that myth." People had seen prisoners—changed by the Living Christ—bringing practical demonstrations of love in the form of hammers and nails and fresh, clean paint to a grimy home in need.

But most important, it gave the prisoners themselves the privilege of making restitution, of making amends for some of the hurt they had caused the community. Not because they had to— but because they wanted to. They also gained a positive self-image about themselves. Restitution!

Daniel Van Ness, president of Justice Fellowship in Washington, D.C., informed me that, at this writing, there is a bill being drafted by one of our United States congressmen that "would have federal minimum security prisoners leave their confinement during the day to work. Of course," he wrote, "they would be well-supervised. The money they receive would be divided between the victim, the prisoner's family, the government (to pay room and board), and some savings for the prisoner. The benefits to the victim and community are obvious," he continued. "Victims would be paid back, and the community would have its costs reduced. But I think there is also a great benefit to the offender, not the least of which is the opportunity to make right the wrong."

How marvelous it would be to finally have a restitution program and one that would benefit the victim, the prisoner's family, the government, and the criminal!

John Calvin said, "In whatever way, therefore, a man should have committed an offense, whereby another is made poorer, he is commanded to make good the loss."[2]

Mary Kay Beard is one who has made good many losses and is now giving her whole life to prisoners. At Charles Colson's Prison Fellowship staff retreat, I spent many hours with Mary Kay, a successful and effective state director of this organization. "My whole life is restitution now," Mary Kay said to me.

But she has not always been bringing Christ into prisons and working with inmates, their families, and released prisoners. Mary Kay is an ex-con herself who was sentenced to serve twenty-one years in prison for armed robbery of mainly cash and diamonds. She was wanted in five states and by the federal government, and there was a contract on her life from the underworld.

She was abused as a child by her alcoholic father who had broken her back, every one of her ribs, and her nose twice. Running away from home at fifteen, then marrying the man she later discovered was a gambler and a thief, Mary Kay traveled for five years with him in a continuous crime spree. Beautiful clothes, furs, jewels, and custom-built cars fulfilled all her childhood dreams. Then the man she worshiped left her and was soon arrested. Eight months later she too was in jail.

Mary Kay, however, was transformed in prison when one day she slipped from her metal bunk onto her knees on the concrete floor of her cell and gave her life to Jesus. She wrote, "As tears streamed unchecked down my face, a flood of joy filled my whole being. I felt light, as though I'd been loosed from a mighty anchor. At that moment on March 16, 1973, God set me free—free from a terrible weight of guilt and shame, and free from the enslavement of sin!"

Graduating with honors in the first group of inmates to participate in the prison-college program at Julia Tutwiler Prison for women, she has gone on to become the first woman in the United States to receive a graduate degree while serving time in a prison.

More than Legalistic Responsibility

Mary Kay now devotes her life to those still in concrete and spiritual prisons. And the exuberance and joy with which she bounces and beams made me know it was not just legalistic responsibility—but wanting to—that motivates her.

"Angel Tree," one of Prison Fellowship's most successful programs, was originated by Mary Kay. Since prison inmates rarely can buy any Christmas presents for their children, these children are asked to write down the four things they want most for Christmas. The requests are then recorded on paper angels that are hung on Christmas trees placed in churches, shopping malls, or other public places by Prison Fellowship volunteers. Then people, taking an angel from the tree, purchase one or more of these gifts which are then wrapped and delivered to the children by Prison Fellowship staff and volunteers.

It is incredible what this now nationwide project is accomplishing. Children who feel forsaken suddenly are remembered, ever-widening rifts between incarcerated parents and their children are narrowed, and many desperate needs are filled. During Christmas 1985, Angel Trees provided Christmas presents for 31,500 children of inmates. The response of these children when the gifts were delivered was absolutely overwhelming.

I asked Mary what the children requested and she replied, "It's amazing. Sometimes it's just a pencil box for school the parent can't supply. One adolescent asked for a *new* item of underclothing, which she had never owned in her whole life. Another young girl asked for just one thing—to be able to visit her daddy in prison in another state for Christmas. Most people puzzled over that 'angel' request and passed it by. But an eighth-grade Sunday School class picked it off the tree, worked to raise the money, and sent her to see her daddy for Christmas!"

I asked Mary whether this project was in any manner her way of making restitution. Surprised at this possible motivation, she said she needed some time to think it through. When we met the next day, she had the answer: "There's no question about it. Yes, this is my way of helping the whole prison population." Then Mary reflected sadly, "Christmas is the hardest time of the year to be away from children and to be absolutely unable to bring any happiness into their lives. It was especially hard to watch mothers in prison receive perhaps a little gift of toothpaste from a caring church group or individual, and then give it to their child for Christmas—the only gift they had."

This is far more than legalistic responsibility. Mary Kay was a terrific example of the Apostle John's admonition in 1 John 3:18 to live out Jesus' love, "Little children, let us not love with word or with tongue, but in *deed* and truth" (NASB, emphasis mine).

Mary Kay also had a lot of restitution to make to her own family. She explained to me, "I had created division between my sisters while I was living with them by lying about what each had said in certain situations."

And she told me that when she prayed, "Lord, where did I go wrong?" He answered by telling her to write a letter, making restitution to her two older sisters. She wrote and rewrote letter after letter, always including in each one something that justified her actions. But God would always tell her that it was not right. "It was when I finally could write confessing it all as a total lie that the Holy Spirit let me put it in the mail." Although it was more than four years before one sister responded, accepting her apology, Mary Kay had obeyed God's answer to her prayer—to make restitution.

It was two years after the crime had been committed that God brought to Mary Kay's mind her need to make restitution for having misused a telephone credit card for more than $100. But she had to ask God to bring to her mind the exact date and the phone number she needed to know in order to make restitution. His answer was to have her mother check all her old phone bills, which surprisingly, included the phone number to which Mary Kay had charged all those bills. Mary Kay was making $25 a month in her prison work-release job, and it took exactly four months to make that restitution. But make it she did!

Restitution is not just paying fines, sending alimony checks, serving a prison sentence, or begrudgingly paying back what we have stolen. It springs from desire of the heart. Restitution is not made from duty—but from love.

Not Always Easy

"To make restitution may open yourself to more liability than you think you can deal with," Mary Kay told me. "When I was wanted in four states but had not yet come to trial, I knew that if I confessed to one crime it would have shown that I had been in Raleigh, North Carolina, and would have implicated me in several other crimes. But I finally could write to that sheriff and admit that I had stolen that car there, so the items could be returned to their rightful owner." But she told me that although she was willing to pay the additional price, God graciously protected her from further charges of more crimes in that area at the time. Restitution may not be easy!

One restitution experience was particularly difficult for her because of the *victim's partial guilt*. After becoming a Christian, Mary Kay pleaded guilty to the crime of stealing cash and jewelry from a member of a certain town's "First Church." But her victim accused Mary Kay of stealing a ring that the woman had had in her safety deposit vault all along, collecting the insurance for the supposed theft. Mary Kay had asked this woman's forgiveness for breaking into her home, frightening her, and stealing not only her possessions but her security in her home as well. But her victim refused to forgive Mary Kay, claiming the worst part was having lost the ring—which, of course, she had all along.

More than a year later, the warden allowed Mary Kay to speak to a Christian Women's Club in that city, and this woman had been invited to attend. With reporters and the chief of detention watching, Mary Kay shared her testimony. The victim's neighbor then asked Mary Kay if she wasn't going to ask for forgiveness since the woman claimed that her life started to fall apart at the time of the robbery and, although her husband forgave Mary Kay before he died, the woman was now a desperately bitter widow.

Mary Kay knew that she had been denied forgiveness and swallowed hard to keep from revealing the truth and incriminating the victim. In this case, it was time for the *victim* to make restitution by asking Mary to forgive her and returning the insurance money. Mary's responsibility ended when she had asked for forgiveness and was paying back what she actually stole. The victim's problems were her own because of her guilt in the crime and her unforgiveness.

Mary Kay's husband, Don, an ex-con who had served two terms of embezzlement and business-related crimes, joined us at that Prison Fellowship retreat. Together, they explained their *joint restitution program.*

First they prayed, asking God how they should go about making restitution. He answered with a specific plan which they immediately put into practice. The first 10 percent of their budget would go to God, then they agreed that 60 percent would be sufficient for their household budget, and that the other 30 percent would go to those from who they had stolen.

Then they carefully sought out and contacted their victims, initially taking care of those who were personally harmed and who suffered personal loss, dividing the 30 percent among them little by little, month by month. Restitution is not paying a fine that goes to the treasury of the community but repaying the victim.

Jesus Makes a Difference

Mary Kay and Don reminded me of Zaccheus, the rich tax-gatherer who climbed a tree that he might see Jesus. Zaccheus and other tax collectors did not receive a salary for their work, but they collected as much money as they could so that they would have a handsome rake-off after paying the Roman government its appointed sum. But when Zaccheus had "received Jesus gladly," he made this startling declaration of his restitution intentions to Jesus, "Behold, Lord, half of my possessions I will give to the poor, and if I have defrauded anyone of anything, I will give back four times as much" (Luke 19:8, NASB).

Surprisingly, there is no indication of Jesus demanding that Zaccheus make restitution. It was simply that once he came into a right relationship with his Lord, all the cheating of his past life loomed before him; and his first thought was to make amends to those he had hurt.

Evidently, he did not think only of clearing his own conscience by making restitution, but a new love and compassion for his victims sprang up within him. In place of greed, Zaccheus seemed to discover the thrill of seeing his victims repaid, and perhaps even lifted out of their poverty.

Should we today do less than Zaccheus? Should we not only

have the blush of a first love that comes with new life in Jesus, but also an ever-growing awareness of how we damage, hurt, and wound our victims even in everyday life?

Since Zaccheus' words, "I give" and "I give back," are both in the present tense in the Greek, we know that he intended a future ongoing process of making restitution. Should we not also strive to keep alive that sensitivity to those hurts we bring to people—even those we love?

For the Sinner's Benefit

As I talked with Don Beard at the Prison Fellowship staff retreat, I was impressed by his insight into the importance to the criminal himself of making restitution. "I am at the point now in my restitution that I can walk around without fear of whom I might run into," he said, smiling victoriously.

"Did all those to whom you made restitution respond in the same way?" I asked Don.

"Oh, no. When I went to them and said that I had a responsibility for the past but could only repay a little at a time, their responses varied. One man was offended. Another former business acquaintance whom I had cheated greatly was overwhelmed. He said that he knew from my actions I was sincere and forgave me the whole debt. Amazingly," Don continued, "those people I harmed the most forgave the most!"

Then Don agreed with me that the victim's response has nothing to do with the responsibility to make restitution. The responsibility is the offender's—but the rewards are also his.

"Making restitution is very rewarding to myself," said Don. "*It has validated what I did in private with God as I repented.*" He explained further, "Restitution gives substance to your repentance." Then, seemingly reflecting on this whole process, he said softly, "Repentance without restitution is pretty hollow."

Don knew about repentance. He had repented when he accepted Christ as his Savior while a prisoner. And then as a Christian, he had repented deeply over the hurts he had caused in so many people. And he had learned well that complete restoration never can come to the offender until there has been the lifting of the guilt in one's own eyes by making restitution.

Then Mary Kay and Don chimed in together, "Restitution is for

the criminal's benefit. It is healing and cleansing!"
  Is there restitution you have to make?

Closing Prayer

Oh, God, forgive me for being insensitive to those I have hurt. Forgive my selfishness. Father, bring to my mind all those to whom I need to make restitution. God, I will wait in silence for You to bring to my mind the steps You want me to take. Please give me Jesus' love for them and Your courage to be obedient to Your expectations of me.

In Jesus' name, **Amen.**

10
When God answers...

Restore That Sinner

When catching a sister or brother sinning, how often we pray, "Oh, God, what do I do now?" And the surprising answer from God is already recorded in the Bible. "Restore that sinner!"

> Brethren, even if a man is caught in any trespass, you who are spiritual, restore such a one in a spirit of gentleness (Gal. 6:1, NASB).

What does it mean to restore? Paul had in mind here the mending of something that had been damaged. Restoration is the responsibility of those Christians surrounding the sinner. Repentance, reconciliation, and restitution are all the responsibility of the sinner; but, shockingly, restoration very likely must be done by the one sinned against, and it may even be the victim's job.

However, restoration does not begin while the person is sinning. It is when he or she is "caught" trespassing that the process begins. There can be no real restoration without the sinner fulfilling the other three "R's" preceding it—repentance, reconciliation, and restitution. Paul leaves no excuse in his teaching for Christians who are sinning, but makes it clear that the person who has sinned can be restored. But it is only the sinner whom God has accepted back through His forgiveness that we should accept back and restore.

This seems to be a lost teaching in recent years. We have been handling the sinning brother or sister one of two ways. Either we have ignored the sin, finding it much more comfortable not to become involved, or we have followed the scriptural injunction to rebuke him but with no further concern for the repentant one's well-being and restoration.

Although sin is not to be tolerated, there are definite steps the Christian church must take when a brother or sister sins. And the final step in this whole process is restoring the sinner to fellowship and ministry.

Jesus told His followers in Luke 17:3: "Be on your guard! If your brother sins, rebuke him; and *if he repents*, forgive him" (NASB, emphasis mine). It is when the sinner repents that Christian action begins.

Who Restores That Sinner?

At a "Lord, Change Me" seminar a few years ago, during a Bible reading exercise, God stopped me at Galatians 6:1, "Restore such a one in a spirit of gentleness" (NASB). As I prayed asking Him who it was He wanted me to restore, His immediate answer was the name of a close friend. Whenever the Lord gives a command as clear as this to me, I immediately promise Him I'll do it— which I did that day.

Then I asked God what needed to be restored, and His answer flooding through my mind was, "Vigor, leadership, self-esteem, shoulders back, and a posture of confidence again." So, for more than two years, I have been actively involved in restoring my friend. And although the price has been high, the rewards and joys for me are indescribable as I've watched one by one those qualities being abundantly restored to my friend.

God, through Paul, gave the "spiritual" Christians in the churches in Galatia the job of restoring sinners. I remember recoiling at that word *spiritual*. In all honesty, I could not see myself as "spiritual." Although I knew God divided Christians into these categories, it felt like horrible pride for me to do so. But it is true that while no Christian is perfect, there are some who are striving to be Christlike while others are living in defiance of His laws. It is to these "spiritual" Christians that God gives the restoring role.

Also, in the great forgiving formula in 2 Corinthians 2:5-11, it is the grieved Christian who is to comfort, get underneath, and buoy up the one who has done the grieving. And it is the Christian whom a brother has something against who is to go to that brother before bringing his offering to God.

Now, if we are not willing to obey God and restore the sinner, then we obviously don't qualify as being spiritual in His eyes. We may prefer to remain bitter, especially if we are the one sinned against. Then we are breaking God's command in Ephesians 4:31 to "let all bitterness and wrath and anger . . . be put away from you, along with all malice" (NASB). Which, of course, marks us as unspiritual also. And a Christian living in sin hardly is in a position or eligible to restore a sinning brother or sister.

"I Don't Want To"

There also is the possibility that we don't want the sinner restored. We may prefer to say, "Good, you got what was coming to you. Squirm in the results of your sin! Retaliation is what you will get from me, not restoration!" But restoration, not retaliation or retribution, is God's New Testament command to us. "See that no one repays another with evil for evil, but always seek after that which is good for one another and for all men" (1 Thes. 5:15, NASB). Then again in Romans 12:17, "Never pay back evil for evil to anyone" (NASB).

There are many reasons why we knowingly or subconsciously really do not want the sinner to be restored. As long as they are not restored, we appear so much more spiritual in contrast to them. We, the victims, get so much more sympathy for the burden we are carrying if they remain in their sinning state. And people may even compliment us on what a great job we are doing holding them up.

Or, perhaps we need the sinner to keep depending on us. We need to be the strong, victorious, forgiving leader. It helps our own self-image when they are groveling at our feet in remorse, shame, and defeat.

I was surprised at the warning to me included in Galatians 6:1, "Looking to yourself, *lest* you too be tempted" (NASB, emphasis mine). Reading verse 3, I cried, "O God, forgive me for thinking I'm better than the one I'm restoring. Search my heart lest I be tempted too—before I am."

Then, of course, there is the possibility of our being jealous of the repentant sinner being restored to a great ministry, feeling they have no right to achieve once more and perhaps even surpass us. But, no matter what our excuses, God says in His Word, *"Restore that sinner!"*

Who Needs Restoring?

We must be careful to identify the sinner about whom Paul is writing in Galatians 6:1. Restoration is possible only in the life of a Christian. Being restored to an upright state (2 Tim. 3:16) is not possible for one still in the state of sin into which he or she was born. What non-Christians need is regeneration—when all sin is forgiven as they repent and accept Christ. Then they are accepted into the body of Christ for nurturing.

Paul was careful to tell us in 1 Corinthians 5:12-13 not to judge the outsider, because God would. Jesus also said in John 3:18 that the one not believing on Him is condemned already. The restoration process is not for him. We are to win that one to Jesus—who at the moment is making that person a new creation in Himself.

My non-Christian father sinned against my mother for many years; and even though she forgave him—and there was complete reconciliation in their marriage, and although he did his best to make restitution for what he had done to her—my father could not be restored to an upright state. It was only after he asked God to forgive all his sins and asked Jesus to become his Savior and Lord (Mark 1:15) that we as a family could watch his restoration begin.

How Do Humans Restore Sinners?

Now that we know restoring the sinning brother or sister is not optional, we ask God, "But how do we go about restoring such a one?" The Bible is full of God's instructions on this oft-neglected subject.

Rebuking the sinner is His first instruction. Just as the Lord sent Nathan to rebuke David after he had sinned, so God also sends people today. Sometimes He sends a Nathan into our lives, and other times He calls on us to be the Nathan.

When Nathan told David he had not just sinned against Uriah but had despised the word of the Lord by doing evil in His sight, David cried out, "I have sinned against the Lord" (2 Sam. 12:13, NASB). And David, accepting Nathan's rebuke, had taken the first step toward restoration.

How important it is to listen to those whom God sends to us. Jesus in Luke 16:19-31 told His followers the story of a rich man calling from his place of torment after death, begging Abraham to send Lazarus to warn his brothers to repent. But Abraham answered, "If they do not listen to Moses and the Prophets, neither will they be persuaded if someone rises from the dead" (Luke 16:31, NASB).

Paul, giving instructions as to what to do with an erring brother or sister, concludes with, "And yet, do not regard him as an enemy, but admonish him as a brother" (2 Thes. 3:15, NASB).

Jesus tells His followers in Luke 17:3, "Be on your guard! If your brother sins, rebuke him" (NASB). So the first step in people restoring a sinning brother or sister is to admonish and warn.

Restore by forgiving. Rebuking the sinning brother is not all we are to do to restore him. Jesus follows this admonition to rebuke the sinning brother with the words, "And if he repents, forgive him" (Luke 17:3, NASB).

The restoration process demands that the one doing the restoring forgive the one being restored. Without genuine forgiveness, the whole process will be a sham; and the insincerity of the restorer will be sensed by the one hopefully being restored.

The step of forgiveness in restoring the sinner may be the most difficult one to take. Sometimes, we resent the person being restored, having deep unresolved feelings that he, or she, "doesn't deserve to be forgiven and restored after that awful sin." But we cannot begin to restore a repentant sinner until we have forgiven him or her.

I watched the hurt in a close friend as his wife was having an affair with a mutual family friend, finally leaving him and their children. Then came the reconciliation period when the husband took her back into their home. One day, the husband and I happened to meet. With his face flushed with deep emotion and his eyes wet with tears, he smiled through it all as he showed me a Bible passage. "Look what the Lord gave me! See, it tells me how I'm to forgive her. And, Mrs. Chris, I did! I did! I've forgiven her!" How exciting now, a couple of years later, to see this marriage and the erring wife completely and joyously restored!

For me, the hardest part of obeying while working with the person God gave me to restore came one afternoon when that person just exploded in confession to me that I was the one against whom that friend had sinned. Although I actually had known about it for years, there always had been that one's denial of the situation. Although I truly had forgiven when it happened, suddenly hearing the awful details sent me reeling in shock. And only God enabled me to stand unflinchingly on all the previous forgivenesses; never once did I feel a twinge of unforgiveness that day.

In the last ten years during our prayer seminar teaching on forgiving, I have seen literally hundreds of marriages restored and snatched from divorce proceedings by the act of forgiving an erring spouse.

Restoration to usefulness in God's kingdom is possible only after involved Christians forgive the repentant leader or layperson. I missed a convention speech as I sat listening to a beautiful Christian leader tell me of the bitter circumstance she had just left at home. Her fourteen-year-old daughter was soon to give birth to a baby fathered by their church's youth director— who was married and had a child of his own. He had come to their home to counsel their daughter, had taken her into the bedroom, and she came out pregnant.

Devastated, he deeply repented before God, appeared before the church body asking for their forgiveness, and unremittingly did all he could to make it right with the family and the girl against whom he had sinned.

This mother recounted that just before she left for this convention he had come to see how her little girl was doing. Then she repeated to me the incredible thing she said to him: "You have a theological education and were called by God to serve Him the rest of your life. Now, when Satan gets other people to say that you have forfeited the right to serve God because of the awful thing you did, you look them right in the eye and say, 'Oh, but even her mother forgave me!' "

A highly qualified administrator had been hired by a Christian college, only to be fired at the insistence of its ruling board because of a past immoral act. Although he had deeply repented to God, to his wife, and before his church publicly and had been forgiven and taken back by all, the members of the college board still were skeptical and understandably protective of the reputation of their school and the possible influence on the student body. But even though he definitely had turned from his former lifestyle, he was not given the opportunity to be restored to ministry.

After sinning, how many Christians, gifted by God for His kingdom's work, are using those talents in the world because Christians refused to do their part in obeying God's command to forgive and restore after the offender had taken the steps of repentance, reconciliation, and restitution?

Restore by what we are. It is not only what we say but what we are in our relationship to God that is extremely important in our human restoration of repentant sinners. The ones being restored will "catch" what we are, much more than what we tell them. Our unshakable trust and faith in God; our striving to be holy in spite of all the ugly circumstances in which we are living or people with whom we are associating; an upbeat, victorious attitude toward life; a sweet spirit of gentleness permeating our whole being—these will help restore that sinner.

I watched this in my mother, one of the greatest restorers God ever put on earth. Unshakable, childlike trust in God no matter how her world was falling apart; never wavering in her faith as she restored sinning relatives and my repentant father; tenderly caring for him in his last, bedridden years—my mother!

In fact, it was during a period when I was deeply seeking God's holiness for myself and praying for revival, that the one I was restoring said, "It was watching your striving to be holy and my realization that I am not spiritually eligible to be part of revival that I couldn't stand. It led to my being unable to stand my deceit—and ultimately to confess."

Restore by prayer **for** *that sinner.* Praying is the most powerful thing we can do to restore the sinner. Why? Because it releases the God of the universe to reach down and touch that repentant sinner with His omnipotent restoration.

Also, there may be times in the depth of guilt and remorse that the sinner is spiritually or emotionally unable to pray for himself or herself; and then our prayers will be all the prayer there is. There also may be times that praying is the only thing we can do.

However, this is praying *for*, not *about*, the repentant sinner. Jesus exhorted His followers in Matthew 5:44 to "Pray *for* them which despitefully use you." It is rather easy to pray *about* the person we are restoring, but sincere intercession *for* them requires much more of us. We can experience a deep agony of soul as we wrestle in prayer for them. By interceding *for* the sinning Christian, we enter into the very work Christ Himself is now engaged in at the right hand of the Father.

After witnessing much sinning by God's chosen people, the Prophet Samuel said to them, "God forbid that *I* should sin against the Lord by ceasing to pray for you (1 Sam. 12:23, NASB). This also is true of the "spiritual" Christians God calls to restore sinning brothers and sisters.

Aradam Tedla, whose escape from Ethiopia was written up in the December 1983 issue of *Reader's Digest* magazine, smiled at me following my "Gaining through Losing" seminar in Washington, D.C. After most of his friends were executed or imprisoned without the right to defend themselves, and after his own release from prison, this former chairman of Ethiopia's Urban Dweller's Supreme Tribunal and head of their Property Consolidation Commission fled his country. He then trekked through minefields and enemy fire for fifteen days. Exhausting his food and water supply, he made his way across Ethiopia's border and finally to America. With deep emotion, he told me after the seminar, "I learned to forgive today—even though they took every possession I ever owned. And," he added, "God has shown me that He is going to work all of this out for my good."

But the exciting meeting with Aradam came over a year later when we met at Prison Fellowship's International Symposium at Queen's University in Belfast, Northern Ireland. After I had taught and we all had participated in "praying for those who despitefully use you," a breathless Aradam caught up with me at the elevator. "I've done it all now. I've done it! Today I was able to pray *for* them!" he beamed.

Real praying *for* a sinner must be done in love, not just from human concern or Christian duty. We can pray *about* them without loving them. But praying *for* them requires that we put our feelings and rights out of our minds and concentrate in prayer only on their needs. And the more deeply we have been hurt the greater the tendency is to pray *about* them and not *for* them. But Jesus said, "But I say to you who hear, love your enemies, do good to those who hate you, bless those who curse you, pray for those who mistreat you" (Luke 6:27-28, NASB).

By praying **with** *that sinner,* amazing strides in his or her restoration can be accomplished. Why? Together we spend time, not offering or rehearsing human counsel which may or may not be correct or timely, but interacting with the Ultimate Restorer, our Father in heaven. His answers are always true, correctly timed, and exactly right for every circumstance.

The precious hours I spent in prayer *with* that friend I was restoring were by far the most fruitful of all my efforts. Together, we lingered in His holy presence. How sweet it was just to pour out our hearts together to the Lover of our souls and feel His sweet love surround us and His powerful arms undergird us.

What happens when God answers this praying together with the repentant sinner? His restoration just seems to flow—amazingly—not only to the one being restored but also to the restorer.

Restore by loving, not legalism. So much of restoration of the repentant sinner hinges on our loving him or her. If we follow the Bible's instructions with rigid legalism, it will be perceived by this person, and our attempts at restoration may be rejected. But, if we love that one sincerely and selflessly, our actions and attitudes will be automatically supportive and restoring.

At this point, you probably are saying, "But I don't love that sinner very much. How do I get the love God wants me to have?"

One of the most effective exercises of my "What Happens When We Pray" seminars has been our praying through the scriptural formula for handling someone who has grieved us, as given in 2 Corinthians 2. Although we study it from the perspective of the responsibility of the one who has been grieved, the needs of the offender are in this portion of Scripture as well. After forgiving and promising to comfort that sinner (lest they become overwhelmed with too much sorrow), we then promise to confirm our love to him or her.

Of course, we realize that it is not possible to confirm something we don't have; so, in prayer, we ask God to give us all the love He wants us to have. Then we wait in silence after that prayer, feeling the love come from God. And it does! So, if you don't feel much love for that sinner you are restoring, get on your knees—and wait until God gives it to you.

When the repentant sinner being restored is truly loved, he or she usually responds to that love and begins the process of loving us and, even more important, himself again.

How Does God Restore the Sinner?

Humans at best can create the environment in which God can work to restore the soul. The ultimate restorer of the sinner, of course, is God. The complete work of restoring comes as He answers the pleas of the repentant sinner, as when the one I was restoring finally cried out, "Father, restore my soul!"

This prayer must follow the prayer of repentance, for a forgiven soul is not the same as a restored soul. A forgiven soul is one reconciled to God, but there still may be much to be restored.

God uses Scripture to answer the prayers for restoration. "The law of the Lord is perfect, restoring the soul" (Ps. 19:7, NASB).

In the Bible verse, "All Scripture is given by inspiration of God, and is profitable for doctrine, for reproof, for correction, for instruction in righteousness" (2 Tim. 3:16), the word *correction* means "to restore to an upright state." God does restore with Scripture.

The friend I was restoring knew theologically from 1 John 1:9 that "if we [Christians] confess our sins, [God] is faithful and just to forgive us our sins, and to cleanse us from all unrighteousness" but my friend had struggled for several years trying to accept forgiveness, doing everything humanly possible to secure it. And after confessing to me, my friend still agonized for two months over God's actual forgiving. But the reality of forgiveness came dramatically from the Bible.

It was Psalm 32 that finally did it for my friend. "Look at this!" my friend just exploded, and slowly we read together:

> How blessed is he whose transgression is forgiven, whose sin is covered! How blessed is the man to whom the Lord does not impute iniquity, and in whose spirit there is no deceit! (vv. 1-2, NASB)

And then God gave that beautiful and oh-so-true picture of my friend's life:

When I kept silent about my sin, my body wasted away through my groaning all day long. For day and night Thy hand was heavy upon me; my vitality was drained away as with the fever-heat of summer (vv. 3-4, NASB).

But the victory was there:

I acknowledge my sin to Thee, and my iniquity I did not hide; I said, "I will confess my transgressions to the Lord" and Thou didst forgive the guilt of my sin (v. 5, NASB).

Then verse 11 produced the thrill of assurance for my friend:

Be glad in the Lord and rejoice you righteous ones, and shout for joy all you who are upright in heart (Ps. 32:11, NASB).

Forgiven! Restored to an upright state! Rejoicing!

Four months later, God gave my friend, "For Thou, Lord, art good, and ready to forgive, and abundant in loving-kindness to all who call upon Thee" (Ps. 86:5, NASB). In the margin of my Bible, I recorded, "My friend just opened to this today, and took it as as personal promise!"

So God powerfully uses His written Word, the Bible, to answer the prayer of, and for, the repentant sinner for restoration.

Forgive Yourself

But the forgiven sinner must accept God's forgiveness. How often God cries, "I forgave you. Won't you please let Me open the curtain to that beautiful room called 'forgiven'?" A room filled with the sweet aroma of God's forgiveness. Its sweetness is surprisingly pleasant, not only to the nostrils but to the whole being. Saturating, engulfing, it completely obliterates any lingering stench of that sin. But the response is up to us.

A young woman who had had an abortion later married and tried for years to become pregnant. After exhaustive medical tests and experiments, the final conclusion was—pregnancy impossible. In the depths of despair, she cried, "I killed the only baby I'll ever have!" How tragic to be unable to accept God's forgiveness when there has been deep repentance. How sad not to be able to walk once again with God in the cool of the garden—forgiven.

God cannot restore the sinner until that sinner accepts His forgiveness. My son-in-love, Skip, said this to me the other day, "After God has forgiven you and you have gone to your brother, if you can't forgive yourself, you are setting your standards higher than God's."

The greatest enemy of restoration may be ourselves. Complete restoration can come to the repentant sinner only when the self-loathing and the sometimes paranoid existence is exchanged for God's loving acceptance.

I sat listening to the widow of a prominent pastor who, after sinning grievously, had committed suicide. "When he repented deeply, the children and I forgave him, the church forgave him, God forgave him—but," she hung her head and sighed, "he could not forgive himself."

If Only

When there has been a devastating sin in our lives, we say, "If only! What if I had not done it? What would I be, what could I have accomplished if only I had not sinned?" These are bitter words that plague the repentant sinner, causing seemingly never-ending shudders of the soul—"If only!"

To be sure, there are consequences of sinning with which we must live. "For he who does wrong will receive the consequences of the wrong which he has done, and that without partiality" (Col. 3:25, NASB). And again in Galatians 6:7, "Do not be deceived, God is not mocked; for whatever a man sows, this he will also reap" (NASB).

There will be the inevitable consequence of sin—broken relationships, ravaged bodies, a child out of wedlock, lost years the locusts have eaten. Those we will have with us always.

An emaciated, faltering young man who had found Christ after years of being on hard drugs drove up to me on his motorcycle at a youth convention and labored to say, "Mrs. Ev-elyn, y-y-you re-ally mi-mi-ministered to me to-to-today." Then he poured out his brokenheartedness at a body and a mind crippled for life. "If only!"

One repentant pastor cried, "Will I ever be able to have the trust and confidence of others again?"

David, even though forgiven by God, for the rest of his life paid the price for his sin against Bathsheba and her husband. God said the child she was bearing would die—and he did (2 Sam. 12:10-14). Also, David was not allowed to build the temple, and his family had to live by the sword from that time on. In his deep repentance, David often must have thought, *Oh, if only! If only I had not done it!*

Only God Restores Ministry

But, wonderfully, while we are crying "If only!" God is answering "Since." He answers our "if only" lament with, "Now then, *since* you have been forgiven, I am in charge of restoring your ministry."

David, after his deep repentance, found a very important word—*then*. Psalm 51 tells us that he bowed down acknowledging his sin, deeply repented of it, begged God to create in him a clean heart, and asked Him to restore the joy of His salvation. *"Then,"* David said, "I will teach transgressors Thy ways, and sinners will be converted to Thee" (Ps. 51:15, NASB). Restored ministry!

And incredibly, God still used that repentant, restored sinner's lineage to produce the Messiah, Jesus! The New Testament opens with these words, "The book of the genealogy of Jesus Christ, the son of David, the son of Abraham" (Matt. 1:1, NASB).

However, we must add that there is no way to know what glorious things God had planned for David had he not sinned. C.S. Lewis in his novel *Perelandra* said it like this, "Whatever you do, He will make good of it. But not the good He had prepared for you if you had obeyed Him. That is lost for ever."[1] We never will know what David's later life would have been without his horrible sin.

Many people have said to me, "God never can use me again because of that awful sin I committed." But God not only forgives when there is genuine repentance, He can restore status and position in His kingdom. We can be cleansed again for His holy ministry.

But we must remember that only God can decide if or how much ministry He will restore. We humans have nothing to do with God reinstating His call to that person. We may hire that one in a new job, or even restore his or her status in a former position, but only God can choose to once again pour out His power and blessing upon and through that one again. The decision is God's—not ours.

Peter is a tremendous example of one whose ministry was restored by God after sinning grievously. After denying his Lord the night Jesus was betrayed, Peter went out and wept bitterly. The words, "If only I had not done it," must have kept surfacing through those bitter tears. And Peter must have been convinced he was finished in the work of his Lord's kingdom.

What agony of soul Peter must have felt on that beach after the Resurrection when Jesus kept asking, "Lovest thou Me?" But what confusion, and then twinge of hope, must have stirred within him when Jesus said, "Feed My lambs" (John 21). In his grief, it is possible that Peter did not grasp the magnitude of Jesus' restoration of his ministry.

He was restored to ministry—shoulders back, step quickened, self-image restored, and, most important of all—a fruitful ministry for God.

But Who Restores the Restorer?
In the depths of restoring a penitent sinner, what happens when the restorer finally cries out, "Oh, Father, who restores me, the restorer?"

Perhaps we have been disgraced by our teenaged child's lifestyle, devastated by a mate who has sought greener pastures, or humiliated by someone we love in Christ who is bringing shame to His holy name and ours. Does God expect us to restore that one without any concern or provision by Him for our own needs?

Since the "spiritual one" commanded to do the restoring in Galatians 6:1 is likely to be the one who has been deeply hurt by the sinning one, we ask, "Who restores the restorer?"

The Restorer Is God
I remember lifting up and praying for that one God gave me to restore for nine months. But when I was suddenly told the details of how the sinning had been against me, I felt a deep, tearing

wound inside me. Then as I continued to struggle for another year in the restoring process, the burden seemed to become unbearable. And I bowed my head and sobbed, "O God, who restores the restorer?"

Astonishingly, God's answer immediately filled my mind. "It's the Twenty-third Psalm," He said. Assurance flooded my soul. There it was: *"He* restoreth my soul!" God!

Restoring the restorer was part of God's original intention when He instructed us to restore the fallen one. Before telling us to "restore such a one," in Galatians 6:1, He already knew it would include His having to restore us—the restorers. Amazingly, "restore such a one" is in the continuous present Greek tense, suggesting a process of perhaps long duration, not just a once-for-all action.

Then, at the end of this portion of Scripture on restoring, God gives a promise. My heart leaped within me as I read, "And let us not lose heart in doing good, for in due time we shall reap if we do not grow weary" (Gal. 6:9, NASB).

It is admirable and tremendously helpful if the repentant sinner spends time and effort trying to make restitution to the one against whom he or she has sinned. The loving tenderness, the myriad of kind words and actions to make up for the hurting they caused are wonderful and do help so much. But the deep hole that we feel has been punched right in the middle of us only can be restored to wholeness by God. It is only God who can fill the devastating void left by severed relationships with children, relatives, and friends and by broken marriage vows. Only God can restore the *soul.*

The Restorer's Needs

Restoring someone who has sinned can be a tremendously exhausting process. Sincerely working with, praying for, and emotionally undergirding the one who needs restoring can leave the restorer emotionally, and perhaps physically, bankrupt. There may be nothing left with which to cope.

The restorer's own self-image may have been severely damaged, especially if his or her parenting or leadership capabilities have been questioned or he or she no longer is "number one" in the eyes of the mate. Or, one may appear to be a failure when, no matter how hard you try, the sinner will not let you restore him or her. And the searching question, "Where have I failed?" seems to have no answer. So, who restores the restorer?

Also, most people tend to ignore or even be unaware of the restoration the restorer may need. It hurts when people acclaim the progress of the one being restored, but ignore the sweat, blood, and tears we have put into their recovery. Few seem to care about the hours, days, and perhaps years we have spent keeping that head above water—treading water ourselves. Nor do they seem to notice the deep wounds inflicted on us, especially if we *seem* to be strong and are "handling it beautifully."

Other people probably see only the attitudes out in public of the one being restored, while we have had to live with, and perhaps suffer in silence with, that person's mood-swinging existence, depression, self-incrimination, wrestling to admit the sin, hopelessness, and perhaps even suicidal tendencies. Others also may see their brave cover-up in public while we must live with the inevitable collapse when they reach home. So, who restores us?

Or, even worse, the hardest part is being blamed for causing the problem in that one we're trying to restore, when we know the real cause and that basically we are innocent. But because of our fierce loyalty, we are protecting that one we are restoring and will not defend ourselves by revealing the facts or order of events, when just a few words would clear our reputation.

Also, the sinning one usually sees only his or her own need, and is unaware of any need the restorer might have.

So, who restores the restorer? God says, "I will!"

When Circumstances Don't Change
Even when the circumstances don't change, and frequently they don't, God still restores us.

"Dear Evelyn," a seminar participant wrote, "I was absolutely at the end of myself. I no longer could live under the circumstances of my life. I was ready to end it all when I found your book *Lord, Change Me!* I took to heart those principles, turned to God's Word—and He restored me! My circumstances haven't changed, but my relationship with the Lord has. And He has picked me up and sent me rejoicing!" Yes, ultimately, the restoration of the restorer must be his or her relationship with God.

"My pastor-husband, who has his Ph.D. in psychology," wrote a seminar attendee, "gives away three books in counseling; and one of them is your *Lord, Change Me!* Then they let him know how the Lord is changing *them*. Even when their circumstances don't change!"

A beautiful Christian television personality shared with me her incredible restoration after her husband's suicide. He was brilliant and an extremely successful pastor, building a several-thousand-member church. "He could preach better in the flesh than most men could all prayed up," she quipped, "which, of course, was what he was doing when he fell into sin with another woman."

When he realized his church, his wife, his family, and all he was equipped to do and all he had worked for were gone, he wallowed in a pool of remorse. And finally, instead of taking the necessary steps and then accepting God's forgiveness, he committed suicide.

"We all did everything we could to restore him," she sighed sadly, searching my eyes for understanding. "But he would not let us!" But she had let God restore her!

Although crushed and devastated, this beautiful woman was able to turn to God and receive the strength to sustain her and her family through it all. Now she not only has been restored by God but she also has a nationwide ministry to hurting singles.

When the mother of her teenage daughter's friend collapsed and had a nervous breakdown under similar circumstances, this restored woman's daughter said, "Thanks, Mom, for being a godly woman!"

Let God Be God

Don't expect other people to be your only source of restoration. Don't depend on your pastor, your mate, your family, or friends to fill all your lonely hours and the devastating void. Let God be God in your life.

How can I be restored to being the loving restorer when attitudes surface in me such as, "I'd rather retract my hand than touch," "I'd rather run away than walk beside," or, "I'd rather throw in the towel than pick up the apron"? Who can handle these negative feelings in me? God—as He restores my soul!

Give God a chance. Spend at least as much time with Him as with others to whom you are clinging for support. A woman whose husband had left her called again last week, saying she was so confused by all the conflicting instructions and advice different people were giving her.

"Stop talking to people for a while," I replied. "Instead keep taking your Bible and reading it until God speaks to you. Then stop reading and talk to the Author of that Book—God. See what advice and comfort He has for you. Then you will have what is true and also what is right for you at the moment."

People Also Restore the Restorer
God also uses people to answer our prayer, "Who restores the restorer?"

People can play a huge part in restoring the restorer by undergirding, listening, understanding, supporting, and spending time with them. Even when they don't know why the restorer needs restoring, they frequently are sensitive enough to that hurting one to give their needed support.

The Christian church is intended to be a place, not where we ignore, gossip, and criticize, but where we restore our hurting ones. Immediately following the instructions to restore the sinner, in Galatians 6:1 we are told to "bear one another's burdens" (v. 2, NASB). One of the important ways to do this is by taking time to affirm others through our caring and support.

I watched my own church obey this admonition as our members flocked around a beautiful wife who was struggling to restore her wandering husband. Sometimes, it was a squeeze or a handshake while our eyes met hers with an affirming, "I understand," "We're with you all the way," or, "Hang in there!" Sometimes, we helped with a myriad of little and big actions needed to fill the empty moments, lonely prayer times, missed conversations—or even financial needs.

But the most important way relatives and friends can restore the restorer is to pray for that struggling one. Here too prayer releases God's healing balm on the wounds, His strength for sagging knees, and His courage to the fainting heart. A letter arrived one day from a woman who asked why God woke her nightly for the past two weeks to pray for me. Another day, a member of our Twin Cities metropolitan prayer chain, whom I'd never met and who was totally unaware of the kind of prayer I needed, told me that she has been rising at 3 o'clock every morning to pray for me. Many times, I have been acutely aware that without all their prayers I never would have made it.

When I left a luncheon in Fort Worth, Texas during my period of devastation, a former missionary to Korea evidently sensed my need, squeezed me, and told me she would pray for me during my trip home. Oh, how I could sense those prayers. And I felt myself taking a huge step forward in my own restoration on the plane.

His Answers to Our Prayers

Perhaps the greatest way God restores us, the restorers, is to answer our own prayers for help.

I had prayed, "Lord, heal me!" for several days during my time of restoring my friend. But it was on a Saturday morning after a long dry spell without rain in our city, and then two days of refreshing rain, that I was sitting on our deck and asking Him to heal me again. I was just waiting quietly in His presence, in that washed air as the birds sang, and my heart suddenly soared. I was thrilled as I let the warm sun and the Son relax me, fill and thrill my whole being. My eyes were moist with teardrops of thanks and love for God! I felt Him streaming into me—as real as the warm, morning sun. I brushed away a stray tear of joy that crept down my cheek. God!

This was just one of a long series of answers to my original prayer, "God, who restores me, the restorer?" But I have learned I must allow Him to restore me. There is a law involved here: The speed and completeness of my restoration is determined by what I let God do in me as He answers this prayer.

But there is another kind of prayer. A member of the Godhead is praying for me, the restorer. One day during my prayer time, I was feeling the brunt of Satan's attacks and was emotionally drained. Then a smile spread across my face as I suddenly envisioned Jesus praying for me—sitting up there at the right hand of the Father, interceding for me! "He always lives to make intercession for them" (Heb. 7:25, NASB). I thanked Him with great joy in my heart as I asked Him to continue the praying He started in

His High-Priestly Prayer "[Father], keep them from the evil one" (John 17:15, NASB).

The Enemy of Restoration

Why did Jesus pray that prayer just before leaving Earth? And why did He teach us, His followers, to pray, "[Father] . . . deliver us from the evil one" (Matt. 6:15, NASB) in His model Lord's Prayer? Because Jesus knew how our enemy Satan would operate, trying to negate God's will on earth just as he tried in heaven before God cast him out. The battle is a spiritual one as Satan desires to thwart God's restoration.

There will continue to be times when places, things, and people remind both the restorer and the one being restored of the sin. Painful memories flash in the mind as they pass the building or city in which the sin took place, when they suddenly are face-to-face with the person with whom the sin was committed, or pass nearby but are unobserved by that person—initiating renewed grief or remorse.

At one such time, I was engulfed in past hurts, and the friend I was restoring was in deep sorrow because of the hurt caused me. The next day as we were talking through this devastating experience, my friend asked, "How do you handle these flashbacks? How come you have victory, but I don't? The only way I can handle them is finally just to dismiss them. I am able to agonize in the remorse and regrets just so long, and then I have to put them out of my mind—and get very, very busy filling my mind so I won't think about it anymore."

As I pondered the reason, I suddenly was aware that I did have victory already the next day. I had returned to a state of peace and even joy in that short time. "I think the difference is that, rather than dismiss them, I handle my feelings," I replied. When my friend asked how, I explained the steps.

"First, recognize the source of these flashbacks. Satan is the enemy of restoration. The last thing he wants is for the one he has trapped in a deep sin to be restored. (Of course, God too may have reasons for bringing warnings and teaching through His recalling.)

"So, instead of dismissing my feelings," I continued, "I flee to my prayer closet. Yesterday, I spent an hour and a half with the

Lord praying this through. Then I echoed Jesus' intercession for me, 'Father, deliver me from the evil one, Satan.'

"The next step," I explained, "is not prayer, but addressing Satan himself. With unshakable faith in Jesus' finished work on the cross and the resultant power of His blood, I tell Satan I'm claiming this blood against him. I even visualize that irresistible force of Jesus' shed blood rushing through my body and my mind, dislodging Satan and sweeping all of his influences right out of me.

"I then ask God to forgive me for all my negative thoughts and however I have let Satan have the upper hand in my thoughts as I succumbed to his fiery memory dart.

"The next step is asking God the Holy Spirit to fill me with Himself. The vacuum that has been created in me by God emptying and forgiving me," I concluded, "needs to be filled with Him."

And God does it! Peace, His positive thoughts, His stability inside me like a solid rock. Victory is there! And, incredibly, there is love in me for the one who sinned against me—renewed and reinforced—and even enlarged.

Elva Stump, a ninety-seven-year-old who was at our Lakeland, Florida seminar, stood and gave us all her secrets for such a long and victorious life. "It's Romans 12:2," she said. "I've quoted it every day of my life." Then she explained, "Because Jesus loves me and I love Him, I keep filled with the Holy Spirit. First, Jesus helps me to love everybody, and pray for the unlovely, for their salvation. Second, He helps me to hold no grudges or resentment. Confession and forgiveness are a must. Third, He helps me to reject negative thoughts. The devil uses our minds as his playground—if we let him. So, reject the first negative thought. How do you do this? Discipline, and work at it!"

So, instead of Satan cackling his hideous laugh of victory, chalking up one more Christian having "bitten the dust," he retreats, whipped, his prey snatched from his grasp.

And the kingdom of God marches on—victorious, restored, powerful, and conquering—just as God intended it to do. This is not without struggles and battles, but with His children taking seriously the mandate from Him to restore the repentant sinner—and to be restored themselves!

"Lest You Too"

There is a warning for the restorer in the portion of Galatians 6 about the spiritual ones restoring the one caught in a sin. While reading this Scripture in a recent "Lord, Change Me" seminar, God stopped me on the words, Looking to yourself lest you too be tempted" (v. 1, NASB).

"Lord," I prayed, "search my heart *lest* I be tempted too. Search me *before* I am. O God, what kind of temptation will it be? Surely not the same kind. I've never had those thoughts. O God, what kind of temptation?"

Then, shocked, I cried, "Is that the answer in verse 3? 'For if anyone thinks he is something when he is nothing, he deceives himself.' The sin of pride? Thinking I am greater than the one I'm restoring? O God, forgive me! I already have been tempted to think too much of myself."

Reverse That Trend

As my friend and I talked about all the leading Christian national and even international musicians, writers, and pastors who had fallen into sin, I said, "What we really need to break this insidious trend in Christian leadership today is for one of them—one of the famous ones—to repent publicly. Perhaps on radio or TV or in a national magazine to call it what it is—sin—and ask the Christian community to forgive him or her. Then promise to do everything possible to make restitution for all the shattered trust in their leadership.

"Maybe if just one would do it," I continued, "it would give Christians a chance to obey the scriptural commands to forgive and restore that penitent sinner. Give us a chance, not to cancel their appearances in our churches and their concerts, not to take their books off our shelves or programs off Christian radio and TV stations—but to forgive when God forgives.

"This would give all those hundreds, thousands, and even millions following their leadership not only the right to see their hero or heroine's error in their sinning and their unworthiness to be followed, but it would also be a courageous example of what God expects from and will do for the followers if they sin."

The problem is, we all have a tendency to want to be restored without paying the price. We expect to jump from our gross sins right back to ministry, fellowship, and respect. We have convinced ourselves that, when we pray, "Lord, I have sinned," only restoration is necessary—while God is insisting on repentance, reconciliation, and restitution first.

Rest

Amazingly, when these scriptural instructions have been obeyed and applied, and the seemingly endless struggles and hurts finally are past, the end result of that restoration is found in its first four letters—R-E-S-T.

But it is only when we obediently have followed all the steps of repentance, reconciliation, restitution, and allowing God to restore us that we experience His ultimate for us—*rest:* that beautiful state free from guilt, estrangement, and burdens. Only then are we able to relax in the joy of unbroken fellowship with God and others.

The process producing enmity, anger, and wounds has been reversed. And Satan, defeated, goes slinking offstage while God pulls the curtain open on a new era in our lives—peace with Him, with others, and with ourselves. Restored!

Closing Prayer

Father, teach me Your steps in the restoration process. Help me to examine where I am in all my relationships with others. Make me aware of how I am hurting them, and help me correct it. Make me a restorer to those who need me. Take my hurts from other people and in Your time, and in Your way, restore me to perfect oneness with them and to perfect rest in You.

In Jesus' name, **Amen.**

11

When God answers...

Now Obey Me

What happens when God answers prayer? What God always expects to happen—our *obedience.*

After God has answered our prayer, whether exciting, mind-boggling, or difficult, the next step is obedience. When God answers our prayer with a command, instruction, or an open door, He fully expects us to obey. We must put into practice what God has told us in His answer. And our obedience to His answer to our prayer opens the curtain on the next act of our lives. "So shall My word be which goes forth from My mouth, it shall not return to Me empty, without accomplishing what I desire, and without succeeding in the matter for which I sent it" (Isa. 55:11, NASB).

This is the God of the universe speaking, the One whom all the stars, planets, weather, and seasons obey. The One who spoke, and the universe came into being. The One who spoke, and the sea was calm. Who spoke, and the dead came alive. The One who expects obedience to His words.

However, God does not coerce us into obeying His answers to our prayers. He has given each of us a free will, with the privilege of responding as we choose. And, astoundingly, we humans frequently ignore, rebel, make excuses, refuse to obey, or even laugh at a certain answer from Him. This is amazing in light of the fact that it is the omniscient God of the universe who has answered us.

Our son, Kurt, said to me this way: "Remember, when dealing with the Great Potter, the quality of the pot is solely determined by the malleability of the clay." It is our ability and willingness as clay to obey and be shaped by God, the Potter, that ultimately fashions what we are—and what God can do through us.

What Are You Missing?

Have you ever wondered what you have missed in life because of a wrong response to God's directions?

For years, I have wondered what Jesus' disciples missed on the day of His resurrection because of disobedience. How had Jesus planned to return in His risen body to that little grieving, disillusioned band? What kind of joyous reunion did He have in mind for them?

Somehow, I feel Jesus had planned a jubilant, victorious appearance—turning their shattering grief into instantaneous rejoicing. Celebrating in Galilee, rather than hiding in Jerusalem. Galilee—where He could reveal Himself—alive and victorious over sin and death. What a reunion! Their crucified leader, risen from the dead—suddenly in their midst!

Jesus had instructed His disciples twice to go to Galilee and meet Him there; but, because of their wrong response to His words, they missed what He evidently had planned for them.

First, before His death, Jesus had given them instructions as to where He would go and that they should follow, saying, "But after I have been raised, I will go *before you* into Galilee" (Matt. 26:32, NASB, emphasis mine). But instead of obeying Him after His death, their response to this instruction was to hide in fear behind locked doors in Jerusalem, thereby missing the planned reunion in Galilee.

The second time the disciples' response was wrong was on Easter morning before Jesus had appeared to any of them. The angel and Jesus Himself both sent word to them through the women at the tomb:

> And the angels answered and said to the women, "Do not be afraid; for I know that you are looking for Jesus who has been crucified. He is not here, for He has risen. . . . And go quickly and tell His disciples that He has risen from the dead; and behold, *He is going before you into Galilee; there you will see Him.*" . . . And they departed quickly from the tomb

with fear and great joy, and ran to report it to His disciples. And behold, Jesus met them and greeted them. And they came up and took hold of His feet and worshiped Him. Then Jesus said to them, "Do not be afraid; go and take word to My brethren *to leave for Galilee, and there they shall see Me*" (Matt. 28:5-10, NASB, emphasis mine).

Mark, in his Gospel, tells us that the angel at the empty tomb even reminded the women of Jesus' command, "Go tell His disciples and Peter, He is going before you into Galilee; there you will see Him, *just as He said unto you*" (Mark 16:7, NASB, emphasis mine).

This time, the disciples' wrong response was *unbelief*. Luke tells us that "these words appeared to them as nonsense, and they would not believe them" (Luke 24:11, NASB). Words telling them that Jesus was alive! Words telling them that they still could have that reunion in Galilee!

So Jesus had to settle for second best. And the reunion that had to take place in Jerusalem was so much less than He had hoped. When Jesus finally did appear to the disciples, they were huddled behind locked doors, "startled and frightened and thought they were seeing a spirit" (Luke 24:37, NASB).

Also, after Jesus appeared to the two on the Emmaus Road, they hurried back to tell the grieving disciples. But Mark tells us they did not believe them either. "And afterward [after appearing to the women and the two], He appeared to the eleven themselves as they were reclining at table, and *He reproached them* for their unbelief and hardness of heart, because they had not believed those who had seen Him after He had risen" (Mark 16:14, NASB, emphasis mine). Reproach instead of triumph!

How disappointed Jesus must have been. His return to His disciples after His death and resurrection filled them with fear, mourning, weeping, unbelief, and fright. They even had to be scolded by their beloved Master. His plans for the greatest moment of their lives were ruined—all because they refused to believe and obey His words.

Perhaps there were excuses for their disobedience—they forgot Jesus' words, they didn't understand in the first place, or they were too grieved to think rationally. But even when the angel prodded their memories by sending the message "as He told *you*" with the women, their response was still unbelief and disobedience.

Then, their response, even when Jesus Himself sent a personal message to them, was seemingly inexcusable—unbelief. Was it their hopelessness, their grief? Was it their view of the messengers—women, unfit to be witnesses in those days? Yet, the women were entrusted by both the angel and Jesus with "He is risen"—the most significant piece of information ever to be released on Planet Earth!

Yes, the only ones who didn't miss the glorious impact of that first Easter were the women and the two on the Emmaus Road. The rest missed the greatest opportunity ever offered to mankind: a mind-exploding reunion with their supposedly dead leader—the risen, triumphant Lord! Oh, what might have been!

It was only when the disciples finally did go "to Galilee, to the mountain which Jesus had designated" (Matt. 28:16, NASB), that they received their orders for the future—the Great Commission.

I wonder how many of my Galilees I have missed? Missed because I'm aghast at the prospect of a cross, too grieved to see clearly, or have an inadequate view of the Messenger, my Lord. Missed because of unbelief, disobedience. Missed because of not responding to a simple, seemingly unimportant little piece of instruction like, "Go to Galilee, and there I will meet you." Oh, what my today might have been had all my responses to my Lord been belief and obedience!

What are you missing that Jesus had planned for you? Joy, hope, peace? An intimate walk with Jesus? Renewed fellowship with Him? Are you living like the disciples—in despair, defeat, fear, tears, unbelief, and disobedience? Then it is because your response to His words also has been wrong. Perhaps you are feeling that there are good reasons why you should not believe and obey. But the hard fact is that you are missing the triumphant, joyous relationship with Him that He is longing to have with you—if you were obedient.

"Just Trust Me!"

What God actually is saying to us when He gives us commands, directions, and open doors is, "Just trust Me!" In return, what response does He expect from us to His "Just trust Me"? Just trusting Him!

There are three kinds of people: those irresponsible beings who eat, drink, and are "merry" for tomorrow they may die; those who perpetually worry about what might happen; and those who live in that wonderful state of trusting God, who have learned to take the hassle out of their lives by casting all their cares on Him—and then relaxing in Him.

The air controllers had gone on strike the day I was due in Oklahoma City. I was told by an airline official, "Lady, we can get you as far as Dallas, but there's absolutely nothing going out of there to Oklahoma City." I could almost feel the quizzical look on his face as I replied, "OK, I'll take your plane as far as Dallas."

With mixed emotions, my executive director, Sally, took me to the airport and deposited me with a waiting skycap. Then she returned home to pray. She and Jeanne, her prayer partner, added their prayers to those of the telephone prayer chain already asking God to intervene in a humanly hopeless situation, as I was due to start speaking that afternoon at a denominational annual meeting in Oklahoma City.

When Sally and Jeanne finished praying, they looked at each other and confidently giggled, "I wonder how God is going to get Ev out of *this* one?"

Unaware of their spirit of expectant confidence in God, I couldn't wait to get off that plane in Dallas to see what God was going to do. It never dawned on me that He might not have a solution. For years, in answer to multiplied prayers, I had practiced an abandonment to God that produced such exciting results. There was not even a twinge of doubt that God had His plan all worked out.

As I walked the Dallas Airport jet-way from the plane to the terminal, my chest was almost bursting with exhilaration. I felt like a young colt, nostrils slightly flared in anticipation, tail flying high, prancing into a challenging headwind.

But I was not prepared for what I saw in that terminal. Even though I'd missed a plane once and had been stranded overnight in this new mega airport, I was stunned. Baggage was piled high everywhere. Stranded passengers of all sizes, races, and financial means were sprawled, trying to sleep with heads propped on baggage. Some just sat dejectedly, while others wended their way over and through the people and suitcases hoping to find some way to go someplace.

A long makeshift row of airline ticket booths had been set up for agents to try to assist the almost hopeless sea of passengers. They herded us into a long line, and as openings occurred, they sent each one to the next available official.

My agent looked at me and said, "Lady there's *nothing* going to Oklahoma City any time today." I nodded my understanding. "Except . . . that man who just left my booth. He's around that corner trying to make a telephone call to see if there is a car he can rent to drive to Oklahoma City. Of course, all the cars have been gone for hours. But if you hurry you should catch him just as he comes back around that corner—" His voice trailed off as I dashed away.

Then I did something I've never done before—or since. With absolute assurance in my heart that it was right, I rushed up to that unknown man and gasped, "Are you going to Oklahoma City?" His startled response was, "Well I, ah, my wife and I are." Then with an incredulous expression on his face, he explained that, just as he made that call someone canceled a car reservation and rather than checking the whole reservation mess, they just gave it to him.

He led me to his weary wife, propped up on their baggage, both protecting it and trying to get a little rest. While he went to get the car, his wife and I exchanged pleasantries. "Oh, you are going to a convention too? That's nice. In the same hotel I'll be in? How interesting. Your husband is what? Eastern director for the Holiness Association? Oh, that's the convention where I'm going to speak!" We hugged and laughed, amazed at our God's incredible working.

Her husband returned with the car, and we set out walking those long terminals trying to get a glimpse of my luggage. Just as a porter put his hand on my suitcase to "store it who knows where?" we just happened to be walking by! Another miracle.

We missed the first session, along with almost everybody else; but on the way, our car was filled with praise and gratitude as we pieced together God's plan. And joy and laughter filled our hearts. "Just trust Me!"

But, Can God Trust You?

Are you secretly longing to get out of your status quo and into something you think would be more glamorous, more important for the Lord? The secret of God being able to do greater things through us is found in 1 Corinthians 4:2, "It is required of stewards that they be found trustworthy" (NASB).

Stewards are those to whom something has been entrusted for which they are responsible and accountable. In the Bible, stewards include the manager of a household, a governor of young children, an official of a city, elders and bishops in the church, and those entrusted with the mysteries of God. Each of us has been entrusted with differing gifts from God—a household, children, a civic position, work in the church, money, and the mysteries of God—making us all stewards. And according to God's Word, stewards are required to be faithful—trustworthy.

So how can being a steward determine whether or not God can trust us with bigger things? Our track record. Jesus said, "He that is faithful in a very little thing is faithful also in much" (Luke 16:10, NASB). So it is he who is faithful over a few things who can be entrusted with greater things. We demonstrate our faithfulness and trustworthiness by what we have done with what God has given us in the past.

Jesus explained this in His Parable of the Talents in Matthew 25. The servants to whom the master entrusted the five and two talents (money) each doubled them for him. It didn't matter how many talents had been entrusted to each for, upon returning, the master commended them both by saying, "Well done, thou good and faithful servant" (v. 21).

The master did *not* add, "You have been faithful over a few things—so go on vacation and rest." Nor, "You have been faithful over a few things—so you deserve an early retirement." No. Instead, he said a shocking thing, "Now I will make you ruler over many." When the master found the steward faithful, he gave him a bigger job to do.

Frequently, I am asked, "How can I do something great for God?" Or, "I have this fabulous idea; how can I write a million-copy book?" And surprisingly, these questions often are asked by someone not involved in serving Christ in any way. God knows if He can trust us with a bigger job by what we are doing right now with that seemingly insignificant or monotonous task.

Only when we are obeying His answers to our previous prayers will God open bigger and wider doors of service.

He Will Do It—If He Calls

Since God expects us to trust Him and obey Him, what, in turn, can we expect of Him? That God fully expects to do it through us! It is in those times when I honestly respond, "Lord, I can't," that He answers, "No, you can't. But I can—and will."

Discovering our God-given gifts and talents is good, but there is one more step: obeying when God calls us into a job we feel sure we do not have the gifts or talent for. This is stepping out on faith. But, of course, this is only done when we are positive that God has specifically called us. And then He will do it through us.

It was the first Sunday night of April 1981, and the next morning I was to participate in my first Prison Fellowship national board meeting with Charles Colson. I knelt struggling in prayer in my motel room in Washington, D.C., telling the Lord how incapable I felt, how I was not smart enough to be on that board, how I was not able to do the job. Feelings of total inadequacy swept over my being as I continued there in prayer, crying, "God, I can't."

Finally I asked God for some Scripture so that I would have *His* words for me. I turned to 1 Thessalonians 5, where I was in my daily devotional reading. And there it was, verse 24: "Faithful is He who calls you, and He also will bring it to pass" (NASB). The *King James* translation says, "He will do it!"

The answer exploded within me. *I* don't have to do it. God will! *I* don't have to be all those things I know I can't be. *I* don't have to do those things I know I can't do. God will do them through me.

But then I wondered: Am I eligible for God to be faithful in performing that prison board task? He has promised to be faithful only when *He* had called me to a task, when it was *His* voice I was obeying. Carefully I reviewed His call.

Three years before, while I was standing silently and alone in Fellowship House in Washington, God unexpectedly had said "prison ministry" to me. It was almost as if a mantle had dropped out of heaven and wrapped around me as He spoke. And I had simply and immediately told Him I would go—if He opened the door. Yes, I knew that I had been called by Him, and so I was eligible for Him to do it. Just as He had done it in the prisons where I had ministered—when I didn't know how—those three intervening years.

I jotted a note in the margin of my Bible by 1 Thessalonians 5:24: "God's answer, The joy and excitement are here." My attitude completely changed from apprehension to joy because I had received God's answer promising that He didn't expect *me* to do it, *He* would! How about you? Are there many times, as with me, when you wallow in a mire of self-doubts, feelings of inadequacy, unworthiness?

In our prayer seminars, just before confessing sins aloud to God, I read a list of Scripture verses with questions. After reading Ephesians 3:20, "Now unto *him* that is able to do exceedingly abundantly above all that we ask or think, according to the power that worketh in us," I follow with these questions: "Do you fail to attempt things for God because you are not talented or wise enough?" "Do feelings of inferiority keep you from trying to serve God?" A yes answer, according to God in James 4:17, is a sin that needs to be confessed.

If it is true in your life today that you feel you are not talented or wise enough to serve God, confess it as sin and accept His promise that, if *He* has called you, *He* will do it!

Expect Him to Do It

At the first seminar series I did in England in 1981, I said to my husband, "This is the first place I feel their expectancy exceeds mine. I usually am the one who gets the vision and motivates others. But there is an unbelievable spiritual hunger and expectancy here."

I was baffled as they introduced me at times "for such a day as this." But they then told me it was because of their taking seriously the turn-of-the-century predictions by a Russian monk recorded in a current bestseller. He had predicted that Germany would be divided in two, France would lose her power, Italy would be devastated by natural disasters, Britain would lose her empire and all her colonies, and would be on the brink of disaster—all of which to that time had come true. But the last part of

England's prediction was that she would be saved by her praying women.

Sensing the magnitude of it all, I knelt in my morning devotional time in a motel in Plymouth, England, overlooking the bay from which the Pilgrims had sailed for America. It was the day of my first full seminar in the British Isles, and I asked God to bring to my mind any sin that I needed to confess, that would hinder Him from working in my audiences there. Immediately His answer shot into my mind—stark, singular—"UNBELIEF!"

Stunned and bewildered, I started questioning Him—almost in self-defense. "Lord, am I not the one who flew to Taiwan all alone, completely trusting You for safety, strength, and power in ministry? God, didn't I give You my body in 1965 and haven't had an anxious thought about it since then? Lord, don't You remember that when I lost the use of my left leg for a while I never once questioned Your wisdom or purpose? Father, don't You remember how in Florida this spring when that infection went into my bloodstream, with complete faith in You, I got out of bed and taught that all-day seminar? Father, You know that I not only teach absolute faith in the God who never makes a mistake—but also believe it—and live it. Don't You, God?"

God patiently waited for me to finish defending myself and then clearly brought His answer to my mind. "Yes, all those things are true. However, that is *obedience*. But—" The silence of His pause was deafening. "But," He finally continued, 'you do not have enough *faith in what I am going to do* when you are obedient. You aren't thinking big enough!"

After I had begged God to forgive me and then waited silently before Him in prayer, He again recalled my favorite "faith" verse for me, the one He had used for years to enlarge my faith— Hebrews 11:6. "But without faith it is impossible to please [God]."

Our daughter, Nancy, had much greater expectations when she wrote on my birthday card, "Dear Mom: Your 58th year brought us the Churchwoman of the Year, your millionth copy of *What Happens When Women Pray* and many fabulous seminars all over the world. I can't wait to see what God does for an encore during your 59th year! Love, Nancy." But to me, it was God who kept saying, "You still haven't discovered what I will do when you are obedient!"

Yes, our obedience needs faith. It takes faith to submit totally to His will and then more faith to step out in obedience. Not faith in our own faith—as it sometimes is—but faith in God and who He is. The omniscient God who, with more than 4 billion people on Planet Earth, can give each His undivided attention all the time—while keeping a running total of all past actions, motives, and the outcome of all the current action. This is our God.

You Haven't Finished the Task Yet

Obedience is not just an occasional burst of obeying God. The Apostle John wrote in 1 John 3:22 that we have power in prayer "because we keep His commandments and do the things that are pleasing in His sight" (NASB). And the words *keep* and *do* are in continuous tenses, meaning that we keep on keeping His commandments and doing the things that please Him.

Obedience is ongoing, not just one quick act. It involves stick-to-it-iveness, tenaciously persevering as long as God does not withdraw the call or command.

The first night of our International Prayer Assembly in Seoul, Korea, God reminded me powerfully to "take heed to the ministry which you have received in the Lord, that you may *fulfill* it" (Col. 4:17, NASB, emphasis mine).

Then, at the end of that summer, I was feeling emotionally and physically exhausted, and I was reluctant to keep going full time with seminars and writing, plus my new grandbabies and such a full family life. I even had discussed with my husband how I might pull back.

For that September's United Prayer Ministries annual retreat, God had directed me to use Revelation 2 and 3. As I was preparing from these chapters, He abruptly spoke to me out of 3:2, "Wake up, and strengthen the things that remain, which were about to die; for I have not found your deeds complete in the sight of My God" (NASB).

You may think you are done, Evelyn, but God doesn't see your task completed. He is not finished with you yet!

"My Door, Not Yours"

It was at that retreat when we were reading individually Revelation 2 and 3, seeking His direction for the future of our organization, that God reminded me that it was *His* door, not mine, through which our prayer ministry had gone.

I still was having feelings of "throwing in the towel," or at least part of it, when God spoke to me dramatically through Revelation 3:7. In 1967, it was Revelation 3:8 that He used to call me to my prayer ministry, "Behold, I have set before [you] an open door." So the verse preceding it shocked me; and for the first time, I saw the whole picture. It is Jesus "who opens and no one will shut," and also Jesus "who shuts and no one will open."

Who did I think I was, deciding whether or not to shut or at least partially shut a door that wasn't even mine? When the Lord opens a door, no human has the right to shut it; but also, when He shuts it, no person has the power to open it.

As we met back together to pray aloud about what God had told us in the Scripture reading, I wept as I confessed before the others, "Please, Father, forgive me for looking only at myself, my weariness, my life too full of the tyranny of the urgent, and how old I'm getting. I have taken my eyes off the One who opened the door, Jesus. Forgive me for seeing it as my door. Oh, not my door, Jesus—Your door!"

Waiting

One of the most difficult parts of obedience is waiting. It almost seems like seeing the flash of His lightning, and having only to wait and wait for the boom of the thunder of His power, accomplishing what He called us to do.

There are two kinds of waiting for answers to our prayers. First, there is the kind where we wait in His presence until He answers. We practice this in our prayer seminars while praying through the 2 Corinthians 2 forgiving formula. I ask all to pray aloud in their groups of four for God's love for the one they just forgave. Then I request that they wait—in silence—until they feel that love come. And it is amazing how we can feel God's love just descending on all of us—answering immediately, while we wait.

I do this same waiting personally in my daily devotions. Before each seminar or speaking engagement, I always pray, "Lord, fill me for today." And many times, the answer comes immediately with the warm, powerful filling for that day's ministry. But it does not always come so quickly. Sometimes, even after exhausting all the requirements in my life that need to be prayed through, I finally pray, "Lord, I will not rise from my knees until You bless me! I will not even take time to eat breakfast before this huge day if You don't bless me!" Then I wait on my knees, often struggling in prayer, for His answer until it comes. This is like Jacob wrestling at the Jabbok River, not letting go until God had granted his request.

But there is a second kind of waiting for answers to our prayers in which we must give God much more time to answer. We must pray and trust in His sovereignty while we wait for Him to answer—in His timing. But this waiting sometimes is spent persisting in prayer; and other times, God assures us that we have done our part and can release it to Him. But it is always waiting—hours, days, or perhaps even years.

The Bible is full of accounts of those called by God who waited for Him to carry out their commitment. Moses' heart burned within him to rescue his people from their taskmasters in Egypt, but God sent him to the backside of the desert for forty years before consummating that call into action.

Paul also, after receiving his dramatic call on the road to Damascus obeyed God's instructions to "rise, and enter the city, and it shall be told you what you must do" (Acts 9:6, NASB), waited for three days, blind and neither eating nor drinking. He waited until God sent Ananias to lay his hands on him, to have his sight restored, and to be filled with the Holy Spirit. Then Paul was ready for the ministry to which God had called him.

Even Jesus, after His resurrection, told His followers that they had to wait before they could bring this earth-shaking news to the world. So, after His ascension, they waited for ten whole days—in prayer. Waited for His Pentecost promise of power!

Obedience Is Born in the Closet
Obedience is born not while purchasing a plane ticket or enrolling in a school, but in the closet—the prayer closet.

As I communicate with God in prayer for guidance, He answers with His plans and goals for me. And the way I respond in submission to Him determines the extent and depth of my obedience. It is in the prayer closet that I do my deciding, resolving, promising—and then make plans to work them out in the corporate board meeting, committee meeting, or with my family.

I set all my life's goals in my prayer closet. This not only makes them a joint project between God and me, but they actually are not my goals at all—but God's for me. Then, when I pray in obedience making His goals my goals, He goes to work fulfilling them—because they are His will.

The goals I set without including God so often fail because, though they seem like such good goals, they may not be God's will for me. Then, of course, He will not bring them to pass.

Also, human goals so frequently fizzle or are forgotten like New Year's resolutions. But never God's goals! He is only looking for willing and obedient people through whom He can accomplish His goals for this world.

Not Doing?

One of the most difficult aspects of obedience is being willing *not* to do something. Obedience isn't only going and doing, it also is *not* going and *not* doing. This is especially hard when we feel that the job or activity is so right and so necessary.

There is an important step to take in most major tasks to which I feel God is calling me. After the excitement and emotional thrill have died down, I pray a different kind of prayer: "Lord, I give this back to You—not to do it—if that is Your will." These are not just mouthed words but a total submission of my whole being to what He wants.

This prayer helps avoid many wrong turns on the road of life. It eliminates much overextending of ourselves in doing things which humanly seem so right, but can be disastrous to His plans for us. Jeremiah said it so well: "For I know the plans that *I* have for you, declares the Lord, plans for welfare and not for calamity to give you a future and a hope" (29:11, NASB, emphasis mine).

Paul must have been surprised and even confused when the Spirit did not permit him to speak the Word to those in Asia when he was so convinced that they needed to hear of Jesus. But God's plan was so right, and Paul's obedience opened Europe to the Gospel.

Also, when a position or job would bring prestige, honor, and favorable exposure to the world, it is especially hard to release it back to God. But when we are willing to decrease so that He and His kingdom may increase—this is real obedience.

Surprisingly for me, it frequently is *only* after I have prayed that prayer of release that God flings the door open wide to what He originally called me to do. To God, my complete obedience seems to include being willing not to do it; and then He says, "Now go!"

The Price

Obedience, also, does not mean that we are always thrilled about going to some exciting or perhaps exotic place to share Jesus. Real obedience is going when it hurts.

My obedience has been deeply tested in relation to my grand-babies. Our Nancy was long overdue with her Kathleen this fall, overlapping the start of my fall speaking schedule with her birth. So while Nancy was in the hospital delivering her baby, I was boarding a plane for an out-of-state seminar. I desperately wanted to be near my daughter, and the price of obedience loomed high. My heart ached as I flew farther and farther from her, praying through every step of that birth. The minute I arrived in Omaha, I phoned the recovery room, and the first sound I heard was the cry of my new granddaughter—too far away to hold in my arms or even to see. But Jesus said, "He who loves son or daughter more than Me is not worthy of Me" (Matt. 10:37, NASB).

When it was time for me to leave for India in 1982, my heart was heavy over being gone for five weeks while my new grand-babies were being bonded to their paternal grandmothers. We had waited ten years for these first grandchildren, and our two daughters delivered just five weeks apart.

But while reading in Luke 14 between Cindy's and Jennifer's births, God stopped me on Jesus' words in verse 33: "So therefore, no one of you can be My disciple who *does not give up all his own possessions*" (NASB, emphasis mine). And I knew that the words *give up* literally meant "bid farewell to."

"Lord," I prayed, "does that include grandbabies?" And His yes answer sent me to my knees, weeping. I struggled long over having empty arms at leaving tiny Cindy, and perhaps the right to even see my other grandchild before I left for India.

Drying my tears, I read on into Luke 15. Jesus was speaking again, "I tell you that in the same way, there will be more joy in heaven over one sinner who repents, than over ninety-nine righteous persons who need no repentance" (v. 7, NASB).

A new prayer emerged, "Oh, God, *replace* the joy of holding my newborn babes in my arms with the joy of a sinner coming to Christ in India." Then I changed my prayer to, "No, Lord, *many sinners!*"

I wrote to each of those wee ones from India, "God has answered Grandma's prayer. Thousands have prayed here, making sure they have a personal relationship with Jesus." And God had drawn back the curtain of heaven, and let me glimpse the angels, also rejoicing over lost ones finding Christ.

But that was not the only joy I found in obeying God by going to India. The sixth night there, I was struck with severe diarrhea. The next day, I spoke shakily from 8 A.M. to 8:30 P.M., with Chris taking just two of the hours. I finished the last two hours physically propped up because my muscles suddenly were quivering like jelly from a pill a doctor gave me right there on the platform for the terrible pain in my stomach. Then, the very next morning, I woke with all the symptoms of a respiratory infection. However, instead of fear and panic at the possibility of becoming too sick to carry on the heavy schedule before me, I relaxed in God's unbelievable joy that engulfed me and bubbled up from within.

In my diary, I described it "as tiny, soft droplets spraying tenderly from a fountain somewhere within me in that parched and dusty city." Asking God for a word to describe that rare and extraordinary joy, He immediately brought to my mind *effusive.* Back home, my dictionary defined effusive as "pouring out, overflowing, lacking reserve like effusive greetings or an effusive person, unrestrained . . . " Exactly what my sick body was feeling that morning in India—effusive, overflowing, unrestrained joy.

But the most surprising joy came my first morning back home. After having been exactly halfway around the world with my internal circadian time-clock operating twelve hours off home time, I awoke at my usual United States time. However, instead of the dreaded jet lag of disorientation and befuddlement, I was lying wide awake in bed praising God. Then joy just flooded the whole room and enwrapped me in itself like the down comforter under which I was snuggling in the Minnesota chill. Joy instead of horrible jet lag!

However, God did not give me that joy by letting me stay home, by not facing me with hard things. He gave it in my obedience. It was the same joy that Jesus surprisingly had in the face of impending death when He said, "These things have I spoken unto you that My joy might remain in you, and your joy might be full" (John 15:11, NASB).

Jesus left His divine joy with His followers on Earth when He went back to heaven. Are you settling for only a quickly evaporating mist or an occasional light shower of joy which barely dampens the surface of a soul parched with anxiety, fear, and apprehension? Or is the fountain of Jesus' effusive joy welling up within you, unrestrained and overflowing? It comes from obedience.

Jesus paid a tremendous price for His obedience to the Father. When agonizing in the Garden of Gethsemane, He *could* have prayed "alternate plan B" instead of submitting to the will of the Father that He go to the cross. He *could* have said, "Father, do You remember that committee meeting You, the Holy Spirit, and I had before the foundation of the world? Do You remember Our 'alternate plan B'? It didn't have a cross in it, Father. Why don't We use that plan?" Jesus *could* have said, "Oh, just until We get to Easter morning, Father. I'd be glad to pick up this plan then." As we so frequently do, Jesus *could* have prayed "alternate plan B."

But He did not. He chose to be obedient and bear all the world's sin in His sinless body. "Although He was a Son, He learned obedience from the things which He suffered; and having been made perfect, He became to all those who obey Him the source of eternal salvation" (Heb. 5:8-9 NASB).

Something I have learned to expect is that God frequently uses me to answer the prayer that I have prayed. He expects my obedience in doing and saying those things which, at least partially, will bring about that for which I've prayed.

Peter tells us in 1 Peter 1:14-15, *"As obedient children,* do not be conformed to the former lusts which were yours in your ignorance, but like the Holy One who called you, be holy yourselves also in *all* your behavior" (NASB, emphasis mine). And in the forgiving formula of 2 Corinthians 2, Paul says he expects forgiving, comforting, and confirming love to be extended to the one who has grieved them (and us), so that he might put them to the test—"whether you are obedient in *all* things" (v. 9, NASB, emphasis mine). The price? Obedience in all things.

Rewards

God's requirements for obedience may be extremely high, but the reward usually equates with the price of the obedience. Although He expects a lot, He also has fabulous rewards for those who obey Him. Jesus said, "Truly I say to you, there is no one who has left house or wife or brothers or parents or children, for the sake of the kingdom of God, who shall not receive many times as much at this time, and in the age to come, eternal life" (Luke 18:29-30, NASB). Yes, rewards on earth today and eternity in heaven. But only for those who obey: "Not everyone who says to Me, 'Lord, Lord' will enter the kingdom of heaven; but he who *does the will of My Father* who is in heaven" (Matt. 7:21, NASB).

Jesus also said He, the actual Son of God, would abide in those who keep His commandments (1 John 3:24); and God promised to give the third member of the Trinity, the Holy Spirit, to those who obey Him (Acts 5:32).

Could there be a greater reward than to be regarded by Jesus as His friend? He said, "You are My friends *if* you do what I command you" (John 15:14, NASB). It also is shocking to think of what the opposite is—not being Jesus' friend if we don't obey Him!

Then the complete, indescribable circle of the obedient life is summed up by Jesus in John 14:21, "He who has My commandments and keeps them, he it is who loves Me; and he who loves Me shall be loved by My Father, and I will love him, and will disclose Myself to him" (NASB). Rewards!

As I kissed the warm forehead of my sleeping grandbaby recently to say good-bye before leaving for Australia and Guam, I said to her daddy, "The price gets higher every time." True. But so does the reward!

Responses

It is awesome to realize that at the end of our lives we will be the sum total of our responses to God's answers to our prayers, for

God has chosen to be limited in His next action by our response to His previous answer.

The final outcome of our lives is decided by a life-long series of responses to God's answers to our prayers. The way we respond to God and then He, in turn, to us actually determines the direction our lives will take.

It would be wonderful if each response to God affected only our lives at that point and no more. But not so. One response triggers the domino principle that affects all the rest of life. A major wrong response slips or hurtles us into the path of lost opportunities and missed spiritual growth, limiting God from taking us down the path He intended and planned for us.

As I grow older, it is interesting to look back on what seemed to be my correct responses and wonder "what if" I had not followed God's leading in that initial word from Him. What if I had not obeyed His initial call of "behold, I set before you an open door" (Rev. 3:8), when I sought His face about the original prayer experiment that produced my prayer ministry? What path would I have taken? How far astray might I have gone before He would have given me another chance to respond correctly?

We really do determine our own spiritual growth rate, usefulness to God, and new opportunities by the way we respond to Him. At any point, we can hinder or stop His plan for our lives by our rebellious response to Him. Only in eternity will we see "what might have been" had our responses not thwarted God's plans for us. But with each step of obedience to God's answer to our prayers, He holds us gently yet firmly in that perfect path He has for us—walking hand in hand with Him.

Closing Prayer

Dear Father, I know the plans You have for me are best. Forgive me for all the times I have stubbornly gone my own way. Teach me to listen to Your answers to my prayers, and then to obey exactly what You have told me to do—or not to do. Thank You, Father, for all the wonderful rewards You have ready for me when I do obey You.

In Jesus' name, **Amen.**

12
When God answers...

Have a Thankful Heart

What happens when God answers? The ultimate, final response on our part should be to thank Him. No matter how God has answered our prayer, the one thing He expects from us is thankfulness.

People tend to insert their thanksgiving at different places in the prayer process. Some never bother to thank God no matter how great and wonderful the answers He sends. Most people, but not all, are thankful when God anwers the way they requested and has given them what they wanted. Then, some Christians have matured enough spiritually to thank Him in spite of how He has answered, trusting His divine wisdom.

But the Bible has an even greater requirement as to where the thanksgiving belongs in the whole prayer process. Philippians 4:6, surprisingly, reads, "Be anxious for nothing, but in everything by prayer and supplication *with thanksgiving* let your *requests* be made unto God" (NASB, emphasis mine).

It is rare indeed to find those who actually put their thanksgiving right in with the request. Few are able to be thankful *while* they are asking, because they are concentrating on the way they want God to answer. And the deeper the personal need or hurt, the more difficult it becomes to be thankful while begging God to intervene. Our minds usually are totally consumed by the problem, not with thanksgiving, during our wrestling and striving in prayer. It takes deep maturity indeed to be able to thank God *before* He answers, to be able to include the thanks *with* the request!

Attitude of Gratitude

Thanksgiving is a lifestyle. Long before He answers, God requires an *attitude* of thanksgiving. "Devote yourselves to prayer, keeping alert in it with *an attitude of* thanksgiving" (Col. 4:2, NASB, emphasis mine).

Our ultimate goal is to be engulfed by, saturated with, and completely controlled by an attitude of gratitude. Not some emotional high, or an escape from reality, but the actual living in a state of thankfulness—before, during, and after we receive answers to our prayers.

Paul explains in 1 Thessalonians 5:18 that this is not an option, but it is God's will for us, "In everything give thanks; for this is God's will for you in Christ Jesus" (NASB). While we are *in* every situation and while we are praying about it, we are to be thankful. Thanks should not have to be legislated through God's Word, but it should be the spontaneous response of our whole being toward Him.

I shivered in my hotel room in Australia one winter Sunday evening. Chills from a flulike sore throat, plus sitting all that day in buildings with so much less heat than I was used to in America, left me miserable. Alone in that room, I kept getting sicker and sicker. I took a bite of an apple, but my throat hurt too much to swallow it. And I was scheduled to speak all day, starting early the next morning!

Knowing that no doctor could cure me fast enough for the next day's seminar, I just knelt down by my bed to pray. But I didn't panic, I didn't ask God to get a replacement speaker ready, I didn't even ask to be healed. No, rather I just stayed there, kneeling in prayer with my whole being wrapped in His presence—with feelings of thanks spontaneously flowing to God for the privilege of once again being absolutely dependent upon Him.

I wasn't asking for or expecting what resulted from that prayer, but rising from my knees, I was surprised to find my throat completely healed. Filled with an attitude of gratitude!

Our attitude while we are making the request greatly influences the way we handle God's answers to our prayer. When the thanksgiving is there at the time of asking, it completely changes how we respond to God's answer, whatever it may be. Our attitude toward God's answer will be largely dependent upon our attitude toward Him during our request.

I was due to leave Dulles Airport in Washington, D.C. at 5:30 Friday evening, November 2, 1984 on Continental flight #383. But it didn't leave. All the radar had gone out in our whole nation's capital, and nothing was leaving that jammed airport the Friday night before election day until they let our planes limp out, one by one, on the dark runways, hours late. But God had an incredible "just trust Me" lesson waiting.

Since this was the last connection that could get me to San Jose, California in time for the next morning's seminar, and since I had only a half-hour layover in Denver to catch my plane for San Jose, I called to alert the seminar committee. Then I called my prayer chain at home. But the chances of getting to San Jose looked bleak, in fact, humanly impossible.

As my plane droned on in the night, I scribbled on the back of my flight schedule: "As we approached Denver, the announcement came. 'For those of you who are late for connections, there will be one of our people to assist you as you deplane. Just tell him your destination, and he will tell you your plane's gate number—or—if it's gone!'"

I settled back in my seat, almost snuggling down with a smile inside me. Most of my flight had been spent in prayer—not begging God to make my connection, but praying for tomorrow's seminar, His will in my life, my desire to be His handmaiden, to do only what He wanted me to do.

So it was just continuing our conversation when I prayed, "Oh, God, what an incredible feeling! The *privilege* of once again being totally dependent on You. The privilege of once again completely trusting You."

I continued writing on the back of my flight schedule in the darkened plane as the hours dragged on: "There is no anxiety, no worrying, no 'what if's.' Just the overwhelming security and peace—knowing that God is in absolute control."

Then I was once again quoting to Him, but mostly for me, "Be anxious for nothing, but in everything by prayer and supplication with thanksgiving let your requests be made known to God" (Phil. 4:6, NASB). *"The thankfulness just rolled,"* I wrote.

Even when "their man" sent me to the wrong gate, which was

in the opposite direction of mine, the assurance in my heart was still there. Completely out of breath, I dashed back—only to see the door of my plane, which miraculously had waited, being closed, then being opened again. And, as I darted in, to hear the call, "That's the last one!"

I shot a quick glance at my Heavenly Father, grinned, and breathed a prayer, "Thanks, Father, I knew You would!"

"Through Him then let us *continually* offer up a sacrifice of praise to God, that is, the fruit of lips that give thanks to His name" (Heb. 13:15, NASB, emphasis mine).

Why does God expect us to live continuously with an attitude of thanksgiving? Because He knows how it will be of benefit to us. There is a surprising fringe benefit from a lifestyle of thankfulness. A medical doctor in Michigan said with great wisdom that the best way to handle stress is with an "attitude of gratitude." An Old Testament proverb agrees: "A joyful heart is good medicine" (Prov. 17:22, NASB). Why? Because there evidently are chemicals released in our bodies from such an attitude. The single best way to remove stress from life, the doctor had wisely concluded, is an *attitude of gratitude.*

In Advance
When we leave a lovely dinner party or a special vacation time with a friend, we often say, "Thanks *for* everything." Also, after God has sent us successes and victories, we tend to say the same to Him. And this is good and scriptural, for Ephesians 5:20 does tell us to be thankful *for* all things. But the real test of our relationship with God is being able to say sincerely, "Thank You," *before* He gives us anything. To be able to say, "Thanks for everything," by our whole lifestyle of gratitude and by our prayer requests including "thanks in advance."

How is this possible? It is through a *relationship with the Father.* Frequently, our thanksgiving *for* God's answer comes from circumstances that have been changed by God or when He has removed the trial, illness, or heartache in answer to our praying, but thankfulness during the request requires a relationship of unequivocal trust in God that what He will answer will be right and best.

It almost seemed as though God was putting me to the test

recently one morning before dawn. Our daughter Nancy was more than two weeks overdue, and her doctor had decided to start the procedure to bring the baby on that day.

I had watched Nancy getting larger and larger as her unborn baby became less and less active—exactly as it had been with my two handicapped babies; and, just two weeks before, we had watched our Jan dangerously lose half her blood giving birth to her Crista. The apprehension and anxiety were growing in me. I remembered Nancy's Cindy with the cord wrapped three times around her neck at birth, and the possibility of what might go wrong with this birth loomed menacingly.

"Lord," I cried, "how can I thank You in advance with all these concerns in my heart?" I knew the scriptural teachings well, yet applying them at a time like this was not easy. But then God so clearly brought Philippians 4:6 into my mind, and I lay in the predawn blackness reciting over and over, "Be anxious for nothing, but in everything by prayer . . . *with thanksgiving* let your requests be made known to God" (Phil. 4:6, NASB, emphasis mine).

Suddenly, unsolicited, the thanksgiving welled up within me and permeated my entire being and, it seemed, the whole bedroom. My furrowed forehead automatically gave way to the smile that came. My eyes were moist with tears—of thanksgiving!

What had happened? Somehow, my focus changed direction—from possible earthly, human problems—to God. The thanks to Him just flowed. Who He is! He never makes a mistake. It is He who will take that child from the womb! And Kathleen Mae finally arrived—healthy and beautiful.

Who God Is
Last week God showed me a secret of being able to thank Him right at the time of my requests. I had just asked Him to help me praise and thank Him more, and I was reading through the Psalms for specific wordings of praise and thanksgiving, when He stopped me on 7:17, "I will give thanks to the Lord according to *His* righteousness" (NASB, emphasis mine).

According to. There it is again, that little prepositional phrase. I am to thank God, not according to my righteousness, nor my pastor's, nor my parents', but according to *His* righteousness.

But what is God's righteousness? It is the quality of actually *being* right and just, and then of being this way in His treatment of His creatures. So, I can know that what God answers is right and just, and can trust His answers unquestioningly. Then I can thank Him while I ask, not according to what I want, but according to who He is—righteous—in His dealings with me.

Also, God's righteousness is without prejudice or partiality. Other people's responses to my requests are influenced by their attitudes toward me. But not God's. He answers my prayers without any unfair prejudice against me or harmful indulgence toward me. So I can be secure in His answers.

God's righteousness is His holiness as it affects us—His transitive holiness. Since His holiness is the chief subject of rejoicing and adoration in heaven, when I give thanks unto the Lord according to His righteousness, I actually am joining the attitude and activities of those in heaven—rejoicing and adoring Him.

Often, prisoners who accept Christ while incarcerated tell me that they have prayed, "O God, get me out of this hell-hole." Then they expected God to answer their prayer with a miraculous pardon, change in a parole law, or some other divine intervention. Now, God has done this occasionally, but usually He has answered no to that prayer. Then their response to His no has been, "If that's the kind of God I'm serving now, I don't want anything to do with Him any more. He let me down." However, I'm surprised how frequently inmates, who have recently become Christians, share with me that they already have grasped who God is, that He knows what He is doing, and it is for their ultimate good—and that they can trust Him completely. Then their response to God's answer to that prayer has been, "Thanks, God, for leaving me here. You have a purpose. What is it?"

There is a difference in thanking God for what He does and for who He is. It is easy and almost natural to thank Him when He answers our prayers with something obviously good or what we wanted. But it is not as easy to thank Him for being what He is— right and just—before He answers.

Faith in Who God Is
Thanking God in advance takes not only knowing who He is but an unshakable faith in the God to whom we are praying. Only

when this adequate view of God has been arrived at *before* making the request can this attitude of thanksgiving be there *during* the request.

Actually, we have been practicing this principle in our prayer seminars for years. After teaching the participants who God really is (He never makes a mistake and does all things for our good), I ask them to pray aloud in small groups, giving God the most important thing in the whole world to them right then. The next prayer is thanking Him—in advance—before they have any idea what He might decide to do with what they just gave Him. This thanksgiving prayer is only possible because they have firmly grasped who God really is.

In my seminars, I always pray what I expect the audience to pray. Last March, I had just asked the audience to give that most important material or human possession, relationship, or circumstance to God when I knew i had to pray a very difficult prayer. We were expecting our second set of grandbabies in five months, and I knew I had to give God the thing I wanted more than anything in the world right then—two healthy, normal babies!

I struggled, momentarily remembering the heartache of my own two spina bifida babies. But this was erased from my mind almost immediately as a spirit of thankfulness welled up within me—thankfulness for all the wonderful lessons and gains God had given me through those two babies. And, with unequivocal assurance in my heart that God is right and just, I gave these precious, unborn wee ones to God—for anything He knew to be best—according to His righteousness.

It was the following July when God assured my heart with Psalm 100:3, "It is He who has made us, and not we ourselves." And I marked it in my Bible with a huge asterisk in the margin. Then His next words to me were the fifth verse, "For the Lord is good; His loving-kindness is everlasting" (NASB). Tears burst into my eyes as I cried, "Babies. I *can* trust His loving-kindness." Who God is!

Our Jan phoned one day announcing, "Mother, I was talking to my friend Diane last night and I have something for your new book. They want another baby so badly, but she just had her second miscarriage. But she told me she is actually thanking God for this miscarriage, because He knows exactly which egg He wants fertilized to produce their next baby. It is a deep-down attitude of thankfulness she has, not just words." I listened in awe.

"Mother," Jan continued, "it isn't when people say, 'I will be thankful because the Bible says I must be.' But real thankfulness depends on who is in control of your life. Who is in the driver's seat of your life. Who is sovereign. This is what produces joy in all circumstances, Mother. When you see God as sovereign and never making a mistake, you can thank Him for whatever happens—even a second miscarriage when you desperately want a baby."

David had an incredibly accurate view of who God is. And it produced his beautiful prayer of thanksgiving:

> So David blessed the Lord in the sight of all the assembly; and David said, "Blessed are Thou, O Lord God of Israel our Father, forever and ever. Thine, O Lord, is the greatness and the power and the glory and the victory and the majesty, indeed everything that is in the heavens and the earth; Thine is the dominion, O Lord, and Thou dost exalt Thyself as head over all. Both riches and honor come from Thee, and Thou dost rule over all, and in Thy hand is power and might; and it lies in Thy hand to make great, and to strengthen everyone. Now *therefore*, our God, *we thank Thee*, and praise Thy glorious name" (1 Chron. 29:10-13, NASB, emphasis mine).

David's word *therefore* explains his whole prayer. "Therefore"— because of who You, God, really are—we thank Thee.

Who God is. With no environment and no heredity, God alone chose who He would be. He alone decided what He would dedicate and consecrate Himself to be. Then He revealed it to us through His Word and His involvement in our lives so that we, with David, also could explode with our prayers of thanksgiving.

Keep Alert
But occasionally, I have trouble and slip from thankfulness into grumbling. It was at one of those times in August of 1984, while on vacation, that I recognized this attitude in me while reading

Colossians 4:2, "Devote yourselves to prayer, keeping alert in it with an *attitude of thanksgiving*" (NASB, emphasis mine).

Deeply rebuked, I cried out, "O God, forgive me. Bring me back to a right relationship with You. Make my testimony positive before others. I have taken my eyes off You. Replace my uptightness with your peace and joy—and thankfulness!" And it worked—as it always does!

Why do we have to keep alert in prayer? Because the Bible clearly tells us that Christians are in a spiritual battle and that we have an enemy, Satan.

In Ephesians 6, God describes the armor that will enable us to stand firm against the devil. But most of the time, we stop short of God's warning at the close, to be on the alert—*in prayer*. Verse 18 cautions: "With all prayer and petition pray at all times in the Spirit, and with this in view, be on the alert with all perseverance and petition for all the saints."

Obviously, Satan wants us to grumble, to be negative and powerless, thus destroying our own well-being and witness. However, being alert isn't one of the things we usually associate with prayer. But God does. He expects us to be fighting the only battle known where the soldiers go forth on their knees.

In, with, For

Thanking God *in* everything (1 Thes. 5:18) and *with* our requests (Phil. 4:6) does not cancel out His command to thank Him *for* everything. All three of these prepositions describe a relationship of the pray-er to God, which are commanded in the Bible.

God must be horrified at how ungrateful His children can be for His answers. A woman who had been in a wheelchair for years walked spryly up to me at a large denomination's weekend retreat last month. She complained bitterly to me that she could not get any faith in God—even after He had miraculously healed her in answer to prayer, and she had not had to use her wheelchair since. I cringed at her inability to thank God *for* something as spectacular as that.

We are shocked at the nine out of ten lepers Jesus healed who did not bother to come back to thank Him, but I wonder what our ratio is today—even when He answers with exactly what we requested. Is it more than one out of ten?

Ephesians 5:20 says that God expects us to be thankful *for* His answer, no matter how He answers our prayer—even when it is not what we wanted. "Always giving thanks *for* all things in the name of our Lord Jesus Christ to God, even the Father" (NASB). Then *always* giving thanks every time—even when we had asked for something different. His answers are the source of our praise and thanks, no matter how our opinions differ from God's.

A friend, Ruth Johnson Jay, wrote me a note several years ago in which she expressed her thanks to the Lord for a pair of crutches! She had just completed thirty years with the Back to the Bible broadcasts when she wrote, "I fell, broke my ankle in three places and dislocated the bone. Surgery was necessary . . . but I even find myself thanking the Lord for crutches. I cannot put any weight on the cast for four to six weeks, and none (on the foot) after that for another four weeks. So you can see why I am thanking the Lord for crutches!"

I'm sure that another reason why we don't thank God *for* His answer is that frequently we don't recognize events and gifts *as* answers to our prayers. We just take His bountiful supply or dramatic action for granted when it comes. This is why I teach my prayer seminar participants to jot down their prayer request and then what happened so they can put the two together. Often I hear their surprised, "Oh, that *was* His answer!"

Even worse, of course, is when God answers and we have forgotten that we even prayed. Keeping a list of our requests helps tremendously here, also. Then a periodic reading through the list of requests can be quite revealing: "Oh, yes, that provision, healing, or circumstance really *was* an answer to one of my prayers!" Then the thankfulness for it comes.

There are also those times when I believe God deliberately waits long enough to answer so that there will be no doubt who gets the credit for what happens. It is only when I have exhausted all human resources that He finally answers—so that I will recognize the answer as coming from Him. And thank Him for it. And give Him all the glory!

Thanks For
The list of things *for* which I thank God in my prayers would fill many books, but here are just a few:

For redemption. Thanking God for transferring me out of the state of sin into which I was born into His glorious kingdom— forgiven and bound for eternity with my beloved Savior. "Joy-ously giving thanks to the Father, who has qualified us to share in the inheritance of the saints in light. For He delivered us from the domain of darkness, and transferred us to the kingdom of His beloved Son, in whom we have redemption, the forgiveness of sins" (Col. 1:11-14, NASB).

For peace. Thanking God for the formula which has produced peace in my life. Here it is: "Be anxious for nothing, but in everything by prayer and supplication with thanksgiving let your requests be made known to God. And [then] the peace of God, which surpasses all comprehension shall guard your hearts and your minds in Christ Jesus" (Phil. 4:6, NASB). The prerequisite, usually omitted as we try to claim this promised peace, is a life-style of an attitude of gratitude—before, during, and after the prayer requests. But the whole formula really works.

For His omniscience. Although there are more than 4 billion people on Planet Earth, God the Father can give His undivided attention to each one of them all the time. So, although I'm just 1/4 billionth of the world's population, God watches over me, sorts through the intents of my heart, listens and cares when I cry for help, never makes a mistake in His moment-by-moment guid-ing of my life, and will judge me according to His righteousness.

For Jesus' blood. Almost daily, I thank God that the blood of Jesus is the only positively irresistible force against evil. For many years, He has proved in my life that there is no immovable object from Satan that the irresistible force of His precious blood—once and for all victorious on the cross—cannot and will not dislodge and wash away. "Now the salvation, and the power, and the kingdom of our God and the authority of His Christ have come, for the accuser of our brethren has been thrown down, who accuses them before our God day and night. And they overcame him because of the blood of the Lamb" (Rev. 12:10-11, NASB).

For setting me free. "If therefore the Son shall make you free, you shall be free indeed" (John 8:36, NASB). How grateful I am for Jesus' promise that I could be free *in* all circumstances—not *from* them. No intellectual bondage, no spiritual enslavement because of sin, no confinement of my spirit because of a wheelchair or a hospital bed, no restriction of my vision, in a nursing home room, no mental imprisonment to others' ideologies, no emotional enslavement to those who would demand my will, no restraint of spiritual insight and hope because of a weakened body. No imprisonment of the real me—because Jesus has set me free.

For God using my body. For the progressively growing thankfulness of having given God my body in 1965, in that once-for-all action of Romans 12:1. For frequently being healed but, much more important, for the privilege of having God always take all the anxiety out of bodily infirmities. Thanks for His replacement of that anxiety with absolute trust in Him as the One who owns, is in charge of, and is responsible for my body.

But even more, I am thankful for the privilege of God using my still-living sacrifice in any way He chooses—to teach others the power of their prayers for me, that the works of God might be displayed in me (as in the man born blind whom Jesus healed), or to lead someone to Jesus in a redemptive way because of watching His power to transcend and use me through, and in spite of, physical weaknesses.

For you, dear prayer partners. I "do not cease giving thanks for you, while making mention of you in my prayers" (Eph. 1:16, NASB). You who have prayed diligently, faithfully, and sacrificially for me year after year, and seeing God answering with wisdom, courage, and sometimes supernatural strength—I bow in humble thanksgiving and gratitude to God for you.

"And He will yet deliver us, you also joining in helping us through your prayers, that thanks may be given by many persons on our behalf for the favor bestowed upon us through the prayers of many" (2 Cor. 1:10-11, NASB). Your prayers!

Preserved and Enhanced

What happens when God answers? After all God does with and through His answers to prayer, He still has a final step. He does not discard them after answering, but preserves and enhances them in heaven: "And when He [the Lamb] had taken the Book, the four living creatures and the twenty-four elders fell down before the Lamb, having each one a harp, and golden bowls full of incense, which are the prayers of the saints" (Rev. 5:8, NASB).

"MY PRAYERS!!!" I wrote in the margin by the Bible verse. "I am one of God's saints—true believers in Jesus Christ. My prayers didn't disappear when God answered them! No, they are preserved in heaven!"

"And this is the song they sang before Jesus the Lamb," I continued to write, "holding *my* prayers": "Worthy are Thou to take the book, and to break its seals; for Thou wast slain, and didst purchase for God with Thy blood men from every tribe and tongue and people and nation. And Thou has made them to be a kingdom and priests to our God; and they will reign upon the earth" (Rev. 5:9-10, NASB).

Then, joined by millions of angels, they said with a loud voice: "Worthy is the Lamb that was slain to receive power and riches and wisdom and might and honor and glory and blessing" (Rev. 5:12, NASB).

Still holding my prayers and yours, they were joined by every created thing which is in heaven and on the earth and under the earth and on the sea, all saying: "To Him who sits on the throne, and to the Lamb, be blessing and honor and glory and dominion forever and ever" (Rev. 5:13, NASB).

I wept as I realized all the agonizing, wrestling, and tears; all the praise, worship, submission, and intercessory prayers from my whole life are there. Not lost, or cast aside once they are answered—but preserved for eternity.

Yes, the final reason for our thanksgiving in the prayer process is that God has chosen only special words of ours—our prayers—to keep forever.

But even more astounding, they not only will be preserved—but enhanced! Enhanced by the grace and cost of the vessels that hold them. The Apostle John on the Isle of Patmos, as he was penning these things to come, saw our preserved prayers in precious, valuable, golden bowls. Broad, shallow, saucer-like bowls, made of the most precious commodity known on earth in that day—costly gold.

Then the final scene in the long journey of our prayers' life is recorded in Revelation 8:3-4. When all the seals are broken on that Book in the Lamb's hands, this climactic celestial scene will unfold:

And another angel came and stood at the altar, holding a

golden censer; and much incense was given to him, that he might add it to the prayers of all the saints upon the golden altar which was before the throne. And the smoke of the incense, *with the prayers of the saints, went up before God* out of the angel's hand (NASB, emphasis mine).

"O God, I am not worthy!" my heart cried. "Thank You, Lord!"

How wonderful to know that—after all the other things that have happened to us and to those for whom we pray, through God's answers to prayers—there is one more thing. God feels every one of them is important enough to preserve—and precious enough to enhance—in golden bowls before His throne.

When we get to heaven, will we be embarrassed at how few prayers of ours God received to put in golden bowls? And of those He did get, will their content bring a blush to our cheeks? Selfish prayers—to glorify ourselves, to be consumed on our lusts? "Grocery lists" of our endless wants?

Or will we be overwhelmed at the sight of them all—preserved because of their permanent significance in God's sight? Then we will suddenly realize that prayer has been one of God's chief means of accomplishing His will on earth—our prayers!

What happens when God answers prayer? He pulls back the curtain to the next act of our lives. And, through His answer, lets us step into that next room of our lives—open doors, spiritual maturity, accomplishing His will on Planet Earth. One step nearer to the Christlikeness He had planned for us before the foundation of the world.

And when we finally take that last step into God's throne room, our prayers will be there—waiting for us—with our Lord Himself.

ENDNOTES

Chapter 2

1. J.J.S. Perowne, ed., *The Cambridge Bible for Schools and Colleges* (London: C.J. Clay and Sons, 1895), 102.
2. Augustus Hopkins Strong, *Systematic Theology* (Philadelphia: Judson Press, n.d.), 287–88.
3. E.M. Bounds, *Power through Prayer* (Grand Rapids: Zondervan Publishing House, 1964), 35.
4. Evelyn Christenson, *What Happens When Women Pray* (Wheaton, Ill.: Victor Books, 1975).

Chapter 8
1. From *Tabernacle Hymns Number Five,* © 1953 by Tabernacle Publishing Co., Chicago, Illinois, 1963.

Chapter 9
1. Henry Rogers, ed., *The Works of Jonathan Edwards,* vol. 2, rev. Edward Hickman (London: Ball, Arnold, and Co., 1840), 226.
2. John Calvin, *Commentary on the Four Last Books of Moses,* vol. 5 (Grand Rapids: Wm. B. Eerdmans Publishing Co., n.d.), 149.

Chapter 10
1. C.S. Lewis, *Perelandra,* © 1954 by Clive Staples Lewis (New York: Macmillan Co., 1958), 125.

BEATRICE MODUPE
LAD- OGUNKOYA
06/11/04.